THE ULTIMATE ENCYCLOPEDIA OF

GOLF

THIS IS A CARLTON/HODDER & STOUGHTON BOOK

Copyright © Carlton Books Limited 1995

First published in 1995 by Hodder & Stoughton,
a division of Hodder Headline PLC

10 9 8 7 6 5 4 3 2 1

A CIP catalogue record for this book is available
from the British Library

ISBN 0 340 64952 6

Project Editor: Martin Corteel
Project Art Editor: Paul Messam
Picture Research: Sharon Hutton
Designer: Simon Wilder
Production: Sarah Schuman

Printed and bound in Spain

Hodder and Stoughton Ltd
A division of Hodder Headline PLC
338 Euston Road
London NW1 3BH

THE ULTIMATE ENCYCLOPEDIA OF

GOLF

The definitive illustrated guide to world golf

Ted Barrett & Michael Hobbs

CARLTON

Hodder & Stoughton

ACKNOWLEDGEMENTS

The authors would like to thank the USGA for permission to use their Centennial Logos (*see* page 198), and for the cooperation of their Technical and Library Support staff at Far Hills, New Jersey. Thanks are also due to John Glover, R&A Rules Secretary, Touche Rosse, Michael Harvey, chairman of the trustees of the Golf Course Wildlife Trust, Richard Doyle-Davidson and Juliette Brindley of the Wentworth Club, Phillips Auctioneers of Chester and "Joe the Pro" Hardwick, lately of Royal Hong Kong Golf Club.

PREVIOUS PAGE: IT HAPPENS IN MONTEREY *The 18th hole at Pebble Beach*

CONTENTS

GARY PLAYER *South African golfing legend*

AUGUSTA'S 12TH *Play it well and say "Amen"*

EXCLUSIVE EQUIPMENT *A Ryder Cup golf bag*

FOREWORD
BY NICK PRICE

In July 1994 I experienced my greatest thrill in golf, winning the Open Championship at Turnberry. It was a dream come true, especially after coming so close at Royal Troon in 1982 and at Royal Lytham in 1988. Standing at the prize-giving with both hands on that famous old claret jug was a feeling that is difficult to put into words. Then, a few weeks later, I managed to sustain my good play and concentration by capturing my second US PGA Championship in the heat of Southern Hills in Tulsa, Oklahoma.

There's no doubt about it, winning one of the four major championships is the goal of every professional golfer. Becoming a major champion is the greatest reward one can pay oneself for all the practice and hard work put in over the years. There is nothing like winning and while I might experience those moments of glory, so can the average player by winning his or her club championship, medal event or company match play tournament. That is what makes golf the great game it is.

Even when golfers are not swinging away on the fairways, they love reading about the game, which brings me to this book. Within its pages it covers the world game in such depth that it will provide all golfers with many hours of great reading. If you are looking for the game's early history, facts about the great championships, the game's legends, the great courses and players, even bizarre happenings, it's all here. For me, it really is the *Ultimate* Encyclopaedia of Golf, and I hope you enjoy it.

Nick Price
Orlando, Florida
March 1995

THE EARLY HISTORY OF GOLF

Golf belongs to the group of sports best described as target ball games. This also includes snooker, pool, ten-pin bowling, bowls, pétanque, croquet, curling and several varieties of billiards. Yet it stands proudly apart from them all, for only golf can claim to be both Royal and Ancient.

Eleven years before his death in 1513 during the disastrous Scottish defeat at Flodden, James IV of Scotland, known as "James of the Iron Belt", had golf clubs made by a Perth artisan whose usual stock in trade was bows and arrows. More clubs and balls were bought the following year, for a match with the Earl of Bothwell.

These purchases by James, the record of whose golf transactions is the earliest historical evidence of a golfer's name, were utterly at variance with previous royal attitudes to golf. In the previous century several bans on "fute-ball, golfe and uther sik unproffitable sportis" were imposed by the Scottish parliament, the last as late as 1491.

The reasoning behind the bans was that time wasted on "the green" – the old Scots term for a course, and not just the putting surface, hence greenkeeper and Green Committee – should have been spent in mastering the martial arts, the better to discomfort the English.

Yet this game despised by the Scottish leadership has conquered, half a millennium later, vast areas of land in every continent, and, like football, the allegiance of millions. The English have never quelled the Scots half as effectively as this Scot-

ROMANTIC RECONSTRUCTION *Forestier's 1905 impression of Mary Queen of Scots at St Andrews, 1563*

tish game has colonized the five continents.

The relatively sudden change of heart in the Stuart camp followed close upon James's marriage to the daughter of Henry VII of England. The royal alliance did not, as Flodden and the Jacobite uprisings of the eighteenth century attest, mean the immediate end of war between the two nations, but longer spells of peace and prosperity supervened.

Moreover, for more than 180 years – until William of Orange replaced James II of England – there was an unbroken line of royal Stuart golfers, including Mary Queen of Scots, who may or may not have been insensitive enough to have played golf shortly after the murder of her husband Darnley, but whose reputation has suffered ever since from the suspicion that she did. Mention of William, who,

like the Hanoverians who followed him on the English throne, was no golfer, reopens the great debate as to whether the game is utterly Scottish, or an adaptation of pastimes like *kolven*, popular in Holland, or *chole*, from Belgium and northern France, or *jeu de maille*, a pursuit of Louis XIV. *Jeu de maille*, however, contains even fewer of the essential elements of golf than *kolven* which, as clearly shown in a Rembrandt

KOLVEN ON ICE *Usually playing indoors, Dutch kolf players used frozen rivers, too, as shown in this painting by Dutch artist Hendrik Averkamp*

drawing, was played with a ball the size of a cricket ball, usually in a courtyard or on a frozen river, or even in churches in the days before pews. The object was to drive the ball against a mark or post.

Chole, which dates from at least as early as the middle of the fourteenth century, was a cross-country event, with the target a distant door or pillar. *Chole* still survives in Belgium, and in France by the name of *soule*. Golf historian Robert Browning believes *chole* may have been brought back and adapted to Scottish usages by Scots fighting on the side of the French in the Hundred Years' War after Henry V's victory at Agincourt. *Chole* had hockey-like features absent from golf, since a player was at liberty to hit his opponent's ball into trouble if he had failed to hit the target within the number of strokes he had declared. This rule of *chole*, benefiting the *chole* player's opponent or "*decholeur*", is directly opposed to the principle that the golfer, and never his opponent, shall enjoy the exclusive, unhindered and uninterrupted right to strike his own ball. This principle has stood the test of

time throughout the long history of golf, and has been a major factor in preserving the civility of the game.

There are pictures, dating from the early seventeenth century, showing the playing of *kolven* and *chole* that are highly convincing arguments that these games are the forerunners of golf. On the other hand, golfers must have been active, to the annoyance of the Scottish parliament, well before that body first banned the sport in the middle of the fifteenth century (indeed St Andrews claimants back-date the sport to the twelfth century); since Scotland was not rich in graphic art in that era, all we know for certain is that golf was being played two centuries before *kolven* pictures were being painted. Moreover, there is no known form of the Scottish word golf that begins with a "k" sound.

The novelist Sir Walter Scott doubted that the word golf came from the verb "to gowff", meaning to hit. Others theorize that the verb derived from the game. The correlation between verb and game seems too close and too clear, however, to be mere coincidence.

Another possible origin for the game of golf from nearer home is shinty, but no recorded variant of this ancient Celtic hockey-like game has ever included mention of putting a ball into a hole, though in an early sixteenth-century German book of religious and sporting illustrations on vellum there is a depiction of a child apparently putting a ball into a depression. These fragmentary clues, like the club-swinging figure in a stained glass window in Gloucester Cathedral in England (dating from the middle of the fourteenth century), provide no definite answers, and Andrew Lang, the poet who leads the great roll of golf's literati, put the Scots' points of view succinctly with his dictum that "Clearly, kolf is no more golf than cricket is poker."

Putting the ball into the hole is the crucial, and some would say, diabolical, contribution of golf to the cross-country target ball game. The other contribution which can be seen in courses throughout the world is the nature of the Scottish landscape over which golf was developed. Great sums of money have been spent in the United

States and Japan, to name only two countries, on earth-moving carried out frequently on a vast scale in order to replicate in turf and sand the characteristic features of natural Scottish courses – formed by wind and water and the depredations of domestic and wild animals.

The world-wide spread of golf received a racing start when Elizabeth I died without issue, and the Stuarts assumed the English throne in 1603 in the person of James I of England and VI of Scotland. He was the son of Mary Queen of Scots and the unfortunate Lord Darnley, and great-grandson of Margaret Tudor. Margaret was the English wife of James IV, none other than our first (known) golfer.

No doubt exists that James I was a powerful influence in favour of golf. Though a century had passed since the Scottish ban on golf had been lifted, James I was moved to make his view known that the common people's right to enjoy sport on Sunday was to be respected, as long as religious observances had been completed first. Charles I repeated this sentiment a few years later. James I, Charles I and II and James

COCKED HATS AND CRAVATS *Four gentlemen golfers, vintage 1798, at St Andrews, complete with tail-coats and caddies*

II all golfed, and so did Bonny Prince Charlie, who succeeded James II as pretender to the throne of England.

Many a 40-shilling fine was imposed on those who persisted in playing "in tyme of sermonis" – notably in Scotland, where the kirk looked down upon such flibbertigibbet behaviour. Despite these hindrances, golf flourished, like cricket, in all classes of the community. Early in James I's reign, bishops, noblemen, and folk of every rank were busy on Scottish links, while James's two sons were making golf fashionable south of the border by taking it up at their father's behest. The eldest son Henry died at 18, the second son Charles surviving to succeed to the crown, only to lose his head after the Civil War. Charles was golfing on Leith Links, near Edinburgh, on the day he received the news of a rebellion in Ireland.

The Restoration of the Monarchy in 1660 brought royal golfers

into play again, the most notable being James, Duke of York, later James II. His example is being keenly followed by Andrew, the present Duke. James is credited with setting up and playing in the first international match, partnered by a Scottish shoemaker named Patersone, who was no novice at the tee. This Scottish team of Stuart and shoemaker beat two English noblemen, and Patersone was rewarded with enough cash to build a house in Cannongate, Edinburgh (which stood until 1961).

Not until the middle years of the following century did golf take the next great step forward. The engine of golf's further development was the social device of the club, until then strictly a political entity. No matter how powerful the ruling bodies of the game, no matter how rich the professional tours become, it is the club that remains the beating heart of the game.

A golf course was just that, a place where people could play golf.

They did not pay for the privilege: there was no one to pay, no committee, and no greenkeeping costs, since the land over which the game took place was common land, untended apart from grazing animals and rabbits and the more damaging attentions of wind and tide. The links at St Andrews in Fife had since 1552 been given under licence by Archbishop Hamilton for free and unfettered use of citizens at football, golf and other games. That was the only formal convention.

The rules under which people played were a matter of local custom, on-the-spot agreements and wagers. Score cards were yet to be thought of. All golf was of the match play variety, and handicaps a rudimentary give and take between individuals, be they dukes or cobblers. Leading players were, however, already sufficiently celebrated to be the subject of poetry. The next step was to see who was the best player of all.

The defining moment came in 1744, when a group of players,

"gentlemen of honour" it goes without saying, well known on Leith Links, presented a petition to the City of Edinburgh to provide a prize for the winning player in an open competition. This was granted in the shape of a Silver Club, by the magistrates, who were quick to indemnify themselves, after the fashion to be expected from careful guardians of public funds in those days, from any further expenditure which might be incurred in running the competition.

The new trophy was carried on the appointed day through the streets of Edinburgh, to the tuck of drums. The entry (of 10) was in the event strictly a local one. An Edinburgh surgeon named John Rattray came out on top, and repeated the dose the following year. The poet Mathison had a year earlier sung of "Rattray for skill… renowned".

This man of medicine was certainly a cool hand. He went at Bonny Prince Charlie's behest to the aid of the wounded in the

Young Pretender's army during the second Jacobite rebellion of 1745. Owing perhaps to the leading Edinburgh golfers having a heavy presence in the law – they still do – he was not arraigned for treason as he might well have been. His escape has been attributed mainly to the efforts of Duncan Forbes of Culloden, which only goes to show what useful contacts can be made at golf clubs, since Forbes was himself a "Gentleman Golfer". After Rattray's second victory the aftermath of the Jacobite troubles prevented further competition for the Silver Club for two years.

Ten years after the Edinburgh initiative, 22 "Noblemen and Gentlemen" of St Andrews subscribed for a Silver Club of their own. As at Edinburgh, competition for the silver trophy was the only cement binding together the group of local players. The winner each year was captain of the group, and entrusted with the resolution of any disputes between players. Not for another 80 years did the St Andrews men have a regular meeting place, and even then they shared it with the local Archers' Club.

A second key date in the slow, piecemeal development of the idea of a club came in 1764 when, with no sign as yet of the hoped-for challenge for the Silver Club from other parts of Britain, the Edinburgh men moved to restrict entry to competition to "admit such Noblemen and Gentlemen as they approve to be members of the Company of Golfers". The cornerstone of the Honorable Company of Edinburgh Golfers had been laid 20 years earlier, and thus in 1994 the Company celebrated their 250th anniversary – 10 years before their rivals in St Andrews are at liberty to do so.

Edinburgh also scored a first in the matter of setting up a code of rules. This they did in 1744, to govern play for their Silver Club, though it is possible that the players at Leith had already put together a rudimentary list of do's and don'ts. The St Andrews men, following suit in 1754, were to abide by a similar codification, employing the principles of simplicity and brevity.

Today's mighty tomes detailing definitions and settling abstruse queries are a world away from the 13 rules issued in 1754: "back to basics" is an inadequate description. The first of the 13 makes strange reading to the modern golfer, since it directs that the player must tee off within a club's length of the hole, which gives an immediate and daunting idea of what the putting surfaces must have been like in the mid-eighteenth century. The main burden of the other 12 rules is "Play it as it lies", except when the player's ball comes to rest against his opponent's, or is unplayable in "water or watery filth", in which latter case the player may lift his ball, but must allow his opponent a stroke. Removing "stones, bones, or any break-club for the sake of playing your ball" was forbidden, except "upon the fair green, and that only within a club length of your ball". Putting green standards obviously improved over the next hundred years, and needed to be protected, because half-way through the nineteenth century Rule 1 was relaxed to the extent that the ball was allowed to be teed as much as six club lengths from the hole.

All these early rules were, as has been indicated, for match play. Once stroke play became widespread – and stroke play has always been the most popular form of the game in America – the need arose for exact definitions as to what constituted, to give an obvious example, an unplayable ball. A competitor at stroke play needed to know precisely whether the circumstances involved a penalty or not. Otherwise it would be impossible for him to continue his round and complete his card.

A century after the first simple codification of the rules, an attempt by the St Andrews club to define "unplayable" required almost as many words as the whole of the original 13 rules. The process of

devoting further words to this intractable problem has used up a quantity of ink since then.

With the Leith Links deteriorating as the city pressed in upon them, the Honourable Company had to move, initially to Musselburgh, while the duties of regulators and adjudicators were assumed little by little by St Andrews. Finally they were shared by the United States Golf Association, and in 1951 a conference made the first real attempt to provide a code for golf worldwide. In doing so, it also got rid of the hated stymie.

Within a few years, the irresistible attractions of golf were

spreading south of the border. Just as with the two pioneer Scottish clubs, the presentation of a trophy in 1766 set Blackheath golfing activities in motion in Kent, to the south of London. Not surprisingly, Blackheath's foundation owed much to the presence of expatriate Scots. Such men were often prime movers in helping the game spread further afield.

It did so with great rapidity, and in 1810 came the first mention of a women's competition, at Musselburgh. There had already been reports of Scottish officers playing in New York, and of the formation (1786) of a club in South Carolina, though the game was slow to take root in the United States, a process which took more than another

APPROVED DRESS *Lemuel Francis Abbott's painting of Blackheath captain William Innes, and caddie*

hundred years, and was pre-dated by the founding of Royal Montreal in 1873.

Golf had already followed the Union flag to Calcutta in 1829, and Bombay in 1842. Conversely, though the British began business in Hong Kong in the 1840s, golf did not flower there until 1889. Nor did it make the short journey to the Continent until 1856, when Pau in the shadow of the Pyrenees was founded for holiday visitors. Scottish soldiers of the Duke of Wellington's Peninsular Army are said to have played at Pau in 1814, some of them returning 20 years later on holiday – which places them among the very first of the great army of golf tourists, though many English players belonged to the leading Scottish clubs, and journeyed north for their regular silver club and gold medal meetings.

Australia joined the throng in 1870, with the Royal Adelaide Club, and South Africa in 1885, with the Royal Cape Club.

The rate of golf course construction in the British Isles was prodigious in Victorian times, mostly with horse, cart and shovel. The railways helped, from St Andrews to Blackheath, and from Shering-ham, where the line ran within a few feet of the 17th green, to Aberdovey in west Wales, and from Ganton in Yorkshire to Lytham in Lancashire, where there were also gas trams on a line that was later electrified.

Course building reached a feverish pitch in the 1890s, as proved by the number of clubs celebrating their centenaries in the last decade of the present century. Curiously, there had been little golf in Ireland before the boom of the '90s, though Belfast set up their club in 1881. Unsurprisingly it was a Scot, Sir David Kinloch, who brought the game to Dublin.

The popularity of the game had greatly increased because it was given a focus by two competitions. 1860 saw the staging of what has gone down to history as the first "Open" Championship, though as we shall see in the next chapter it was not Open at all, and the crucial value of the events of that year took many years to make themselves apparent. Second, 25 years later, came what eventually was styled as the Amateur Championship, which meant that for players both paid and unpaid there was a summit to strive toward.

Among the catalysts leading to the foundation of golf's first major championship was Blackheath's victory, gained by George Glennie and Lieut. J. C. Stewart, in the Inter-Club Foursomes of 1857, a competition suggested by the Prestwick club. This constituted the first Championship Meeting to be played at St Andrews, and the host club were beaten finalists. The St Andrews club had assumed authority as the game's law-givers, and their decision to cut the number of holes on their course from 22 to 18 made 18 the magic number world-wide.

Significantly the winning pair in 1857 were both Scots; Glennie's natural talent was such that when he was studying at St Andrews University his fellows insisted he should play with only one club. He still won.

The following year a singles event was held, attracting a field of 28 from which the publisher, Robert Chambers, emerged victorious. In 1859 another publisher, Robert Clark, who wrote about golf, was much fancied to win, but a big hitter called George Condie strolled to the title 6 & 5.

These three competitions were amateur, but the leading players were celebrated in newspaper reports and verse, and attained the status of national sporting heroes.

The links were the haunt of a great variety of folk quite apart from the gentlemen amateurs, some of whom played in tall hats – a powerful inducement to keep the head still – and their caddies, whose name, it seems clear, derives from the French word *cadet*. This was the term used to describe the young French noblemen who came to Edinburgh with Mary Queen of Scots when she returned after her years at the French court.

Scottish humour, ever sardonic, extended the usage to mean something less complimentary, and in a classic sequence of semantic change, the meaning of *cadet* journeyed by way of "hanger-on" and "odd jobber" to "porter". Latterly, over the last two centuries, the word has slowly gone up-market again, certainly in the world of the major tours, to mean well-paid golf-bag carriers who keep their player dry when it is wet, watered when it is dry, fed when hungry, and well supplied with advice at all times on how far it is to the hole, which way the wind is blowing, and exactly how far the next putt will

THE FIRST NO. 1 *Allan Robertson (bare-headed, seventh from left), the first acknowledged champion, at St Andrews circa 1853*

OPEN FOR BUSINESS *Members gather outside the newly-constructed Royal & Ancient clubhouse*

swing on its way to the hole.

Many wanderers across the courses were simply out to take the air; others kicked a ball about, or flew kites. Soldiers drilled, horses were raced, cricket matches were played: but on the days of big challenge matches, sometimes with hundreds of pounds at stake, crowds surrounded the growing band of professionals. They got much closer to the action than would be countenanced today. The classlessness of the game, at least in Scotland, is indicated by the story of the caddie who, when he judged that spectators were getting a little too close, grabbed one, who happened to be a magistrate, by the ear, and invited him to stick his nose into the hole, so that he could *feel* the ball was there.

After the success of the events they had set in motion in 1857–59, the innovative members of Prestwick turned their attention to the professionals, many of whom started their golfing life as caddies.

It hardly needs saying that the professionals around the middle of the nineteenth century could not make a living from tournament winnings alone: there was no programme of events, and what money they won with their clubs, which they usually fashioned themselves, came from challenge matches for cash.

Club-making, which in the early days seemed to become the natural fiefdom of bow-makers, was, along with the manufacture of feathery golf balls and teaching, the staple source of income of the early Victorian professional. This state of affairs continued long after the establishment of the first regular Open events.

Allan Robertson, the first golfer to beat 80 at St Andrews, was accepted as the leading player of the day. With his assistant Tom Morris, Robertson ran a thriving feathery-ball business out of the window of their workshop, which was the kitchen of Robertson's house. Stuffing a top hat full of feathers into a leather casing was a job for an expert, though even the best could manage no more than three balls a day.

The era of the feathery, preceded almost certainly by lathe-turned wooden balls as used in such games as *chole*, ended, to Robertson's dismay, with the development of the solid gutta-percha ball during the last years of his life: he died in 1859, aged only 44. The popularity of the cheaper "gutty" must have been an especially severe shock to Robertson, because the family feathery trade had been in existence for so long, run by his grandfather Peter and father Davie before him. The gutty was a solid ball made from the juice of the Malayan percha tree and, unlike the feathery, could be remoulded when damaged – the feathery simply burst open when mistreated, especially in wet weather.

Moreover, the Robertson and Co. output is reckoned to have been well in excess of 2,000 featheries a year. At half a crown each (12.5 pence in sterling metric terms, or about 20 US cents) that came to an annual revenue of about £300, a fair sum in the mid-nineteenth century. The high cost of a feathery in the last days of its dominance no doubt kept many would-be golfers off the course. Robertson proved himself the complete professional, for after first declaring of the new projectile, "It's nae gowff", he reacted positively to the playing problems set by the new ball, which was much less responsive and more difficult to get into the air than the feathery. He made much greater use of the mid and short irons to fly the ball to the target. Pitching had previously been performed with wooden clubs. Never a long hitter, Robertson obeyed the first rule of golf: he kept the ball in play, and used his new iron technique to get close to the hole with his approach shots.

His death posed the question: who is champion now? Prestwick provided a way of finding out in October, 1860, with the game's first formal competitive tournament at stroke play, what we know as The Open. The golfing calendar has for nearly a century been dominated by this and three other majors: two of them, both amateur events, were replaced as social changes reshaped golf. How appropriate that the youngest of the majors, the Masters, is the first great international event of the year.

THE GREAT CHAMPIONSHIPS

With the increasing popularity of golf throughout the twentieth century, four championships have so captured the imagination of players and public alike that they have become known as the majors. The four majors march through the calendar nowadays like this: Masters (held in April), United States Open (in June), British Open (in July) and US PGA (in August) ... *nowadays* because the majors used to be the two Opens and the British and American Amateur Championships, while other tournament organizers style their events as "the fifth major".

DELAYED DOUBLE (left) *Greg Norman welcomes back the Open Championship trophy with a kiss at Royal St George's, Sandwich, in 1993; (opposite) Curtis Strange lands a second US Open in a row in 1989, at Oak Hill, Rochester*

After Bobby Jones won all four majors in 1930 it gradually became clear that changes were necessary. They did not occur overnight. When Ben Hogan, uniquely, won the first three of the "modern" majors in 1953, the fourth, the US PGA, was out of reach because it clashed with the British Open. It was a decade later before the idea of a latter-day Jones to hit all four targets in a season seized many minds. The Masters, the youngest major and the only one always played on the same course, got the nod from players, public and Press despite the misgivings of its creator, Jones. Carefully engineered attempts to invent a fifth major have failed. In other words, the majors have a life of their own ...

THE MASTERS

It took a long time for the full effects of the years 1930–34 to register upon the world of golf. Indeed, things were never the same again from the moment Bobby Jones, at the age of 28, retired from competitive golf. He had no more peaks to climb after 1930, when he exceeded even the massive expectations of his adoring public on both sides of the Atlantic by winning in one season all four of what were then accepted as the four major championships – the British and United States Opens, and the Amateur championships of the same two countries.

It is difficult for a golf fan under 80 or so who has not skimmed the contemporary media to take on board the scale of the adulation, respect, affection and general awe commanded by Jones, even before the Grand Slam, a term taken from the game of bridge by his faithful biographer, O. B. Keeler. Jones's fame eclipsed by a fair margin that of such outstanding professionals as Walter Hagen and Gene Sarazen. Besides, they could not play for the two amateur titles, and though the Professional Golfers Championship, founded in 1916, was gaining in importance, its quality was never franked by the presence of the undisputed top golfer of the day, Jones.

Three years after Jones retired, Johnny Goodman won the United States Open. No amateur has won it since, or won any other major. So the amateur titles rapidly lost their honoured position at the topmost level of the game. Playing in high-class amateur golf cost money, and there was little about in the depths of the Depression, as President Franklin Roosevelt began his efforts to revive the nation.

Another major, open to paid and unpaid, was needed, and there was more than a touch of poetic justice in the fact that the greatest amateur of them all, Jones, was to provide it, unknowingly, in 1934. His offer-

ing was a uniquely lovely course and an event which admitted pros and amateurs, and would, in time, slot into the calendar alongside the two main Opens and the PGA Championship, which was to move into the top bracket of competition now that the amateur challenge had faded.

Jones had decided to return to his law practice on retirement and to make some money with instructional films and books. He also intended to fulfil a long-held ambition: to found a golf club with a superior course, somewhere near his home in Georgia, which his golfing friends could join. A year before his retirement, Jones had conversations on the subject with Dr Alister Mackenzie at Pebble Beach during the Amateur Championship, in which Jones was beaten by Goodman from Nebraska. Mackenzie had turned, during the First World War, from doctoring to a camouflage unit, and later took up course architecture. He and Jones sought a different marque of course, one which Mackenzie characterized as "adventurous". With the assistance of a New York businessman, Clifford Roberts, who had started out as a suit salesman and enjoyed golf trips to Georgia and friendship with Jones, Thomas Barrett, of the Augusta Chamber of Commerce, the journalist Grantland Rice and several financiers, the project took a big step forward when Barrett suggested the purchase of what had been one of the first nurseries in Georgia, Fruitlands.

Jones fell in love with the site at once. "It seemed that this land had been lying here for years waiting for someone to lay a golf course upon it." The money for the purchase was obtained piecemeal – this was so soon after the Wall Street crash of 1929 that some of his backers were still strapped for ready cash.

Once the purchase had been underwritten, however, more cash

GRAND SLAMMER *J.A.A. Berrie's 1930 portrait of Bobby Jones*

flowed in from all over the world to meet building costs. It was built to Mackenzie's design in about a year, incorporating the latest in irrigation systems. Augusta National, as it was to be called, was right up to date in this regard. Jones struck a great many balls to verify shot values around the lay-out, which was designed with massive fairways and greens, little rough and few bunkers. Instead of these, mounds were used to produce a rolling topography much after the style of Jones's beloved St Andrews with its seaside humps and hollows. One of the underlying aims had been to produce a course which would look far more difficult than it really was. Jones wanted all his friends, expert or not, to enjoy the course.

By the time the first Augusta

National Invitation was issued in 1934, the final touch had been added – that every hole should be named after a blossom, and decorated with that blossom, among others.

The idea that this was no more than a jolly spring meeting for Jones's friends at the close of the professional winter tour lasted no time at all. No one knows if Roberts had a long-term vision of Augusta as a world-class event, but his promotional skills and the box office appeal of Jones did the trick with bewildering speed. Roberts made a fuss of the Press, always a good Public Relations move, and paid old-time pros to sit around in front of the clubhouse. He later hit a promotional jackpot by enrolling Eisenhower as a member: schmaltz, class and flowers make a potent mixture. Roberts persuaded Jones to play in the first and (as it turned out) only Augusta Invitation event. That followed a get-together for members and friends (a few members had started to play on the course at the end of 1932), at which, at Rice's behest, Roberts and Jones were to be given *carte blanche* to run Augusta National.

Jones did not like the idea of calling the Invitation event the Masters, deeming it presumptuous. However, as soon as the notion that the competition might have been called the Masters got out to the Press, they adopted the name right away, though the official programme made no mention of "Masters". Many years passed before Jones joined the general approbation of the title, and indeed before the entry became anything more than merely invitational. The other majors were never so restricted.

Jones finished 10 shots behind the first winner, Horton Smith, one of the very few players who had beaten Jones in his climactic year of 1930. Yet Jones as usual got more column inches!

The only leading player missing from the field in the first year was Gene Sarazen, who was playing on a tour of South America. He made up for his initial absence in a big way in 1935. He needed three birdies to catch Craig Wood, who had finished with 282. He got the three shots he needed in a flash by holing his four-wood second shot at the par five 15th. Walter Hagen, in a piquant pairing with Sarazen, and Jones, as a spectator, were among the few witnesses of the shot "heard round the world", the description given to it by the media.

Sarazen parred 16, 17 and 18, and as usual when a player is overtaken by such a cruel stroke as Sarazen's, Wood lost the play-off. No one, not the big three of the '60s, Palmer, Nicklaus and Player, nor even Ballesteros, specialist in the spectacular, has topped Sarazen's Masterly touch. Smith won again in 1936,

by which time the title Masters was, for all but Jones, set in stone. More Masterly golf, with the new shafts of steel, came from Texan Byron Nelson, who set new standards in 1937 with a flying start of 66, hitting every green in regulation figures (except the par fives, which he reached in two). Still they poured out of Texas: stars like three-time winner Jimmy Demaret, Ralph Guldahl and Ben Hogan helped ticket sales to soar, and yet another, Lloyd Mangrum, shook the the Masters firmament, but not the eventual winner, Demaret, with a scintillating opening round of 64 in 1940.

Amazingly, though Jones's golf was on the decline, the same could seldom be said right up to the Second World War of the space newspapers reserved for his rounds. All this finished after Nelson's second Masters in 1942, when the club was wound down for the duration, with cattle keeping the grass short, and profit made from turkey farming.

Private contributions from rich members revived the club and course, improved the clubhouse, and got things rolling once Jones, Snead, Hogan and company got out of uniform.

The Masters was still far short of the riches it has attained in the television age. Yet the strong flavour of exclusivity it has always had began to work in its favour more and more, aided by the flowering of Ben Hogan as the first great post-war player. His astonishing recovery from dreadful road crash injuries in 1949 added to the public sense of wonder at his achievements. He lost by a stroke to Herman Keiser in 1946, was within a stroke of the best four-round total in winning his first Masters in 1951, and beat it by five shots with 274 two years later, when he went on to win both the big Opens.

Hogan's quality was succeeded just at the right moment for Augusta by the irrepressible showmanship of a player born to be a television star, for Arnold Palmer won his first Masters (1958) in the early days of sports coverage on the box. He perfectly complemented Roberts's relentless eye for detail and flair for presenting the players as stars upon a green and flowery stage which might have been invented for television.

The exclusive nature of the Masters has been enhanced (and since aped elsewhere) by the outward symbol of success: the symbolic green jacket, made of a specially reserved cloth, that can be worn only by club members and Master golfers. Only the champions may wear it off the course, and only as long as they remain champion and provided it is not demeaned by its use for commercial purposes.

Roberts made sure the course was so policed and roped off that there was space around the players (and no reporters inside the ropes). There is always more room for the players in another important sense: in 1994, for example, only 51 players qualified for the final 36 holes when José-Maria Olazabal got his first green jacket out of a total entry of 86. Nearly twice as many play in most top-line pro events.

Roberts, who was laid low by a terminal illness and died by his own hand in 1977, made the Masters ticket by far the most difficult to obtain in world golf. He was not the most popular of golf's dictators, but proved a truth that many a club should heed: committees are frequently not the best government.

Roberts's skill was to present

FAME AT A STROKE *Gene Sarazen, remembered for his double eagle*

CLOSING IN ON VICTORY *José-Maria Olazabal drives off Augusta's 13th, during the final round in his 1994 success*

world-class golf with an amateur, country club ethos in many subtle ways, for little is made of mundane items like money, though plenty of it is available for the leading finishers. The entry is no longer solely a matter of invitation, and the highly successful gain entry whether the club likes it or not. All the same, for the first 38 years no black player was admitted to the Masters, though such men as Charlie Sifford, in 1973, had performed as well as many white players who had gained a place. But he did not get enough points on a scale Roberts had developed, and was excluded despite grumbles from US congressmen. Next year Lee Elder won the Monsanto Open, and cut the Augustan knot for black players. Black *caddies* have always been the norm at Augusta.

Palmer's four Masters triumphs were trumped by Jack Nicklaus's six, the last, in 1986, a tonic to every golfer over 40. Gary Player, thrice a winner, was, in 1961, the first non-American to succeed at Augusta. Nineteen years passed before another foreigner followed suit – the Spaniard Severiano Ballesteros, who began an unprecedented European domination of an American event. Five European wins in the 1980s (Ballesteros 2, Bernard Langer, Sandy Lyle and Nick Faldo) have been followed up by Faldo, completing a rare double, Ian Woosnam, Langer (again), and Olazabal.

Faldo's double was performed the hard way, for he beat Scott Hoch

FINAL STRETCH *(Facing page) Jack Nicklaus on the way to his 1986 win*

at the second extra hole in 1989, and repeated the feat to overcome a doughty Augusta campaigner and a former green jacket man in Raymond Floyd in 1990. A convenient explanation for repeated success is that broadly the same group of international stars play the course every year and become used to Augusta's foibles. Less easy to explain is why the Europeans have

coped so well of late with the huge, fast greens, and the need not merely to hit greens but the right areas on the putting surfaces to facilitate holing out. Europeans manage less well on the narrow courses lined with heavy rough set up for the US Open and PGA Championships.

Whoever wins, the fans, Press and television cameras lap it all up, and it is hard to resist the thought that Jones's ability to make things happen has been transferred to the course that was his last rich gift to golf; how else to explain that while last nines excite in so many events, the drama seems more knife-edged amid Augusta's flowery elegance?

Defeat seems crueller here, notably Greg Norman's second extra hole loss to Larry Mize's giant chip-in. The associated faint praise for Mize was also cruel, for Norman had his touch of luck on the previous hole, where Mize's birdie putt seemed sure to drop but didn't. Cru-

ellest of all was the play-off with Bob Goalby that was denied to Roberto de Vicenzo in 1968 because he signed for one more shot than he had taken. "I am a stupid", said the Argentine, whose courteous acceptance of his fate must have charmed Jones. A spinal illness kept the founder of Augusta from the Masters for the last three years of his life, ended by an aneurysm in 1971.

V FOR VICTORY *Olazabal salutes his first major championship*

Masters results at Augusta National, Georgia

Year	Winner	Runner-up	Score	Year	Winner	Runner-up	Score
1934	H Smith	C Wood	284	1969	G Archer	T Weiskopf, W Casper G Knudson	281
1935	G Sarazen	C Wood	282	1970	W Casper	G Littler	279
	WON PLAY-OFF 144 TO 149				*WON PLAY-OFF 69 TO 74*		
1936	H Smith	H Cooper	285	1971	C Coody	J Miller, J Nicklaus	279
1937	B Nelson	R Guldahl	283	1972	J Nicklaus	T Weiskopf, B Crampton, R Mitchell	286
1938	H Picard	R Guldahl	285				
1939	R Guldahl	S Snead, W Burke, W Lawson Little	279	1973	T Aaron	J C Snead	283
				1974	G Player	D Stockton, T Weiskopf	278
1940	J Demaret	L Mangrum	280	1975	J Nicklaus	J Miller, T Weiskopf	276
1941	C Wood	B Nelson	280	1976	R Floyd	B Crenshaw	271
1942	B Nelson	B Hogan	280	1977	T Watson	J Nicklaus	276
	WON PLAY-OFF 69 TO 70			1978	G Player	R Funseth, H Green T Watson	277
1943–45	No tournament						
1946	H Keiser	B Hogan	282	1979	F Zoeller	T Watson, E Sneed	280
1947	J Demaret	B Nelson, F Stranahan	281		*WON PLAY-OFF AT SECOND EXTRA HOLE*		
1948	C Harmon	C Middlecoff	279	1980	S Ballesteros	G Gilbert, J Newton	275
1949	S Snead	J Bulla, L Mangrum	282	1981	T Watson	J Nicklaus, J Miller	280
1950	J Demaret	J Ferrier	283	1982	C Stadler	D Pohl	284
1951	B Hogan	S Riegel	280		*WON PLAY-OFF AT FIRST EXTRA HOLE*		
1952	S Snead	J Burke, Jnr	286	1983	S Ballesteros	B Crenshaw, T Kite	280
1953	B Hogan	P Oliver, Jnr	274	1984	B Crenshaw	T Watson	277
1954	S Snead	B Hogan	289	1985	B Langer	C Strange, R Floyd, S Ballesteros	282
	WON PLAY-OFF 70 TO 71						
1955	C Middlecoff	B Hogan	279	1986	J Nicklaus	T Kite, G Norman	279
1956	J Burke, Jnr	K Venturi	289	1987	L Mize	S Ballesteros, G Norman	285
1957	D Ford	S Snead	283		*WON PLAY-OFF AT SECOND EXTRA HOLE*		
1958	A Palmer	D Ford, F Hawkins	284	1988	S Lyle	M Calcavecchia	281
1959	A Wall, Jnr	C Middlecoff	284	1989	N Faldo	S Hoch	283
1960	A Palmer	K Venturi	282		*WON PLAY-OFF AT SECOND EXTRA HOLE*		
1961	G Player	A Palmer, C Coe	280	1990	N Faldo	R Floyd	278
1962	A Palmer	G Player, D Finsterwald	280		*WON PLAY-OFF AT SECOND EXTRA HOLE*		
	WON PLAY-OFF 68 TO 71 TO 77			1991	I Woosnam	J-M Olazabal	277
1963	J Nicklaus	A Lema	286	1992	F Couples	R Floyd	275
1964	A Palmer	D Marr, J Nicklaus	276	1993	B Langer	C Beck	277
1965	J Nicklaus	A Palmer, G Player	271	1994	J-M Olazabal	T Lehman	279
1966	J Nicklaus	T Jacobs, G Brewer	288	1995	B Crenshaw	D Love III	274
	WON PLAY-OFF 70 TO 72 TO 78						
1967	G Brewer	R Nichols	280				
1968	R Goalby	R de Vicenzo	277				

US OPEN

Late twentieth-century competitive golf is dominated by the professionals, but the amateurs of America were the fashionable end of the game as the US golf boom throbbed into action in the last decade of the nineteenth century. All the same, early attempts to stage both Amateur and Open Championships were a shambles. Neither the United States Golf Association (USGA) nor the US PGA recognize, as some record books do, the 1894 affair at the St Andrew's Club, in New York City's Bronx, won by Willie Dunn from Musselburgh at match play against fellow Scot Willie Campbell by two holes. This is not surprising, because the USGA was not founded until the winter of 1894, by representatives of St Andrew's and four other clubs, Chicago, Newport, Shinnecock Hills and The Country Club, Brookline.

Their primary purpose was to decide when, where and on what basis the Amateur and Open titles were to be decided. For the first three years both were played at the same time and course; the USGA's first choice was Newport's nine-holer, in September, 1895, but the double-header was put off until the following month because of a clash with the America's Cup yacht races, which says a good deal about golf's standing at the time.

Moreover, the Open was relegated to a one-day, 36-hole affair to follow the three-day Amateur event, won from a field of 32 by Charles Macdonald, founder of the Chicago club. Most early American pros hailed from Scotland; their throaty accents were difficult to understand. Many had started out as caddies, and they had a reputation, deserved or not, as hard drinkers: they were not about to be admitted to the cream of East Coast society.

So Macdonald's victory was considered to be of far greater import than that gained on October 4 by Harold Rawlins, at 19 the youngest

of all US Open champions. This Englishman, recently arrived to become assistant at the Newport club, scored 172 (91, 82) with a gutty ball, and won $150, a $50 gold medal and the Open Championship Cup for his club. He had beaten nine other pros and one amateur.

Though the US Open was dominated by Scottish and English pros until the 1911 victory of Johnny McDermott from Atlantic City, it quickly became the one to win for paid or unpaid Americans, and there were some highly resourceful unpaid swingers about. The elevation of the pro to teacher, writer of instructional books and designer and endorser of all manner of golf gear and clothing made it, above all others, the crown that bestowed the Midas touch.

Modern pros have a true-blue amateur, Francis Sales Ouimet from Boston, to thank for putting golf on the front page. His defeat of a formidable English pair in Harry Vardon and Ted Ray in a play-off for the 1913 Open that lit the touch-

ON TARGET *Jack Nicklaus putting towards his first major win, in the 1962 play-off with Arnold Palmer at Oakmont*

paper of a further American golf explosion: and Ouimet was merely the scout, not the Seventh Cavalry.

It says much for the easy assumption of his prolonged status as American Sporting Hero grade one by Ouimet's modern counterpart, Arnold Palmer, that although he won the US Open once only, with his most cavalier finish, he was the first of golf's major tycoons. Within 10 years of his victory at Cherry Hills in 1960, Palmer's businesses had an annual turnover in excess of $15,000,000.

By contrast, Willie Anderson, four-time winner from North Berwick in Scotland, died at 31, some said because he drank too much. Anderson would strike a bizarre figure on the course today, for he deployed a flat swing with a bent left elbow. Although no one has equalled Anderson's feat of a hat-trick of Opens, from 1903 to 1905, his record of four victories is shared by an illustrious threesome in Bobby Jones, Ben Hogan and Jack Nicklaus, all giants of the game and all totally different from each other in style and temperament.

Jones, the southern gentleman, with degrees in mechanical engineering, literature and law, and with more victories than any other amateur, added to his four US Opens two lost play-offs, a second place and (at 19 years of age) joint fifth. Apart from his saving shot from the sand at Royal Lytham's 17th in 1926, the most remarkable of his career must surely have been at Interlachen, during the third leg of his 1930 Grand Slam, when he was five shots ahead with 18 holes to play. A miscue on the long 9th hole in the second round proved a godsend: although he almost topped his second shot, his ball, instead of diving into the lake guarding the green, skipped across it, ducks and drakes fashion, and was eventually holed for a birdie four.

Hogan, almost universally recognized as the purest striker of the ball in golf history, gained all his Opens in a time span of only six years. He would certainly have earned a fifth and perhaps even a sixth US Open had his life at the top not been limited by the aftermath of the 1949 road crash injuries from which he recovered by a great effort of will to win his second Open in 1950, the Golden Jubilee of the Championship. Even more remarkably, though every step of the extra 18 holes must have been a challenge, he triumphed in a play-off, scoring 69 against Lloyd Mangrum's

73 and George Fazio's 75. Mangrum would have come closer, with 71, had he not picked up his ball to blow a fly off it.

Further Open successes followed in 1951 and 1953, when Hogan led after every round, a feat unequalled since 1921, and finished (at Oakmont!) with three threes, a par and two birdies. He lost a play-off in 1955, and was joint second the following year.

Of the ones that got away, none would have caused him more regret than the 1960 Open, for it came close to his 48th birthday, and offered the juicy possibility of upstaging two young tigers in one fell swoop, none other than Palmer and Nicklaus. Hogan required pars on the 71st and 72nd holes for 280, which would have equalled Palmer's winning score. He scored a six and a seven, four over. A fired-up Palmer ravenous for success might have been more than even Hogan could manage in a play-off, but the prospect of two generations in mortal combat is, to say the least, enticing.

Nicklaus, who had set an amateur scoring record of 282 in achieving second place at Cherry Hills, went one better in 1962, and won his fourth Open 18 years later. How typical of Nicklaus's career, high level from the first, that his first professional win should be in the 1962 Open at Oakmont. He was a little over 23; best of all, perhaps, it was gained at the expense of Arnold Palmer in a play-off.

Nicklaus was surely the best heeled as a youngster of all the professional giants of the US Open, for his father was a well-to-do owner of pharmacies. Financial security for Nicklaus did not mean security for his opponents: his single-minded pursuit of excellence and major titles has no parallel in golf's history.

While Nicklaus hit the target with his first professional attempt at the Open, Andy North has won only three titles, the first a PGA Tour event in 1977. The other two are US Opens, similar victories in that his final round in each case, at Cherry Hills in 1978 and Oakland Hills in 1985, was a nervous 74.

It seemed for some time at Oakland Hills that the first Open win by an Asian, Tze-Chung Chen from

Taiwan, was about to burst on the world of golf. But a double hit at a crucial juncture led to a final 77, after rounds of 65, 66, 69. Even then he was only one shot away from a tie with North.

By contrast, David Graham played a final round to win in 1981 at Merion that was almost without flaw. He strode past George Burns to become the first Australian to win the title, and the first foreigner since Tony Jacklin 11 years earlier. He missed one fairway, the first, and that by not very much: he still birdied that hole, and his final 67 gave him a total of 273, one more than Nicklaus's record Open score, set at Baltusrol the previous year. The round suited Graham's character: straight-backed, very correct in his manner.

His error-free round was succeeded 12 months later by a Tom Watson coup to rob Nicklaus of a coveted fifth Open. Watson's chip at Pebble Beach's short 17th recalls the defining moment of Sarazen's career, his double eagle to turn the 1935 Masters upside-down. Before long Watson was writing a book on

STRAIGHT AND NARROW *David Graham kept it on the hard-to-find fairways for his 1981 victory at Merion*

the short game: how to get "up and down". He showed the world how on the Californian clifftops. Needing a birdie to get past Nicklaus, he overshot the 17th but, from dense semi-rough, he told his caddie he would hole a chip shot – and did hole it, the ball running in downhill from a cuppy lie: a triumph of nerve and touch, for as Bobby Jones once wrote, "the delicate shot, if it fails, fails completely". Watson laid up at the long last hole, but still got a birdie to win by two.

Lack of a first English win since Jacklin's has not been for want of trying on the part of Nick Faldo, most successful of post-war British players. Curtis Strange landed a rare Open double in 1988–89, the first by beating Faldo by four shots in a play-off at Brookline. Faldo came close again in 1990, sharing third place with Billy Ray Brown, a stroke behind the play-off pair of Irwin and Donald.

The 1988 event brought joy for Strange, his Open crowning a year of three other first places. In the 1989 Open, his only win of the year, he held off Ian Woosnam, Mark Mc-Cumber and Chip Beck by a stroke. Not since Hogan (1950–51) had the double been performed.

Since Graham's marvellous round, no foreigner had stormed the USGA's most closest guarded citadel – until Ernie Els, the immensely powerful South African, at 24 years of age beat off Loren Roberts and Colin Montgomerie in a sweltering 1994 Oakmont at the second extra hole of a sudden-death play-off after a tie with Roberts in the 18-hole play-off round which is a feature of this championship.

Over the years the Championship has been given an added spice by the USGA's policy of setting courses that stretch nerves and (some say) exact undue punishment for off-line shots. This was perfectly illustrated in 1995, when Corey Pavin's winning score was a level-par 280 at Shinnecock Hills. Not every critic – or golfer – is in love or agreement with the way US Open greens are cut to lightning speed and the rough is encouraged to the extent that recoveries are often a matter of damage-control rather than par-saving. This, say the

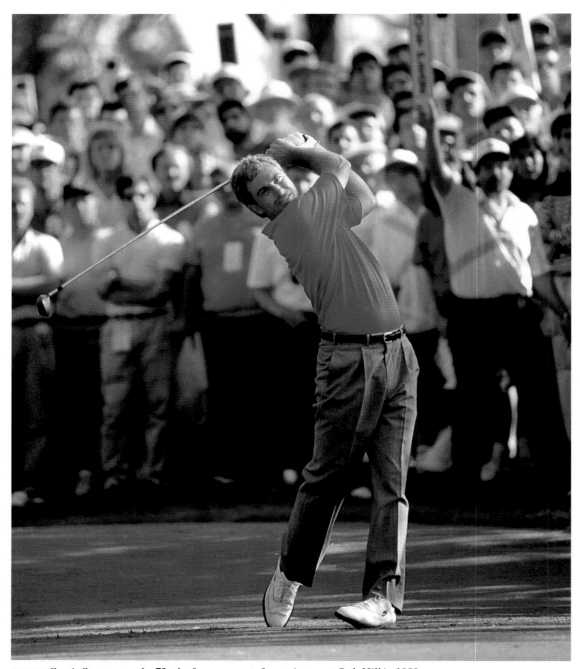

LAST LAP *Curtis Strange on the 72nd a few moments from victory at Oak Hill in 1989*

USGA's detractors, gives safety-first golfers an undue advantage. This view was widely expressed when Sam Parks, known only in the immediate catchment area of the 1935 Open course, Oakmont in Pennsylvania, won with the only sub-300 score – 299. This was the highest score since the 1914–18 war, apart from Tommy Armour's 301, also at Oakmont, and Walter Hagen's 301 in 1919 at Brae Burn, Massachusetts. Parks's stroke average of 74.75 rather bore out cynical comment that Parks could score

75 on any course, but that that was about the sum of his abilities. For all that, Open courses, even justifiably feared Oakmont, have on occasion received rough treatment, notably Johnny Miller's final 63 at that very course in 1973.

No other champion of a major Open has ever won with a final round as low as that, though Greg Norman's missed tiddler on the 17th at Royal St George's in an otherwise unflawed fourth round in the British Open of 1993 cost him a share of

Miller's record. Of the current players Els, his long-hitting perfectly complemented by a mature touch at close range, is the best bet to put up a stern chase of the four-time winners of the US Open, especially as he has determined to concentrate on the most demanding tour, that of the American PGA.

It is not difficult to imagine that at the Far Hills HQ of the USGA, the planning staff will not be preparing a bed of roses for Els or any of his fellows.

Year (36 holes till 1898)	Winner	Runner-up	Venue	Score
1895	H Rawlins	W Dunn	Newport, RI	173
1896	J Foulis	H Rawlins	Shinnecock Hills, NY	152
1897	J Lloyd	W Anderson	Chicago, IL	162
1898	F Herd	A Smith	Myopia, MA	328
1899	W Smith	G Low, V Fitzjohn, W H Way	Baltimore, MD	315
1900	H Vardon	J H Taylor	Chicago, IL	313
1901	W Anderson	A Smith	Myopia, MA	331
	WON PLAY-OFF 85 TO 86			
1902	L Auchterlonie	S Gardner, W J Travis	Garden City, NY	307
1903	W Anderson	D Brown	Baltusrol, NJ	307
	WON PLAY-OFF 82 TO 84			
1904	W Anderson	G Nicholls	Glen View, IL	303
1905	W Anderson	A Smith	Myopia, MA	314
1906	A Smith	W Smith	Onwentsia, IL	295
1907	A Ross	G Nicholls	Philadelphia CC, PA	302
1908	F McLeod	W Smith	Myopia, MA	322
	WON PLAY-OFF 77 TO 83			
1909	G Sargent	T McNamara	Englewood, NJ	290
1910	A Smith	J J McDermott MacDonald Smith	Philadelphia CC, PA	298
	WON PLAY-OFF 71 TO 75 TO 77			
1911	J J McDermott	M J Brady G O Simpson	Chicago, IL	307
	WON PLAY-OFF 80 TO 82 TO 85			
1912	J J McDermott	T McNamara	Buffalo, NY	294
1913	F Ouimet	H Vardon, T Ray	Brookline, MA	304
	WON PLAY-OFF 72 TO 77 TO 78			
1914	W Hagen	C Evans Jnr	Midlothian, IL	290
1915	J D Travers	T McNamara	Baltusrol, NJ	297
1916	C Evans Jnr	J Hutchison	Minikahda, MN	286
1917-18	No championship			
1919	W Hagen	M J Brady	Brae Burn, MA	301
	WON PLAY-OFF 77 TO 78			
1920	T Ray	H Vardon, J Burke, L Diegel, J Hutchison	Inverness, OH	295
1921	J Barnes	W Hagen, F McLeod	Chevy Chase, MD	289
1922	G Sarazen	J L Black	Skokie, Glencoe, IL	288
1923	R T Jones Jnr	R A Cruickshank	Inwood, NY	296
	WON PLAY-OFF 76 TO 78			
1924	C Walker	R T Jones Jnr	Oakland Hills, MI	297
1925	W Macfarlane	R T Jones Jnr	Worcester, MA	291
	WON PLAY-OFF 147 TO 148			
1926	R T Jones Jnr	J Turnesa	Scioto, OH	293
1927	T Armour	H Cooper	Oakmont, PA	301
	WON PLAY-OFF 76 TO 79			
1928	J J Farrell	R T Jones Jnr	Olympia Fields, IL	294
	WON PLAY-OFF 143 TO 144			
1929	R T Jones Jnr	A Espinosa	Winged Foot, NY	294
	WON PLAY-OFF 141 TO 164			
1930	R T Jones Jnr	MacDonald Smith	Interlachen, MN	287
1931	B Burke	G Von Elm	Inverness, OH	292
	WON SECOND 36-HOLE PLAY-OFF 148 TO 149: FIRST TIED AT 149			
1932	G Sarazen	T P Perkins, R Cruickshank	Fresh Meadow, NY	286
1933	J Goodman	R Guldahl	N. Shore, IL	287
1934	O Dutra	G Sarazen	Merion CC, PA	293
1935	S Parks	J Thomson	Oakmont, PA	299
1936	T Manero	H Cooper	Baltusrol, NJ	282
1937	R Guldahl	S Snead	Oakland Hills, MI	281
1938	R Guldahl	D Metz	Cherry Hills, CO	284
1939	B Nelson	C Wood, D Shute	W. Conshohocken, PA	284
	WON PLAY-OFF 138 TO 141			
1940	W Lawson Little	G Sarazen	Canterbury, OH	287
	WON PLAY-OFF 70 TO 73			
1941	C Wood	D Shute	Colonial, Ft Worth, TX	284
1942-45	No championship			
1946	L Mangrum	B Nelson, V Ghezzi	Canterbury, OH	284
	WON PLAY-OFF 72 TO 73			
1947	L Worsham	S Snead	St Louis, Clayton, MO	282
	WON PLAY-OFF 69 TO 70			
1948	B Hogan	J Demaret	Riviera, L Angeles, CA	276

Year	Winner	Runner-up	Venue	Score
1949	C Middlecoff	C Heafner, S Snead	Medinah, Chicago, IL	286
1950	B Hogan	L Mangrum, G Fazio	Merion, PA	287
	WON PLAY-OFF 69 TO 73 TO 75			
1951	B Hogan	C Heafner	Oakland Hills, MI	287
1952	J Boros	P Oliver Jnr	Northwood, Dallas, TX	281
1953	B Hogan	S Snead	Oakmont, PA	283
1954	E Furgol	G Littler	Baltusrol, NJ	284
1955	J Fleck	B Hogan	Olympic, CA	287
	WON PLAY-OFF 69 TO 72			
1956	C Middlecoff	B Hogan, J Boros	Oak Hill, Rochester, NY	281
1957	R Mayer	C Middlecoff	Inverness, OH	282
	WON PLAY-OFF 72 TO 79			
1958	T Bolt	G Player	Southern Hills, OK	283
1959	W Casper	B Rosburg	Winged Foot, NY	282
1960	A Palmer	J Nicklaus	Cherry Hills, CO	280
1961	G Littler	R Goalby, D Sanders	Oakland Hills, MI	281
1962	J Nicklaus	A Palmer	Oakmont, PA	283
	WON PLAY-OFF 71 TO 74			
1963	J Boros	J D Cupit, A Palmer	Brookline, MA	293
	WON PLAY-OFF 70 TO 73 TO 76			
1964	K Venturi	T Jacobs	Congressional, MD	278
1965	G Player	K D G Nagle	Bellerive, MO	282
	WON PLAY-OFF 71 TO 74			
1966	W Casper	A Palmer	Olympic, CA	278
	WON PLAY-OFF 69 TO 73			
1967	J Nicklaus	A Palmer	Baltusrol, NJ	275
1968	L Trevino	J Nicklaus	Oak Hill, Rochester, NY	275
1969	O Moody	D Beman, A Geiberger, B Rosburg	Cypress Creek, TX	281
1970	A Jacklin	D Hill	Hazeltine, MN	281
1971	L Trevino	J Nicklaus	Merion, PA	280
	WON PLAY-OFF 68 TO 71			
1972	J Nicklaus	B Crampton	Pebble Beach, CA	290
1973	J Miller	J Schlee	Oakmont, PA	279
1974	H Irwin	F Fezler	Winged Foot, NY	287
1975	L Graham	J Mahaffey	Medinah, Chicago, IL	287
	WON PLAY-OFF 71 TO 73			
1976	J Pate	A Geiberger, T Weiskopf	Duluth, GA	277
1977	H Green	L Graham	Southern Hills, OK	278
1978	A North	J C Snead, D Stockton	Cherry Hills, CO	285
1979	H Irwin	J Pate, G Player	Inverness, OH	284
1980	J Nicklaus	I Aoki	Baltusrol, NJ	272
1981	D Graham	W Rogers, G Burns	Merion, PA	273
1982	T Watson	J Nicklaus	Pebble Beach, CA	282
1983	L Nelson	T Watson	Oakmont, PA	280
1984	F Zoeller	G Norman	Winged Foot, NY	276
	WON PLAY-OFF 67 TO 75			
1985	A North,	D Watson, D Barr, T-C Chen	Oakland, Hills, MI	279
1986	R Floyd	L Wadkins, C Beck	Shinnecock Hills, NY	279
1987	S Simpson	T Watson	Olympic, CA	277
1988	C Strange	N Faldo	Brookline, MA	278
	WON PLAY-OFF 71 TO 75			
1989	C Strange	I Woosnam, M McCumber, C Beck	Oak Hill, Rochester, NY	278
1990	H Irwin	M Donald	Medinah, Chicago, IL	280
	WON PLAY-OFF AT FIRST EXTRA HOLE AFTER TIE (74) OVER 18 HOLES			
1991	P Stewart	S Simpson	Hazeltine, MN	282
	WON PLAY-OFF 75 TO 77			
1992	T Kite	J Sluman	Pebble Beach, CA	285
1993	L Janzen	P Stewart	Baltusrol, NJ	272
1994	E Els	L Roberts, C Montgomerie	Oakmont, PA	279
	18-HOLE PLAY-OFF SCORES: ELS 74, ROBERTS 74, MONTGOMERIE 78; ELS BEAT ROBERTS AT SECOND EXTRA HOLE OF SUDDEN-DEATH PLAY-OFF.			
1995	C Pavin	G Norman	Shinnecock Hills, NY	280

BRITISH OPEN

Considering that the British Open Championship is a movable feast, it ranks as one of the best organized major sporting events in the world, though it is, perforce, not nearly as well travelled as the US Open, which has visited nearly 50 courses across the North American continent. The Open has drifted into the doldrums from time to time. Nowadays such a fate for the oldest of the major championships (founded 25 years before the second championship to be accepted as a major meeting, the British Amateur), is unimaginable. Attendance soars regularly past 20,000 a day, a huge tented village offers golf gear, food and drink, and media coverage is massive, notably on television.

All this stems from the idea put forward by Prestwick Golf Club in 1860 to find a successor to the late, great Allan Robertson. Only eight players competed for the red morocco Championship Belt put up by Prestwick for competition over three rounds of the club's 12-hole course. Willie Park from Musselburgh won from seven rivals (all pros, so this was not technically an Open at all), but the early history of the Open, which involved amateurs from 1861 onwards, is dominated by Tom Morris, runner-up in this first staging of the event, and his son, also called Tom, whose brilliant scoring in 1870 was not bettered until 1904. After Old Tom won for the fourth time, Young Tom achieved a hat-trick of Opens, and so took the Belt outright before going on to win for the fourth time in succession, a record still, and becoming the first holder of the present trophy, a silver claret jug, in 1871.

Sport knows no more poignant story than the death of Young Tom in 1875, heartbroken after the death of his wife in childbirth while he and his father were playing Willie and Mungo Park in a challenge match at North Berwick across the Firth of Forth. Old Tom's assessment of his son's golf skills was that he could never cope with young Tom, though he could with Robertson, which rather demolishes the legend of Robertson's invincibility.

It is well documented that Young Tom had no weakness in his game. A long hitter with uncanny touch on and round the green, he had a full house of talents that has never been paralleled, except possibly by Bobby Jones. Sixty golfing societies put together the fund to erect a fine monument to Young Tom in St Andrews Cathedral yard.

His father lived until 1908. "A legend in his own lifetime" could truly be said of Old Tom, for many years greenkeeper of the Old Course. He played in every Open until 1896, a year that linked two golfing eras . . . the year of Harry Vardon's first victory.

Before the golfing giant of America was fully awake, three British champions (16 Opens between them) ruled the roost in the years before the First World War. Harry Vardon edged in 1914 to his record sixth Open, upstaging J. H. Taylor and James Braid (five apiece). Tom Watson has come closest among the moderns to emulating Vardon.

Two names are inseparable from an account of the resurgence of the Championship over the last 35 years: Keith MacKenzie, who officiated as Royal and Ancient Club secretary for the last time in 1983 before Michael Bonallack took over, and Arnold Palmer. The strength of US golf since the First World War has meant that when a representative entry has failed for whatever reason to cross the Atlantic, the British Open's significance has been much diminished.

The persistence of the Great Depression, fewer events on the US PGA tour, and less prize money, meant that few Americans could afford to participate after the early 1930s, as evidence the string of British winners following the almost unbroken run of American champions from 1921, including such box office favourites as Walter Hagen, Gene Sarazen and Bobby Jones. In 1937, however, when the US Ryder Cup team was in Britain, Henry Cotton proved his world class by finishing comfortably ahead of a daunting phalanx of the leading American players.

Sam Snead, who won the first Championship after the 1940–45 hiatus, found that the prize money

KNICKERBOCKER GLORY *Harry Vardon won his sixth Open in 1914*

(about $600) did not cover his expenses. The fact that he at first mistook the stark topography of St Andrews, the scene of his only major Open success (for he invented one unlikely method after another to miss out on his own national Open), for an abandoned golf course may have put him in the right frame of mind to overcome any nerves.

South Africa and Australia provided the stars of the 1950s, in Bobby Locke and Peter Thomson respectively, Locke having surprised the American pros by winning sackfuls of money from them, a spree which was restricted after the US PGA banned him from their events in 1949 for allegedly failing to honour playing contracts.

The exception to this southern hemisphere to-ing and fro-ing provided one of the Open's defining moments: a player of legendary skill focusing his powers on a difficult course, and getting the better of it a little more each day.

This was Ben Hogan's one attempt on the Open. Not a man given to adulterating golf with sentiment, he had won the 1953 Masters and the US Open, and no one had ever won these two and the British Open in one season. The thought must also have occurred, as it did in times past to Walter Hagen and Bobby Jones, that he must prove his standing in the game's history by winning in Britain.

He could hardly have chosen a more difficult challenge. His preparations for Carnoustie were thorough; he spent a fortnight sizing up this longest of Open courses, which the R&A dropped from the Open circuit after 1975, but which is to be used again in 1999. His attitude was characteristically taciturn, but more forthcoming with the Press than his laconic legend suggested. His four rounds demonstrated that he could harness the accuracy of his striking to any course, no matter how different from the lay-outs he was used to; in any case, his mastery of long, low shots controlled with a touch of fade was ideal for Carnoustie.

He scored 73, 71, 70, 68, and won by four shots from four players, Frank Stranahan, an American amateur, Antonio Cerda from Argentina, Thomson and Dai Rees. Roberto de Vicenzo was another stroke adrift, and the only other notable American in the field, Lloyd Mangrum, was 19 behind Hogan. Mangrum was used to trailing the new Open Champion by this time. He had been third to Hogan in the Masters – but eight strokes in arrears; and third in the US Open – nine behind. He cannot have enjoyed Carnoustie much, joking that the undulating fairways had made him feel seasick.

Hogan promised to come back to defend his title, but he never did. It would have been difficult to top his performance in any case: it was his last major success, and a date clash with the US PGA Championship meant he was ruled out of that. The clash demonstrates that the four modern majors were not yet seen as the four premier events in world golf. When Gary Player took his first major at Muirfield in 1959, the American challenge was non-existent.

The following year Arnold Palmer, who like Hogan in 1953 had already won the Masters and US Open, came, saw, but did not conquer in the golfing sense, finishing second to Kel Nagle in the Centenary Open. Instead, he captivated the British public, and won the next Open at Birkdale, where his 73 in the worst of a gale in the second round fitted his publicity: heroic. He seemed to have scored 72, but called a penalty stroke on himself on his assertion that his ball moved in the sand at the 16th. Next year he won again at Troon, where he established a record aggregate of 276 and won by six strokes.

The trickle of US participation did not immediately become a flood, but by the mid 1960s Palmer's initiative, followed by that of Jack Nicklaus, a winner at Muirfield in 1966, had ensured that the winner of the Open was again unarguably the top of his profession.

Thus the victory of Tony Jacklin in 1969 at Lytham by two shots from Bob Charles, the first and only left-hander to win, in 1963, raised the British game as nothing else could – barring, perhaps Jacklin's victory in the US Open in 1970. Jacklin's win had foreign players like Nicklaus, Nagle, Thomson, Gay Brewer, Orville Moody, Bert Yancey, Gary Player, Billy Casper, Ray Floyd and Lee Trevino all labouring in the Briton's wake.

His final drive to the tough-to-locate 18th fairway ("a corker", said Henry Longhurst, a favourite commentator in the United States just as in Britain) summed up the confidence and precision of his game as his greatest opportunity beckoned. He put his second shot just inside that of playing partner Charles as if to rubber-stamp his win.

Next year came the bitter disappointment of a thunder and lightning interrupted first round at St Andrews, where Jacklin quickly holed three birdies plus an eagle two (with a nine-iron second) at the ninth. Starting home with another birdie, his luck ran out when a shout of "Fore" put him off his stroke, and he deposited his ball in a gorse bush. Play was suspended, and next day the magic had gone, Jacklin finishing in "no better" than 67.

His anguish was in minor key compared to that suffered at the climax of this Championship by Doug Sanders, whose restricted swing still sent the ball a fair distance. On the 72nd hole came the moment every golfer longs for and dreads: a downhill four-footer for the Open. Disappointingly, he interrupted his routine to pick up some minute object. Instead of starting again, he putted, and the ball, as so often on the green named after Old Tom

Morris, second Open Champion of all, drifted marginally right. A recent comment from poor Sanders, when asked if he still thinks about the miss, is that sometimes he goes five whole minutes without the thing crossing his mind at all.

More eyebrow-raising stuff came the next day in a play-off with Nicklaus, who drove *through* the 385-yard 18th, but still managed to chip back and hole his birdie putt to gain a second Open by a stroke from oh-so-nearly man Sanders.

Jacklin was in the same doleful situation in 1972, Lee Trevino's luck being thoroughly in at Muirfield when a series of iffy shots turned up trumps, notably his chip in for his par at the 71st hole after missing the green – with his fourth shot.

Turnberry 1977 is a popular choice as the most thrilling Open of them all, as Tom Watson and Nicklaus both broke the aggregate record, and Watson took the title by a stroke. Spain's Severiano Ballesteros (even if his routes to Lytham's greens in 1979 tended to be circuitous) and Gary Player were the only players to break the American run of success that followed Jacklin's Open and persisted until a great sea change took place at the Open in the mid-1980s.

Willie Auchterlonie (1893) was the last home-based Scot to win the Open, but Sandy Lyle, a Scottish international although living south of the border, redressed the balance a little in favour of the land that gave golf to the world by winning at Royal St George's in 1985. A fluffed chip from the side of the 72nd hole could have been expensive, as Payne Stewart, seldom far from the leaders in recent British Opens, and David Graham were chasing hard. Errors crept in, however, and Lyle, waiting in the clubhouse, found his final 70 (par) was just good enough.

Turnberry in 1986 was not about to provide the low-scoring conditions that the Watson-Nicklaus show had featured in 1977. The weather was brutal, the rough seemingly bottomless, and Greg Norman needed every ounce of his strength and determination to keep afloat as his tee-off times condemned him to endure the worst of the weather on day three. A 69 as Turnberry relented on the last day gave him a five-shot margin.

More severe weather at Muirfield the following year brought the long-awaited Nick Faldo victory that seemed sure to follow his brilliant amateur career. Faldo was single-minded and brave enough to spend years remodelling his swing, and the fruits of this intense effort were a secure method that enabled him to par every hole of his fourth round and hold off Rodger Davis from Australia and a closely following group of leading Americans, led by Ryder Cup star Paul Azinger, who faltered at the last.

Faldo dominated the 1990 St Andrews Open with a record aggregate 270 and a five-shot win over Mark McNulty, of Zimbabwe, and the persistent Payne Stewart. A third Faldo Open at Muirfield two years later was a nerve-shredding affair for golfer and fans, after he started 64 ("best round of my life", said Faldo), 66 = 130, equalling the 36-hole record.

Yet he seemed to have thrown the title away as he started for home on the final day, and was overtaken by American John Cook, who, fatally, returned the compliment by missing a tiny birdie putt on the 17th, and dropping a shot at the 18th. Faldo, behind him, was carrying out his last-ditch task of "playing the best four holes of my life". In this critical situation two birdies and two pars was a stalwart and, as it transpired, winning effort.

Scoring reached a new low – 267, 13 under par – at St George's in 1993 as Faldo chased Norman home, Stewart finished with a fruitless 63, and the Australian's final round of 64, a prodigy of accurate driving, earned a two-shot win from the Englishman, and these words from Gene Sarazen, whose judgment can be trusted: "This was the greatest Championship I have known."

But who can tell? The best is usually yet to come.

"THE GREATEST" *Sarazen's view of Greg Norman's Open win at Sandwich*

Year	Winner	Runner-up	Venue	Score
(36 holes until 1892)				
1860	W Park	T Morris Snr	Prestwick	174
1861	T Morris Snr	W Park	Prestwick	163
1862	T Morris Snr	W Park	Prestwick	163
1863	W Park	T Morris Snr	Prestwick	168
1864	T Morris Snr	A Strath	Prestwick	167
1865	A Strath	W Park	Prestwick	162
1866	W Park	D Park	Prestwick	169
1867	T Morris Snr	W Park	Prestwick	167
1868	T Morris Jnr	R Andrew	Prestwick	157
1869	T Morris Jnr	T Morris Snr	Prestwick	154
1970	T Morris Jnr	R Kirk, D Strath	Prestwick	149
1871	No championship			
1872	T Morris Jnr	D Strath	Prestwick	166
1873	T Kidd	J Anderson	St Andrews	179
1874	M Park	T Morris Jnr	Musselburgh	159
1875	W Park	B Martin	Prestwick	166
1876	R Martin	D Strath	St Andrews	176
	STRATH REFUSED TO PLAY OFF			
1877	J Anderson	R Pringle	Musselburgh	160
1878	J Anderson	R Kirk	Prestwick	157
1879	J Anderson	J Allan, A Kirkaldy	St Andrews	169
1880	R Ferguson	P Paxton	Musselburgh	162
1881	R Ferguson	J Anderson	Prestwick	170
1882	R Ferguson	W Fernie	St Andrews	171
1883	W Fernie	R Ferguson	Musselburgh	159
	WON PLAY-OFF 158 TO 159			
1884	J Simpson	D Rolland, W Fernie	Prestwick	160
1885	R Martin	A Simpson	St Andrews	171
1886	D Brown	W Campbell	Musselburgh	157
1887	W Park Jnr	R Martin	Prestwick	161
1888	J Burns	D Anderson, B Sayers	St Andrews	171
1889	W Park Jnr	A Kirkaldy	Musselburgh	155
	WON PLAY-OFF 158 TO 163			
1890	J Ball	W Fernie	Prestwick	164
1891	H Kirkaldy	A Kirkaldy	St Andrews	166
1892	H H Hilton	J Ball, H Kirkaldy, A Herd	Muirfield	305
1893	W Auchterlonie	J E Laidlay	Prestwick	322
1894	J H Taylor	R Rolland	St George's	326
1895	J H Taylor	A Herd	St Andrews	322
1896	H Vardon	J H Taylor	Muirfield	316
	WON PLAY-OFF 157 TO 159			
1897	H H Hilton	J Braid	Hoylake	314
1898	H Vardon	W Park Jnr	Prestwick	307
1899	H Vardon	J White	St George's	307
1900	J H Taylor	H Vardon	St Andrews	309
1901	J Braid	H Vardon	Muirfield	309
1902	A Herd	H Vardon, J Braid	Hoylake	307
1903	H Vardon	T Vardon	Prestwick	300
1904	J White	J H Taylor, J Braid	St George's	296
1905	J Braid	R Jones, J H Taylor	St Andrews	318
1906	J Braid	J H Taylor	Muirfield	300
1907	A Massy	J H Taylor	Hoylake	312
1908	J Braid	T Ball	Prestwick	291
1909	J H Taylor	J Braid, T Ball	Deal	295
1910	J Braid	A Herd	St Andrews	299
1911	H Vardon	A Massy	St George's	303
	WON PLAY-OFF AT 35TH HOLE			
1912	E Ray	H Vardon	Muirfield	295
1913	J H Taylor	E Ray	Hoylake	304
1914	H Vardon	J H Taylor	Prestwick	306
1915-19	No championship			
1920	G Duncan	A Herd	Deal	303
1921	J Hutchison	R H Wethered	St Andrews	296
	WON PLAY-OFF 150 TO 159			
1922	W Hagen	G Duncan, J Barnes	St George's	300
1923	A G Havers	W Hagen	Troon	295
1924	W Hagen	E R Whitcombe	Hoylake	301
1925	J Barnes	E Ray, A Compston	Prestwick	300
1926	R T Jones Jnr	A Watrous	Lytham	291
1927	R T Jones Jnr	A Boomer, F Robson	St Andrews	285
1928	W Hagen	G Sarazen	St George's	292
1929	W Hagen	J Farrell	Muirfield	292
1930	R T Jones Jnr	Macdonald Smith, L Diegel	Hoylake	291

Year	Winner	Runner-up	Venue	Score
1931	T Armour	J Jurado	Carnoustie	296
1932	G Sarazen	Macdonald Smith	Prince's	283
1933	D Shute	C Wood	St Andrews	292
	WON PLAY-OFF 149 TO 154			
1934	T H Cotton	S F Brews	St George's	283
1935	A Perry	A H Padgham	Muirfield	283
1936	A H Padgham	J Adams	Hoylake	287
1937	T H Cotton	R A Whitcombe	Carnoustie	290
1938	R A Whitcombe	J Adams	St George's	285
1939	R Burton	J Bulla	St Andrews	290
1940-45	No championship			
1946	S Snead	A D Locke, J Bulla	St Andrews	290
1947	F Daly	R W Horne, F R Stranahan	Hoylake	293
1948	T H Cotton	F Daly	Muirfield	284
1949	A D Locke	H Bradshaw	St George's	283
	WON PLAY-OFF 136 TO 147			
1950	A D Locke	R de Vicenzo	Troon	279
1951	M Faulkner	A Cerda	Portrush	285
1952	A D Locke	P W Thomson	Lytham	287
1953	B Hogan	F R Stranaham, A Cerda, P W Thomson, D J Rees	Carnoustie	282
1954	P W Thomson	A D Locke, S Scott, D J Rees	Birkdale	283
1955	P W Thomson	J Fallon	St Andrews	281
1956	P W Thomson	F van Donck	Hoylake	286
1957	A D Locke	P W Thomson	St Andrews	279
1958	P W Thomson	D C Thomas	Lytham	278
	WON PLAY-OFF 139 TO 143			
1959	G Player	F van Donck, F Bullock	Muirfield	284
1960	K D G Nagle	A Palmer	St Andrews	278
1961	A Palmer	D J Rees	Birkdale	284
1962	A Palmer	K D G Nagle	Troon	276
1963	R J Charles	P Rodgers	Lytham	277
	WON PLAY-OFF 140 TO 148			
1964	A Lema	J Nicklaus	St Andrews	279
1965	P W Thomson	B Huggett, C O'Connor	Birkdale	285
1966	J Nicklaus	D C Thomas, D Sanders	Muirfield	282
1967	R de Vicenzo	J Nicklaus	Hoylake	278
1968	G Player	J Nicklaus, R J Charles	Carnoustie	289
1969	A Jacklin	R J Charles	Lytham	280
1970	J Nicklaus	D Sanders	St Andrews	283
	WON PLAY-OFF 72 TO 73			
1971	L Trevino	Liang Huan Lu	Birkdale	278
1972	L Trevino	J Nicklaus	Muirfield	278
1973	T Weiskopf	N C Coles, J Miller	Troon	276
1974	G Player	P Oosterhuis	Lytham	282
1975	T Watson	J Newton	Carnoustie	279
	WON PLAY-OFF 71 TO 72			
1976	J Miller	J Nicklaus, S Ballesteros	Birkdale	279
1977	T Watson	J Nicklaus	Turnberry	268
1978	J Nicklaus	S Owen, R Floyd, B Crenshaw, T Kite	St Andrews	281
1979	S Ballesteros	B Crenshaw, J Nicklaus	Lytham	283
1980	T Watson	L Trevino	Muirfield	271
1981	W Rogers	B Langer	St George's	276
1982	T Watson	P Oosterhuis, N Price	Troon	284
1983	T Watson	H Irwin, A Bean	Birkdale	275
1984	S Ballesteros	B Langer, T Watson	St Andrews	276
1985	S Lyle	P Stewart	St George's	282
1986	G Norman	G J Brand	Turnberry	280
1987	N Faldo	R Davis, P Azinger	Muirfield	279
1988	S Ballesteros	N Price	Lytham	273
1989	M Calcavecchia	G Norman, W Grady	Troon	275
	WON PLAY-OFF OVER FOUR HOLES			
1990	N Faldo	M McNulty, P Stewart	St Andrews	270
1991	I Baker-Finch	M Harwood	Birkdale	272
1992	N Faldo	J Cook	Muirfield	272
1993	G Norman	N Faldo	St George's	267
1994	N Price	J Parnevik	Turnberry	268

US PGA

Rodman Wanamaker is a name that does not loom large in the minds of most followers of golf, yet he set in motion the Championship which is today the fourth "major" in the world game…not only fourth in the golfing calendar (except for an unpopular and short-lived February experiment in Florida in 1971) but also ranked fourth in most people's estimation behind the two Opens and the Masters.

This does not mean it is the easiest to win, since the ranking US professionals are involved. While Australians and South Africans have done the trick, Europe-based players have found the going tough, though moves have been made in recent years to make the US PGA and US Open more accessible to leading foreign players and so more representative of the world game.

The genesis of the US PGA Championship stemmed from attempts to better the lot of club professionals who, during the first years

of the twentieth century, were about as far removed from the millionaire status of today's tour stars as were most operators of small retail businesses of the time. They were in an even worse plight in many ways, since they were not able to command the merchandise they wanted but were supplied by middlemen who reaped the profits and paid the pro a pittance for manning his shop. Many clubs even took the profit from the sale of golf balls.

Rodman Wanamaker was himself in the business of selling, in New York, and a keen golfer. It did not take a genius to see that the professionals needed organizing, and, slowly, regional groups were formed, leading to a national Professional Golfers Association, to whom Wanamaker presented a trophy for a national professional championship. The name Wanamaker is still there on the trophy.

The man himself did well out of the deal, getting the concession to sell golf gear more cheaply than the pros could in their shops. His greatest service to the professional game was to be the prime mover in calling the first founding meeting of the Association, at a luncheon at a New

York club on January 17, 1916. Now the professionals had a voice, and an event of their own.

The first winner was born in Britain, as were most of the early winners of the US Open. Long Jim Barnes, whose nickname "Long" was on account of his great length off the tee, came from Lelant, in Cornwall. He beat a Scot, Jock Hutchison, at Siwanoy Country Club, Bronxville, New York, by one hole in the final of what was, for many years, a match play event.

Owing to the war, the second US PGA Championship was not played until 1919, when Barnes won again against Fred McLeod at the Engineers Club, Long Island. McLeod was Scottish also, from North Berwick, and already a US Open winner. For many years, and long after the Second World War, McLeod, who was as short in stature as Barnes was tall, formed the traditional starting twosome in the Masters with Hutchison, who was from St Andrews, and finally got his hands on the Wanamaker Cup, a mighty piece of silverware, in 1920. He defeated a talented English pro, John Douglas Edgar, from Newcastle-upon-Tyne, in the first US

BOGEY BEATEN *Leo Diegel ended Walter Hagen's 22-match unbeaten run*

PGA played outside New York, at Flossmoor, Illinois.

Three of American golf's big "names" now took over, for Walter Hagen (for five years), Gene Sarazen (two) and Leo Diegel (two) won the right to look after Wanamaker's gift throughout the rest of the 1920s (and Sarazen won again in 1933).

To tell the truth, Hagen did not look after the trophy all that well. He could not recall where he had left it ("In a taxi?" he pondered), after Diegel's 1928 victory at Baltimore Country Club. It was not located until 1930, parcelled up in a Detroit factory.

Hagen's record in Open championships either side of the Atlantic attests to his stroke-play ability, but he was surely of all golfers who ever lived the most richly endowed with every match play talent. Having become champion at the expense of the inaugural winner, Barnes, in 1921, Hagen did not defend in 1922, but from the time he lost the 1923 final (at the 38th hole) to Sarazen, Hagen was unbeaten till Leo Diegel gained revenge in the third round in 1928 for many Hagen defeats.

One of Hagen's victims, Wild Bill Mehlhorn, must have feared the worst after Hagen's first tee shot against him in the 1925 final, for it went into the hole. Mehlhorn went down 6 & 5.

In addition to self-confidence,

US PGA FOUR-TIMER *Walter Hagen beating Joe Turnesa to complete a perfect record 1924–1927*

US PGA Results

Year	Winner (match play until 1958)	Runner-up	Venue	Score
1916	J Barnes	J Hutchison	Siwanoy, NY	1 hole
1917-18	No championship			
1919	J Barnes	F McLeod	Engineers, NY	6 & 5
1920	J Hutchison	J D Edgar	Flossmoor, ILL	1 hole
1921	W Hagen	J Barnes	Inwood, NY	3 & 2
1922	G Sarazen	E French	Oakmont, PA	4 & 3
1923	G Sarazen	W Hagen	Pelham, NY	38th hole
1924	W Hagen	J Barnes	French Lick, IN	6 & 4
1925	W Hagen	W E Mehlhorn	Olympic Fields, IL	2 holes
1926	W Hagen	L Diegel	Salisbury, NY	4 & 3
1927	W Hagen	J Turnesa	Dallas, TX	1 hole
1928	L Diegel	A Espinosa	Five Farms, MD	6 & 5
1929	L Diegel	J Farrell	Hillcrest, CA	6 & 4
1930	T Armour	G Sarazen	Fresh Meadow, NY	1 hole
1931	T Creavy	D Shute	Wannamoisett, RI	2 & 1
1932	O Dutra	F Walsh	St Paul, MN	4 & 3
1933	G Sarazen	W Goggin	Blue Mound, WI	5 & 4
1934	P Runyan	C Wood	Buffalo, NY	38th hole
1935	J Revolta	T Armour	Twin Hills, OK	5 & 4
1936	D Shute	J Thomson	Pinehurst, NC	3 & 2
1937	D Shute	H McSpaden	Oakmont, PA	37th hole
1938	P Runyan	S Snead	Shawnee, PA	8 & 7
1939	H Picard	B Nelson	Pomonok, NY	37th hole
1940	B Nelson	S Snead	Hershey, PA	1 hole
1941	V Ghezzie	B Nelson	Cherry Hills, CO	38th hole
1942	S Snead	J Turnesa	Atlantic City, NJ	2 & 1
1943	No championship			
1944	R Hamilton	B Nelson	Manito, Spokane, WA	1 hole
1945	B Nelson	S Byrd	Morraine, Dayton, OH	4 & 3
1946	B Hogan	E Oliver	Portland, OR	6 & 4
1947	J Ferrier	C Harbert	Plum Hollow, MI	2 & 1
1948	B Hogan	M Turnesa	Norwood Hills, MO	7 & 6
1949	S Snead	J Palmer	Hermitage, VA	3 & 2
1950	C Harper	H Williams Jnr	Scioto, Columbus, OH	4 & 3
1951	S Snead	W Burkemo	Oakmont, PA	7 & 6
1952	J Turnesa	C Harbert	Big Spring, KY	2 & 1
1953	W Burkemo	F Torza	Birmingham CC, MI	2 & 1
1954	C Harbert	W Burkemo	Keller, St Paul, MI	4 & 3
1955	D Ford	C Middlecoff	Meadowbrook, MI	4 & 3
1956	J Burke	T Kroll	Blue Hill, Boston, MA	3 & 2
1957	L Hebert	D Finsterwald	Miami Val., Dayton OH	2 & 1
1958	D Finsterwald	W Casper	Llanerch, PA	276
1959	B Rosburg	J Barber, D Sanders	St Louis Pk, MI	277
1960	J Hebert	J Ferrier	Firestone, Akron, OH	281
1961	J Barber	D January	Olympia Fields, IL	277
	WON PLAY-OFF 67 TO 68			

Year	Winner	Runner-up	Venue	Score
1962	G Player	B Goalby	Aronimink, PA	278
1963	J Nicklaus	D Ragan	Dallas Athletic, TX	279
1964	B Nichols	A Palmer, J Nicklaus	Columbus, OH	271
1965	D Marr	W Casper, J Nicklaus	Laurel Valley, PA	280
1966	A Geiberger	D Wysong	Firestone, Akron, OH	280
1967	D January	D Massengale	Columbine, Denver, CO	281
	WON PLAY-OFF 69 TO 71			
1968	J Boros	R J Charles, A Palmer	Pecan Valley, TX	281
1969	R Floyd	G Player	NCR, Dayton, OH	276
1970	D Stockton	R Murphy, A Palmer	Southern Hills, OK	279
1971	J Nicklaus	W Casper	PGA National, FL	281
1972	G Player	T Aaron, J Jamieson	Oakland Hills, MI	281
1973	J Nicklaus	B Crampton	Canterbury, OH	277
1974	L Trevino	J Nicklaus	Tanglewood, NC	276
1975	J Nicklaus	B Crampton	Firestone, Akron, OH	276
1976	D Stockton	R Floyd, D January	Congressional, MD	281
1977	L Wadkins	G Littler	Pebble Beach, CA	282
	WON PLAY-OFF AT FIRST EXTRA HOLE			
1978	J Mahaffey	J Pate, T Watson	Oakmont, PA	276
	WON PLAY-OFF AT SECOND EXTRA HOLE			
1979	D Graham	B Crenshaw	Oakland Hills, MI	272
	WON PLAY-OFF AT THIRD EXTRA HOLE			
1980	J Nicklaus	A Bean	Oak Hill, NY	274
1981	L Nelson	F Zoeller	Atlantic Ath Club, GA	273
1982	R Floyd	L Wadkins	Southern Hills, OK	272
1983	H Sutton	J Nicklaus	Riviera, Los Angeles, CA	274
1984	L Trevino	L Wadkins, G Player	Shoal Creek AL	273
1985	H Green	L Trevino	Cherry Hills, CO	278
1986	R Tway	G Norman	Inverness, Toledo, OH	276
1987	L Nelson	L Wadkins	PGA National, FL	287
	WON PLAY-OFF AT FIRST EXTRA HOLE			
1988	J Sluman	P Azinger	Oak Tree, Edmond, OK	272
1989	P Stewart	A Bean, M Reid, C Strange	Kemper Lakes, IL	276
1990	W Grady	F Couples	Shoal Creek, AL	282
1991	J Daly	B Lietzke	Crooked Stick, IN	276
1992	N Price	J Cook, N Faldo, G Sauers, J Gallagher Jnr	Bellerive, St Louis, MO	278
1993	P Azinger	G Norman	Inverness, Toledo, OH	272
	WON PLAY-OFF AT SECOND EXTRA HOLE			
1994	N Price	C Pavin	Southern Hills, OK	269

and the ability to scrape a way out of trouble and slot the most daunting putt, Hagen's armoury included a smile that must have seemed crocodile-like to his opponents.

It didn't always work: before getting down to a 20-foot putt at a critical moment in the third round of the US PGA in 1928, he turned and directed the full force of one of these smiles at Diegel, a frequent victim of his match playing ability. Hagen holed the putt, but Diegel, though he had lost an early four-hole lead and was clearly shaken, managed to survive. He went on to record a crushing final win against Al Espinosa (6 & 5), and followed up the following season with a 6 & 4 victory over Johnny Farrell, one of the few to have beaten Bobby Jones over 36 holes . . . for the US Open too.

There was no suggestion at first that the US PGA was a "major" title. The leading amateurs of the day were still to be reckoned with as the elite of golf. Between 1913 and 1933 the two big Opens were won by an amateur on 11 occasions.

Tom Creavy, like John Daly in 1991, was among the most surprising winners of a national championship. He won the US PGA in 1931, aged 20, beating Denny Shute at Wannamoisett, Rhode Island, in the final, and two other Open champions on the way to it. He lived until 1979, but illness restricted his golf after he reached the last four in 1932 and the last eight in 1933, and finished eighth in the Open of 1934.

The US PGA Championship remained a match play event until 1958, providing in 1942, soon after Pearl Harbor, Sam Snead's first national title. He was able to play only because he persuaded his recruiting officer to let him enlist a few days late so that he could compete at Seaview, Atlantic City, where he beat Jim Turnesa 2 & 1.

The Second World War caused only one year's inaction, for Bob Hamilton beat Byron Nelson at Spokane, Washington, in 1944, and the following year Nelson was back to regain the title he first won in 1940, at Snead's expense. The US PGA was also Ben Hogan's first national title, and with the growth of the PGA Tour, and the absence of amateurs good enough to beat the pros, the event grew in importance.

Americans love the pencil and card game, and in its new guise as a medal competition (from 1958) the US PGA gained more and more attention. It also caused agonized disappointment as Arnold Palmer took the place of Hogan in the nation's high regard, for this is the one major

Palmer did not win. He certainly tried hard, finishing joint second in 1964, 1968 and 1970.

Discounting early immigrant winners like Barnes, Hutchison, Tommy Armour and (in 1947) the Australian Jim Ferrier, long based in the United States and a heavy money-winner on the PGA Tour, the first foreign winner was Gary Player in 1962 on the occasion of the US PGA's only visit to Aronomink, Pennsylvania. Three years later, by winning the US Open, Player became, with Sarazen and Hogan, the third golfer to have won the modern quartet of majors. Jack Nicklaus made it a foursome when he became Open champion at Muirfield in 1966. Australia's David Graham beat Ben Crenshaw in a play-off only after an excruciating 72nd hole at the difficult Oakland Hills course near Detroit in 1979.

He began with a misplaced drive, and an over-strong approach. Two indifferent chips and a missed putt left him wanting a downhill putt to equal Crenshaw's 272. He holed it, and then made two lengthy putts to keep the sudden-death play-off going to the third hole, which he birdied for victory.

The suspense attached to John Daly's 1991 triumph, his first on the PGA Tour, started for this Californian-born long hitter from Arkansas before he even reached Crooked Stick, Indiana, to which the Championship was making its first visit. He was ninth "reserve" in line for a place in the event, and got in because Nick Price departed to be with his wife, who shortly afterward gave birth to Gregory, their first child. Daly, 25, decided to take a chance and make the seven-hour drive to Crooked Stick before he knew of Price's decision.

His gamble paid off. After two rounds he led on a 7,289-yard course he had never seen before. Daly, known to about one golf fan in a million, was a huge hit with the media, gaining instant fame as "Wild Thing" with his fulsome swing and 300-yard plus drives, not to mention sand wedges that flew 150 yards. His winning total of 276, three strokes ahead of Bruce Lietzke, also owed

a good deal to a sharp short game. He received a 10-year exemption on the Tour, life-time US PGA exemption, and a $230,000 (£137,000) start towards finishing 17th on the 1991 money list. Naturally, he was also voted Rookie of the Year.

Price was back for the 1992 US PGA at Bellerive, with his caddie Jess "Squeaky" Medlen, whom Daly had taken over the previous year in Price's absence. The South African Price, so close to "major" fame in the British Opens of 1982 and 1988,

ZINGER'S BIG DAY *Paul Azinger with the Wanamaker Trophy after his play-off win over Greg Norman*

won by three shots, and repeated the dose, this time by six shots, two years later at Southern Hills, Tulsa, a month after his Open at Turnberry. His second US PGA put him at the head of the Sony World Rankings. At Tulsa, at the age of 37, Price set new US PGA scoring standards. His 269 (11 under par on this 6,834 yard lay-out) beat Bobby Nichols's 1964 record by two shots; 269 is also the lowest score achieved in winning a major in the United States.

Price's first nine in the final round ruled out much chance of excitement later on, for he reached the turn in 32, though three birdies on the back nine were cancelled out by three bogeys, which cost Price his chance of taking Nicklaus's championship record winning margin which stands at

seven shots. Despite these blemishes no one got to within three shots of Price. Proof of Arnold Palmer's lasting popularity came on the eve of the Championship, when Palmer, making his 37th and final appearance in the US PGA, which he never won, was presented with the PGA of America Distinguished Service Award. Daly failed to qualify by a stroke: he confessed to a couple of shanks and said, "Now I know how amateurs feel."

His disputes with other players, officials and his girlfriend, and the need to attend a drying-out clinic had robbed the Tour of the full range of the star qualities of the longest hitter the game has yet known. There was disappointment too for Nicklaus, like Hagen a winner of five US PGAs. He started with a 79, missed the cut by five strokes and determined to take up a fitness programme.

Between Price's twin triumphs, which meant that "Squeaky" had carried for three winners in four years, came a most popular win by Paul Azinger. The New Englander beat Greg Norman in a play-off at Toledo, making the reigning British Open champion the unhappy owner of a unique record: he has lost play-offs for all four majors. Also, in 1986, he lost this very championship when playing partner Bob Tway birdied the 72nd hole (also at Toledo) out of a bunker.

Azinger, the choice of many good judges to be America's next dominant player, soon had to begin treatment for lymphoma cancer. His Ryder Cup colleagues in particular and golfers in general have been watching his steadfast campaign to regain fitness with admiration.

A footnote to the majors of 1994 reads like a warning headline to the game in the United States. Price's second US PGA was the last stage in the breaking of a mighty mould: for the first time since the US PGA and Masters became majors, not one had been won by a native of the United States.

RYDER CUP

From the first Ryder Cup match between the United States and Britain up to the first between the US and Europe, the American advantage in points scored, in 22 matches, surpassed three figures. In the first eight US vs. Europe Cup meetings, total American advantage was 12 points. The improvement was not immediate, for Europe did not get into gear until their third outing, and in the last six matches the Europeans have actually scored three more points than the Americans.

Even the most rock-ribbed European (Community) sceptic could not discount the value to the Ryder Cup and golf in general of the European connection, which was first mooted seriously at the last "old style" Cup match at Lytham. The late Earl of Derby, who was President of the PGA, discussed the idea with Jack Nicklaus, Henry Poe, Lord Derby's opposite number at the US PGA, and senior British professional Neil Coles.

Two years later, at The Greenbrier, West Virginia, with Severiano Ballesteros and Antonio Garrido of Spain in the team led by John Jacobs, a leading figure in the creation of the European Tour, the new series began – not too well, as it turned out, for the brand, sparkling new team of Europe.

Discipline was not a strong point to start with: Jacobs considered sending Mark James home when he turned up at Heathrow Airport (London) not clad in the team uniform. James and Ken Brown set teeth on edge in both camps by lounging about at the flag-raising ceremony. The pair of them lost their four-ball to Lee Trevino and Fuzzy Zoeller. Brown made it clear that he wished to play only in partnership with James, but, when James was injured, had perforce to partner Des Smyth,

with whom his attitude was not conducive to a happy and winning blend.

Europe's great banker, Ballesteros, ran into a jinx in the smooth-swinging shape of Larry Nelson, to whom he lost in singles and three times in partnership with Garrido, though the two Spaniards did beat Fuzzy Zoeller and Hubert Green.

All told, the result was dustier than the usual one. The pattern of the Billy Casper-led American victory by six points was also familiar.

His men were only one point ahead at the end of the first two days of four-ball and foursome play, but in the singles on day three they drew away to six points clear.

The second European match, at Walton Heath, south-west of London, was dominated by an American side which many good judges believe to have been the equal of any sent forth by the US PGA. Moreover Europe, again led by Jacobs, were handicapped by the absence of Ballesteros and Tony Jacklin, who was less than pleased that Mark James was chosen in his stead. The Spaniard was demanding appearance money in Europe; there was talk of his resigning his European Tour membership. On this basis European professional sentiment opposed his selection.

Non-selection of these two players, who alone in the European ranks had won major championships in Britain and the United States, was an even bigger mistake in hindsight than it seemed at the time. This was the team in which Bernhard Langer, Scotland's Sam Torrance, José-Maria Canizares and Manuel Pinero were all making their first appearances. All were to play a part in European victories, and the missing pair's experience might have inspired these new boys to even greater heights. Dave Marr, a US PGA Championship winner whose salty comments in beguiling Texan drawl are a feature of television coverage, was non-playing captain of this daunting aggregation of talent, who were five points ahead when the singles began: Lee Trevino (beat Sam Torrance 5 & 4), Tom Kite (beat Sandy Lyle, who was six under par at the time, at the 16th), Bill Rogers (current Open champion, halved with Bernard Gallacher), Larry Nelson (beat Mark James to make his Cup record played nine, won nine), Ben Crenshaw (beat Des Smyth 6 & 4), Bruce Lietzke (halved with Langer), Jerry Pate (lost 4 & 2 to Pinero), Hale Irwin (beat Cani-

zares one hole), Johnny Miller (lost to Nick Faldo 2 & 1), Tom Watson (lost to Howard Clark 4 & 3), Raymond Floyd (beat Peter Oosterhuis one hole), and Jack Nicklaus (beat Eamonn Darcy 5 & 3). This brought up a final score of 18½ to 9½.

At the PGA National, Palm Beach Gardens, Florida, in 1983, Europe came within a putt or two of beating the US on their own soil. Even in the days when there were only 12 points at stake, Britain and

Ireland had never got closer than a four-point deficit in America. To start with, strength in depth and depth of experience were at last approaching American standards . . . but not yet quite close enough, it transpired.

There was certainly experience at the helm, where non-playing captain Jacklin was getting powerful support from his top-of-the-draw men. Nick Faldo was fulfilling his early promise, and won three times out of four in company with Langer. He also beat Jay Haas. After an initial stumble, Masters champion Ballesteros partnered new boy Paul Way to two wins and a half. Then, after being three up against Fuzzy Zoeller, he had to claw his way back to a half, notably with a wood shot from a bunker that impressed many witnesses as the best shot they had ever seen. It was certainly among the most daring.

Hearts pounded faster on both sides as, in the last three matches, Brown easily beat Raymond Floyd, but Lanny Wadkins was relentlessly cutting back Canizares's three-hole lead, and Gallacher was in a pressure cooker of a match against Watson. Wadkins's pitch almost to "gimme" range at the 18th squeezed a half out of Canizares, and Gallacher said later of his four-footer for a half against Watson, after both men had fluffed their first chip at the 17th: "I still think to this day that I hit a good putt. There was a subtle break but I missed and that was it, two and one." And that was it, 14½ to 13½ for the United States, a score that sold any number of tickets for the 1985 battle at British PGA HQ, the Belfry.

This new course, not far from the centre of Britain's motorway system, had several holes that were, in the view of some critics, not up to scratch for a Cup match. Moreover the flat terrain greatly restricted spectators' view of play. Nevertheless 27,000 of them celebrated a victory for Europe, with Concorde flying over the course in a roaring celebration of European togetherness not yet achieved by the European Commission in Brussels.

The Belfry does have a finish

made for shredding the nerves of all but the bravest. The long dog-leg 17th, to an elevated green, is followed by a final par four where both first and second shots have huge water hazards, the second demanding accurate judgment of length because the green has three tiers.

A five-point win for Europe was promise of giant gates for future Cup matches, and total vindication for the words of Jack Nicklaus almost a decade earlier: "It is vital to widen the selection procedures if the Ryder Cup is to continue to enjoy its past prestige."

In the British Isles the Cup had never lost its prestige, for it still attracted wide media coverage and big attendances even when the US were handing out hidings every two years. This was because opportunities to see the leading American players were limited, and for the most part eagerly taken up. However, the American media and golf-going public were low-key on the Cup matches while they were so one-sided. Three US defeats in 56 years, and two of those having come in the first four matches, did little to build up suspense.

But it is not true of golf that it is better to travel hopefully than to arrive, because when the European team "arrived" at the Belfry in 1985 the whole Ryder Cup ethos, not to mention its attractions to sponsors, was elevated to Open Championship standards and, in the opinion of some, even beyond.

The players are not paid, yet zealously husband selection points, or failing these, cultivate the good opinion of their captains, giving rise to jokes about how sycophantic macho players can be towards the captain if they are on the edge of Cup selection. Lanny Wadkins, the 1995 US captain and among the most combative yet outgoing of players, has expressed mock surprise at how nicely his fellows behaved towards him from the time of his appointment. The pattern of team selection has been similar for both sides – most of the team chosen strictly on performance in official Tour events, the last few places filled by the captain's choices. Dispossessing the

PLUCK OF THE IRISH *Eamonn Darcy earned the crucial point in 1987*

American team, led by (non-playing) Lee Trevino, of the Cup for the first time since Dai Rees scored his greatest triumph as player and leader in 1957 at Lindrick was achieved at last with gratifying ease at the Belfry. Here, Europe performed the rare feat of

winning the singles by three points after finishing four-balls and four-somes two ahead. Ironically, the two leading European players of the era contributed only half a point in singles, Faldo losing to Hubert Green and Ballesteros halving with Tom Kite.

It was now that the new-found strength in depth came to the aid of Jacklin in his second stint as captain, for Pinero gave Europe a flying start on the final day by beating Lanny Wadkins, and Lyle, Langer, Torrance and Clark made a clean sweep of the middle four matches in the singles order. To Torrance fell the great moment: his opponent Andy North put his drive into the water at the 18th, Sam Torrance hit a vast distance into position A, and slotted the birdie putt offered by his accurate approach.

Concorde took the British team to Ohio for the 1987 match, Jacklin having insisted that all of the European planning for the defence of the Cup should be top bracket. The excitement around Muirfield Village, Jack Nicklaus's pet exercise of his architectural

career, was not merely intense over the last couple of hours; it was almost insupportable. The Ryder Cup, 1980s style, had been given the imprimatur of live coverage by US television, a complete reversal of previous media disinterest. An all-ticket crowd of 25,000 was another reward for the success of the Nicklaus European initiative.

Ballesteros and José-Maria Olazabal netted three points out of four, and Faldo and Woosnam dropped only a half point out of four, in the process beating Wadkins and Masters champion Larry Mize after falling four holes behind. Lyle and Langer also contributed three points. So Europe led by five as the singles began; but the match was far from decided.

America won five and halved one of the top eight singles, Andy Bean beginning the rally with a last hole victory over the previously unbeaten Ian Woosnam. It was with considerable relief that Jacklin took in the sight of what looked like the world's happiest golfer, by name Eamonn Darcy, repeatedly shaking his fist after holing a testing downhill putt to beat Crenshaw by one hole. Darcy's elation may have been fuelled by the fact that this was his first Cup win in 11 starts. It was a good time to start winning, though he has not been selected since.

On the American side, Nelson suffered his first defeats, three of them, in 13 starts, and Nicklaus's score as captain was now one win, one defeat. This was the first time America had lost a home Ryder Cup match.

The Ryder Cup fortunes of the two captains had never lacked dramatic qualities, notably in the only halved series of the US vs. Britain and Ireland series, in 1969 at Birkdale, where 16–16 was the result under the ruling 32-match format. After getting his four on the final green from three feet, Nicklaus gave an 18-inch putt to Jacklin which brought up the tied score, saying that he was sure Jacklin would have holed it, "but I was not prepared to see you miss". Jacklin, the Open champion, was not to see Nicklaus and Co. beaten for many years. The

32-match format gave Jacklin two singles against Nicklaus, and he had halved one and won the other.

Beating the leading golfer of the age was given to few in match play. Nicklaus won 17 Cup matches and lost eight, two of them on the same day to Brian Barnes in the 1975 Ryder Cup at Laurel Valley. Barnes was suitably modest about his feat, rather discounting 18-hole matches as a bit of a lottery if one or other golfer was a touch off form. Yet Barnes had done the trick twice, at a time when Nicklaus was at his best and had just won his fourth US PGA title.

The next Ryder extravaganza at the Belfry in 1989 went all the way through hours of tension to a final cliff-hanging and decisive moment: a Cup-saving long iron shot across the lake at Belfry's finishing hole that Christy O'Connor Jr will never forget, nor the multitudes who saw him ... the television audience was estimated at 200,000,000.

Europe, without Sandy Lyle at his own request owing to lack of form, were two clear as the singles began. Paul Azinger and Chip Beck, both making their first Cup appearances, rapidly evened the score against the seasoned Ballesteros and Langer. They had already gained two points in two starts as partners. Prospects now began to look bleak, with Mark James the only leader lower down the order. He beat Mark O'Meara at the 16th, and Olazabal and Ronan Rafferty fought back to right the ship. The crux of the matter came with that O'Connor shot to foil Fred Couples, and Canizares' cool long putt on the last, where, as it turned out, his opponent three-putted the Cup away.

A draw at 14 each fired the Americans to prepare a hot welcome in 1991 for the team led by Jacklin's successor, Bernard Gallacher, at a new lay-out on Kiawah Island, South Carolina. The media hyped "The War on the Shore", a phrase which was anathema to traditionalists and and not too well received by the players.

Again the tension was almost beyond bearing, especially as this time the reckoning was 8–8 with the sin-

MEASURING UP *Chip Beck figured it right at Kiawah Island in 1991*

BELFRY BONANZA *Tom Watson, behind the trophy, and his winning team*

gles to come, which had so often produced a final day bonanza for the Americans. Only seven singles were to be played, since Steve Pate, bruised in a car crash the previous Wednesday, had played in one four-ball, with Corey Pavin, and lost, and now withdrew. So a half was agreed with David Gilford. Pate had been due originally to play Ballesteros, who had dropped only half a point throughout, so the arrangement turned out well for Stockton.

Azinger and Beck were again singles heroes for the US, as were Pavin, Couples and Wadkins, though an effective first appearance was made by Paul Broadhurst for Europe, and Colin Montgomerie too, for he got a half against Mark Calcavecchia by winning all of the last four perilous holes. This time the clincher was not a long iron, but a not very long putt. Langer, who had come back from behind against

Hale Irwin, faced it for par and a win and a tied match, for Irwin had already bogeyed. He missed, right edge, and – to a mighty roar – the Cup was held aloft by Stockton.

The 1993 meeting was again at the Belfry, but with the next European staging earmarked for Spain, whose players had done so much to bring a new vitality to Ryder Cup play. Tom Watson took up the American leadership with Floyd, captain when they were beaten in 1989, in the team; for Europe, Gallacher led again, and had problems. Ballesteros asked to be dropped from his partnership with Olazabal on the grounds of loss of form, though the pair had won twice in three starts. Gallacher, controversially, conceded to him. Joakim Haeggman joined Olazabal, and they lost. Sam Torrance was side-lined by a poisoned toe.

Gallacher was buoyed up by a wonderful display by new Cup

selection, Midlander Peter Baker, who had little sleep, because of his daughter's illness, before he beat Corey Pavin on the final day. But elsewhere in singles the old American magic worked again, washing out their one-point overnight deficit. In the bottom six matches only Azinger was held, by Nick Faldo, who registered a stunning hole-in-one, but that did not matter, for Payne Stewart, Davis Love, Jim Gallagher (against an out-of-sorts Ballesteros), Floyd (now aged 51) and Kite (5 & 3 over Langer) all won. Costantino Rocca, the first Italian to gain Cup selection, endured a sad debut. He was one up against Davis Love III on the 17th tee, but an over-bold attempt at a birdie putt led to a bogey and Love drew away to win at the 18th, where Rocca's second

barely made the far bank of the final lake hazard.

All of which means the lovely gold trophy given by Samuel Ryder is now a hotter property than it ever was in the days when Britain, even with considerable reinforcement from Ireland, seldom had the strength in depth to withstand teams not only led by players like Walter Hagen, Ben Hogan, Sam Snead, Byron Nelson and Arnold Palmer, but including plenty of golfers who would never admit being inferior to these worthies, and who often enough proved that they were not.

All manner of factors have combined to make the Cup matches such compelling affairs, but none more important than the development of the European Tour and its production line of polyglot, world-class, golfers.

Year	Venue	United States	GB and I
1927	Worcester, MA	9½: W Hagen	2½: T Ray
1929	Moortown, Leeds	5: W Hagen	7: G Duncan
1931	Scioto, Columbus, OH	9: W Hagen	3: C A Whitcombe
1933	Southport and Ainsdale, Lancashire	5½: W Hagen	6½: J H Taylor*
1935	Ridgewood, NJ	9: W Hagen	3: C A Whitcombe
1937	Southport and Ainsdale	8: W Hagen*	4: C A Whitcombe
1939–45	No matches		
1947	Portland, OR	11: B Hogan	1: T H Cotton
1949	Ganton, Yorkshire	7: B Hogan*	5: C A Whitcombe*
1951	Pinehurst, NC	9½: S Snead	2½: A J Lacey*
1953	Wentworth, Surrey	6½: L Mangrum	5½: T H Cotton*
1955	Thunderbird Club, CA	8: C Harbert	4: D J Rees
1957	Lindrick, Notts	4½: J Burke	7½: D J Rees
1959	Eldorado CC, CA	8½: S Snead	3½: D J Rees
1961	Lytham, Lancs	14½: J Barber	9½: D J Rees
1963	Atlanta, GA	23: A Palmer	9: J Fallon*
1965	Royal Birkdale, Southport	19½: B Nelson*	12½: H Weetman*
1967	Houston, TX	23½: B Hogan*	8½: D J Rees*
1969	Royal Birkdale, Southport	16: S Snead*	16: E C Brown*
1971	St Louis, MO	19: J Hebert*	13: E C Brown*
1973	Muirfield, Scotland	19: J Burke*	13: B J Hunt*
1975	Laurel Valley, PA	21: A Palmer*	11: B J Hunt*
1977	Lytham, Lancs	12½: D Finsterwald*	7½: B Huggett*
		United States	**Europe**
1979	The Greenbrier, WV	17: W Casper*	11: J Jacobs*
1981	Walton Heath, Surrey	18½: D Marr*	9½: J Jacobs*
1983	PGA National, FL	14½: J Nicklaus*	13½: T Jacklin*
1985	The Belfry, West Midlands	11½: L Trevino*	16½: T Jacklin*
1987	Muirfield Village, Columbus, OH	13: J Nicklaus*	15: T Jacklin*
1989	The Belfry, West Midlands	14: R Floyd*	14: T Jacklin*
1991	Kiawah Island, SC	14½: D Stockton*	13½: B Gallacher*
1993	The Belfry, West Midlands	15: T Watson*	13: B Gallacher*

(* = non-playing)

BRITISH AMATEUR CHAMPIONSHIP

Allan MacFie was the first British Amateur champion, but never attained the fame of Horace Hutchinson (more properly Horatio Gordon Hutchinson), whom he he beat in the inaugural final at Royal Liverpool's course, Hoylake. Hutchinson won the second and third finals, the third against John Ball. The Hoylake-bred Ball was accounted the greatest of them all long before 1912, when he won his eighth title, which is still a record.

In any case the first Championship, organized by the Royal Liverpool, was not recognized as official until 1920, when the Royal & Ancient finally took over full control of the event; Hutchinson was also a celebrated writer on golf and other sports.

In 1995 the R & A, who like the USGA have a well-developed sense of tradition, marked the 100th Amateur by bringing the event back to its Hoylake birthplace. Besides, Michael Bonallack, secretary of the R&A, is the most successful living competitor in the Amateur, with five titles, including a hat-trick in 1968-70.

Before the turn of the century the entry had reached 100, and by 1958 almost 500. Lower and lower handicaps were demanded to keep down the flood of would-be competitors. In 1983, 36-hole qualifying was introduced, the leading 64 reverting to match play over four days.

Bonallack's feat in the days of greatly increased competition from a world-wide entry is at least the equal of John Ball's achievements, in the days when a small handful would meet year after year in the closing stages of the Championship. Indeed, from 1887 to 1895 either Johnny Laidlay or Ball or both figured in every final. At the same time, Ball was the first Englishman (in 1890) and another amateur, Harold Hilton, two years later, the second, to win the Open.

Freddie Tait, a long hitter who managed to play golf with an extraordinary regularity considering his position as an officer in the Black Watch, might well have emulated Hilton, but in 1900, aged 30, he was killed leading his men against the Boers at Koodoosberg.

The British Amateur was to attract a growing number of Americans, but the first to win, Walter Travis, in 1904, did not improve transatlantic golf relations. Ironically, the cause of the rift was that Travis, a triple US Amateur champion, won with a brand new putter, adopted in desperation for the Amateur at Royal St George's because, during his preparations for the event, his putting, his greatest strength, suddenly "went off".

But the instrument he chose was looked upon by the British establishment as unfair. It was called a Schenectady putter, invented and patented by Arthur Knight of that particular New York city, and had its shaft attached to the middle of a mallet-shaped head.

No one had ever seen putting such as Travis now deployed against one opponent after another, beating Hilton and Hutchinson in turn to reach the final, where he won at the 33rd against Ted Blackwell, who towered above and outhit Travis throughout. Travis relished a victory which was received with a minimum of applause, which cannot have surprised him, for he felt he had not been accorded the usual courtesies, particularly in the matter of clubhouse facilities and an effective caddie.

TWENTIES STAR *Cyril Tolley, returned from a German prisoner-of-war camp to capture his first Amateur title*

The Travis Schenectady, centre-shafted wand of victory, though approved by the USGA, was banned by the R&A, though not, contrary to popular legend, directly as a result of Travis's 1904 victory. The ban was imposed in 1910, and even then only after Nga Motu GC, New Zealand, asked if a small croquet mallet was legal. No, said the R&A. Not until mid-century was such a weapon unbanned. Ben Hogan used the same type in his one (triumphant) tilt at the British Open in 1953.

From 1920, when the Championship resumed after the war, it became far more difficult to put together even as few as two wins, and Ball's eight began to look as

HOYLAKE TRIUMPH *Michael Bonallack lifts his fourth title in 1969*

British Amateur Championship Results

Year	Winner	Venue	Year	Winner	Venue
1885	A F McFie	Hoylake	1940-45	*NO CHAMPIONSHIP*	
1886	H G Hutchinson	St Andrews	1946	J Bruen	Birkdale
1887	H G Hutchinson	Hoylake	1947	W P Turnesa	Carnoustie
1888	J Ball	Prestwick	1948	F R Stranahan	St George's
1889	J E Laidlay	St Andrews	1949	S M McCready	Portmarnock
1890	J Ball	Hoylake	1950	F R Stranahan	St Andrews
1891	J E Laidlay	St Andrews	1951	R D Chapman	Porthcawl
1892	J Ball	St George's	1952	E Harvie Ward	Prestwick
1893	P C Anderson	Prestwick	1953	J B Carr	Hoylake
1894	J Ball	Hoylake	1954	D W Bachli	Muirfield
1895	L M B Melville	St Andrews	1955	J W Conrad	Lytham
1896	F G Tait	St George's	1956	J C Beharrell	Troon
1897	A J T Allan	Muirfield	1957	R Reid Jack	Formby
1898	F G Tait	Hoylake	1958	J B Carr	St Andrews
1899	J Ball	Prestwick	1959	D R Beman	St George's
1900	H H Hilton	St George's	1960	J B Carr	Portrush
1901	H H Hilton	St Andrews	1961	M F Bonallack	Turnberry
1902	C Hutchings	Hoylake	1962	R D Davies	Hoylake
1903	R Maxwell	Muirfield	1963	M S R Lunt	St Andrews
1904	W J Travis	St George's	1964	G J Clark	Ganton
1905	A G Barry	Prestwick	1965	M F Bonallack	Porthcawl
1906	J Robb	Hoylake	1966	R E Cole	Carnoustie
1907	J Ball	St Andrews	1967	R B Dickson	Formby
1908	E A Lassen	St George's	1968	M F Bonallack	Troon
1909	R Maxwell	Muirfield	1969	M F Bonallack	Hoylake
1910	J Ball	Hoylake	1970	M F Bonallack	Newcastle, Co. Down
1911	H H Hilton	Prestwick	1971	S N Melnyk	Carnoustie
1912	J Ball	Westward Ho!	1972	T Homer	St George's
1913	H H Hilton	St Andrews	1973	R Siderowf	Porthcawl
1914	J L C Jenkins	St George's	1974	T Homer	Muirfield
1915-19	*NO CHAMPIONSHIP*		1975	M M Giles	Hoylake
1920	C Tolley	Muirfield	1976	R Siderowf	St Andrews
1921	W I Hunter	Hoylake	1977	P McEvoy	Ganton
1922	E Holderness	Prestwick	1978	P McEvoy	Troon
1923	R H Wethered	Deal	1979	J Sigel	Hillside
1924	E Holderness	St Andrews	1980	D Evans	Porthcawl
1925	R Harris	Westward Ho!	1981	P Ploujoux	St Andrews
1926	J Sweetser	Muirfield	1982	M Thompson	Deal
1927	Dr W Tweddell	Hoylake	1983	A P Parkin	Turnberry
1928	T P Perkins	Prestwick	1984	J-M Olazabal	Formby
1929	C Tolley	St George's	1985	G McGimpsey	Dornoch
1930	R T Jones Jnr	St Andrews	1986	D Curry	Lytham
1931	E Martin Smith	Westward Ho!	1987	P M Mayo	Prestwick
1932	J De Forest	Muirfield	1988	C Hardin	Porthcawl
1933	Hon. M Scott	Hoylake	1989	S Dodd	Birkdale
1934	W Lawson Little	Prestwick	1990	R Muntz	Muirfield
1935	W Lawson Little	Lytham	1991	G Wolstenholme	Ganton
1936	H Thomson	St Andrews	1992	S Dundas	Carnoustie
1937	R Sweeney Jnr	St George's	1993	I Pyman	Portrush
1938	C R Yates	Troon	1994	L James	Nairn
1939	A T Kyle	Hoylake			

War. Even when James Bruen, the Irish Ryder Cup player, won in 1946, he had to beat an American, Bob Sweeney, to do it. So did Sam McCready, another Belfast golfer, in 1949, holding off Willie Turnesa, the 1947 champion, 2 and 1 at Portmarnock.

Joe Carr carried on the Irish tradition with three wins, but since the war there has been an even stronger American tradition, which lasted until 1983 and was unbroken except in 1963: that is, whenever the US Walker Cup team was, at four-year intervals, visiting Britain, there was an American winner of the Amateur.

On six occasions – 1947, 1951, 1959, 1967, 1971 and 1979 – *both* finalists were American. None of Bonallack's five wins came in years of American Cup visits, but he did win the English Championship five times, shooting a 61 at Ganton, Yorkshire in 1968.

Since Jay Sigel's win over Scott Hoch in 1979, another change has come over the Amateur, for continental invaders from France (1981), Spain (1984), Sweden (1988) and Holland (1990) have replaced US winners. Otherwise it has been British Isles players only, with Gary Wolstenholme gaining a measure of personal satisfaction by beating Bob May of the successful 1991 Walker Cup team 8 and 6 at Ganton.

Bonallack is sure of the best Amateur final he has ever seen, and he should know: it was played in 1993 at Portrush in Ireland, Yorkshire's Iain Pyman beating Kent's Paul Page at the 37th hole.

unrepeatable as time has proved it to be. Cyril Tolley, an England international for a quarter of a century, managed two wins. He and Robert Gardner relaunched the Amateur with a 37-hole cliff-hanger of a final at Muirfield. Both men had survived war service (Tolley, who won the Military Cross, was a POW).

Three thousand cheered as Tolley birdied the extra hole, for amateur golf was thoroughly fashionable, and was to become the more so with the advent of Bobby Jones, though he won the Amateur only once, in his Grand Slam year of 1930,

beating Roger Wethered in the St Andrews final. His closest call came in the semi-final, against Tolley, whose 37th hole luck was out this time, Jones going through with the aid of a stymie which was, as Jones himself said, "a cruel way to lose".

William Lawson Little followed Jones's Grand Slam with two "Little Slams" in 1934 and 1935, capturing both the US and British Amateurs twice. Six American victories in the British Amateur between the wars was succeeded by five more in seven years immediately following the Second World

CUP CONSOLATION *Gary Wolstenholme was a comfortable winner at Ganton*

US AMATEUR CHAMPIONSHIP

The first United States Amateur Championship started three days before the nation's first Open, and play lasted three times as long, a pecking order that was not quickly disturbed. Across the Atlantic the Open pre-dated the Amateur by a quarter of a century, and rapidly became the Holy Grail for all golfers.

There is a direct personal link between the US Amateur and the British Open. Old Tom Morris, winner of four Opens, coached the first winner of the American Amateur, a well-built, self-willed Chicagoan named Charles Blair Macdonald. He had first fallen in love with golf in Scotland as a student at St Andrews in the 1870s, and in the early 1890s built the Chicago club, then a much improved 18 holes at Wheaton, a Chicago suburb.

Macdonald first came to public notice in his campaign to become American Amateur champion. Since golf lacked a national authority, the clubs of Newport, Rhode Island, and St Andrew's, New York, put on "Championships" in 1893 and 1894.

Macdonald came second in both, but discounted the quality both of the venues and of his opponents. He was an influential man, a stockbroker on the New York ex-

UNIQUE DOUBLE *Young Chick Evans took the US Open and Amateur in 1916 – a record*

change, but the game was clearly in need of leadership a little less egotistical than his. So the US Golf Association came into being at the end of 1894, and the first president, Theodore Havemeyer, a sugar baron, gave an extra veneer of authority to the inaugural Amateur starting on September 1, 1895, by donating a championship trophy.

Macdonald won it, easily.

ARNIE'S FIRST BIG ONE *Palmer in quarter final action in his first national title triumph, the US Amateur of 1954*

His victim in the final, by 12 and 11, at Newport, was Charles Sands, who preferred lawn tennis. Although Macdonald went on to perform great service as a USGA committee man and (unpaid) course designer, his fame was as nothing compared to that of Walter J. Travis, the champion in 1900, 1901 and 1903.

Travis came from Australia as a child and did not take up golf until he was 35. At 37 he reached the semi-final of the US Amateur, and the following year, 1900, he won it. He was also second in the 1902 US Open.

Travis was a short hitter but a devastating putter. His most celebrated single feat was his British Amateur title, his last major win, in

1904. His "trade-mark" was his eternal black cigar.

Travis's victory on foreign soil, for the British title, was answered seven years later by Harold Hilton, who had two British Opens to his credit. Having won the British Amateur in 1911, he went for the transatlantic double at the age of 42. He strolled through the early rounds, but Fred Herreshoff took Hilton to the 37th before surrendering.

Ouimet's Amateur title in 1914 sounds pallid after his 1913 giant-killing in the US Open, but it had been the great ambition of his life to lift the Amateur. For a former caddie like Ouimet, or a caddie like Chick Evans who graduated to the Stock Exchange to finance his golf, the Amateur was still the thing.

Evans followed recovery-expert Jerome Travers's record fourth Amateur success with a unique double in 1916. First he recorded a total of 286 to win the US Open at Minikahda, Minnesota, a figure not beaten for 22 years. Three months later he beat Bob Gardner in the Amateur final at Merion in Pennsylvania. Gardner had got into the last four by virtue of a 5 and 3 victory over a 14-year-old from Georgia playing in his first USGA championship. This

US Amateur Championship Results

Year	Winner	Venue
1895	C B Macdonald	Newport, RI
1896	H J Whigham	Shinnecock Hills, NY
1897	H J Whigham	Chicago, IL
1898	F S Douglas	Morris County, NJ
1899	H M Harriman	Onwentsia, IL
1900	W J Travis	Garden City, NY
1901	W J Travis	Atlantic City, NJ
1902	L N James	Glen View, IL
1903	W J Travis	Nassau, NY
1904	H Chandler Egan	Baltusrol, NJ
1905	H Chandler Egan	Wheaton, IL
1906	E M Byers	Englewood, NJ
1907	J D Travers	Cleveland, OH
1908	J D Travers	Garden City, NJ
1909	R Gardner	Wheaton, IL
1910	W C Fownes Jnr	Brookline, MA
1911	H H Hilton	Apawamis, NY
1912	J D Travers	Wheaton, IL
1913	J D Travers	Garden City, NY
1914	F Ouimet	Ekwanok, VT
1915	R Gardner	Detroit, MI
1916	C Evans	Merion, PA
1917-18	*NO CHAMPIONSHIP*	
1919	S D Herron	Oakmont, PA
1920	C Evans	Engineers Club, NY
1921	J Guilford	Clayton, MO
1922	J Sweetser	Brookline, MA
1923	M R Marston	Flossmoor, IL
1924	R T Jones Jnr	Merion, PA
1925	R T Jones Jnr	Oakmont, PA
1926	G von Elm	Baltusrol, NJ
1927	R T Jones Jnr	Minikahda, MN
1928	R T Jones Jnr	Brae Burn, MA
1929	H R Johnson	Del Monte, CA
1930	R T Jones Jnr	Merion, PA
1931	F Ouimet	Beverley, IL
1932	C R Somerville	Baltimore, NJ
1933	G T Dunlap	Kenwood, OH
1934	W Lawson Little	Brookline, MA
1935	W Lawson Little	Cleveland, OH
1936	J W Fischer	Garden City, NY
1937	J Goodman	Portland, OR
1938	W P Turnesa	Oakmont, PA
1939	M H Ward	Glen View, IL
1940	R Chapman	Winged Foot, NY
1941	M H Ward	Omaha, NE
1942-45	*NO CHAMPIONSHIP*	
1946	S E Bishop	Baltusrol, NJ
1947	R H Riegel	Pebble Beach, CA
1948	W P Turnesa	Memphis, TN

Year	Winner	Venue
1949	C R Coe	Rochester, NY
1950	S Urzetta	Minneapolis, MN
1951	W J Maxwell	Saucon Valley, PA
1952	J Westland	Seattle, WA
1953	G Littler	Oklahoma City, OK
1954	A Palmer	Detroit, MI
1955	E Harvie Ward	Richmond, VA
1956	E Harvie Ward	Lake Forest, IL
1957	H Robbins	Brookline, MA
1958	C R Coe	San Francisco, CA
1959	J Nicklaus	Broadmoor, CO
1960	D R Beman	St Louis, MO
1961	J Nicklaus	Pebble Beach, CA
1962	L E Harris Jnr	Pinehurst No. 2, NC
1963	D R Beman	Des Moines, IO
1964	W C Campbell	Canterbury, OH
1965-73 DECIDED BY STROKE PLAY		
1965	R Murphy	Southern Hills, OK
1966	G Cowan	Merion, PA
1967	R Dickson	Broadmoor, CO
1968	B Fleisher	Columbus, OH
1969	S N Melnyk	Oakmont, PA
1970	L Wadkins	Portland, OR
1971	G Cowan	Wilmington, DE
1972	M M Giles	Charlotte, NC
CHAMPIONSHIP REVERTED TO MATCH PLAY		
1973	C Stadler	Inverness, OH
1974	J Pate	Ridgewood, NJ
1975	F Ridley	Richmond, VA
1976	B Sander	Bel-Air, CA
1977	J Fought	Aronomink, PA
1978	J Cook	Plainfield, NJ
1979	M O'Meara	Canterbury, OH
1980	H Sutton	Pinehurst, NC
1981	N Crosby	Olympic, CA
1982	J Sigel	Brookline, MA
1983	J Sigel	North Shore, IL
1984	S Verplank	Oak Tree, OK
1985	S Randolph	Montclair, NJ
1986	S Alexander	Shoal Creek, AL
1987	W Mayfair	Jupiter Hills, FL
1988	E Meeks	Hot Springs, VA
1989	C Patton	Merion, PA
1990	P Mickelson	Cherry Hills, CO
1991	M Voges	Honours Course, TN
1992	J Leonard	Muirfield Village, OH
1993	J Harris	Houston, TX
1994	E Woods	Sawgrass, FL

was R. T. (Bobby) Jones Jnr, five times a winner between 1924 and 1930.

Only one man had two wins in the 1930s, William Lawson Little, but he added the novelty of winning the British Amateur in the same years, 1934 and 1935.

With Jones's retirement, and the fitful but sure growth of the professional tour, the fascination of the amateur game began

SOMETHING TO SING ABOUT Bing Crosby's youngest son, Nat, was US Amateur champion in 1981

to fade. After the war, the names of the outstanding professional players Byron Nelson, Ben Hogan and Sam Snead dominated the sports pages, and with the coming of television the process accelerated.

Gene Littler, Arnold Palmer and Jack Nicklaus used the Amateur as a stepping-stone to wealth, yet the continuing high standards of the amateur game in the US were never more clearly demonstrated than at Broadmoor, Colorado, in 1959, when Charles Coe, at 35 twice a winner, took Jack Nicklaus, then a student at Ohio State University, to the 36th hole of the final. The winner was about to begin a run of second/fourth/first in the US Open. At 19 years and eight months Nicklaus was the second youngest Amateur champion being three months older than Robert Gardner when he won half a century earlier.

Eight years of stroke-play format, begun with Bob Murphy's win at Southern Hills, Oklahoma, in 1968 (including a win by Lanny Wadkins in 1970), were abandoned in 1973, when more future PGA stars began to take the title, notably Craig Stadler, Jerry Pate, John Cook, Mark O'Meara and Hal Sutton.

In 1981 a stir was caused by a famous name from quite another sphere: Crosby. The singer's son Nathaniel, aged 19, won at Olympic, San Francisco, close to his home. Bing, who once got down to a handicap of two, and attracted a huge crowd when he tried for the British Amateur at St Andrews and birdied two of the first three holes, did not live to see Nat's triumph. He died in 1977 after playing a round in Spain in company with Manuel Pinero.

This was Nathaniel Crosby's sole moment of glory: Jay Sigel, champion for the next two years, was far more consistent. When he won in 1982 at Brookline, he was 38, twice as old as Crosby had been the previous year.

A hand injury 20 years earlier dissuaded Sigel from a professional career, and in any case he earned a living in insurance. His services to US golf are legion, and recently took a new turn when he joined the Senior PGA Tour and showed what a power he might have been in the paid ranks by starting to win serious money right away: his total in 1994 was well past the half million dollar mark.

Phil Mickelson, a left-hander who hits long and chips with a velvet touch from the tightest lies, was 1990 champion and within a year, still an amateur, won a PGA tournament at Tucson. Even cynics were ready to believe that here at last was the next great American player.

Another candidate emerged in 1994 when Californian Eldrick "Tiger" Woods won the Amateur

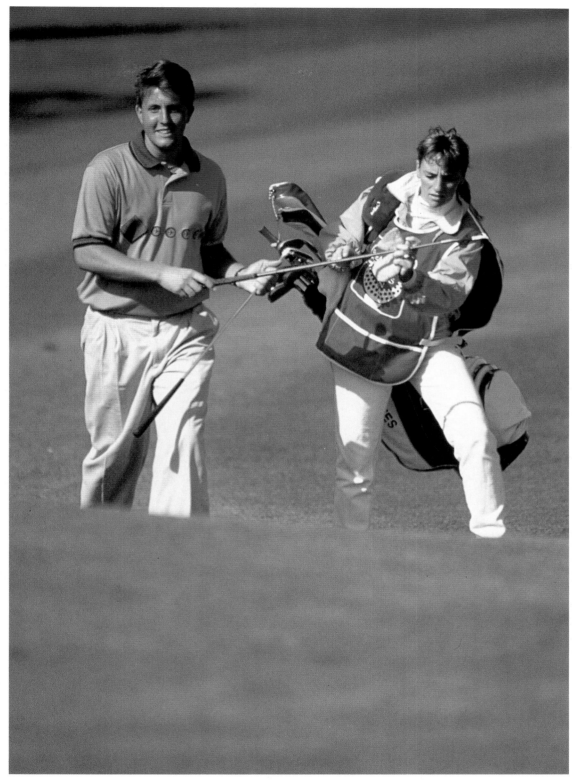

HIGH HOPES *Phil Mickelson, America's answer to to golf's only other world-class left-hander, Bob Charles*

at the Tournament Players' course at Sawgrass, Florida. He is the first black to win in the 94 years of the event, and the youngest champion, at 18. Not only that, but he got the better of Trip Kuehne from Texas by two holes, winning the last three holes in a hair-raising final in which he was six holes adrift on the 14th tee of the first circuit. At that point Kuehne had holed seven birdies. Woods's swing and attacking style are exceptional, and despite his youth he was the hottest favourite for the title in years. His double of US Junior (which he won three times) and Amateur titles is a feat missing from even Jack Nicklaus's CV.

WALKER CUP

By the time the first professional international for the Ryder Cup was played between the two countries, the amateurs had already met four times for the Walker Cup.

This particular Cup competition has been over the years the most difficult of the four major trophies to prise out of American hands. The deep US reserve of amateur talent has been so well organized, coached and led as to win 30 of the 34 matches. Not until the 32nd match did the Americans lose at home, though they were held to 12–12 at Baltimore in 1965.

William Fownes, U.S Amateur champion in 1910, took a team to Hoylake for an informal international on the eve of the 1921 British Amateur Championship. Fownes's team won 9–3.

The R&A sent an official team to the National Golf Links of America at Southampton in New York State to compete for the Walker Cup, presented by a president of the USGA, in 1922. With Fownes at the helm once more, the US sent the R&A select home 8–4 losers. The visitors were handicapped; their captain, Robert Harris, was indisposed and unable to play. Bernard Darwin of *The Times*, who had made the trip as a reporter, took over as captain, and won his single 3 and 1 against Fownes, though Darwin was three down to his opposite number when they stood on the fourth tee.

WALKER TRIO *(L–R) Marvin Ward, Reynolds Smith and Johnny Goodman*

Eight more US Cup victories followed, in which the leadership was passed on to Robert Gardner to Bobby Jones to Francis Ouimet. These three held most of the cards, with such men as Chick Evans and Johnny Goodman, both winners of the US Open, to call upon.

The US, after five big wins in a row, looked certain to get through the 1930s unbeaten . . . until, in the 10th Walker Cup match, at St Andrews in 1938, Ouimet's team, which included American Amateur champion Goodman and the outstanding Marvin Ward, fell to a side coached by Open champion Henry Cotton and led by John Beck, who refined the selection process with painstaking trials.

Though James Bruen from Belfast gained only half a point, in the top foursome with Harry Bentley, and lost his single, he was the life and soul of the party for the home team. He and Bentley got their half with an inspirational rally; they were three down at lunch, after which they toured the Old Course in about four under par to hold John Fischer and Charles Kocsis.

The US, a point behind in foursomes, were unable to gain the five singles they needed to keep their hands on the Cup. Indeed they lost the singles (5–3) for only the second time in the series.

The Second World War meant that the Walker Cup remained under Royal & Ancient care for nearly a decade. The series was resumed in 1947 with a return to American dominance.

Signs of a challenge to US superiority were few. Ronnie White, from Wallasey on Merseyside, had a fine record with six wins from 10 appearances between 1947 and 1955, but the Americans had almost a monopoly of the won/lost credit balances

The matches of the 1950s never produced a winning US margin of less than three points in a 12-match format. Worse was to come in 1961 with an 11–1 defeat at Seattle.

In terms of cash and time, being a top-class amateur was becoming ever more expensive in Britain. A change of format in 1963 increased the matches to 24, but did not alter the result, though that was in doubt until the second day at Turnberry, an improved performance by Britain and Ireland thrillingly maintained at Baltimore in 1965.

There was plenty of fresh blood in the side . . . Gordon Cosh, Rodney Foster, and Clive Clark all in their twenties, teenager Peter Townsend, and Gordon Clark, just into his thirties. Townsend won three points out of four, defeating Billie Joe Patton, who was playing in his last Walker Cup, finishing with an 11–4 record. Britain and Ireland led 10–5, and one match halved, as the final singles began.

WILLIAM FOWNES JNR *First US captain, seen here at Oakmont in 1920*

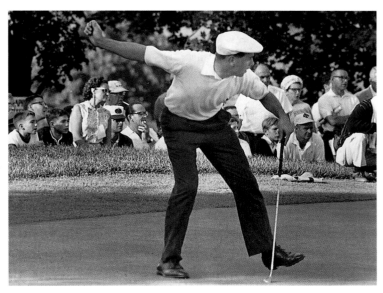

CLIVE CLARK *Urging home the 34-footer that tied the 1965 Walker Cup match*

Only Cosh won as America hit back hard, Edgar Tutweiler, at 46 the only American unbeaten throughout, setting the pace with a winning rally against Ronnie Shade. Nothing routine about the climax though, in which Clive Clark had to hole a 34-foot putt to halve with John Mark Hopkins and tie the whole match ... and this Clark did. He and Townsend soon turned pro, and that was the extent of British pretensions to victory for six years, when a second win was gained.

Like the first it came at St Andrews, where the key in 1971 was the final singles series, won 6-2 by the team led by Michael Bonallack, five times British Amateur champion, whose record as captain (two matches, one win) is much superior

to his playing record of eight wins in 25 matches.

A supremely brave and accurate three-iron approach shot to the Road Hole green (the 17th) was the decisive blow. David Marsh struck it to go dormie against Bill Hyndman, who lost at the next ... his one defeat, against six wins, in five Cup appearances.

Many of the best US amateurs tend to stay amateur, leavening the youthful ambition of the products of collegiate competition. This is certainly borne out by the record defeat inflicted by the US in 1993, 19-5 at Interlachen, Minnesota. Britain and Ireland looked to Iain Pyman, who had a month earlier achieved the record low Open score by an amateur, to inspire a side with an

average age of 21 against a team averaging 31.

The experience of players such as local hero and Walker Cup debutant John Harris, 41, and Jay Sigel, 49, in his ninth Cup match, and Danny Yates, 43, was crucial.

How then to explain the third defeat of the US in 1989 (in Georgia too) by another youthful British selection, in which only resourceful Peter McEvoy, in his fifth match, and Garth McGimpsey, in his second, had played Cup golf before?

McEvoy, than whom no more determined amateur breathes, certainly did his bit, winning more than losing. Most crucial were the misadventures of Sigel, in his seventh Cup match for the US, who lost after a series of most un-American chip shots against Jim Milligan in the final single.

After the Interlachen disaster, however, voices were being raised calling for European amateurs to be brought into the equation. Neither side likes the idea. Besides, while the Continent has provided the handful of pros who have made the Ryder Cup into a contest at last, the same contribution from the amateur game is not in sight.

IN CREDIT *Peter McEvoy, more wins than losses in the first-ever Britain & Ireland away win in Georgia in 1989*

Walker Cup Results

Year	Venue	GB & I	United States	Year	Venue	GB & I	United States
1922	National Links, Southampton, NY	4: R Harris (ill: acting captain B Darwin)	8: W Fownes	1961	Seattle, WA	1: C D Lawrie	11: J Westland
1923	St Andrews	5½: R Harris	6½: R Gardner	1963	Turnberry	10: C D Lawrie	14: R S Tufts
1924	Garden City, NJ	3: C Tolley	9: R Gardner	1965	Baltimore, MA	12: J B Carr	12: J W Fischer
1926	St Andrews	5½: R Harris	6½: R Gardner	1967	St George's	9: J B Carr	15: J W Sweetser
1928	Chicago, IL	1: Dr W Tweddell	11: R T Jones Jnr	1969	Milwaukee, WI	11: M F Bonallack	13: W J Patton
1930	R St George's	2: R H Wethered	10: R T Jones Jnr	1971	St Andrews	13: M F Bonallack	11: J M Winters
1932	Brookline, MA	2½: T A Torrance	9½: F Ouimet	1973	Brookline, MA	10: D M Marsh	14: J W Sweetser
1934	St Andrews	2½: Hon M Scott	9½: F Ouimet	1975	St Andrews	8½: D M Marsh	15½: E Updefraff
1936	Pine Valley, NJ	1½: Dr W Tweddell	10½: F Ouimet	1977	Shinnecock Hills, NY	8: A C Saddler	16: L W Oehmig
1938	St Andrews	7½: J B Beck	4½: F Ouimet	1979	Muirfield	8½: R Foster	15½: R Siderowf
1947	St Andrews	4: J B Beck	8: F Ouimet	1981	Cypress Point, CA	9: R Foster	15: J Gabrielsen
1949	Winged Foot, NY	2: P B Lucas	10: F Ouimet	1983	Hoylake	10½: C W Green	13½: J Sigel
1951	Birkdale	4½: R H Oppenheimer	7½: W P Turnesa	1985	Pine Valley, NJ	11: C W Green	13: J Sigel
1953	Kittansett, MA	3: A A Duncan	9: C R Yates	1987	Sunningdale	7½: G C Marks	16½: F Ridley
1955	St Andrews	2: G A Hill	10: W C Campbell	1989	Peachtree, GA	12½: G C Marks	11½: F Ridley
1957	Minikahda, MN	3½: G H Micklem	8½: C R Coe	1991	Portmarnock	10: G MacGregor	14: J Gabrielson
1959	Muirfield	3: G H Micklem	9: C R Coe	1993	Interlachen, MN	5: G MacGregor	19: M M Giles

WOMEN'S CHAMPIONSHIPS

The ambitions of the Ladies' Professional Golf Association of the United States know few bounds. Their collaboration with the state of Florida in general and the City of Dayton Beach in particular, involving more than 4,000 acres, is not intended merely to provide a two-course backdrop to their new headquarters (until 1989 the LPGA were based in Texas). Their aim is to create a full-scale resort, with residential and commercial property.

Millions of dollars are being devoted to improving road links with the Interstate highway; 21,000 jobs will be created at the resort, the main offices of the LPGA and its Academy and Teaching Complex.

Britain's Laura Davies clinched the Order of Merit of the LPGA in November, 1994, with $687,201 (nearly £450,000), in a year when the top European tour prize (in the British Open) reached £52,500 ($82,000).

The existence of these massive investments and prizes owes much to the Women's PGA pioneers (vintage 1944) such as Hope Seignious, Betty Hicks and Ellen Griffin, and those of the LPGA which replaced the WPGA in 1950. The LPGA owed much to the organizing flair of Fred Corcoran, who made optimum use of the skills and attention-getting exploits of such players as Babe Zaharias and Patty Berg.

The sheer scale of the fixture and prize structure of the world's five major women's tours (US, European, Asian, Japanese and Australian) gives the lie to Horace Hutchinson's patronizing advice to women golfers eager to set up the Ladies' Golf Union of Britain, the world's first women's national organization.

Pioneering Ladies

Writing in April, 1893, to Blanche Martin, who was to become Union treasurer, Hutchinson, one of the leading amateurs of late Victorian times, issued what might today be termed a triple whammy. Women were, he pontificated, incapable of pushing any scheme to success: they would soon quarrel. Secondly, they would never get through a single ladies' championship with credit. Thirdly, they were unfitted for golf because they were incapable of lasting through two rounds of a long course in a day.

Regardless, within a few weeks of the receipt of his letter the LGU was formed and the first British Women's Amateur Championship completed at St Anne's. Lady Margaret Scott, aged 18, won, and did so again twice. Contrary to Hutchinson's expectations, Lady Margaret could not only propel the gutty ball close to 150 yards, despite the long skirts she wore, but also excite the admiration of seasoned male pros at the graceful way in which she did so.

Her third win was followed by the first women's international, in which England beat Ireland. This match might have afforded Hutchinson minor consolation, since several hurry-ups had to be issued to players by the secretary, Issette Pearson, to get to the tee on time, a happening which may have been connected with a dance that lasted deep into the previous night.

Ninety-five years later, in November 1990, the Solheim Cup match between the US and Europe at Lake Nona, in Florida, the inaugural US vs. Europe professional international, demonstrated that the women's game was entering its most sophisticated era. The trophy is named after Karsten Solheim, the engineer who built a club-making empire, most famously with his distinctive Ping putter.

The US won it 11–4, with one match halved, but fears that this was to become another one-sided series like the Walker Cup were dispelled by Europe's 10–5 victory, with three matches halved, at Dalmahoy in Scotland in 1992.

The Cup had speedily become a compelling contest. There was some hand-wringing over the fact that Dalmahoy had received such poor media coverage, particularly on television, but it was clear to officials that the fixture would be a money-making event which would prove a magnet to the media in the future, and to sponsors.

So it proved in 1994 when the Greenbrier, in Virginia, provided a second US victory, 13–7, watched by enormous galleries in stark contrast to the meagre admissions achieved by the first Cup match. More anxiety is expressed, it often seems, by golfers, male or female, about their prospects of gaining Ryder or Solheim selection than they ever divulge about their hopes of winning a major. Being left out of the gang prompts feelings in them of total inadequacy. Once in the gang, players agonize over their fears of letting team-mates down.

GRACEFUL PIONEER *Lady Margaret Scott, three times the British champion*

International competition

Persistent is an inadequate term to describe America's pioneer of international team golf for women, Margaret Curtis. The game was in her blood, and that of her sister, Harriot: they were nieces of Lawrence Curtis, who had much to do with the formation of The Country Club at Brookline, Massachusetts, was present at the meeting that formed the USGA in 1894, and became the second USGA president.

Margaret, a woman of energy, compassion and considerable organizing skill, was engaged before the First World War in social service and relief work. During the war, and for six years afterwards, she worked in France for refugees under the banner of the Red Cross.

The idea of a US vs. GB match had been born, in the mind of the British LGU secretary, Issette Pearson, as early as 1898. The visits of Margaret, Harriot and several other prominent US women golfers to British events in 1905 and 1907 (the year when Margaret beat Harriot in the US Amateur final) brought the first international closer, but the 1909 offer from the USGA of a cup for such a match was not taken up by the LGU. Nor were two unofficial matches followed up : in 1907 England beat America 6–1, and in 1911 Britain won 7–2 against "American and Colonial".

Financial considerations defeated initiatives for an international series in the 1920s. A guarantee of $5,000 per match by Margaret Curtis in 1928, and a third unofficial match in 1930 were not in themselves enough to start the transatlantic golf ball rolling, but perhaps they gave officialdom the necessary nudge … for in 1931, the year of the first official women's international (between Britain and France for the Vagliano Cup), the LGU and USGA agreed to biennial matches. The idea was to involve France – all comers if possible – but that option was never adopted.

Fifteen thousand turned up on May 21, 1932, at Wentworth, southwest of London, to see the American tourists, who were led by Marion Hollins and included the outstanding US golfer of the era, Glenna Collett Vare. She and Opal Hill beat the British captain, Joyce Wethered, and Wanda Morgan in foursomes, all of which the US won.

Wethered beat Collett Vare 6 and 4 in singles, but despite further victories by Enid Wilson over Helen Hicks and Diana Fishwick over Maureen Orcutt the Curtis Cup, a silver Revere bowl donated by the Curtis family, went back to the US, by 5–3, with one match halved. The cup is inscribed with the hope that it would stimulate friendly rivalry between the golfers of many lands, but it has remained a two-sided event from that day in May, 1932.

Collett Vare captained a successful defence at Chevy Chase in 1934, and the whole match was halved four years later, thanks to a huge putt by Jessie Valentine on her debut for Britain and Ireland.

The US kept defeat at bay until 1952 at Muirfield, where Elizabeth Price, a diabetes sufferer, took the deciding match. Her opponent, Grace DeMoss, unaccountably lost all semblance of form at the 14th, after she had hit straight down the middle and seemed sure to win as Price ran into bunker trouble. Instead DeMoss was racked by an attack of the sockets, repeatedly catching her ball with the bottom of the shaft instead of the blade. She took six to reach the green. Price took full advantage, winning the next also and putting stone dead at the 16th to complete a 5–4 win for her team.

Polly Riley was the inspiration of the US team that wrested back the Cup at Merion, Pennsylvania, two years later. Then Britain and Ireland managed a four-year tenure of the Cup by winning 5–4 at Prince's in Kent in 1956 and halving the 1958 event at Brae Burn, Massachusetts, Frances Smith beating Polly Riley at the penultimate hole to tie the match. No visiting team, amateur or professional, had done so well in America.

There followed 26 years of US domination, the longest one-sided run yet, but suggestions that European players should be brought in to redress the balance have fallen on stony ground, certainly as far as the Americans are concerned. A resounding 13–5 victory by the Great Britain and Ireland side so meticulously prepared for the Cup match of 1986 by their captain, Diane Bailey, put an end to the run of 13 US victories. The win, achieved at Prairie Dunes, Kansas, was another first against the US, who in more than 60 years had never lost a home match to a visiting international side, male or female, pro or amateur.

SISTERS ARE DOING IT FOR THEMSELVES *Harriot Curtis – a doughty golf pioneer*

REVENGE IS SWEET *Laura Davies and her fellow Solheim Cup winners*

ALL SMILES *Betty Jameson shows off the US Amateur trophy*

Bailey completed an unprecedented double by leading Britain and Ireland to another win at Royal St George's in 1988, but the US replied in some style in 1990 with a 14–4 trouncing at Somerset Hills, New Jersey. After this Vickie Goetze, the 1989 Amateur champion, summed up the appeal of the Curtis Cup with her remark that she had never been so nervous as when standing on the first tee with her partner Anne Sander at the start of play …and it wasn't even her tee shot.

Britain and Ireland next claimed the Cup for at least another four years with an exciting last-hole victory at Hoylake, clinched by Caroline Hall's fine four iron to the last hole of the last match against Goet-ze, and another halved match at Chattanooga, Tennessee. Visiting stars on the first occasion the Cup had been staged in the South were Catriona Matthew, unbeaten with 3½ points out of four in her Curtis swansong before turning pro, and Janice Moodie with an imperious six-iron approach to the 17th in the final match for a two-hole win over Carol Semple Thompson, playing in her eighth match. That still left the US with 20 wins against five defeats in the series.

Part of the US strength in the 1960s and 1970s derived, according to Anne Sander, from the long service and hence experience of such players as herself and JoAnne Gunderson. Moreover, US losses to the professional game were relatively small in those years.

The sea change that has come over the Curtis series since the mid-1980s, with the US holding the Cup for only two years in a decade, suggests that American losses to the LPGA are becoming heavier. Consider these five golfers who played only one Curtis Cup match apiece, and who have earned more than $10 million between them as LPGA members: Patty Sheehan, leading the way with more than $4 million, Dottie Mochrie, Brandie Burton, Juli Inkster and Danielle Ammaccapane.

Stars of the US Tour

Men pros had long since outclassed the amateurs when American women were struggling to set up a professional circuit in the late 1940s. In the women's game, the amateurs were not only dominant, but fashionable, indeed glamorous. The "bewitching blonde" Edith Cummings, winner of the 1923 Amateur, was reputed to be the model for one of F. Scott Fitzgerald's beautiful high-society women in his novel *The Great Gatsby*. Another lissome blonde golfer, Betty Jameson, took the Amateur in 1939 and 1940, and won the Western Open both as an amateur and as a pro. She was the first to break 300 for 72 holes in any tournament, her 295 taking the 1947

SOLHEIM AVENGER *Dottie Mochrie was a key figure in the 1994 United States Solheim Cup triumph*

Year	Winner	Year	Winner
1946	Patty Berg	1971	JoAnne Carner
1947	Betty Jameson	1972	Susie Berning
1948	Babe Zaharias	1973	Susie Berning
1949	Louise Suggs	1974	Sandra Haynie
1950	Babe Zaharias	1975	Sandra Palmer
1951	Betsy Rawls	1976	JoAnne Carner
1952	Louise Suggs	1977	Hollis Stacy
1953	Betsy Rawls	1978	Hollis Stacy
1954	Babe Zaharias	1979	Jerilyn Britz
1955	Fay Crocker	1980	Amy Alcott
1956	Kathy Cornelius	1981	Pat Bradley
1957	Betsy Rawls	1982	Janet Anderson
1958	Mickey Wright	1983	Jan Stephenson
1959	Mickey Wright	1984	Hollis Stacy
1960	Betsy Rawls	1985	Kathy Baker
1961	Mickey Wright	1986	Jane Geddes
1962	Murle Breer	1987	Laura Davies
1963	Mary Mills	1988	Liselotte Neumann
1964	Mickey Wright	1989	Betsy King
1965	Carol Mann	1990	Betsy King
1966	Sandra Spuzich	1991	Meg Mallon
1967	Catherine LaCoste (Amat.)	1992	Patty Sheehan
1968	Susie Berning	1993	Lauri Merten
1969	Donna Caponi	1994	Patty Sheehan
1970	Donna Caponi		

US Women's Open Results

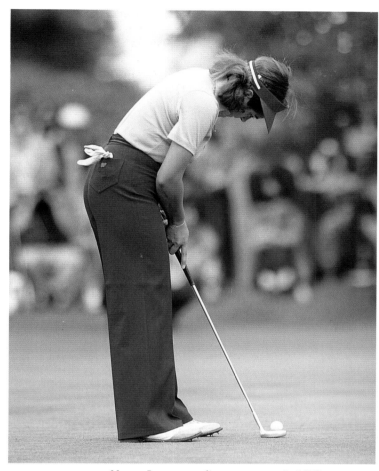

RECORD SHATTERING DEBUT *Nancy Lopez standing over a putt in 1978*

TOUR TREASURE *Babe Zaharias was invaluable to the LPGA's success*

US Women's Open at Starmount, Greensboro, North Carolina.

There was no better amateur than Polly Riley, who played six Curtis Cup matches from 1948 to 1958, and beat Babe Zaharias 10 and 9 in the 36-hole final of the 1948 Texas Open. When the LPGA got started in 1950 after the fade-out of the WPGA, Riley won their first tournament, the Tampa Open.

All the same, Zaharias was the glittering star of the early years of the LPGA. The tour, with such players as Patty Berg to back her up, would doubtless have become prosperous without her, eventually, but she was the catalyst to its more rapid development.

Fame followed Zaharias around, starting from her two 1932 Olympic gold medals and one silver in athletics (as Mildred Didrickson before her marriage to George Zaharias). At 16, she could reputedly drive a golf ball more than 250 yards, but she did not take the game at all se-

riously until she was 23. The range of her skills, from baseball to ballroom dancing and playing the harmonica, is scarcely credible. Yet as a golfer there were few tournaments and little money Zaharias could try for after she had been reported for breaking the amateur status rules and designated a pro by the USGA, a decision which Jack Burke termed "the dirtiest deal I've heard of in a long time".

Her strength was her strength, and after taking a raft of amateur titles when her status was restored, Zaharias turned pro again (voluntarily, upon accepting an offer of $300,000 to make golf films), and proceeded to outhit every rival.

She is also reputed to have commanded bigger fees than Ben Hogan in exhibition matches. Her appearance in LPGA events was a guarantee of public interest.

She tended to be a prima donna, using her fame to get her own way, which irritated rivals, but they had

much to thank her for as sponsors, especially makers of products that interested women, recognized the attractions of women's golf. At the same time the emerging talents of Louise Suggs, Betsy Rawls and Peggy Kirk enlivened competition. A decade after that amateur victory by Polly Riley in the LPGA's first event, the tour prize money was $200,000, and events numbered 26.

The supreme stylist Mickey Wright, then Nancy Lopez, were the next dominating figures.

Though Kathy Whitworth achieved a career record of 88 tournament wins between 1959 and 1991, the immediate and lasting impact of Lopez had a publicity value second only perhaps to that of Zaharias. Lopez, second in the Open as an amateur, took nine events in 1978, her first full year on the Tour, including five in a row. This galvanized the golfing public, sent gate receipts soaring, and earned for Lopez simultaneous Rookie of the

Year and Player of the Year awards.

The professional women's set of majors has varied over the years with the nature of sponsorship. There have not always been four. Two players have managed a seasonal sweep of the available majors, Zaharias with the three available in 1950 (US Open, Titleholders and Western Open), Sandra Haynie with the two on offer in 1974, the US Open and LPGA title.

Pat Bradley came closest to the current feminine version of Bobby Jones's Impregnable Quadrilateral. She won the 1986 LPGA title, the du Maurier Classic, and the Nabisco Dinah Shore, but finished third in the Open to Jane Geddes. Bradley, a former skiing instructor, has constructed an LPGA record of marvellous consistency, with nearly $5 million in official prize money. She has 13 times finished in the top ten money-winners, and was No. 1 in 1986 and again, with $763,118, in 1991. Not surprisingly, in that year

AYATO OKAMOTO *From Hiroshima, she has won 17 times on the LPGA tour, earning over $1 million*

she was also leader in three other categories, achieving 21 top ten finishes in 26 starts, the best scoring average and 314 birdies.

Patty Sheehan, the first double Open winner in 1992, with the US title at Oakmont, Pennsylvania, and the British at Woburn, has managed to reach six figures in prize money annually since 1981.

The late Dinah Shore added to her fame as a singer by becoming the Bing Crosby, so to speak, of women's professional golf. Her tournament, richly sponsored by Colgate, who also owned the Ram golf company, began in 1972 at Palm Springs, California, and attracted plenty of Shore's Hollywood and music-business friends, in the tradition of Crosby's celebrity "Clambake" event on the Monterey courses. Like the Masters, this major is always played at the same venue, the Mission Hills course in California, at which the 1991 winner Amy Alcott jumped into the lake with Dinah.

The success of Chako Higuchi, an LPGA champion, and Ayako Okamoto, 1987 Player of the Year, gained the attention of Japanese sponsors; these and other supporters swelling the average tournament purse from $30,000 in the early 1970s to more than half a million dollars in the mid-1990s – that is, a total of more than $20 million.

The Tour has unearthed heart-warming stories of struggles against ill fortune, none more remarkable than that of Martha Nause. She won the LPGA title in 1994 by a shot in Ottawa, with four birdies in the last seven holes to beat her playing partner Michelle Gann by a stroke. Nause, 39, from Wisconsin, had just spent a year recovering from an infection causing nerve damage in her ear, destroying her sense of balance. "I had to hold on to things to walk. I couldn't drive a car at all," Nause explained.

Her doctor said she should consider never playing again. Nause's feeling was that she had everything needed to be a winner, and proved it. Betsy King, who had lost the two-stroke lead she held when the final round started, no doubt admired Nause's feat, but must have breathed a sigh at her own joint fourth place, because she needed only one more win to enter the LPGA Hall of Fame, 30 being the required figure.

The European tour

European women began breaking into the rich, charmed circle of the US Tour. Laura Davies won the US Open in 1987, following up by ranking first in prize money seven years later. Trish Johnson (with back to back wins in 1992), Liselotte Neumann, and Helen Alfredsson (with a Dinah Shore title in 1993) have also prospered in LPGA events.

The European women's tour was a good deal slower achieving rich and piping times than the American. Total prize money, around £2 million (over $3 million) is still only about one-seventh of the US figure. The first British Women's Open in 1972, won by Jenny Lee Smith, now a golf-gear entrepreneur, post-dated the American version by a quarter century. It was not played at all in 1983, for lack of a sponsor. Since 1987 it has been safe-guarded under the banner of Weetabix.

Sponsorship has generally been hard to come by from the inception of the European tour, when prize money totalled £80,000. Cathy Panton-Lewis, the first winner of the tour's inaugural Order of Merit, earned £2,494.50. These relatively meagre pickings did not suggest to the best amateurs that turning pro would make their fortunes.

Early standards of play were patchy, and helped depress the number of tournaments from an initial 18 to 10 in 1982. Steady progress was resumed under the aegis of the PGA and Colin Snape, but faltered after a prize-money peak of £1,999,325 in 1990 with the onset of the recession. The mid-1990s are more encouraging, with thorough (satellite) television coverage.

Above all, battles for Karsten Solheim's trophy provide the supreme test of excellence in women's golf ... and they are sure-fire winners at the turnstiles.

British Women's Open		
	Year	**Winner**
	1976	Jenny Lee Smith
	1977	Vivien Saunders
	1978	Janet Melville
	1979	Alison Sheard
	1980	Debbie Massey
	1981	Debbie Massey
	1982	Marta Figueras-Dotti
	1983	*NO COMPETITION*
	1984	Ayako Okamoto
	1985	Betsy King
	1986	Laura Davies
	1987	Alison Nicholas
	1988	Corinne Dibnah
	1989	Janet Geddes
	1990	Helen Alfredsson
	1991	Penny Grice-Whittaker
	1992	Patty Sheehan
	1993	Karen Lunn
	1994	Liselotte Neumann

WORLDWIDE WINNER *Liselotte Neumann, showing off the British Open trophy at Woburn in 1994, earned richly on the US, European and Asian tours*

US PGA TOUR

Now the powerhouse of world golf, the American PGA Tour in its early, cash-strapped, play-it-by-ear days had need of the spirit of the frontiersman. There were huge distances to cover, usually by automobile, cheap lodgings to find if prize money had been elusive of late, and even if it hadn't in most cases. Tournaments were loosely organized (golfers who got there first teed off first), and players had to have other sources of income because prize money was short, and the available cash did not go far down the list of also-rans.

Since the tour began as a winter event in Florida, Texas and other southern states, the players could combine playing for prize money with a club job in the north during the months when play was difficult or impossible, and custom at professional shops correspondingly light. The tournaments, often at tourist resorts, were usually sponsored by the local chamber of commerce, for the results would be reported in the great cities of the north-eastern seaboard and middle west, giving publicity at a reasonable rate to the fact that where the golfers were, there the sun was. Chilly northerners were made well aware of the best places to take vacations.

There was, if your imagination is allowed to run riot for a moment, a touch of the western gambler/gunslinger about the early tour pro, travelling from town to town chancing his luck. Wild Bill Mehlhorn, whose father had left Germany rather than join the ranks of Kaiser Wilhelm's army, kept dollars in his pocket by giving lessons *en route* to the winter tour, and selling magazine subscriptions.

There is a restless streak in many Americans; many are forever ready to up sticks and seek a new job in the next state, or the next but one time zone.

Besides, the living from a pro's shop was not all that magnificent. Ability to teach the game was not always accompanied by marketing skills, which were the forte of the suppliers of golf clubs, clothing and the like. These middlemen made it a hard life for many club pros, and clubs were wont to command profits on ball sales, the pro's main stock-in-trade.

Hence the establishment in 1916 of the US Professional Golfers Association, which was and is basically an organization to protect the interests of the club pro. This was to be a certain source of friction when tour players grew away from their shop counters and club-repairing, became "names" and wanted privileges the PGA would not grant, of which more later.

A good many British prejudices still ruled in America, inimical to professional golf, for the amateur was still king, and the paid man looked down upon. Pros in England commanded a good deal more respect (but not yet entrée to club-

WILD BILL MEHLHORN *Nicknamed for his brilliant scoring bursts, not for his temper, he was a Tour pioneer who often finished high in the US Open*

houses) thanks perhaps to the mighty reputations, in technique and competitive drive, of players such as Harry Vardon and J. H. Taylor, first and second in the 1900 US Open, and the excitements of watching money matches. What a treat for the Scottish islanders of Islay to watch Vardon and Taylor vs. James Braid and Alex Herd in an international fourball on the newly consecrated Machrie course.

Tournament life took a different route in the United States. The PGA gave the pros a peg to hang their season on (Open Championship apart) with the US PGA Championship, for which the first (1916) winner, Jim Barnes, received $500 – about what Vardon would get in a big money challenge match in the old country. The US PGA and Open were far from becoming the central events in a well-ordered tour, the growth of which began haphazardly in the Sunbelt of the south immediately around the turn of the century, with prize money reaching three figures in Florida resorts. No detailed chronology exists of how it began, except to say that winter tournaments in California, Texas and Florida in the early 1920s were crucial elements.

Amateur events were held at the resorts long before the First World War, and pro events grew up alongside, usually with less notice being taken of them by the Press.

The power of the pro

What the pro game needed was a hero. Amateurs in particular and US golf in general certainly found a hero at the 1913 Open in Francis Ouimet. Walter Hagen almost achieved that status in the same championship, but fell just short of the epoch-making play-off in which Ouimet beat Vardon and Ted Ray. Such was his confidence that he might well have surprised all three; 12

MICHTY HITTER *"Long" Jim Barnes left his native Cornwall to win the 1921 US Open by 9 shots*

months later Hagen *was* Open champion, and became leader in the considerable task of transforming the golf pro into an envied – though not always prosperous – and admired – but not always respected – pillar of society.

There is little difference between Hagen's role and that of the touring pro of today, except that he depended less on prize money (there wasn't much, and he sometimes gave it away) and more on exhibition matches. He played such a match rather than defend his first US PGA title, and attracted thousands of spectators to hundreds of his one-day appearances at a dollar or so admission when a dollar was a dollar. He had the happy knack of being able not only to impress the galleries with his golf but to entertain them with a line of chat that would have ensured success as a stand-up comedian.

This stroll-around comedian created his own lucrative theatre of the open air, aided by players such as Gene Sarazen, just out of his teens and winner of the Open and US PGA titles in 1922. This was the US PGA Hagen had passed up to play in an exhibition, so another exhibition, a challenge match between the pair, was set up, expansively billed as being for the Golf Championship of the World: hype is a new word, but not a new phenomenon.

Sarazen, two down after the first two rounds at Oakmont, Pennsylvania, was in pain before the final holes at the palatial Westchester-Biltmore Country Club in New York. In wind and rain Sarazen struggled on, overtook Hagen, and next day had an emergency operation to have his appendix removed. His prize was $2,000, Hagen's £1,000: winning

"FATHER OF THE PGA TOUR" *Bob Harlow (extreme left) with members of the losing 1929 Ryder Cup US team.*

the US Open was not worth $1,000 until 1929.

One rock upon which the PGA Tour was founded was the Texas Open, founded in 1923 by businessmen in San Antonio. The total purse was a record at $5,000. Another Tour foundation stone was laid three years later by the Los Angeles Junior Chamber of Commerce: this one worth $10,000. A year later other Californian cities organized pro events. The tour was now getting into some kind of order, the players starting in the west early in the New Year, moving east to Texas and Florida, then up the east coast to spring and summer events.

Total prize money of $77,000 was available in 1928. This supported a growing band of men who depended almost entirely on their playing, rather than pro-shopkeeping, skills. Walter Hagen was no longer the one and only touring pro. But of central organization was there none, until a succession of newspapermen,

who had every reason to want the tour to expand, took a hand. Of these the most influential was Bob Harlow, son of a Congregationalist minister. Unsurprisingly, he was also Hagen's manager.

No man has a better claim than Harlow to be the chief begetter of the PGA Tour, though his main difficulty was ... the PGA. Like those before him who had tried to bring order to the tour, he wanted to supplement his income from newspaper articles, and as agent for Hagen and other leading players, with a salary or commission for putting tournaments together and persuading sponsors to part with cash.

He at length got a $100 a week salary, but in 1932 was sacked by the PGA, some of whose officials looked upon touring pros as a pampered, footloose gang of opportunists, who unjustly commanded too many choice club pro jobs on the basis of their playing prowess. Ostensibly he was dismissed because

he was spending too much time on his extra-tour activities.

Maybe, but it was Harlow who rationalized the tour with a showman's flair. He used every contemporary method of advertising to publicize tournaments, issued lists of tournament pairings and tee-times (no first come first served with Harlow), got golf gear makers to buoy up prize money when local sponsors were short of promotional dollars, issued orders of merit, encouraged club volunteers to help in running tournaments (they still do), and in his first year almost doubled the tour purses.

When the PGA re-employed Harlow in 1933, the economy had become chronically sick, yet he invented the minimum purse and worked out a system by which the best players were exempted from qualifying. Already the players, avid for more cash and freedom from the PGA and its club-pro fixation, were looking at ways to set up a rival

organizational shop of their own.

Another journalist, Fred Corcoran, was next to ride the tour tiger, beginning in 1936 at $5,000 a year ... golf had moved on quite a way. A born publicist, he improved information services for the public, with coloured scoreboards, and brought a greater range of sponsors, including financial firms and airlines, into play.

The final rift between the PGA and the players widened to involve threats of boycott in the 1960s. Though the sums pocketed by the leading performer on Tour had declined radically at times in the depressed 1930s, better times, looser corporate purse-strings and the sheer quality of pros such as Ben Hogan, Sam Snead and Byron Nelson made life easier for tour managers as peace broke out in 1945. The advent of the greatest crowd pleaser since Hagen, Arnold Palmer, taken together with the advent of televised golf, changed many things. Television started with local coverage of the 1947 US Open at St Louis, Missouri, and soon progressed, under the influence of George S. May, promoter of the Tam O'Shanter National (*sic*) Open in Chicago to national coverage.

The Midas touch

May's tournament in particular and golf in general had a golden stroke of luck in 1953. May was not present when ABC television offered national coverage for $32,000. Chet Posson, May's assistant, took a chance and accepted. May, a management consultant in a big way of business, said when he heard what Posson had done: "I don't care if it costs us a million. Do it!"

So more people – an estimated two million – saw the Tam O'Shanter of 1953 than had witnessed any previous event in golf history: lo and behold, Lew Worsham won it with a 135-yard wedge approach shot to the final green. It went in ... an eagle two. In a flash Chandler Harper, who had finished and must have counted the $25,000 first prize as good as in his bank account, had lost by a stroke. Worsham's shot, which also brought him a contract for 25 exhibitions at

$1,000 each, is said to have caused early television couch potatoes to fall off their couches.

Television gave golf the Midas touch. It enabled prize money to double in 10 years from $6.7 million in 1970, and this had tripled again by 1990. Sponsors could now use golf to hit consumers right across the nation. Golf's top man (Palmer) in 1963 took $128,230. The first recorded leading money winner, Paul Runyan in 1934, had earned $6,767.

The leading post-war players would soon be thinking airplane instead of automobile. The younger ones, many of them not long out of college, had no knowledge of mending clubs and selling chocolate bars across the counter. Once television rights began to swell, tour pros could not see why the PGA should get much of what their skill alone, as they saw it, was channelling into the prize pot.

Boycott threats by the touring pros in 1967 were followed by an overt move for independence…an announcement that the breakaway American Professional Golfers had a $3.5 million tour programme for 1969. In this particular poker game

GOLF'S GIFT TO TV *Lew Worsham (second left) astounded viewers with his eagle in the 1953 Tam O'Shanter event*

the PGA held two pairs, the touring pros held a royal flush, and a gun to the head of the PGA. Without the leading players, which now included Jack Nicklaus, a prime mover in the negotiations with

Gardner Dickinson, television and sponsors didn't fancy PGA golf at all: only Sam Snead stuck by the old regime.

So the players became free men, their Magna Carta granted unconditionally under what was no more than a convenient fiction, the creation of a new PGA division. Harlow would have enjoyed living at this hour, but he died in 1954, still married to his golf reporting career. He would have been totally at ease with the fact that golf is the only sport whose professionals run their own events. In recent years the PGA Tour players have even built their own courses. Needless to say, no other professional group in the world of sport owns the bricks and mortar, so to speak.

The golf pros of America are going about ownership to even greater degree in the closing years of the twentieth century. They plan a world golf village in Florida, close to the PGA headquarters near Jacksonville. An international museum is planned, together with a Hall of Fame comprising sections for the American Tour, the Ladies' Professional Golf Association, and the PGA, whose exhibits are being moved from Pinehurst, North Car-

olina. There will also be two golf courses and 7,200 homes, plus extensive commercial property … a counterpart to the LPGA's complex at Daytona Beach.

There is no "them" (the bosses) and "us" (the players) about golf, a schism which has of late been so costly to baseball, even to the extent of the loss of the 1994 World Series. Moreover, hockey players were off the ice for half the 1954–55 season.

There was a lasting bitterness between the club pros and tour players after the split. Club-makers MacGregor, it was reported, got requests from club pros to remove Jack Nicklaus's name from their products. They perhaps forgot that Nicklaus, Palmer and Co. have enticed battalions of their fans to buy golf gear in pro shops across the world. Sport is contagious: every time a Finn excels at his nation's athletic speciality, the pole vault, the nation's hospitals can be sure of an influx of young would-be record breakers who manage only to break legs. Fears that the clubs hosting tour events might consider the players had taken too much upon themselves and withdraw course facilities proved to be without foundation.

Year	Winner	($)	Year	Winner	($)
1934	Paul Runyan	6,767	1965	Jack Nicklaus	140,752
1935	Johnny Revolta	9,543	1966	Billy Casper	121,944
1936	Horton Smith	7,682	1967	Jack Nicklaus	188,998
1937	Harry Cooper	14,138	1968	Billy Casper	205,168
1938	Sam Snead	19,534	1969	Frank Beard	164,707
1939	Henry Picard	10,303	1970	Lee Trevino	157,037
1940	Ben Hogan	10,655	1971	Jack Nicklaus	244,490
1941	Ben Hogan	18,358	1972	Jack Nicklaus	320,542
1942	Ben Hogan	13,143	1973	Jack Nicklaus	308,362
1943	NO STATISTICS COMPILED		1974	Johnny Miller	353,021
1944	Byron Nelson	*37,967	1975	Jack Nicklaus	298,149
1945	Byron Nelson	*63,335	1976	Jack Nicklaus	266,438
1946	Ben Hogan	42,556	1977	Tom Watson	310,653
1947	Jimmy Demaaret	27,936	1978	Tom Watson	362,428
1948	Ben Hogan	32,112	1979	Tom Watson	462,636
1949	Sam Snead	31,593	1980	Tom Watson	530,808
1950	Sam Snead	35,758	1981	Tom Kite	375,698
1951	Lloyd Mangrum	26,088	1982	Craig Stadler	446,462
1952	Julius Boros	37,032	1983	Hal Sutton	426,668
1953	Lew Worsham	34,002	1984	Tom Watson	476,260
1954	Bob Toski	65,819	1985	Curtis Strange	542,321
1955	Julius Boros	63,121	1986	Greg Norman	653,296
1956	Ted Kroll	72,835	1987	Curtis Strange	925,941
1957	Dick Mayer	65,835	1988	Curtis Strange	1,147,644
1958	Arnold Palmer	42,607	1989	Tom Kite	1,395,278
1959	Art Wall	53,167	1990	Greg Norman	1,165,477
1960	Arnold Palmer	75,262	1991	Corey Pavin	979,430
1961	Gary Player	64,540	1992	Fred Couples	1,344,188
1962	Arnold Palmer	81,448	1993	Nick Price	1,478,557
1963	Arnold Palmer	128,230	1994	Nick Price	1,499,927
1964	Jack Nicklaus	113,284		* War bonds	

Leading US Tour money-winners

EUROPEAN PGA TOUR

Much the same political shenanigans took place on the European Tour, which was not established until the early 1970s, but has grown a great deal more quickly than the pioneering US Tour did.

In less than a quarter of a century since John Jacobs, Ryder Cup player and prominent teacher, became Tournament Director-General of the PGA in 1971, the prize money has soared from £250,000 to more than £25 million. The following year the Tour took on its crowd-pleasing European dimension as the European Tournament Players' Division. Ken Schofield, the present director of organization, now the PGA European Tour, succeeded Jacobs in 1975, prize-money growing 50-fold under his administration. A great fillip to the European Tour has been the extension of Ryder Cup teams to take in Continental players. Most Cup places depend on European Tour success.

The European Tour has shadowed its US predecessor in setting up the all-exempt tour, under which pre-qualifying for tournaments was discontinued, and places are gained through performance in majors championships and on a sufficiently high ranking in the Order of Merit based on tour events.

The all-exempt tour was logically followed in the US and Europe by qualifying schools for players with tour ambitions. These "schools" have big fields but few prizes – a limited number of highly sought-after tour "cards" that afford entry into PGA tour events.

This did not satisfy the ambitions of youth, and so in Europe the Challenge Tour as a feeder competition for the main Tour developed from the Satellite Tour begun in 1986.

DESERT DEFEAT *The top money earner in 1994 Colin Montgomerie hits out in the 1995 Dubai Desert Classic*

Leading European Tour money-winners					
Year	Winner	(£)	Year	Winner	(£)
1962	Peter Thomson	5,764	1979	Sandy Lyle	49,233
1963	Bernard Hunt	7,209	1980	Greg Norman	74,829
1964	Neil Coles	7,890	1981	Bernhard Langer	95,991
1965	Peter Thomson	7,011	1982	Sandy Lyle	86,141
1966	Bruce Devlin	13,205	1983	Nick Faldo	140,761
1967	Gay Brewer	20,235	1984	Bernhard Langer	160,883
1968	Gay Brewer	23,107	1985	Sandy Lyle	254,711
1969	Billy Casper	23,483	1986	Seve Ballesteros	259,275
1970	Christy O'Connor	31,532	1987	Ian Woosnam	439,075
1971	Gary Player	11,281	1988	Seve Ballesteros	502,000
1972	Bob Charles	18,538	1989	Ronan Rafferty	465,981
1973	Tony Jacklin	24,839	1990	Ian Woosnam	737,977
1974	Peter Oosterhuis	32,127	1991	Seve Ballesteros	790,811
1975	Dale Hayes	20,507	1992	Nick Faldo	1,220,540
1976	Seve Ballesteros	39,504	1993	Colin Montgomerie	798,145
1977	Seve Ballesteros	46,436	1994	Colin Montgomerie	877,135
1978	Seve Ballesteros	54,348			

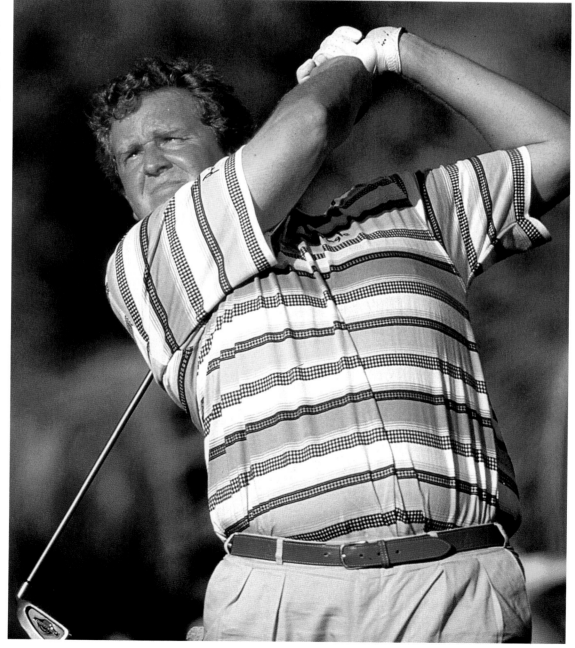

OTHER PRINCIPAL GOLF EVENTS

Amazingly, not only junior extensions have been grafted on to the organization of the two major tours: even greater success has been achieved by the return of senior players to regular competition in their own tour. Fred Raphael, producer of the popular "Shell's Wonderful World of Golf" series, was mustard keen to make Sam Snead's idea of an old timers' circuit work. Some players were fearful that they would not look good in their (relative) old age. This did not apply to Snead, of whom Raphael said: "He knew he was going to play well." Snead did, and, partnered by Gardner Dickinson, won the inaugural event in 1978.

This celebration of mature talents was made into a smash hit by Roberto de Vicenzo and Julius Boros the following year, when they scored in an event named "Legends of Golf". They beat Art Wall and Tommy Bolt in a spectacular low-scoring six-hole play-off that suggested that old golfers do not fade away; they just get more cunning.

Besides, Arnold Palmer, still the darling of the galleries, reached 50 in 1979, his fourth year without a win on the main tour. A four-event Senior Tour was organized in 1980, and the age limit later dropped to 50, and Senior success was assured. Its practitioners are earning far more money than they ever did on the PGA Tour

itself 30 years or more ago. Lee Trevino earned $3.4 million on the regular tour in 20 years, $7.5 million in five years with the Seniors.

Significantly, the great players of the post-war period have cleaned up most prize money on the Senior Tour, their nerve and the security of their technique overcoming the penalties of age. Jack Nicklaus won six times in his first three Senior years, including two US Senior Opens. Trevino won seven events and more than $1 million in his first year. Ray Floyd put one over on young and old with a victory on the regular tour and the Senior in the same season.

None of the foregoing has yet satisfied the hunger of galleries to see

their favourites in action. Nor has it diluted the eagerness of sponsors to hand out prize money.

Hence, after a full 10 months of weekly chances to win "official money" in PGA tournaments, plus further cash and glory on offer in the Masters and the US Open, American Tour players and their peers from other tours look forward to an unbroken series of extra earning opportunities reaching all the way to Christmas and beyond.

Some brave spirits, like José-Maria Olazabal of Spain, prefer family pursuits and will not play as the holiday approaches; others head for an international event such as the Kapalua International, Hawaii, and there are specials events for the superstars, such as the Skins Game, and the Grand Slam. Skins are played by four golfers, with prizes available on every hole, which can be won by one of the quartet outscoring the other three. If the hole is halved, the players progress hole by hole, with the eventual prize money increasing hole by hole, until someone does come out on top. Six-figure sums can rest on one hole.

The Grand Slam involves the winners of the four major championships: in 1994 Nick Price won two, the Open and the US PGA, so Greg Norman was invited to Poipu Bay, Hawaii, as an alternate, since he was second only to Price in the Sony Rankings of world golf. Ernie Els (US Open Champion) and Olazabal (Masters Champion) were the other two players. Norman scored 136 for $400,000 and a $5,000 gold Rolex watch, Price 139 for $250,000, Els 143 for $200,000, Olazabal 144 for $150,000.

Sun City, near Johannesburg, offers the biggest prize of all, $1 million, though the so-called "World Championship" (no such thing is possible in golf) sponsored by Johnny Walker whisky in Jamaica just before Christmas, is not to be sniffed at: prizes total $2.5 million. The event is strictly for the successful – winners of specified events through the year.

Yet another "World" event, Gene Sarazen's World Open, first played at The Legends, Atlanta, Georgia, in November 1994, offers

FOUR MAJORS *(from left) Fuzzy Zoeller, Jack Nicklaus, Arnold Palmer and Tom Watson before the 1985 "Skins"*

GLOBE TROTTERS *Phil Mickelson (known to some as the next Ben Crenshaw) watches as Ernie Els tees off in the 1993 Dunlop Phoenix in Japan*

$1.9 million in prizes. Els won it ($350,000) as the middle segment of a late season treble which started with the Toyota World Match Play at Wentworth in England, and finished with "World Championship" number two in Jamaica. His total take in the three events was more than $1.1 million.

Alternatively, lords of the links can jet off to Japan, where the Tour begins with the $1.5 million Sumitomo Visa Taiheiyo Masters, followed by the $2 million Dunlop Phoenix, Japan's richest event. Johnny Miller won it first, in 1974, since when 12 other Americans have triumphed, but only two Japanese – Tommy Nakajima in 1985 and the ruler of the Japanese circuit, Jumbo Osaki, with a record last round of 65 to beat Tom Watson by a stroke in 1994. The Japanese Open has seldom been won by a foreigner. Seve Ballesteros did so twice (1977 and 1978).

Then there are the Australasian and Asian honey-pots to think about. The Australian Open (which

Jack Nicklaus has won six times, Gary Player seven) dates back to 1904, but the depression years of the late 1980s hit the Australian circuit harder than most. Prize money recovered by the end of the 1994–95 season to A$6.9 million (about £3.4 million, or $5.2 million).

The South African Open, first played in 1903, is older than that of Canada, Australia or New Zealand. Brothers Sid and Jock Brews had dominated South African golf for many years until Bobby Locke won the Amateur and Open in the space of a few days in 1935. He won the Open eight times more – twice as an amateur – and Gary Player has triumphed on 13 occasions.

The ending of apartheid has placed the nation thoroughly back in the mainstream of world golf. The Republic was even made a winter stop on the "European" PGA Tour (Europe = where the PGA Tour pitches its tent, e.g., Manila or Madeira), with a February date at the Wanderers, Johannesburg.

World Match Play Championship Results

Played at Wentworth, Virginia Water, Surrey, England

Year	Winner and Result	
1964	Arnold Palmer bt Neil Coles	2 & 1
1965	Gary Player bt Peter Thomson	3 & 2
1966	Gary Player bt Jack Nicklaus	6 & 4
1967	Arnold Palmer bt Peter Thomson	1 hole
1968	Gary Player bt Bob Charles	1 hole
1969	Bob Charles bt Gene Littler	37th
1970	Jack Nicklaus bt Lee Trevino	2 & 1
1971	Gary Player bt Jack Nicklaus	5 & 4
1972	Tom Weiskopf bt Lee Trevino	4 & 3
1973	Gary Player bt Graham Marsh	40th
1974	Hale Irwin bt Gary Player	3 & 1
1975	Hale Irwin bt Al Geiberger	4 & 2
1976	David Graham bt Hale Irwin	38th
1977	Graham Marsh bt Ray Floyd	5 & 3
1978	Isao Aoki bt Simon Owen	3 & 2
1979	Bill Rogers bt Isao Aoki	1 hole
1980	Greg Norman bt Sandy Lyle	1 hole
1981	Seve Ballesteros bt Ben Crenshaw	1 hole
1982	Seve Ballesteros bt Sandy Lyle	37th
1983	Greg Norman bt Nick Faldo	3 & 2
1984	Seve Ballesteros bt Bernhard Langer	2 & 1
1985	Seve Ballesteros bt Bernhard Langer	6 & 5
1986	Greg Norman bt Sandy Lyle	2 & 1
1987	Ian Woosnam bt Sandy Lyle	1 hole
1988	Sandy Lyle bt Nick Faldo	2 & 1
1989	Nick Faldo bt Ian Woosnam	1 hole
1990	Ian Woosnam bt Mark McNulty	4 & 2
1991	Seve Ballesteros bt Nick Price	3 & 2
1992	Nick Faldo bt Jeff Sluman	8 & 7
1993	Corey Pavin bt Nick Faldo	1 hole
1994	Ernie Els bt Colin Montgomerie	4 & 2

GOLF AROUND THE WORLD

Arnold Palmer says: "If we had the ability to look into the future we would see golf as the biggest participation sport in the world without question." A long way to go then, Arnie, since FIFA believes there are more than 200 million soccer players whereas the largest golfing nation, the United States, has less than an eighth as many players. On the other hand, golf has scarcely started yet in China and Russia ...

THE UNITED STATES

Golf's growth in the United States since the immediate post-war years has been approximately eightfold in numbers of players. There were an estimated 3.2 million golfers in the US in 1950, playing on some 5,000 courses. The latest figures for the 1990s put playing numbers at 24.8 million; courses at 14,000.

Golf is now available to US golf enthusiasts 24 hours a day thanks to the new television Golf Channel, with which Arnold Palmer is inevitably associated. (He remains one of golf's biggest earners, with a finger in a great many commercial pies, including items you might expect, like lawn mower and golf club manufacture, and others that you might not, such as batteries for hearing aids.)

Transmitted from Orlando in Florida, the Golf Channel is getting figures of two million viewers per day, and as more channels take a feed from this cable service, it could reach nine million, and no doubt will at the June–August seasonal peak of interest.

The number of players is, however, not as impressive as it looks at first sight, suggesting as it does that around 10 per cent of Americans are regular golfers. Half the 24.8 million, says the National Golf Foundation, are "recreational golfers" playing between one and seven rounds a year. The "core" golfers, ranging from regular, serious and intense to just plain fanatical, are far less numerous: 80 per cent of the rounds, it is believed, are played by 20 per cent of the players.

This gives a clue as to how America deploys such a depth of playing strength from youth to Ryder Cup level, for that 20 per cent represents a fair number of determined, regular low-handicap players ... and the USGA's handicap system is not a provider of ego-massage or free hand-outs.

Averaging out the cost of a round, from the most exclusive and rarefied clubs to public pay and play courses, gives a figure of about $60. It should be noted that while the US remains a bulwark of free enterprise there are the best part of five thousand more public than private clubs. Here is another of the great strengths of American golf, buttressed as it is by the national golf association's Public Links Championships for men and women.

About one golf ball a year is sold for every one of those 24.8 million players, be they two or two hundred rounds a year players. The price of a golf ball has not increased in real cost over the years, for while the retail price index has been increasing fourfold, a three-ball sleeve has advanced from $3.75 to $8.50.

Ball sales offer a significant exception to economic orthodoxy, for when unemployment is high, sales of this luxury item increase: "At last," many of the jobless must console themselves, "now for a round away from all those weekend crowds."

The average price of a golf club is between $50 and $75, and new equipment tycoons have appeared

CHEERLEADERS *Debbie Couples leads US Ryder Cup wives' cheers at Kiawah Island in 1991*

EXCLUSIVE SHINNECOCK *Members only, but US Open host, 1995*

to take large slices of the market once dominated by Spalding and Wilson. Quite apart from Japanese makers, a cobbler turned engineer, Karsten Solheim, still reputedly a shaky 20-handicapper, has built from his Arizona base a club business with his Ping designs which has placed him among the 400 richest men in the US.

After Solheim rang the bell with a Ping, the latest big hit (literally) on the scene has been made by another career-switcher, this time Ely Callaway, formerly prominent in the textile and wine business. His "big is beautiful" philosophy of club-making has rocketed his company into the top 10 of club-makers world-wide.

An apple for the teacher with the best credentials in recent years, David Leadbetter, will not do, for his advice and coaching cost upwards of $300 a session, and a few days' tuition (conservative estimate only) 10 times as much at a fashionable (sunny) resort in Florida, the Carolinas or the rest of the Sunbelt.

The hotter the better for the caddie cart rental business, for one busy resort club can make a million dollars on rentals in a year. The concept appears to be no older than 1930: Curtis Willock, came up with it at Pasadena, California. He was chairman of the Greens Committee at Annandale GC, and he had a wooden leg. Ben Delanty, manager of Pasadena Power Department, made a three-wheel ve-

hicle, each wheel driven by a battery-powered electric motor.

No developments appeared over the next 18 years until the first patent "Arthritis Special" from R. J. Jackson, a Texas oil man, with a cart developed from a three-wheel vehicle built to take spare parts to aircraft on airfields. "Smokey and smelly" was the reaction to the early petrol-engined caddie carts.

Not until improved batteries were available did the caddie cart come into great public favour. They became more and more fashionable, thanks especially to the influence of cart-drivers such as President Eisenhower, Bing Crosby and Bob Hope, whose preference was for a vehicle equipped with a long nose, ski-jump shaped like his own: a million carts were touring US courses by the mid-1990s.

For about $15,000 (a little under £10,000), the golfer in search of a total style on wheels can purchase one of the carts made by the Classic Golf Car Company of Princeton, Minnesota. Each is hand built to the style of classic US roadsters of the early 1930s, and exudes not a little of the aura of *The Great Gatsby*.

Caddie carts as prizes in Californian ama-

teur events drew the attention of the USGA Amateur Status Committee. Unlimited use was, they held, a violation and would involve the prize-winner being declared a professional because the cart would be worth more than the amateur prize limit of the day. It would be acceptable if no legal possession of the cart were involved. A compromise was reached: the lucky winner could use the cart only 17 times.

A game slow to start

All this prosperity and the development of a professional circuit paying telephone numbers in prize money had started fitfully and taken something like a century and a half to show much acceleration. A colonial

governor named William Burns, who died in 1729, had nine "gouffe" clubs. One was an iron, the estimated value of which was two pounds, worth a small fortune now.

The first mention of golf in American literature was by a Dr Benjamin Rush, in his *Sermons to Gentlemen upon Temperance and Exercise*. It is known that not all golfers are devotees of Temperance, but Rush's recommendation of golf as a healthy pursuit cannot be faulted: it comes as no surprise to discover that Dr Rush studied medicine at Edinburgh.

The first golf club in North America was almost cer-

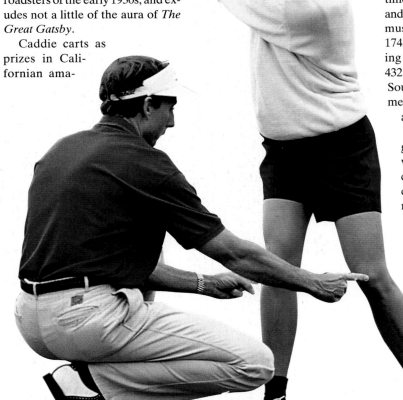

tainly in South Carolina in 1786, and, like the club at Savannah, Georgia, it followed the Scottish pattern of having a social side to club affairs: that is known from advertisements of the time. Although the Carolina club faded from view before the turn of the century – Savannah did not – at about the time of hostilities between Britain and the new United States. Yet there must have been lively interest in 1743, the date of documents relating to the import of 96 clubs and 432 balls from Leith to Charleston, South Carolina, which would have meant no less than £54 for the balls alone, a tidy sum then.

In New York, Maryland, Virginia and Georgia hesitant starts were made on the game, but all came to very little until the last decade of the nineteenth century, despite the efforts of American golf's most steadfast and undeflectable pioneer.

Charles Blair Macdonald, who was to be America's first amateur champion, was only 16 years old when he crossed the Atlantic in 1872 aboard the last of the old side-wheel steamers to make the

COSTLY GURU *David Leadbetter with pointers about posture*

56

trip, the Cunard Line's *Scotia*. The voyage, undertaken because he was to continue his education at St Andrews University, took nine days to Queenstown (now Cóbh) in Ireland, whence Macdonald went on to visit the Blarney Stone. Kissing it cannot greatly have improved his powers of persuasion, to judge from his subsequent brushes with authority.

He went on to Musselburgh, just east of Edinburgh in Scotland, to stay with the mother of an old family friend. Here Macdonald first came into contact with golf. It was the heyday of the Scottish professionals. He watched them and the (amateur) red coats and the "leisurely loungers" on Musselburgh Common.

Young Tom Morris had not long ago won his fourth Open title, but golf seemed "tiddle-de-winks" to Macdonald, who thought it a slow, stupid game for old men; he had never come into contact with a sport that was not strenuous or violent before.

Once Macdonald touched the golf game, however, he was lost, greatly attracted by its code of honour, and the discipline of "play it as it lies".

His grandfather took him to see Old Tom, who sold him clubs and provided a locker in his shop – no juniors were allowed in the R&A Clubhouse. St Andrews had few tourists, but plenty of golfers and not a few intellectuals, including John Stuart Mill, Thomas Carlyle, Charles Kingsley and Anthony Trollope.

Having played with a couple of amateurs against Young Tom's best ball, and lost, and watched and played with most of the other leading British players of the era, it was scarcely surprising that Macdonald went back to Chicago filled with zeal for the game, though he did not emulate Old Tom's example and bathe in the chilly water of the East Bay.

Macdonald set out a rudimentary course back home: the holes were cans left behind by the soldiers at Camp Douglas. He ran into a brick wall of indifference in a city ruined by market crash and fire. These were hard times; the news of Young Tom's death at the end of

THEY LIKED IKE *Former US President Dwight Eisenhower at Wentworth, 1962: he played "fairly well"*

1875 had scarcely improved Macdonald's spirits.

The World's Fair of 1893 in Chicago and the enterprise of two Scots from the industrious town of Dunfermline, close to the Firth of Forth, succeeded where Macdonald had failed. One of his greatest friends suddenly changed his mind after years of indifference to the game after the Fair had brought a number of young English businessmen, who were golfers, into town.

One of the Dunfermline pair, John Reid, was a leader among six citizens of Yonkers, New York, who in 1888 set up the St Andrew's Golf Club. These were the days of endless labour for low wages, and precious little opportunity for most folk for exercise or enjoyment. Racing, boxing and baseball were on the rise, cycling too, but for the generality active sport was not an option. It was badly needed, and in fresh air too, for the majority of Americans now

lived in towns, and the pollution from domestic and factory chimneys was well advanced.

Lockhart starts the drive
The mighty engine of US productivity was just moving into high gear, with the vision of Henry Ford, Thomas Edison and Andrew Carnegie at the controls, and the Wright brothers looking wonderingly at birds in flight.

Wealth would produce leisure,

and Robert Lockhart, who had been at school with Reid, imported the means to brighten that leisure. He had obtained them, six golf clubs and two dozen guttie balls, on a trip to Scotland to do with his linen merchant's business, from none other than Macdonald's supplier, Old Tom Morris.

Lockhart tried them out on what is now Riverside Drive, on New York's Upper West Side. A mounted policeman was watching, and jumped down to have a go. His first effort was (according to Lockhart's son) long and straight, but he could not repeat the feat, and departed, his beginner's luck used up. Where New York's finest faltered, Reid's St Andrew's six went on to glory, for theirs is the club with the oldest continuous existence in the United States.

They cannot boast the longest history in North America: Montreal founded a golf club in 1873. Clearly the extended British influence there must have played a part, compared with the antipathy to many things British revived by the War of 1812. Three holes in a pasture opposite Reid's house in Yonkers was the extent of their first sporting domain. The first game on February 22, 1888, was between Reid and John Upham, for the pioneers had only the six clubs. There

followed weeks of enforced inaction because of snow. When the weather cleared, they had obtained enough clubs for all to play, and quickly determined that their first course was inadequate. Their first "clubhouse" was a wooden table (two boards set upon two barrels) to bear their drinks.

On November 14 of the same year the St Andrew's Golf Club of Yonkers on Hudson was formed at Reid's house. Lockhart was elected as first member, Reid as president. Before 1888, according to the doyen of American golf writers, Herbert Warren Wind, there were fewer than a dozen golfers in the United States.

The St Andreans of the New World did not stay for long at their second course, a six-holer. They moved instead to another six-holer on steeply sloping ground four blocks north in an apple tree orchard, inevitably becoming known as the Apple Tree Gang.

This move, to a spot with a fine view of the Hudson River and New Jersey, was enforced by the extension through their old course of Palisades Avenue, which ran parallel to North Broadway.

The Saints, as they came also to be known, were treated with the same derision as early English golfers, among whom Horace

Hutchinson has described how he and his fellows were regarded as indulging in a "harmless form of imbecility".

Ignorance about the game as the St Andrew's men golfed indomitably onwards, bringing down predictions of hell-fire on their heads from ministers of religion aghast at their habit of playing on Sundays, was still almost as deep in America as it had been at the 1845 publication of *Hoyle's Games*. The name is that of the eighteenth-century Englishman Edmond Hoyle, who in 1740 wrote *A Short Treatise on Whist*.

According to Hoyle in 1845, golfers used light balls when playing with the wind, heavy ones against it, a notion that would intrigue today's Rules Committees. Hoyle's 266 pages included only two on golf, compared to six on breeding game cocks and organizing cock fights.

St Andrew's accommodation at their new third course, which was set up in a day without the loss of a single apple tree, was relatively extensive, a bench around an apple tree serving as the clubhouse, food and drink hanging from its branches. One of these branches is now in the R&A Clubhouse at St Andrews in Fife; another is in the present US St Andrew's clubhouse.

The apple trees dotted about the course made the ability to loft the ball essential. Knowing nothing of the treeless, moonlike terrain of links in Scotland, Americans new to golf thought trees were indispensable obstacles in true golf.

By 1894, St Andrew's had competition. There were a number of clubs in and around New York and Newark in New Jersey by the mid-1890s. John Reid and company had really started something.

The resort of Newport, Rhode Island, soon had a country club and course, financed by some of the giants of contemporary society, among them John Jacob Astor and Cornelius Vanderbilt. Up in Maine, rich vacationers from Boston and New York were making the spectacular Mount Desert island into a resort whose wild beauty was complemented near Bar Harbour by the wooded slopes of the Kebo Valley course; it claims to be the third oldest in the country.

A wind-blown course was built on Long Island at Shinnecock Hills. At first there was a men's course, and nine holes for women members (of which St Andrew's had none in the early days). This form of discrimination was not liked, and the women's course was incorporated with the men's. Moreover, it had a splendid clubhouse designed by no less than Stanford White. Judge O'Brien, on his first round at Shinnecock, said it was not a golf course at all ... "because it had no apple trees over which to loft and play".

Charles Macdonald had designed the only 18-hole course in the country in Chicago, which opened in 1895, then another nearby at Wheaton, which had the first artificial watering systems for greens – all 18 of them. Macdonald would never accept fees for his many course designs.

American golf was able to claim another first in course care, when in 1925 the Brook Hollow Country Club in Dallas, Texas, installed a complete fairway irrigation system.

St Andrew's members, intent on a nine-holer equal to those of their New York rivals, had to move north again, three miles further out of

YONKERS 1888 *(L to R) Harry Holbrook, Alexander Kinnan, John Upham and John Reid*

GOLFING MAN OF STEEL *Andrew Carnegie in his cottage near St Andrew's, NY, 1911*

town, just as thousands were going the other way on to Manhattan Island. Their new home was at Grey Oaks, on a 100-acre farm site, where their first nine-holer was laid out: seven holes had a stone wall running across them. By taking possession of the former farmhouse they had a clubhouse with walls and a roof – and a ghost, the legacy, it was said, of a violent death on the premises.

The list of members lengthened rapidly at Grey Oaks: it included such luminaries as Oliver Harriman, Stanford White, Henry Taft and Andrew Carnegie, who was of the opinion that golf was "the indispensable adjunct of high civilization".

Civilization and the country club

Talking of which, that peculiarly American institution, the country club, was reaching the heights of fashion in the last 20 years of the nineteenth century. Henry James the novelist described the country club as America's only contribution to civilization. It certainly contributed to the development of golf, absorbing the game as one of its members' pleasures along with lawn tennis.

There was no one for tennis among John Reid's friends, who were busy trying to make best use of the same sharply bent left elbow and sweeping, slashing flat swing as the original St Andreans had found effective on their wind-swept links. Reid's clubs were typical of the era back in Scotland. His driver had a long nose, a thick neck, a longer shaft than the modern club, and a fairly massive sole plate.

He and his friends also took on the red coat tradition (and painted the Grey Oaks clubhouse red also). But red coats, decorated with brass buttons and the cross of St Andrew in silver, did not last long in the United States as a general rule, since casual wear was a near essential in summer heat. Besides, unlike coats it did not hamper the swing, nor did sweaters in winter.

The St Andrew's club was not to stay at Grey Oaks for long, moving two miles further out again in 1897 to an undulating site at Mount Hope, where it cost $1,500 to lay out the course, and $65,000 to provide a new clubhouse, for which Carnegie guaranteed the mortgage. He built

a home for himself nearby, steel-shuttered, for he was not popular with his steel workers.

It is said that on the day he sold his company for a quarter of a billion dollars, he parred the fifth hole for the first time. Later a friend, hearing of the deal, commented that he had been hearing great things of him. Carnegie's reply reveals that he had his priorities right: "How did you know I had a par on the fifth today?"

Carnegie, like Reid and Lockhart, came from Dunfermline, the son of a poor weaver, who brought his family to Pittsburgh in 1848. His enthusiasm for golf has a late echo now in Scotland, where he luxuriously refurbished Skibo Castle, near Dornoch, and built a nine-hole course. There he was able to call upon J. H. Taylor for instruction. Skibo is now being developed into a highly exclusive private club, with an updated 18-hole course, by Peter de Savary, whose greatest claim to sporting fame was in a determined but unsuccessful bid for yachting's America's Cup. Fire damaged the castle early in 1995, but Mr de

Savary was confident that his club would open on time.

The Yonkers players' new course in 1897 employed a Scottish professional, Sam Tucker, brother Willy being its first greenkeeper. He helped to construct the course to a design by Henry Tallmadge, a St Andrew's founding member. Willy later designed courses himself, thoroughly absorbed the American enthusiasm for technical improvement, and became a turf expert, putting down the Yankee Stadium playing surface and the original lawn tennis courts at Forest Hills. The Tallmadge/Tucker course is still in use, though it has had a face-lift by way of a Jack Nicklaus re-design.

Transport was ever a problem for the golfer. Before the automobile became widely accessible, St Andrew's members got out of the train five miles north of their club's birthplace at Yonkers, and had to scramble for horse buses and coaches. From New York to Hong Kong the same sort of thing was beginning to happen across the face of the globe.

Shinnecock stole a march on St Andrew's in one particular. It was the first club to be incorporated. It rapidly became a haunt of the élite. Golf was gaining public approval at an extraordinary rate after the years of nil progress that had so disheartened Macdonald.

In 1895 the Christmas message from the *New York Times* was: "In the history of American field sports there can be found no outdoor pastime that developed and attained such popularity in such a relatively short period of time as the game of golf."

The process was accelerated in the next two years by the opening of the nation's first public course, Van Cortland Park, New York City, in 1896, and the launch of the first US golf magazine, *Golf*, in 1897. Also in 1897, Yale got ahead in academia by winning the first collegiate golf championship.

From a state of golf course famine in the early 1890s, it took little over 30 years to reach relative plenty. By 1927 there were 400 courses in Metropolitan New York alone, 200 in the Chicago area, and

4,000 in the US as a whole, against 1,500 in Britain.

In the beginning, women's golf was more of a social occasion than a hard-fought contest to which any great sporting prestige could be attached. Besides, it was known that British champions, like Lady Margaret Scott, were capable of scores 20 shots better than the US pioneers.

The players' outfits were exhaustively described in the Press; the best golfers were already looking around for styles which would least hamper their play. Intricate styles, though sure to attract newspaper attention, seemed to equal high scores. Reports included the names of socially prominent spectators, such as Mrs John Jacob Astor.

Hundreds of spectators crowded on to the Ardsley Club course by the Hudson River for the 1898 Amateur Championship, when Beatrix Hoyt, herself a society girl, secured her third title in a row, hitting accurately to strategies indicated by her caddie, W. H. Sands, an Ardsley member.

The first stirrings of golf among the women of America, apart from the fading echoes of the clubs in the southern states, came sometime after an 1877 article in Frank Leslie's *Popular Monthly* exhorting American womanhood to give golf a chance, if only to "escape from the wearisome monotony of croquet". Golf would be a welcome addition to the meagre list of outdoor sports available to women.

No one took much notice of this, but a little progress was made in 1889, when a mixed foursome was played at St Andrew's. The original male golfers, Reid and Upham, took part. Carrie Low was Reid's partner in a victory over Upham and Mrs Reid.

Another nudge was given by Florence Boit, who had learned the game with Britons at Pau in France, and brought her clubs home to Massachusetts. But, consternation, no courses around Boston, so a start was made by turning the lawns of neighbours and relatives into pitch-and-putt holes. Laurence Curtis of the Country Club, Brookline, was im-

pressed, and suggested the club should take the game up. It has so far hosted two US Opens and five Amateur Championships.

The time of the missionaries

The time was ripe, the St Andrew's club concluded in their splendid new club, to learn from the home of golf. They suggested that a score or so of clubs should contribute $80 each for expenses plus $20 a week salary to Harry Vardon and James Braid, who would then travel to the US to play exhibition matches on an eight-week tour.

It didn't happen, but American golf, now off and running, was speedily conceived as a business opportunity as well as a sport. Among the earliest sporting goods makers to turn their attention to the upwardly-rocketing golf business were A. G. Spalding and Bros Company, founded in 1876 by Albert Goodwill Spalding, a first-class major league pitcher, to make baseballs. Spalding were eager to push their Vardon Flyer guttie ball, and saw a Vardon tour as a sure-fire marketing opportunity.

How utterly right the company were. Vardon's tour began in February, 1900. He was Open Champion at that date, and interrupted his American tour to go back to Britain to defend his title. He lost it to Taylor at St Andrews but, on returning to the US, won the Open at Chicago, relegating Taylor to second place. Vardon, champion by two strokes, could afford to smile about missing his ball altogether when he was a mite casual over a tiny putt on the final green. The

best score by an American was 10 shots worse.

The previous five Opens had been won by two Englishmen and three Scots, all based in the US, so Vardon was the first player to take the trophy abroad. It has been a rare accomplishment this century. (Vardon's record in three attempts on the US Open is played three,

WILLIAM HOWARD TAFT
Presidential preacher of golf gospel

winner once and runner-up twice.)

Vardon was in the best form of his life in 1900, his perfect timing and awesome accuracy inspiring players all over the US – for there was a club in every state by this time, and more than 200,000 players. He lost only one singles match on his tour, and as he usually played against the best ball of two or three other players, his record of 13 defeats in 87 matches speaks for itself on an itinerary of 20,000 miles.

But as it transpired, the Vardon Flyer had appeared as the guttie era was drawing to its close. Two years before the Vardon tour the Haskell three-piece ball, based on the resilience of rubber bands wound under tension, had been patented, a type that would soon command the market.

Another champion came from over the water to charm American galleries in 1903. This one had red hair and the pale complexion that goes with it, and had "made a lifelong study of the second shot". Rhona Adair from Portrush had been unbeatable since 1900 in her native Irish championship, and won the British title in 1900 and again in 1903.

Plenty of practice, and in particular her mastery of the half- or punch-shot approach, a useful talent at breezy Portrush, had brought her to the top in Britain. In the US she beat a strong field at Merion from which only the champion, Bessie Anthony, was missing.

Her public utterances, mainly in exclusive *Illustrated Sporting News* articles, were careful and diplomatic: she proved an accurate talent spotter, praising the potential of Margaret Curtis, who was just out of her teens, and, nearly 30 years before the first Curtis Cup match, she possibly whetted American appetites for battle by predicting that a team of the best British players would trounce an

American team. Possibly she was right – at the time.

She gave credit, in total refutation of Horace Hutchinson's 1893 opinions, to the "army of women golfers ... increasing every year" for being "above the petty squabbles and jealousies which are frequently met with at large gatherings of women".

In 1893, the year of the foundation of the Ladies' Golf Union in Britain, American women staked a claim for golfing emancipation. The women of Morristown in New Jersey set up a golf course of their own.

The opening was at least a social triumph, even though Mrs Arthur C. James whiffed the first shot. The Marquise de Talleyrand-Périgord of Paris and Prince Rospoli, mayor of Rome, and Princess Rospoli were among those present, along with many of the wealthy residents of the leafier New York suburbs.

The club's male associate members, who would have been cheered on by Horace Hutchinson, held that the women officers of the club could not adequately handle the business of the club. Early in 1895 these men obtained control of Morris County, some said by influencing the votes of those of their wives who were members. So the administration soon became all male.

There was a odd sequel: Morris County hosted the second US Women's Amateur Championship. Beatrix Hoyt won, her prize the trophy donated by Robert Cox, of Edinburgh in Scotland, on condition that the 1896 Championship be played at Morris County, where he had helped to lay out the course.

Most trophies are much of a muchness: Cox's slim and elegant silver gift is worthy of close examination, if only for its charming coloured panels of golf scenes.

Hail to the (golfing) chief

Golf's history is replete with royal patrons. In 1909 the game recruited its first major Republican figure, in more ways than one. William Howard Taft was elected US President as Republican candidate in 1909. He weighed well over 200 pounds. He had been captivated

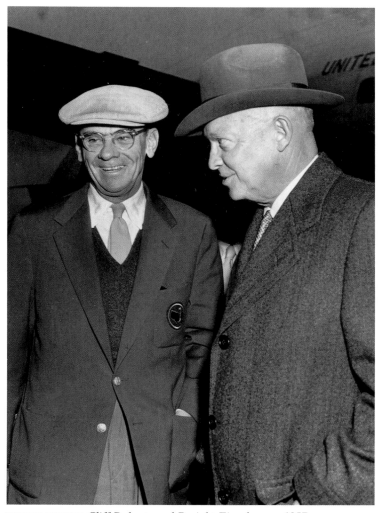

AUGUSTAN INTIMATES *Cliff Roberts and Dwight Eisenhower, 1957*

by the game since 1896. He commended golf in an electioneering speech in 1908 to folks in California as being "full of moments of self-abasement, with only a few moments of self-exaltation. And we Americans, who are not celebrated for our modesty, may find such a game excellent training."

The media were quickly on to this Presidential enthusiasm, in which he was hampered by putting problems. Nothing disturbed his love of the game, not even the arrival of a foreign head of state in the Capitol. "I'll be damned if I will give up my game to see this fellow," said he, and persevered with his round with the self-possession of a latter-day Drake.

Taft's preaching of the golf gospel came at the same time as American golf was coming of age. Tom Mac-Namara's final round of 69 earned

him second place in the 1909 US Open, the highest finish yet achieved by a native-born American.

While Taft was still in office, Johnny McDermott became the first native US Open champion in 1911, and won again in 1912, and while Taft later took up duties as Chief Justice of the Supreme Court, Francis Ouimet beat the best Britain could offer in 1913.

Coincidences no doubt, but Taft had done no harm to golf's social acceptability. Presidents Wilson and Harding followed Taft's lead. Harding, who gave a trophy for the Amateur Links Championship, declared: "It used to be thought that golf was a game for the elderly, but the beauty of golf is that everybody can play it."

Franklin Delano Roosevelt's golf was cut short by polio, but the line of White House golfers continued

through Dwight Eisenhower, John Kennedy, Richard Nixon, Gerald Ford, George Bush and Bill Clinton. Of these it was Eisenhower who, despite his lack of prowess, had the highest profile.

Between the presidency of Taft and that of Eisenhower, the story of golf in America is of the tour professional's gradual climb to supremacy over the amateur as the sport's leader, and America's speedier progress to supremacy over other golfers worldwide. In 1922, only 11 years after the first American-born player won the US Open, Walter Hagen won the British Open. That same year, he became the first professional to set up a company under his own name to make golf clubs.

Not only was the professional game gaining more headlines than the amateur, especially after Bobby Jones retired. The professionals, the vast majority of them native-born between the wars, were light years away, in public perception, from the flock of Scots who had manned professional shops and won the US Open year after year before the Mc-Dermott/Ouimet/Hagen years ... Scots whose brogue was seldom more than semi-intelligible. Many were accused of having too great a liking for the wine of that country.

Most of all, the professional game had Hagen, said by Gene Sarazen to be golf's greatest showman. He was certainly the first true tournament professional. Sarazen did well out of the new social chic and earning power of the the pro, and after his Open/US PGA double of 1922 got himself into the headlines by beating Hagen in the final of the next US PGA Championship, winning at the 38th hole thanks to a tree which prevented his ball from going out of bounds. At the end of the decade, and despite the deepening economic depression, Sarazen won the biggest first prize yet offered, $10,000 in the Agua Caliente Open at Tijuana, Mexico.

Just as the abolition of tax on newspapers allowed the popular Press in Britain to reach the working classes and become a potent force in popularizing football and cricket, golf's quick progress in the US was greatly fostered by news-

USGA EXECUTIVE COMMITTEE 1916 *President Frank Woodward seated centre*

papers and magazines. This was despite a reluctance on the part of tournament officials to grant working facilities or much information on the state of play to reporters.

Typically, Clifford Roberts gave the media "free" lunches and good facilities at the Masters, well aware that tournament golf, like all top-class sport, cannot exist without extensive coverage. All was light and joy as long as commentators toed the line of Augustan propriety, i.e., no mention on television of filthy lucre prize money. One commentator was banned for years for saying that a "mob" encircled the final green, and another one for saying that the bumpy fairways "look suspiciously like body bags".

Prominent among the early writers was Englishman Jim Whigham, Charlie Macdonald's son-in-law, twice a winner of the US Amateur title. Magazines started to appear around the turn of the century. Walter Travis was first editor of *The American Golfer*, started in 1907. Ever increasing demand for tournament news and golf instruction meant there seemed always to be room for one more publication. Bob Harlow started the weekly *Golf World* in 1947, which included international golf news, and in 1959 *GOLF Magazine* appeared, tackling the question of how good, or

how bad, was Ike's game. *GOLF's* circulation in the 1990s is in the high six figures range: *GOLF* and *Golf Digest*, started as a throwaway magazine in Chicago in 1951, are the leading US golf publications.

Like Bob Harlow, Fred Corcoran combined public relations and writing with his administrative pioneering labours for the PGA and LPGA. Grantland Rice and O. B. Keeler (Bobby Jones's biographer) were the best-known writers of the inter-war years, since when Herbert Warren Wind of the *New Yorker* has become the doyen of golf writers and Herb Graffis, who wrote a PGA history, earned a place in the World Golf Hall of Fame.

Radio reporters, meanwhile, found it difficult to get near enough to the action to see what was going on, and far enough away to be inaudible to players. TV solves such problems.

USGA takes helm from start

Though the R&A received its Royal warrant in 1834, and was accepted at the time as authoritative on golf and its rules, nearly a century passed before it took over full responsibility for the organization of the major British Championships.

In contrast, the USGA was founded, first and foremost, to run the men's and women's amateur

events, and the men's Open, and this it did within 12 months of its foundation (but only just, for the Women's Amateur was not contested until November of 1895). It also took over the women's Open when requested (by the LPGA) in 1953, the year of the eighth Championship. The USGA remains active in almost every facet of the game.

The USGA soon had to make its first decision when the inaugural Amateur Championship began in 1895. It was one of the Association's least controversial decisions, forbidding Richard Peters to putt with a pool cue on the Newport greens. Joe Davis, the late world billiards and snooker champion, was sometimes heard to regret this decision when he played in British Press Golfing Society events.

The USGA's history has been riven with disputes about amateur status, in the view of many causing unnecessary friction by too unforgiving a reading of the definition of amateur. On the other hand, amateur golfers are light years nearer a Corinthian state of true-blue no-pay-for-play than those who are still fondly called amateurs in, for example, Rugby Union. The relevant USGA/R&A definition of an amateur golfer is "one who plays the game as a non-remunerative or non-profit-making sport".

Countless words have been printed and spoken and battles fought over the boundaries between pro and amateur. One *cause célèbre* concerned the banishing of Francis Ouimet, Open hero of 1913, to the professional ranks in 1916: his crime was to have opened a sporting goods business. He had been in the business, working for a Boston firm, Wright and Ditson, before his Open win gave him instant fame, proved that Americans could play at the highest level, and demonstrated that the game was for the man on the Boston omnibus, who worked for a living, just as much as for the country club set.

The USGA president at the time was Frank Woodward, a stickler for a strict interpretation of the status rule. The decision was thought unfair, since Ouimet had been in the

sports goods business before the 1913 Open. Thanks in part to the opposition of the Western GA, the decision was rescinded in time for Ouimet to play in the first post-war Amateur in 1919.

Ten years before that, caddies, caddie masters and greenkeepers aged over 16 were deemed to be professionals. Attitudes slowly changed, to the extent that the age limit was 18 from 1930, and 21 from 1945. In 1963, the age limit was rescinded.

Amateur status rules were strengthened because of clubs and colleges enrolling good players with offers of entrance fees and the like. The thinking of the ruling body on this is clearly demonstrated by the decision that Charles Rymer, 1985 Junior champion, should be allowed honorary membership of Tega Cay, South Carolina, as long as no time limit was placed on membership. The awarding of entry fees as prizes, even if they are no more than the amateur prize limit ($500), is a violation.

A major change came when college golfers were allowed to accept scholarships without prejudice to their amateur status. Many foreign student golfers have benefited from the decision. College staff may give golf instruction yet stay amateur as long as the instruction takes up less than 50 per cent of their working hours.

Acceptance of golf equipment from a manufacturer is forbidden, and so is payment of expenses by anyone except family or legal guardian, with exceptions such as for team competitions and young players under 19 or until shortly after graduation. The career of the outstanding US amateur of the 1950s, Harvie Ward, was blighted by the expenses trap.

IMPORTANT ADDRESSES

United States Golf Association, Far Hills, New Jersey 07931

Ladies Professional Golf Association, 2570 Volusia Avenue, Suite B, Dayton Beach, Florida 32114

PGA of America, Box 109601, 100 Avenue of the Champions, Palm Beach Gardens, Florida 33418

PGA Tour, Sawgrass, Ponte Vedra, Florida 32982

CANADA

Few of the leading golfers of the world have not tried for or won the Canadian Open, though Canada itself is still without a winner of a "major". Apart from the British and US Opens, it is the only current tour event listed by the US PGA that dates from before the First World War; that is, long before the US Tour was up and running.

Nor did a Canadian win an American Tour event until 1955, when Al Balding from Toronto did so in the Mayfair Inn Open. He won again, three times, in 1957.

His greatest feat was yet to come, for at the age of 44 Balding, partnered by George Knudson, from Winnipeg, carried off the World Cup at Olgiata, in Rome, beating Lee Trevino and Julius Boros of the US into second place. Balding was leading individual into the bargain, 14 under par.

Team golf is evidently Canada's forte, for further World Cup wins came in 1980 (Dan Halldorson, another Winnipeg man, and Jim Nelford, a right-handed golfer from Vancouver who putts left-handed) and 1985 (Halldorson again, and Dave Barr).

Barr, like Nelford a British Columbian, was top individual in the World Cup won by the US in 1983, then carried on the team-play torch to St Andrews in the 1994 Alfred Dunhill Cup. Barr, 44, and two journeyman pros, Ray Stewart and Rick Gibson, beat a thoroughly up-market US trio of Tom Kite, Curtis Strange and Fred Couples 2–1 in the final. Stewart had never won a significant pro event, and after six years on the US Tour switched to the Asian circuit. Gibson lives in Manila, and has two wins on the Japan circuit.

To say that Canada shook one and all is a considerable understatement. Starting at 28-1 against, and still 7-2 when the final started, Canada had never got past the last 16 before, and in previous years had been obliged to qualify to reach that point, staged always at St Andrews

SWILKEN CELEBRATIONS *Canada's 1994 Dunhill Cup victors at St Andrews*

from the inaugural Dunhill Cup of 1985. This time they did not have to qualify, but progressed into the semi-finals from their group of four (made up by Zimbabwe, Germany and section favourites Sweden) by the narrowest of margins.

During the 40-50 mph gales of the first day, when the average group score was 78, Canada lost to Sweden 2–1, Gibson slumping to Anders Forsbrand 85 to 81. Barr lost too, but had only one reverse thereafter, in the semi-finals against US Open Champion Ernie Els, beating Nick Price, Bernhard Langer and, in the final, Fred Couples. Barr's win over Langer was crucial: if the German had holed his 15-foot putt on the 18th in the decisive match, Zimbabwe would have qualified to meet South Africa, who were beaten by virtue of Gibson and Stewart both getting around the Old Course in 70.

Satellite television covered the event: no Canadian journalist did, which rather sums up Canada's *sotto voce* golf history. That is said to have begun with officers of General James Wolfe's army playing on the Plains of Abraham near Quebec during the British campaign to expel the French from Canada. Victory there cost Wolfe his life, and his opposite number, Montcalm, was killed also.

Golf was also played at Halifax, Nova Scotia, 200 years ago, organized and continuous club existence beginning at Montreal in 1873. Quebec (1874) and Toronto (1875) quickly followed. Montreal and Quebec scored another North American first for Canada by holding the first inter-club match in the hemisphere. The Royal Canadian GA was founded in Ottawa in

1894, contemporaneously with the USGA, when there were only 10 clubs. These swelled to 34 by 1914, and 30 of these are still extant. Canada's PGA was founded in 1911, five years before the US PGA.

The Canadian Women's Amateur title was the target of more anointed heroines of the game in the early days than the Open was of male stars. Dorothy Campbell from North Berwick, first to win the Amateur title of Britain and the US in the same year, landed a hat-trick in the Canadian Amateur (1910–12) and the English champion Cecil Leitch gained the title in 1921.

These feats were modest compared to the achievements of Canada's little giant, Marlene Streit, née Stewart, from Alberta.

Long winters are undoubtedly an obstacle to the acquisition of golf skills in Canada, though the beauty of the courses there is unmatched. That by the Bow River, overlooked by the Banff Springs Hotel, is a prime example, while two further west at Kananaskis, in Alberta, near the site of the Winter Olympics of 1988 in and around Calgary, have a grandeur all their own.

It is something of a curiosity that only Arnold Palmer, and not Jack Nicklaus and Gary Player of the 1960s "big three", has won the Canadian Open (Palmer's first professional victory). One of the very few Englishmen to win the Canadian Open, much revived by Seagram's sponsorship in 1936 after the event showed signs of flagging in the wake of the Depression, is Peter Oosterhuis (1981).

Another Englishman, born in Newcastle-upon-Tyne in 1884, John Douglas Edgar, strolled in 16 strokes clear in 1919. He won again, in a play-off against Tommy Armour (a pupil of his) and Charles Murray, the following year. However, in 1921, this brilliant stylist, tipped to soar to the summit of his profession, met with his still unexplained death in the streets of Atlanta.

IMPORTANT ADDRESS
Royal Canadian Golf Association,
Golf House, RR No. 2 Oakville, Ontario,
L6J 4Z3

CANADA'S WEE MIRACLE WORKER *Marlene Streit at Wentworth in 1959*

GREAT BRITAIN AND IRELAND

From the £40 million ($63 million) London club, designed by the Jack Nicklaus organzation, to the lawn mowers of Niddry Castle in Scotland, golf is in a healthy state of growth in Britain and Ireland. Lawn mowers? Certainly – being pushed up the fairways by members, their wives marching behind with rakes.

Niddry, in the Lothian district near Edinburgh, has progressed since then, and deploys more appropriate machinery. The community effort that produced the Niddry course has been replicated in a number of Scottish regions, with especial emphasis on the more northerly districts of the Highlands and Islands.

Scotland, as befits the land that gave birth to the game, has a ratio of courses to population, one to 13,000, challenged only in Australasia. This happy circumstance for golfers in Scotland extends to one course for 600 people on the Isle of Arran off the west coast.

The Scottish Golf Union has encouraged and guided the building of courses to provide an extra attraction for tourists: more than 10 million visit Scotland each year. Pressure on golf facilities south of the border, and their cost, make a Scottish holiday most attractive to English golfers. In the south-east of England, the course/population ratio reaches one to 43,000.

Nine-hole courses have been and are being built in beguiling areas, notably Ullapool, Dunvegan (on the lovely island of Skye near to the centuries-old stronghold of the MacDonald family), and Eriskay, a tiny island just to the south of South Uist. Members supply labour in the building of the Inverrary nine-holer community project. Lochgilhead's course has been enlarged from nine to 18 holes.

Wild and beautiful Ardnamurchan, which is the most westerly point of mainland Britain, acquired a course through a low-handicap cousin of the Scottish Golf Union's secretary, Ian Hume. Finding the journey to the nearest course a chore, he persuaded a local farmer to turn some of his land into a course.

The farmer's caravan site is well patronized in summer, when the long northern days almost banish night, and the project went ahead, and Hume's cousin, a teacher, is now instructing local youngsters in the royal and ancient game.

Scottish golfers affiliated to the national union number 193,000; juniors total 27,000. There are 518 affiliated clubs, 428 courses – some have playing rights on more than one course.

The English Golf Union has 1,715 affiliated clubs, 20 per cent of them public courses, with 674,260 members, and here too there is much development in progress. (It should be noted that the membership figures of the four home unions [England, Ireland, Scotland and Wales] do not take account of pay-and-play golfers on private and public courses, or society members playing "away". Women golfers are affiliated, through their clubs, to the LGU and women's unions.)

At least 100 courses are under construction or having radical extensions built most of the time; 500 course projects have planning permission, but from past experience it is unlikely that a sizable percentage of them will go ahead. At any particular time there can be more than 30 or 40 courses built and waiting to open. On the same basis, 50 others can have been completed, and have applied for affiliation, and 20 more constructed but not yet applicants to join the EGU. In a phrase, the situation is fluid. Yet the pressure on facilities seldom lessens. About 25 per cent of courses are public.

New and ambitious resort type lay-outs have proved more prone to cash crises soon after opening than courses which do not have other businesses linked to them – luxury hotels, health clubs and the like. Belton Woods Hotel and Country Club at Grantham, in Lincolnshire, birthplace of that stalwart of private enterprise, Margaret Thatcher, cost £20 million and was sold for much less to the De Vere hotel group after running into difficulties. Slaley Hall in Northumberland, a superb project, of championship standard and used for pre-qualifying rounds for would-be European Tour cardholders, suffered much the same type of misfortune.

Remembering that the (Nicklaus designed) London club, which is in Kent, south of the Thames and just off the M25 London Orbital motorway, cost £40 million, and that there is a finite number of players

THE OLD... *John Taylor, captain of the Honorable Company...*

64

AND THE NEW... *Jack Nicklaus's Heritage Course at the London Club, just south of the Thames at Ash in Kent, close to the M25: this is the par 4 12th*

that can be accommodated on the course, and hence subscriptions and green fees that a course can bear, it is clear that the early financial return and, looking ahead, even the mature return, from such an expensive enterprise might disappoint. Then there is the ever present threat of the weather closing the course down for a fortnight, say, so chopping 5 per cent from annual revenue.

While this is a bugbear that any new capital project must face, costly golf infrastructure must be built and then maintained, and the burden absorbed of that highly expensive endeavour, growing good grass and keeping it in order.

By contrast, the ingenious golfers of the Hereford/Wales borders built a course at Ross-on-Wye, which is in the English county of Herefordshire, at a bargain price, to replace the nine-hole course the club had used since 1903. The club, re-sited beside the M50 motorway, has a highly convenient slip road now al-

most on the clubhouse doorstep five miles north of Ross.

Albert Evans, who played for Wales for 30 years until 1961, and Bill Bishop were among the small group who eyed a tract of just over 100 thickly wooded acres, some of it marshy, all of it little better than scrubland. They received a good deal of advice to the effect that a golf course could not be built there. Undaunted, the intrepid members relied on self-help and the first nine holes were completed in 1964 with no more heavy equipment than a £150 tractor and a £300 tipping trailer, plus a contractor's caterpillar to pull out tree roots. Costs were defrayed in part by selling wood for pea-sticks and head-stakes; no wastrels at Ross.

Members cut more costs by tramping up and down with baskets clearing a few acres on the site that were afflicted by stones. Once swathes had been cut through the scrub, the architect Ken Cotton

could see the lie of the land and set out the holes. Cultivation was by discs and harrowing, Evans himself doing much of the seeding. By 1966–67 the course was ready, at the astoundingly low total cost, including clubhouse, of a little over £40,000 (around $80,000 at the time).

All this, by the way, is no pitch and putt, but a serious set of 18 holes, much used for top-class competition. The last three holes – down, up, and down again – are apt to prove to the complacent the truth of the old golfing saw that "Two up and three to play never saw the light of day."

Over the border, Wales itself has expanded steadily: 94 clubs in the Union in 1955, growing fourfold in membership to more than 55,000 members and more than 140 clubs. Which is perhaps why Wales captured the European youth crown. Ireland has added 60 clubs to their roster in as many years to 1994, when the membership of the coun-

try's 321 clubs first exceeded 100,000: another 75,000 also play.

Women's golf can report even greater growth, the Ladies' Golf Union total of affiliations topping 200,000, against 146,000 only 25 years ago.

A social and gastronomic game

Clubs are the backbone of golf, the muscle and sinew of the national associations, but their creation in eighteenth-century Scotland was not indiscriminately welcomed. *The Golf Book of East Lothian* considered that the old free and easy days, when all classes mingled on the links, had been destroyed by the institution of the clubs. First The Gentlemen Golfers of Edinburgh, secondly the St Andrews men, allowed only members to play in the big event of the year, the Silver Club.

What the clubs did not have was permanent premises, or anything faintly resembling a clubhouse, except perhaps that food and drink was served at their tavern meeting-places. Until their Golf House was built in 1768, Leith players ate at Luckie Clephan's tavern.

Silver Club days were followed by members taking dinner together, a habit taken up fortnightly at Bailie Glass's at St Andrews, where a player was called to account for withdrawing from the Silver Club event, and then not dining with his associates. Dinner cost a shilling per member, whether he sat down at table or was absent.

Meals were substantial and drinking was on a generous scale: three-bottle men were proud of their ability to take their liquor.

There was also pride in club uniform, which was changed now and then, but ever colourful, replete with brass buttons, silver badges, velvet capes and other fancies. These grew more and more elaborate in the nineteenth-century, and such dress was obligatory. Finally the Puritan ethic, or perhaps simple parsimony, arrested this trend, and tweed jackets and knickers were the dress for much of the first 50 years of the Open Championship era.

The idea of the Silver Club win-

ner automatically taking the captain's role was no longer appropriate as club life grew more complicated. It became less important for the captain to be the best player, and more useful for him to be a businesslike leader. Captaincy became elective although, after the example set by the Royal & Ancient Club, captains world-wide drive themselves into office. The ritual on the 1st hole of the Old Course, where the caddies scramble to retrieve the captain's drive and claim a reward, is what remains of the old system under which members could win the captaincy.

Westward Ho! club got rid of the old system the year after Horace Hutchinson, aged 16, won the club's gold medal and the captaincy, to sustain which his elders evidently and understandably considered Hutchinson unready.

The North Devon links of Westward Ho! was but one conduit of the spread of the Scottish game into England; the most royal was James I of England and VI of Scotland, whose sons probably played in the royal parks. The first club was Blackheath, to the south of London; though the

most important, in view of its contribution to the amateur game, was undoubtedly the Royal Liverpool Club at Hoylake in Cheshire on the north-west coast, close to major centres of British industrial and commercial might at Liverpool and other Lancashire towns.

There is little doubt that Blackheath, the first club formed south of the border, began in 1766 in the same way as the early Scottish clubs, when Henry Foot presented a Silver Club (in Blackheath's case a Silver Driver), to the Honourable Company of Golfers at Blackheath.

Not until 1818 did the second English club appear, at Manchester, a club which, unlike Blackheath and Liverpool, has not had a continuous existence.

Westward Ho! certainly has, from the time the course was set out by the elder Tom Morris, then working at Prestwick, in 1863. Play began that year and the Royal North Devon Club was founded in 1864, the first set up by English-born golfers. Blackheath had strong Scottish connections.

Hoylake, which was to be the site of the Liverpool, later Royal Liv-

erpool, Club from 1869, had an earlier sporting existence as the racecourse of the Liverpool Hunt Club. Racing continued there into the 1870s, but the fame of the warren at Hoylake was to be founded on the quality of the amateur golfers who learned to play on it, its major part in launching the Amateur Championship, and not least its popularity as an Open course. That privilege has now been lost to it because Hoylake lacks space to house the ever growing facilities offered to the public. Hoylake also staged the first matches between Britain and the US (the 1921 forerunner of the Walker Cup), and the first home international, against Scotland. Contrary to American experience, innovation in Britain has almost always been club-driven.

At the instance of J. Muir Dowie a meeting was held in 1869 in the Royal Hotel, Hoylake. The decision was taken to found a golf club, and this was done a month later. The club was based on the Royal Hotel, and rejoiced in advisers and course designers with impeccable credentials ... Robert Chambers, winner of the forerunner of the Amateur Championship, and Old Tom Morris's brother George, whose son Jack Morris quickly became the first professional.

It is safe to say that no club has ever produced amateurs who achieved such frequent major honours as those achieved by John Ball and Harold Hilton.

Yet a third Hoylake player, Jack Graham, a sporting all-rounder of many talents, was leading amateur in the Open five times before the First World War. He reached the Amateur Championship semi-finals four times, and was held by many to be inferior in very few particulars to Ball or Hilton, added to which he was a considerable Rugby Union player with Liverpool. Graham was killed in action serving with the Liverpool Scottish, at Hooge, in 1915.

Hoylake Opens featured the first won with the Haskell rubber-cored

AMATEUR POWERHOUSE *Royal Liverpool, whose Ball and Hilton are, with Bobby Jones, only amateurs to win the Open*

SUNNINGDALE FOURSOMES, 1993 *Lee James and (right) Andy Beal with trophy*

them out of the circuit of equipment supply, buying direct from factory sources. Scottish professionals had already begun to flex their muscles. In 1892 the Open was switched to the Honourable Company's new Muirfield course, thus cutting out Musselburgh, and ending the long-established three-way roster of the Opens, which had been circulating between St Andrews, Prestwick and Musselburgh for 20 years. The business, and particularly the golfing, community of Musselburgh were appalled at the potential loss of trade, and they put together £100 prize money to hold their own Open, three times the cash on offer in the 1891 Open.

The Honourable Company recognized that this was no idle threat, and responded by raising the Muirfield purse to £110. So the warring pros held their meeting after Muirfield (won, ironically, by an amateur, Hilton) and so had £210 in their sights in all.

Further discontents were expressed as the Open prize money was not regularly increased, and Taylor, while advocating moderation, determined to organize his fellows. Hilton's own *Golf Illustrated* opened the pros' case in a leading article.

Thereafter progress was rapid. Regional then national unity as the Professional Golfers' Association was the pattern, with a £1 membership subscription for pros, half that for assistants. Protection of trade interests, setting up competitions and a Benevolent Fund were among the aims. A professional tournament was quickly organized, with a mere £15 available in prize money, at Tooting Bec. Taylor won. That club and the competition no longer exist, except that the Tooting Bec Cup goes each year to the PGA member with the lowest round in the Open.

Taylor was elected chairman, and there was also the recruitment of a most valuable ally of golf, when Arthur James Balfour, soon to become Prime Minister as head of the Conservative Party, agreed to become PGA President. Balfour was throughout his life a staunch friend of, propagandist for and keen par-

ticipant in the game, and his soubriquet as Father of English Golf was thoroughly earned.

There were no straight political battle lines indicated here, though, for Balfour, productively for the game of golf, had a foot in both professional and amateur camps. The Kent seaside club, Littlestone, had a foot in both parties, for at one time the Liberal Prime Minister, Henry Asquith, was their captain, and Balfour, Leader of His Majesty's Opposition, their president. The Littlestone course, incidentally, was remodelled in the 1920s by Dr Alister MacKenzie, co-designer with Bobby Jones of Augusta National.

The PGA's next problem was the furore over the coming of the Haskell ball, with which Sandy Herd had won the Open in 1902, when the PGA membership was nation-wide, reaching 300, including an Irish section. Midland PGA members wanted the guttie as the prescribed tournament ball, but, fatally for its chances of success, their resolution gave the new ball a sparkling, if unintended, endorsement. It said: "Competitors should be on an equal footing so far as the ball is concerned." This was an unwitting coded statement meaning, "The Haskell is best" – which it was, and opposition to it faded, though not instantly.

The PGA broke new ground with the incorporation, in 1921, of the Professional Golfers' Co-operative Association. The 1920s was a period in which the making of clubs moved from pro shops to small, then major, factory units, and the shortage of hickory and ever greater demand for clubs hastened the dominance of the steel shaft despite the misgivings of many British pros. The USGA's 1926 acceptance of steel came three years before the R&A followed suit, without consulting the PGA, who had earlier opposed the move which, in an era of golf boom, was inevitable.

The boom was reflected in a modest increase in tournaments. By 1924 there were five major pro events each with four-figure purses. Unmistakable signs appeared in the PGA (now with more than 1,000

ball, by Sandy Herd in 1902, and the first won by a foreigner, Arnaud Massy in 1907. Massy rushed home to France with the trophy to see his baby daughter, to whom his Scottish wife had given birth during Open Championship week. He named the newcomer Hoylake.

"J.H." organizes the pros

A young pro called Tom Williamson received a job offer in a letter from the secretary of Notts GC in 1896, towards the end of a quarter century of surging club growth. There were less than 100 clubs in Britain in 1875, 1,300 in 1900. His wages were to be five shillings a week, a couple of dollars or so, and he was to take all profits from making, mending, and selling clubs and balls. (This last, as we have seen, was more than many US club pros were offered).

In return, Williamson (whose sister was stewardess) was to coach at 1s 6d. a round, supervise clubhouse security, manage the caddies, run the draw for Medal competitions, and work for eight hours a week on course maintenance. This was, the letter made clear, a temporary and experimental engagement, which might become a permanence. Williamson took it, for 54 years, and there were others like him, including men who knew little about golf, but developed what aptitude they had for the game, and taught themselves club repair and the like as they went along.

The first pros at English clubs had been mostly Scots, as they were to be in America, but by 1900 half the 300 or so pros at English clubs were English. J. H. Taylor, born to the wife of a working man in the village of Northam, overlooking the links of Westward Ho!, had three Opens to his name in 1901 when he emerged as the man to unite and lead his fellow professionals.

Many of them were suffering because club members were cutting members) of a schism between ambitious young members with tournament aspirations, and the traditional club pros, who looked upon the PGA as their shield and comforter, not primarily as a seeker after tournament sponsors.

So the American experience of tour vs. club pro was mirrored in Britain and Ireland, and the discontent grew more acute in the 1950s, when the tournament programme and purses declined, just when television in America was revealing golf's full potential, and prize money was sky-rocketing. The growth in PGA membership overall in the 16 years from 1975 to 1990 is astounding. Including overseas membership, which increased rapidly with British pros taking jobs on the Continent, there was a 38.8 percent rise. The 1994 total was 4,902.

Progress was slow until the 1960s, when prize money increased more rapidly, thanks in part to the improved cash allotted to the 1960 Open, the date of the arrival in Britain of Arnold Palmer.

All the same it was not until 1976 that the tournament players gained autonomy, with the foundation of the Tournament Players' Division.

The full-time amateur scene

Amateur golf has changed radically over the last 20 years, moulded afresh by two major influences. First, Henry Cotton, knighted just before his death in 1987, was influential in setting up the Golf Foundation, for which clubs raise money to pay for professional tuition for youngsters, who mature to scratch and better at an ever earlier stage. County and international teams now seem to be manned entirely by players whose average age hardly seems out of the teens.

They eye the second great influence, the chimera of riches on the European Tour – chimera because, for all but a tiny percentage, starting places on the Tour are unattainable, especially now that they are fought for by so many Continental players, and ones from even further afield. Parents' support allows the creation of a new class of amateurs, whose description seems almost a contradic-

tion in terms: the full-time amateur.

The route from amateur to pro goes through two channels. Every autumn, hundreds of players are put through the wringer of the Qualifying School. Even those who obtain one of the handful of tour cards on offer and prosper describe the process as the most nerve-racking of their lives. Players can keep their amateur status if they fail in the first section of qualifying, but once they have struck a shot in the final series they are professionals, though there is always an option to apply for reinstatement in the future.

The second channel is through the European Challenge Tour, which is proving a better test of potential than the Schools, for, proportionately, the 10 players who get on tour by finishing in the top 10 of the Challenge Tour fare better than Schools qualifiers. Michael Campbell, 25, a Maori, is a splendid example. He qualified in third place and stepped up, in the first two events of 1995, to tie for third in

Dubai and fourth in Manila, for a take of £48,710 ($75,988).

The competitive amateur scene, despite these professional attractions, is ever more crowded in Britain. J. H. Taylor, as he proved by his pioneering work with the PGA, was a far-sighted individual, but he was well wide of the mark in his *Taylor on Golf* at the beginning of the century. He wrote: "County golf, I regret to say, appears only too likely to die a more or less natural death."

The county game was born in 1894, with the foundation of the Hampshire Union. Yorkshire quickly followed suit, and despite Taylor's doleful view of their future, the two counties have survived to play a centenary match: 'prospered' is more accurate, since Yorkshire often dominate the Northern Counties League, and Hampshire, who also draw players from the Channel Islands, often reach and win the final between the leaders of the northern and southern sections of the Southeast League.

Every county in England plays

in the English Golf Union's County Championship, in which qualifying meetings for the North, Midlands, southwestern and southeastern counties produce four teams for the autumn finals.

Moreover, every county in England is represented in the six English leagues, playing at weekends, and two Welsh counties, Glamorgan and Gwent, are members of the Channel League, along with six southwestern English counties. This system is replicated in the rest of Wales, in Scotland and in Ireland.

A major and recurring difficulty faced by county captains and secretaries is managing to field representative sides when there are too few weekends and too many national and significant regional stroke-play events that serve to dilute team strengths. Another precious weekend on which little amateur competition is possible is that of the Open Championship.

All these competitions are run under the general guidance of the national Unions, whose accent, like that of the PGA, is more and more on training. The professional version of the Golf Foundation, started in 1952, were the training courses begun in 1961. Former tournament players, notably Tom Jones of Maesdu in Wales, instructed assistant pros not just in the primary pursuit of lower scores, but in how to run a shop profitably, how to mend clubs, and how to coach members. One of the first people to benefit from these courses was Maurice Bembridge, who became a widely travelled tournament winner, and at the Masters in 1974 equalled the then Augusta National record with 64.

The European Tour has its Apollo Week: this is a winter break at San Roque in southern Spain that is anything but leisurely for the young card-carrying pros who attend this finishing school of golf. (Talking of school, one in Leicestershire named "playing golf with the family" as the second most frequently used excuse for truancy.)

Experts on the mental and physical fitness aspects of the game are available at San Roque for consultation, and John Jacobs, among

GOLD VASE *Van Phillips and (right) Charlie Challen were joint winners, 1993*

PERILOUS PAR 3 *The 12th at the European Golf Union's new home, at Woodhall Spa, Lincolnshire*

other coaches, passes on his views on the swing. The sponsors are represented too, by an executive who explains what is expected from the players in return for the cash injected by industry and commerce. Chief tour referee John Paramor outlines his job (learn the definitions and all will be revealed, rules-wise, is his creed), guidance is given as to how to choose a manager, and there is plenty of practice time.

There is also a joint scheme worked out by the PGA and club-makers John Letters to help assistants pay training fees with vouchers financed by a percentage of the profits on equipment sales.

British newspapers have of recent years conceived sponsorship for competition at schools level as good for prestige, even if they do not noticeably boost circulation. The scheme run by *The Daily Telegraph* has progressed from a holiday event at a few seaside courses to an event attracting an entry of 25,000 from clubs country-wide, finishing with a final in Portugal.

Ian Woosnam, Peter Oosterhuis and Peter Townsend are successful professionals from among former competitors, for the net result of all these initiatives can clearly be seen from Ryder Cup level downwards in improved levels, and just as important, depth of talent.

EGU set up new golf academy

Woodhall Spa has no peer among the world's inland courses. The decision of the English Golf Union to buy it and move their headquarters there, in the wide open spaces of Lincolnshire, has gladdened the hearts of the nation's amateur golfers. The potential it holds for the good of the English game is considerable.

Woodhall Spa is, as the name suggests, a place where the waters can be taken, but the quality of the course has meant that the excellent hotel accommodation nearby has been taken up more and more by golf visitors. The EGU spent many hours thumbing through course-sale literature, and visiting courses on the market, before deciding on developing Woodhall Spa.

To help them in their final choice they had a trusted adviser to rely on in Neil Hotchkin, owner, and son of the designer of Woodhall Spa, and a leading amateur golf administrator for many years. Hotchkin has run Woodhall Spa in the way you would expect from a champion of the principles of amateurism.

EGU plans for Woodhall are expansive. The overall cost of their scheme is £8 million ($12,640,000), including the purchase of 180 additional acres. The required site had to be at least 300 acres and, if possible, up to 500, because the following facilities are to be added to the championship course: a second course, training centre (with driving range, short game practice area, including bunkers and putting greens), and either a par three course or training holes; EGU administration offices and conference room, to be amalgamated with a clubhouse for 200 people, on a common site. The opening of course No. 2 is expected to be some time after the proposed EGU move in 1996 from their present headquarters in Leicester.

The necessary cash (supplemented by a grant, the EGU hopes, from the National Lottery) will come from a bank loan to be repaid by raising subscriptions from £1 to £3 ($1.58 to $4.74). This would be a small price to pay for the range of facilities offered by the plan, for the Welsh subscription is £4, and the Irish £4.50. Amateurs in developing golf nations such as France and Spain would think this a bargain: they pay £27.50 ($43.45) and £30 ($47.40) respectively.

Since the EGU is based, like most of golf, on the existence of the club, Woodhall Spa will continue in that role as well as its new functions.

The Woodhall Spa plan may prove a solution to a problem which, given the increasing volume of course traffic year by year, may become chronic: seven clubs approached to stage EGU controlled tournaments in future years refused to make their courses available. Possession of Woodhall Spa, and a "spare" course close by, would obviate that poser for the EGU.

A club with a big future in the women's game is the St Pierre Hotel Country Club Resort, near Chepstow in Wales, which has two courses and splendid facilities. (It is also unique in that the parish church is on the property.) Whitbread's the brewers are the sponsors in a deal to stage the Europe vs. US Solheim Cup there.

The Women's European Tour looks in good hands all around, since under Terry Coates's executive chairmanship the number of tournaments has doubled, after hitting a low of only nine events in 1993. The R&A came to the rescue with a pump-priming grant.

On the basis of the response from Irishmen world-wide when the celebrated 7th hole at Ballybunion crumbled into the hungry Atlantic, that course strikes a sentimental note heard thousands of miles away. So much money was contributed towards rebuilding the hole, which demands a hair-raising shot over the waves, that the thought occurred: another Ballybunion course.

After all, players like Tom Watson make a bee-line for Ballybunion *en route* for the Open. Robert Trent Jones was called in to design the new lay-out, the building of which cheered the members in more ways than one, since when weather is bad their course is sometimes the only one playable on that part of the western Irish coast, leading to visitor invasions.

IMPORTANT ADDRESSES
Royal & Ancient Golf Club, St Andrews, Fife, Scotland KY16 9JD
English Golf Union, 1-3 Upper King Street, Leicester LE1 6XF
Irish Golf Union, Glencar House, 81 Eglinton Road, Donnybrook, Dublin 4
Scottish Golf Union, The Cottage, 181a Whitehouse Road, Barnton, Edinburgh EH4 6BY
Welsh Golfing Union, Powys House, Cwmbran, Gwent NP44 1PB

AUSTRALIA

SOUTHERN (AUSTRALIAN) BEAUTY *The 18th hole at Royal Adelaide*

One Australian in 30 belongs to a golf club and, of the other 29, a couple probably play public courses. Australian golf history rather resembles the US story, in that after a fitful start (even golf tends to come second to a gold rush) all is now enthusiasm, powerfully fanned ever since the late 1970s by Greg Norman. Symbolic of Australia's devotion to golf is the New South Wales GC's Botany Bay lay-out at the 1770 landfall of Captain Cook, first Englishman to set foot in Australia. There are upwards of 1,400 courses.

The *Colonial Times* of Tasmania carried a report in 1827 that two young men, Scots of course, were playing golf there. Bothwell GC in the Tasmanian Midlands became the first club, founded by Alex Reid, who arrived in 1829, needless to say from Scotland.

The Royal Adelaide club, founded in South Australia in 1870, claims to be Australia's oldest in continuous existence. Golfers in Victoria, settled 50 years later than Sydney, are, however, among the world's most cossetted. The capital, Melbourne, itself has 60 clubs; 70 per cent of the the state's population of 4.5 million live there, a quarter of the nation's total. Only a 30-minute drive away lies the Port Phillip Bay "Sand Belt". Here, as on the Ayrshire coast of Scotland, is one fine golf course after another: Royal Melbourne, Victoria, Metropolitan, Kingston Heath, Commonwealth and Huntingdale. The latter is the home of the Masters, which Norman has won six times, and which was designed by an Englishman, Charles Alison, who never visited the site itself.

Deep bunkers and lightning fast greens are specialities hereabouts. Royal Melbourne's West Course and Kingston Heath are designs of Dr Alister Mackenzie, of Cypress Point and Augusta fame.

Golf at these premier courses is costly: Royal Melbourne fees are just over a hundred US dollars, around £68. The clubs are also exclusive: often the visitor must be the guest of a member.

Yet there are more than 350 courses in Victoria serving about 150,000 golfers, splendid public courses among them, such as Yarra Bend, where the green fee is 15 Australian dollars (less than £7, or nearly $11).

Asian golfers have the opportunity to join with the locals in buying into new developments in share schemes. The National at Cape Schank, Victoria, was the first in 1985 to raise finance in this way, selling at A$6,000 (£2,727/$4,227), but raising share prices later: they are worth double the initial price now. Members also pay an annual subscription of A$1,400 (£636/$986).

Japanese companies have put together a much costlier development at Terrey Hills near Sydney, opened in 1994 and quickly included on the Australian pro circuit. It has 550 members, 108 of them from Japan and Singapore. They hope for more from Hong Kong, New Zealand and even Europe. The scheme misfired at another Sydney venture: so few shares were sold that the company went into liquidation.

In playing terms, Australia has had a fair share of the majors, Peter Thomson still three British Opens ahead of Norman, whose popularity is not so widely celebrated as it was, possibly owing to his move to Florida, which has led to a new nickname for the Great White Shark ... the Great White Fish Finger.

The recession in Australia was particularly hard on the golf circuit, but prize money was up by nearly a quarter to A$6.25 million (£2.84 million/US$4.4 million) for the 1994–95 season, in which Robert Allenby, the post-Norman hope of Australian golf, took the Open at Royal Sydney despite assembling three bogeys and a double bogey in the last four holes.

IMPORTANT ADDRESS
Australian Golf Union, Golf Australia House, 155 Cecil Street, South Melbourne, Victoria 3205

FUTURE PROSPECT *Robert Allenby, Greg Norman's heir apparent, was quick to win in 1995*

NEW ZEALAND

New Zealand golf, of which Charles Richie Howden, a Scot, is the father, began in Dunedin. After various course moves, the club settled down, red coats and all, with Fogarty's pub as a base. Fogarty's went bust, and *all* the members' clubs were sold for one pound. Howden found them a year later, twisted and useless.

Christchurch revived things, helped by the presence of several Westward Ho! men. Edmund Wilder, fearful perhaps of another Fogarty experience, made a course on his own estate, where he played in blazer, jodhpurs and puttees.

Howden, after a trip abroad, came back to restart Dunedin in 1889, and in 1893 the Amateur Championship began. It was the second in any British colony, India pre-dating it in 1892. It was won by a recently arrived Presbyterian minister, J. A. Somerville, from Scotland.

Soon Hugh Macneil of Otago won it, and lifted the Australian version too. The Maori golfer Kurupo Tareha was the first native New Zealander to win: legends have grown about the long hitting of his son, Kapi.

New Zealand teams held their own against Australia in the six-match Kirk-Windeyer series, which ended at three-all.

Growth was phenomenal after 1945, with 10 per cent in a year not uncommon in the 1950s, when golf's first world-class left-hander Bob Charles was making his presence felt, beating Peter Thomson in the New Zealand Open when the Australian was working towards his British Open Championship hat-trick.

Golf course construction boomed, and New Zealand's one course for 10,000 people is the best per capita in the world of a major golf-playing nation. A fine record in the Eisenhower Trophy for amateur teams completes the picture: Maori Phil Tataurangi could claim in 1992 to be the world's leading amateur. He posted the lowest individual score as New Zealand won the Eisenhower in Vancouver from the US. Another member of the side, Michael Campbell, is making a name on the European Tour.

IMPORTANT ADDRESS

New Zealand Golf Association, PO Box 11842, Dominion Sports House, Mercer Street, Wellington

MAORI MOVERS *Michael Campbell (left), new to the European Tour, has quickly made his presence felt. Philip "Spud" Tataurangi (far left) was best individual when New Zealand won the Eisenhower Trophy in Canada in 1992*

EUROPE

The golf bug crossed 3,000 miles of ocean and, with an ease no invading army could hope to achieve, rapidly assumed occupation of a vast acreage of North America. So why did the 20-odd miles of the English Channel delay golf's conquest of the Continent for so long? After all, the Scots and the French have often shared political and religious causes.

Yet the explosion of interest on the Continent over the last 15 years, with prodigies of course building in the 1980 and 1990s, comes nearly a century after the United States began the same process. Two reasons spring to mind: first, golf, like cricket, spreads fastest where English is spoken. Second, lack of local heroes: before 1979 only one Continental, France's Arnaud Massy, had won a major Open (1907).

FRANCE

Recent up-tempo building has been most marked in France, which can, however, claim to have the oldest club on the Continent, Pau. This is said to be a hangover from the Peninsular War, when Wellington's officers played there in 1814. What is far more certain is that Britons on holiday, including reportedly two of those pioneering officers, founded the club itself in 1856.

Yet France could boast fewer than 200 courses in 1987. The number has raced past 400 not far into the last decade of the century, by the end of which scores, perhaps hundreds, more will have opened. The cliffs of Dover are visible from the Wimereux course near Calais, and it has been said that another of the French clubs closest to England, Hardelot, is also the nation's best, with echoes of The Berkshire thanks to its splendid stands of trees. Needless to say, though worth remembering as an additional plus point in favour of golf in France, is that the food in French club restaurants is, well, French.

France's fast rate of course building is being imitated elsewhere, despite the handicap carried by Alpine courses in particular that because of the weather they are forced to close in winter, usually from November to March.

THE LOW COUNTRIES

In Belgium, whose former monarch Leopold was certainly the most skilful of all Royal golfers, courses have doubled in number since the late 1980s, and are not frighteningly expensive, a happy state of affairs encouraged also by the French authorities, with an eye to augmenting the vast flow of tourists from Britain and America in particular. Also, hotels and guest houses often arrange discounted fees with local courses.

LETHAL LOVELY *Hardelot, on the French coast near Boulogne, has charm, and a fiendish finish at the 17th and 18th*

GALLERY FEVER *Seve Ballesteros, outstayed by Eduardo Romero in this 1991 Spanish Open play-off at Club de Campo, took his third title there in 1995*

It is surprising the boom took so long, as Flory van Donck was a leading player in the 1950s, being nine times in the top ten in the British Open, including twice runner-up – to Peter Thomson and Gary Player. Holland is another late-comer to whole-hearted commitment to golf, despite Dutch claims to have invented the game. The coastal belt offers ideal links country, opportunities well taken by The Hague, frequent and fearsome home of the Dutch Open, and Noordwijk. Courses have increased in number by more than a third since the mid-1980s.

The impetus for this relatively belated activity must have to do, to some degree, with Ryder Cup successes since 1979, when the contest became US vs. Europe rather than US vs. Britain and Ireland. True, the European Tour's solid progress and the world-class scoring needed to win its tournaments have had their effect.

SPAIN

Wreathed in glory above these corporate successes stand Continental Europe's three Ryder regulars and Masters champions, Bernhard Langer, José-Maria Olazabal and golf's box-office banker, Seve Ballesteros. How often the trio must be blessed by golf entrepreneurs, club secretaries and professionals (a great many of them with English and Scottish names) all over Europe.

Spain, however, must be excepted from the list of countries whose golf boom is of most recent vintage. Once jet aircraft brought British holiday-makers within three hours of so of the Costas, particu-

larly the Costa del Sol, and the Algarve in Portugal, course building took off.

Being first in the field is not always a boon, and by the 1980s, golf in the Iberian peninsula had run into problems, some of them of local manufacture to do with soaring green fees and the level of service by course staff; some relating to the saturation of the facilities.

First tees were beginning to take on the look of London suburban municipal courses at sunrise in summer. It was often unwise, especially during British winters, not to be part of an organized golf trip with guaranteed access and tee-times.

The pressure, and prices, have gone down since, and there is no ducking the fact that the quality of many Iberian courses is unequalled anywhere, notably the pride and

joy of the tin magnate Jaime Ortis Patino, Valderrama. This Robert Trent Jones design is a short drive from Gibraltar and will reach its apogee with the Ryder Cup in 1997. High spot at the moment is the Volvo Masters, climactic event of each European Tour season. The Valderrama clubhouse is a wonderful confection of luxury and *objets d'art*.

PORTUGAL

Portugal's oldest club, at Oporto, is a direct outcome of the British liking for port. A nine-holer was laid out near this north-western Portuguese harbour in 1890 by drink-trade Britons.

Penina, the first course of the Algarve, was a, perhaps *the*, key trend-setter for Portugal and Spain. Henry Cotton, the designer, was its life, soul, mordant wit and influential teacher. A massive programme of tree-planting on what was a featureless paddy-field in the 1960s, helped Penina to acquire maturity, fame and many imitators in short order.

Apart from a short period during the Portuguese revolution following Salazar's long, repressive regime, Penina with its luxurious hotel has occupied an enviable position among resorts for the well-heeled – and has often staged the Portuguese Open.

GERMANY AND AUSTRIA

Germany and Austria are other late-comers to the latest golf boom. One of Langer's early experiences in search of golf fame explains a lot. He was told by a career guidance officer that there was no such calling as that of a golf professional. The game was very much for the well-off when he was born, but recent construction, especially of nine-hole courses as in Holland, has opened the door wide. Germany had 60 courses 35 years ago, but now has more than 300, a fair proportion coming with a rush over the past

decade: many more are planned or being built.

Austria too, though on a smaller scale, has joined the rush to be on the rota of European Tour stops. Club names have a splendid resonance: for example Golf Club Bad Kleinkirchheim-Reichenau.

RUSSIA

Russia as golfing territory performs well up to its reputation as an enigma wrapped in mystery. Golf started there in 1895 economically and well, with a half guinea entrance fee at the Mourino Club, St Petersburg (annual subscription £2. 12s. 6d.), by a small village 12 miles from the then capital. All the winners' names that have come down to us were British.

The revolution was not kind to golf: surely no pastime, except perhaps polo, smacks more of royalty and the bourgeoisie. No course of any kind existed for long after the Second World War, despite the zeal of Bindari Pasha, Egypt's minister to Russia, which raised only incredulous stares from collective farmers who watched him, complete with plus fours and caddie, whacking white spheres about a field in 1949.

By 1974, Robert Trent Jones was commissioned to build a course on a site 15 minutes from Moscow's Red Square, following keen lobbying by US lumberman Robert F. Dwyer, a member of the USGA Executive Committee. There was something of the humorous spirit of the *Inspector General* in the lack of progress on this project. Next Armand Hammer, another US magnate, this time in the oil business, seemed to have interested Party Secretary Brezhnev.

Progress has finally been made with a Harold Swan course at Yalta, and the Swedes, thanks to the initiative of ice hockey giant Sven Tumba, got moving with a nine-holer near the Swedish and German embassies. Here John Fite, head pro at Claremont GC, Oakland, California, came to teach; his son was studying on a year's exchange visit at St Petersburg.

A sleeve of balls, however, costs the equivalent of a month's wages, and the only local coaching was by a trio who, until the arrival of Fite, de-

pended for guidance entirely on what they could glean from the writings of Gary Player.

The Russian Golf Association was founded on July 16, 1992, however: here is a nation that may still be rescued from the outer darkness of golflessness.

BERNHARD LANGER *The toast of Europe with Seve and Olly, photographed in action in 1994*

COTTON'S KINGDOM *The ninth at Penina in Portugal, before one of the game's most charming hotels*

REST OF EUROPE

Italy, with courses of outstanding beauty, Switzerland, Denmark and Sweden were into action much sooner, and so purposefully have Swedes coached and built (well over 200 courses, mostly in the south) that it would be a brave man who gave long odds against a Swedish man winning a major before the 21st century dawns, Liselotte Neumann having already done the trick for the ladies with the US Open. Groups of golfers are put together during national service in Sweden, so that military and sports training can go hand in hand.

Danish golf has a friendly, family feeling: the author remembers the opening of the second nine holes at the Storstrommen Golfklub, on the easterly island of Falster, redolent with the succulent aroma of a wild pig roasting on a spit.

The former communist bloc is a different proposition entirely. To begin with, the promising tourist-golf possibilities of the former Yugoslavia remain unrealized owing to the chaos of war, though the European Women's Tour has operated successfully in Slovenia.

Even where there was a welcome locally for golfers in Iron Curtain days, as in Czechoslovakia, there was little movement until the second Prague spring. The author recalls the disappointment of the European Press Golf Association, whose meetings were attended by scores of journalists from all over Europe, when visas were not forthcoming for all of their number: so no one went. In President Vaclav Havel's more welcoming days the European Tour itself became a visitor, though the 1994 Chemapol Trophy Czech Open tournament at Marianske Lazne in the newly created Czech Republic was savaged by frost. Per-Ulrik Johansson won over 63 holes.

IMPORTANT ADDRESSES

Austrian Golf Federation, Haus des Sports, Prinz-Eugen-Strasse 12, A-1040 Vienna
Belgian Royal Federation of Golf, Chemin de Baudemont 23, 1400 Nivelles
Czech Golf Federation, Mezi Stadiony, PO Box 40, 16017 Prague 6, Strahov, Czech Republic
Danish Golf Union, Golfsvinget 12, 2625 Vallensbaek
Finnish Golf Union, Radiokatu 12, SF-00240 Helsinki
French Golf Federation, 69 Avenue Victor Hugo, 75783 Paris, Cedex 16
German Golf Association, Postfach 2106, 6200 Wiesbaden
Hellenic Golf Federation, PO Box 70003, Glyfada, Athens
Iceland Golf Union, PO Box 1076, Reykjavik 121
Italian Golf Federation, Viale Tiziano 74, 00196 Rome
Luxembourg Golf Union, c/o GC Grand Ducal, 1 Route de Treves, 2633 Senningerberg
Netherland Golf Federation, PO Box 221, 3454 ZL De Meern
Norwegian Golf Union, Hauger Skolevei 1, 1351 Rud
Portuguese Golf Federation, Rua Almeida Brandao 39, 1200 Lisbon
Slovenian Golf Association, c/o GC Bled, C. Svobede 13, 64260 Bled
Spanish Golf Federation, Capitan Haya 9-5 Dcha, Madrid 28020
Swedish Golf Federation, PO Box 84, S-182 11 Danderyd
Swiss Golf Association, En Ballegue, Case Postale CH-1066, Epalinges, Lausanne

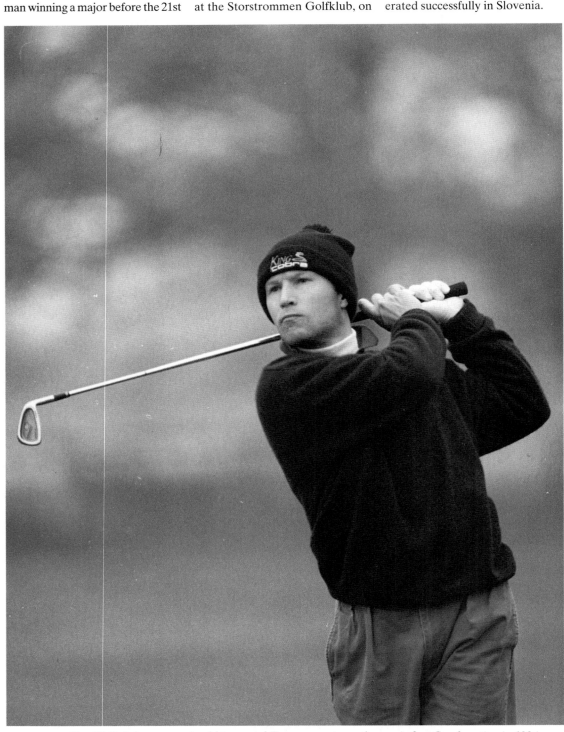

CHILLY WELCOME *Per-Ulrik Johansson gained his second European win on the tour's first Czech outing in 1994*

SOUTH AMERICA AND THE CARIBBEAN

PARAGUAY

Incredible is a frequently misused word. Yet when Raul Fretes, unranked, from Paraguay, beat Colin Montgomerie, then 17th in the Sony Rankings, in the first round of the 1993 Dunhill Cup at St Andrews, it was difficult to object to Fretes's summing-up, "very incredible".

The Paraguayan trio of Carlos Franco, his brother Angel and Fretes had defeated Scotland (Montgomerie, Sam Torrance and Gordon Brand Junior) 2–1 at the home of golf, and in a totally un-Paraguayan style freezing wind too. Brand was the Scots' only winner, beating Angel. "They will not believe this at home," said Fretes. "It is very unreal to me."

Paraguay has fewer golfers than many a single club in Britain has members, and was credited with having fewer clubs (four) than St Andrews, let alone Scotland.

There are only a couple of dozen pros in Paraguay. Six of them are Carlos and Angel Franco and their four brothers. Carlos and Angel are not unused to winning. Both have finished at the head of the Order of Merit of the South American Tour, which was launched in 1991, and Carlos also topped the Asian Order.

Paraguay also beat Wales 2–1, but did not reach the last four because they lost 2–1 on the second day to the team which eventually went on to win the Cup, the USA – far from a disgrace.

The following year Canada's feat in beating the US in the final was hailed as the greatest upset since, well, since Scotland beat Paraguay on the first day, Andrew Coltart doing well in Torrance's place. He beat Fretes at the 19th.

ARGENTINA

Unless the Carlos brothers mount a complete take-over, Argentina will continue to be thought of as Latin America's strongest golfing nation, who look to Edwardo Romero to do great deeds. His compatriot Vicente Fernandez, despite being born with one leg shorter than the other, has seldom been out of the top 40 on the European Tour since the mid-1970s: his fifth win on the Tour, in the 1992 Murphy's Open, was by virtue of an 87-foot birdie putt up the The Belfry's huge triple-tier 18th green. It won him a handsome £92,660 ($142,000).

Like South America's best player of all, Roberto de Vicenzo, Fernandez is a multiple winner of Argentine and Brazil titles, though not such a dominant player as was Antonio Cerda in the 1950s. Cerda was top World Cup individual in 1953, and second to Max Faulkner by two shots in the 1951 British Open. José Jurado came even closer for Argentina in 1931, when a topped shot on the 71st hole into a Carnoustie stream led to his finishing a shot behind the champion, Tommy Armour.

BRAZIL

Brazil has an unusual claim to golf fame: a hat-trick of Brazilian Open wins was completed in 1961 by the

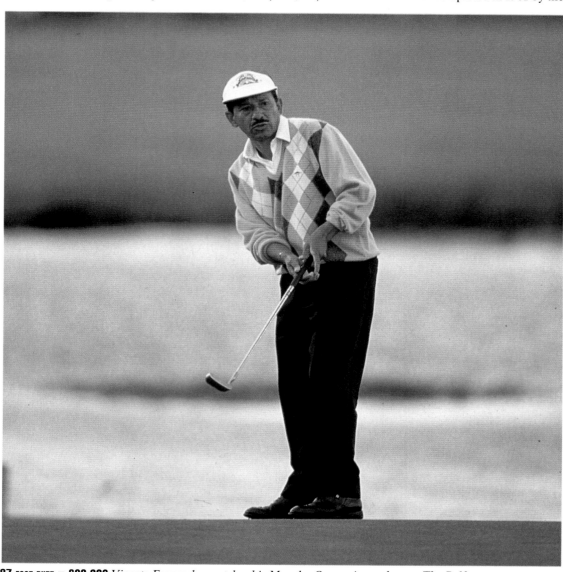

87-FOOT PUTT = £92,660 *Vicente Fernandez watches his Murphy Open winner drop at The Belfry*

American Bob Falkenburg, who had caused something of a furore when winning the Wimbledon lawn tennis title in 1948. In that era when "play shall be continuous" was rigorously enforced, he regathered his strength by lying down now and then on the hallowed Centre Court turf.

The best native Brazilian players have been Mario Gonzales and his son Jaime, who played on the US and European Tours, but never won.

MEXICO

Victor Relagado from Tijuana did manage to win on the US Tour, but the most noteworthy of Mexican golf happenings is also the most tragic. Willie Smith, who won the US Open in 1899 by 11 strokes, still a record, was from Carnoustie, like his brother Alex who also won the US Open. They are the only brothers to do so, and their brother Macdonald is celebrated as being the best player never to win a major event. Willie died after being found in the cellar of the Mexico City club where he was

UNREAL FEELING *Raul Fetes of Paraguay helped shock Scotland in the Dunhill Cup*

serving as a pro. The building had been shelled during the Mexican Revolution of 1914–15.

THE CARIBBEAN

The Bahamas and Bermuda, where the golf tradition is very strong, not to mention Caribbean Islands such as Puerto Rico and Dominica, offer a (much used) sunny escape route for US and Canadian golfers, though the spotlight of publicity has been on Jamaica in recent years, because of the Johnny Walker World Championship at Tryall.

Barbados has one of the most luxurious and fashionable of the golf/hotel complexes in the world, at Sandy Lane (sited on the sought-after western coast), where the course has been renovated and extended with an extra nine holes in a £3 million ($4,650,000) development. A Sandy Lane round costs £75 ($116.25) including caddie cart, but if you can afford Sandy Lane Hotel rates, the golf is free.

To tempt even more players from cooler climes, an old Barbados sugar plantation is being turned into a £300 million ($465 million) project. Royal Westmoreland will eventually be a mix of residential (380 homes) and sports facilities around a Robert Trent Jones course. A US Senior tournament, or regular tour event is the eventual aim, since it

TRYALL JAMAICA *Johnny Walker World title, 1993*

is difficult to see how another tournament on the lines of the Johnny Walker or Sun City event can be shoe-horned into the golfing year between the end of the regular season and Christmas. But if the European Tour can take in Manila, why not Barbados?

IMPORTANT ADDRESSES

South America and Central America
Argentine Golf Association, Corrientes 538, Piso 11, 1043 Buenos Aires
Bolivian Golf Federation, Casilla de Correo 6130, La Paz
Brazilian Golf Federation, Rua 7 de Abril, 01044 São Paulo
Chilean Golf Federation, Casilla 13307, Correo 21, Santiago
Colombian Golf Union, Carrer 7A, 72-64 of Int. 26 Apartado Aereo 90985, Bogotà
Ecuador Golf Federation, Casilla 521, Guayaquil
Mexican Golf Association, Cincinnati, No. 40-104, Mexico 18, DF
Paraguay Golf Association, Casilla de Correo 302, Asunción
Peru Golf Federation, Casilla 5637, Lima
Uruguay Golf Association, Casilla 1484, Montevideo
Venezuela Golf Federation, Local 5, Avda. Avila, La Florida, Caracas 1050

The Caribbean
Bahamas Golf Federation, PO Box N4568, Nassau
Barbados Golf Association, c/o Sandy Lane GC, St James
Bermuda Golf Association, PO Box HM 433, Hamilton HM BX
El Salvador Golf Federation, Apartado Postal 631, San Salvador
Jamaica Golf Association, Constant Spring GC, PO Box 743, Kingston 8

ASIA AND THE FAR EAST

THE ASIAN TOUR

Fact: Frankie Minoza of the Philippines is the only Asian golfer to finish at the head of the Asian Tour's Order of Merit in the six years ending 1994.

That is why the Asian Tour (originally known as the Far East Circuit) began its 33rd year in 1995 with a rival tour to contend with ... the Asian PGA Tour. This new tour is the sequel to years of discontent among Asian pros. Their feeling is that the existing tour, run by the Asia-Pacific Golf Confederation, an amateur organization made up of representatives of member nations, is not helpful in developing the careers of Asian golfers. The leading Asian on the nine-leg 1994 tour was Kyi Hla Han (Burma), who took

21st place on the Order of Merit.

Purse money had not increased remotely as healthily as in the US and Europe, new tournaments were few, and the early Taiwanese domination of the Asian Tour had been followed by an invasion of American, European and Australian players who had consistently made off with a considerable share of the prize money. Payne Stewart was one such.

As if to prove the point, the first event of the 1995 Asian Tour was won by Todd Hamilton, of the US, who headed the Asian Order of Merit in 1992. Americans Brian Claar and Brian Watts (five times a winner in Japan), Rick Gibson (Canada) and Carlos Franco (Paraquay) also took top spot during the six years ending 1994.

Hence the meeting in July, 1994, to set up the Asian PGA. The APGA's circuit, throughout the latter part of the year, was to be launched with a minimum of 20 events, and guaranteed prize money of $4.2 million (about £2.75 million). Four "major" events, worth half a million each, were included.

The Asian Tour announced a 13-event February–April programme, with $4.4 million on offer. A second seven-event section was promised to follow in the autumn. The first section started without a main sponsor for the tour, Newsweek International having withdrawn, and without television coverage.

This turmoil left fans, players and sponsors in confusion, added to by coming Australasian PGA Tour events: the Dunhill Masters in Indonesia, the Epson Singapore Open and a tournament in Shanghai. Basically the Asia PGAs who have worked up the new tour are convinced that the old circuit was put together outside Asia by non-Asians largely for the benefit of non-Asians.

The lack of success of Asian and Japanese golfers at the highest level set against the huge expansion in the number of courses and players remains a puzzle. This has not prevented Arnold Palmer from declaring that Asia is where the next great advance of golf will occur.

Isao Aoki, second to Jack Nicklaus in the 1980 US Open, and Liang Huan Lu, the Taiwanese "Mr Lu" have come closest; Lu was second to Lee Trevino in 1971 at Birkdale.

A YEN FOR GOLF

Japanese pros make lots of money as soon as they get anywhere near the top of their own Order of Merit, and seem disinclined for the most part to seek wider fame. Joe (the Pro) Hardstaff, who retired in 1995 after serving as Royal Hong Kong's pro since 1965 (Mr Lu preceded him there), puts it this way: "They don't travel well." Language and food are particular difficulties. David Leadbetter believes their practice facilities are inadequate, leading to inferior iron play.

There is certainly no financial compulsion for them to travel: it is a chauffeur-driven life for the best of them at home tournaments. Masashi "Jumbo" Ozaki was highest placed, at 38th, of six Japanese players in Nick Price's 1994 Open at Turnberry. Apart from these there was not one player from Asia.

BATTERY GOLFERS *Tokyo's three-tiered Shiba driving range. Despite such facilities, David Leadbetter thinks scope for practice in Japan is inadequate*

ABOVE: **HIGH-RISE BACKDROP** *Tom Watson defends his Hong Kong Open title in 1993*

RIGHT: **SINGAPORE SWINGS** *Tanah Merah club has nearly 3,000 members*

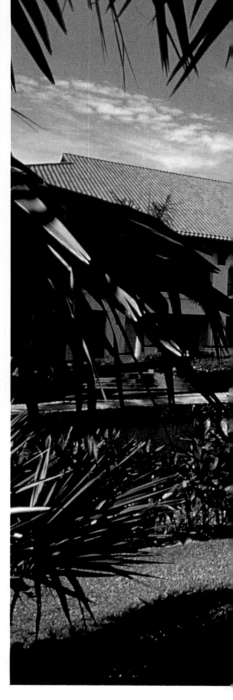

Ozaki won the Japan Open a few weeks later by 13 strokes. His prize was 18 million yen, close to £120,000 ... about £10,000 more than Price earned at Turnberry. Ozaki stood 11th in the Sony World Rankings at the time: none of his colleagues in the Sony Top 30 was in opposition. Japanese purses exceed European Tour rewards. Despite this, none of the Japanese events is included in the Sony Rankings top-40 rated tournaments.

An Englishman, Arthur Groom, "Father of Japanese Golf", chose a spectacular site for the first course in Japan in 1903, a four-hole affair near the summit of Mount Rokko, extended to 18 holes within a year. Groom died after a fall on his way down from the course 14 years later. There were 70 courses by 1934. Tokyo GC was the nation's first, in 1914, to be founded by locals.

Shortage of suitable terrain – Groom's mountainside venture has perforce been followed, expensive as it is, many times – inflates membership fees and subscriptions to the scale of international telephone numbers, and drives Japanese players to fly abroad to buy memberships and courses.

The military regime that led Japan into war in the 1930s was as bad for golf as the communists in Europe; golf was a subversive (US/British) activity. The American military had the opposite effect during the years of occupation, and it cannot be long (though planning authorities not unreasonably oppose the proliferation of courses in some areas) before courses exceed the 2,000 mark.

For all that, golfers short of a few billion yen are struggling. Top club corporate memberships are bought and sold through brokers at six-figure (sterling) terms. Even the moderately rich must be content with golf range golf, like the Shila, a three-tiered range in Tokyo. Some are perched on top of office blocks.

THE FAR EAST

Costly golf is not confined to Japan. The Pacific Ring is as vibrantly expansive in golf as in most other human activities. However, the richest areas, like Singapore and Hong Kong, are also, not unnaturally, the most restricted for course-worthy land in an era of golf boom.

Singapore's *GOLF* magazine lists 14 private clubs (the island is about the size of the Isle of Man). This includes the Singapore Island Country Club, with four 18-hole courses, 6,000 members, and an entrance fee of S$200,000 (£88,500/US$137,175) and where a round with a caddie (A, B, or C class) costs in excess of £100 (US$155). As in Japan, prices vary on a lively market. Then there is the Fairway Country Club – a driving range, where 100 balls will cost a member S$4 (£1.77/ US$2.74) – that is, after the annual membership fee of around S$7,000 (£3,097/US$4,800).

Also listed are 43 clubs in neighbouring Batam and Malaysia, including Kukup on the southwestern tip of the Malaysia peninsula, close to Singapore. These get crowded too, though prices have not attained Singapore levels in general. Kukup has three nine-hole loops (with another to come), a sports centre, a children's miniature course and Kids' Village, six tennis courts, a Conference Centre and restaurant

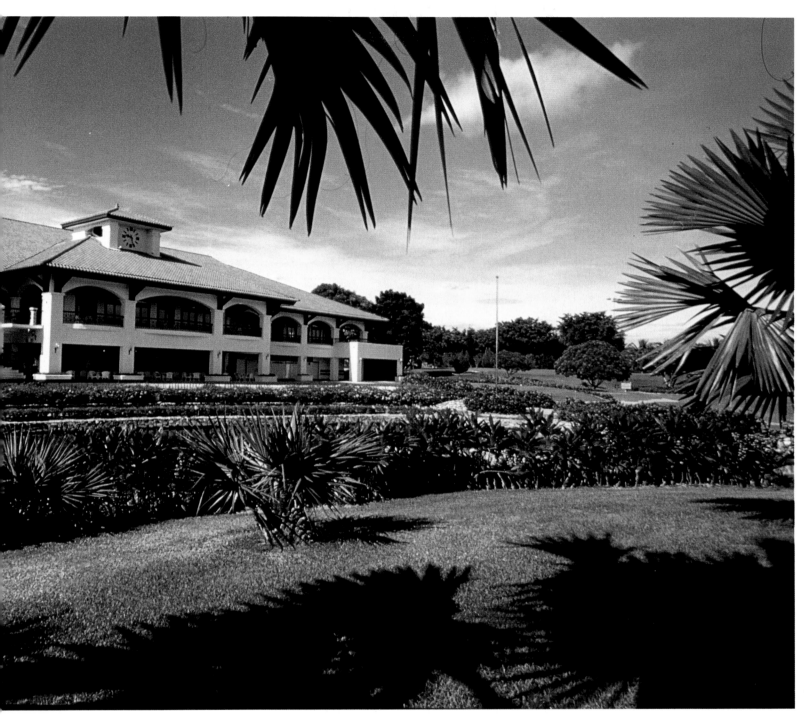

(over a lake), a driving range (with a pond in front of the bays to help quell golfer's hydrophobia), and an island putting green. To join costs a Malay £7,624 ($11,817), a foreigner £11,435 ($17,724); a weekend round £42 ($65).

A brigadier-general drove the Kukup venture forward, and the Royal Thai Army Course at Bangkok is subsidized by the military, its two courses kept parade-ground neat. A twosome playing a weekend round including caddies would fork out 1,500 baht (£38/$59). There is even a golf resort on the River Kwai: tourists can ride on the Death Railway.

Hong Kong, like Singapore, must look outward to extend its golfing facilities. The Royal Hongkong Club, with three courses on the New Territories at Fanling (the home of the charmingly named charitable organization the Fanlingerers, which formerly accrued funds for the war-blinded, and now does so for Cheshire Homes) has 600 registered caddies. That speaks volumes as to the heavy use to which the courses are put, involving well over 10,000 players in the week, including 100 Japanese a day. Also busy is the club's other course on Hong Kong Island itself, Discovery Bay.

Corporate memberships have risen in price from about HK$10,000 (£830/US$1,286) in 1970 to HK$12-million (£998,335/US$1,547,420). No wonder Hong Kong magazines advertise opportunities to buy into courses in Australia. They also pin-point Shenzhen, "the only golf club in China close to Hong Kong". Shenzhen's Mission Hills club (designer Jack Nicklaus) broke new ground in 1995 as the first in China to host the World Cup.

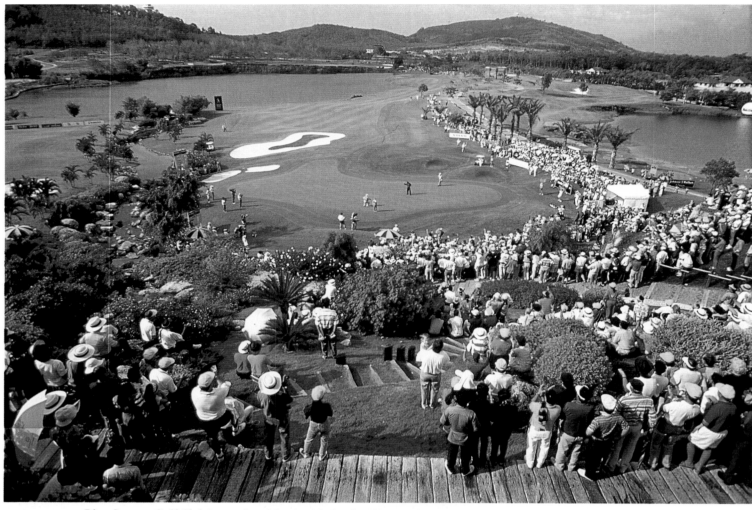

FLOURISHING PHUKET *Blue Canyon Golf Club is as colourful as its title for the 1994 Thailand VW Classic*

CHINA AND INDIA

China's fledgling pros were disappointing at the country's first pro qualifying school at Beijing. None reached the required standard, but six did at the next attempt, and three were given the taxing task of trying to qualify in Thailand for the Shenzhen finals. They were the first golf pro team ever to represent the Republic.

On the other hand, India was among the favourites to qualify along with Hong Kong, Indonesia, Malaysia, Pakistan, the Philippines, Singapore, South Korea and Thailand. Royal Calcutta, founded in 1829, is the oldest club outside the British Isles, with Bombay (1842) not far behind.

Calcutta's New Course is not all that new, though it is 24 years newer than the Old Course, now past its

160th birthday. Despite the longevity of Indian golf, its pros cannot expect to win as much as £10,000 a year. A total of just 130 courses on the subcontinent, many run by the Army, means that golf is not even a dream for most Indians: they fantasize about playing Test cricket instead.

Many courses are on the way in China, which Napoleon called a sleeping giant that would surprise the world. However, the Shenzhen authorities, like their Japanese counterparts, make it clear they will restrict the course building boom to protect land and promote better usage where appropriate.

In stark contrast to the perturbation felt in the west about the Chinese regaining Hong Kong in 1997, many expatriate Chinese are going back there, confident that prosperity will outlast the changes.

The betting is that golf will too. The polite Chinese ought to be hot on etiquette: relations have eased somewhat since the Treaty of Nanking, in which the Imperial Chinese Government agreed, among other things, not to refer routinely to Westerners in official documents as "barbarians".

IMPORTANT ADDRESSES

Asia-Pacific Golf Confederation, 52, 1st Floor, Jalan Hang, Lekiu 50100, Kuala Lumpur

Asia Professional Golf Circuit, 230 East Foothill Drive, Phoenix, AZ85020, USA

China Golf Association, 75 Lane 187, Tunhau S Road, Taipei, Taiwan 10647

Hong Kong Golf Association, Suite 1420, Princes Building, 10 Chater Road, Hong Kong

Indian Golf Union, Tata Centre (3rd Floor), 43 Chowringhee Road, Calcutta 700071

Indonesian Golf Association, c/o Bank Bumi Daya, Jin Imam Bonjol 61-PO Box 106, Jakarta Pusat

Japan Golf Association, 606-6th Floor, Palace Building, Marunouchi, Chiyoda-ku, Tokyo

Korean Golf Assocation, 13th Floor, Manhattan Building, 36-2, Yeo-Eui-Do-Dowg, Yeong Deung Po-Ku, Seoul

Malaysian Golf Association, 12a Persiaran Ampang, 55000 Kuala Lumpur

Pakistan Golf Federation, PO Box 1295, Rawalpindi

Philippines Golf Association, 209 Administration Building, Rizal Memorial Sports Complex, Vito Cruz, Manila

Singapore Golf Association, Thomson Road, PO Box 0172, Singapore 9157

Sri Lanka Golf Union, 2 Gower Street, Colombo 5, Sri Lanka

Thailand Golf Association, Railway Training Centre, Vibhavadee Rangsit Road, Bangkok 10900

THE MIDDLE EAST

Courses are few in the Middle East. Israel's lone gem is at Caesarea, the port Herod built and named for Augustus Caesar. The course is not long, but picturesque, and a perfect holiday set-up, especially for its proximity to a Dan Hotel, some of the best of Mediterranean beaches, and a splendid Roman aqueduct and theatre. The southern Israeli resort of Eilat plans a course, but water engineering difficulties are great there, and as yet the project is not far advanced.

Such problems have been solved in the United Arab Emirates sufficiently well to reach a standard which satisfies the officials of two professional tours, for golf hereabouts, founded on oil money, scored a double in 1995. The European Tour again visited the Emirates Course, and the Dubai Creek course of the Dubai Yachting and Golf Club was on the schedule of the new Asia PGA Tour. Both were designed by Karl Litten.

The Emirates lay-out, created out of the desert in the late 1980s, was voted the best course on the 1994 European Tour by the pros. Ernie Els explained, "The greens are always in good condition and the bunker sand is perfect."

TAKING SHAPE *Dubai Creek golf course and marina*

GREENING THE DESERT *The Dubai Desert Classic in full swing on the much praised Emirates Course, with its innovative and stylish clubhouse*

AFRICA

SOUTH AFRICA

The Bedford Club of Cape Province, founded in 1892, was granted permission in a municipal minute "to make a golf links…provided the holes were covered with large flat stones". Despite this insensitive request, the club prospered by 1896 to the extent of being able to employ a pro named Johnstone, for two weeks at £2 a week.

Golf began in South Africa with the Royal Cape club at Wynberg. Five years later the powerful engine of Transvaal golf, the Johannesburg club, was formed, with John Tudhope as the head of affairs. The club inaugurated the Transvaal Golf Union, which for the first 20 years of its existence was run exclusively by Johannesburg members.

Six years later, for their involvement in the Jameson Raid which foreshadowed the Boer War, the club president, Sir Lionel Phillips, was sentenced to death and the club captain, H. Becker, imprisoned.

A hundred years later and there is a million dollar first prize on offer at the Sun City course designed by Gary Player in Bophuthatswana alongside a hotel, casino and entertainment complex out of Las Vegas by Walt Disney, you might say. Spectacular is the name of the Sun City game, which has a backdrop of the Pilanesberg Game Reserve.

The original name of the site, Letsatsing, means "sun", and the Sun City Classic began in December of 1979. Two years later the first $1 million (now £645,000) prize was offered. International stars performed on stage and on course at Sun City, yet the South African game itself was becoming isolated.

Visiting players were excluded from golf in many countries after their names had appeared in newspaper reports as having played, for example, on the Sunshine Tour in South Africa and subsequently put on a blacklist by the United Nations Anti-Apartheid Committee. South African teams vanished from the World Cup and similar events. Where the professional game was powerful enough and there was no governmental action in the relevant territory, South African players could and did play.

Black players' careers were stunted, and there were well documented cases of out and out cruelty in areas of particularly stony apartheid rule. Sewsunker Sewgolum, of Indian parentage, distinguished himself as the only first-class player to operate with left hand below right on all clubs, a practice seldom adopted except as a cure for putting horrors. He won the Dutch Open three times, but was seldom allowed to play in his native land.

Gary Player followed another Transvaaler, Bobby Locke, putter without peer, as South Africa's shorts-odds prospect wherever he teed off. Player said after winning his second US PGA title (while protected by armed police because of extremist threats) that he was encouraging excellent young black players. One, Vincent Tshabalala, a Bantu, obliged by winning the French Open. He later refused selection for the World Cup, believing it would suggest he condoned apartheid, and then was refused entry to the South African Open.

South Africa's return to the world stage of golf coincides with the rise of another of her sons, Nick Price from Durban, to the head of the world rankings. Clearly Ernie Els, who won his first major, the US Open title, in 1994, is a good bet to succeed him in the short term. Further along, South Africa can look to Retief Goosen and former South African infantryman David Carter, who won the European Tour Qualifying School in 1992 and 1994 respectively, Carter with the aid of an eight under par 64 over 6,913 rain-sodden yards at Massane. Goosen began 1995 by taking South Africa's Open title, rounding things off with an eagle at Randpark's long 18th.

Another golfer of whom the South African PGA have high hopes is black, set free at last with others of his race to follow their golfing stars now that his country has been readmitted to the full range of world sport. Mawonga Nomwa, 24, a former caddie from Soweto who started playing at 14, got through in 13th place at the Tour Qualifying School of 1994, when he turned pro. He went on to earn his first cheque early in 1995, in 29th place in the Masters at Sun City's "Lost City" course. He finished three over par, but, significantly, he made great progress over the crucial last nine holes, where most tournaments really begin, coming home in 32 with four birdies.

THE SAFARI CIRCUIT

The lovely Nairobi courses at Karen (where screaming, mocking monkeys and the possibility lurking in the mind that there might be a cobra or two about are good tests of concentration) and flowery Muthaiga, where some of the events dramatized in the film *White Mischief* occurred, are splendid touristic adjuncts to the game parks, and the holiday courses on the north African littoral grow in popularity.

The Safari Circuit, across the continent from Nigeria to Kenya, has been a fine proving ground for young pros: Sandy Lyle, among others, gained his first tournament success there. Officials at one West African tournament had obviously taken to heart the R&A's "Red Route" scheme of roping off fairways to control galleries. They roped off only one fairway, but as the crossing point on it was usually deserted . . .

IMPORTANT ADDRESSES

Botswana Golf Union, PO Box 1362, Gaborone

Ghana Golf Association, PO Box 8, Achimola

Kenya Golf Union, PO Box 49609, Nairobi

Malawi Golf Union, PO Box 1198, Blantyre

Namibian Golf Union, PO Box 2989, Windhoek 9000

Nigeria Golf Union, National Sports Commission, Surulere, PO Box 145, Lagos

Sierra Leone Golf Federation, Freetown GC, PO Box 237, Lumley Beach, Freetown

South African Golf Federation, PO Box 391994, Bramley, South Africa 2018

Swaziland Golf Union, PO Box 1739, Mbabane

Tanzania Golf Union, PO Box 2569, Dar es Salaam

Uganda Golf Union, Kitante Road, PO Box 2574, Kampala

Zaire Golf Federation, BP 1648, Lubumbashi

Zambian Golf Union, PO Box 31943, Lusaka

Zimbabwe Golf Association, PO Box 3327, Harare

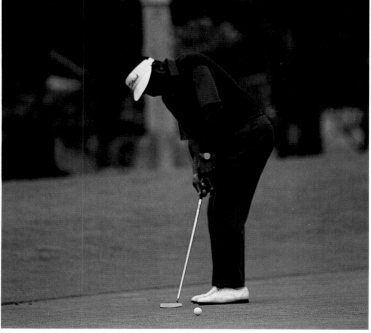

CAREER HAZARD *Apartheid checked Vincent Tshabalala's progress*

LEGENDS

In golf, as in other sports, the epithet "legendary" is over-used and much devalued, having been applied to almost every player who has savoured victory at the highest level. But at the summit of the game there is a small elite group whose golfing exploits make them worthy recipients of exaggerated and romanticized praise. Most of all, their game did not wilt when they neared the winning post.

SEVERIANO BALLESTEROS

Blessed with a supreme natural talent, the man from Pedrena is beloved of the fans in the gallery worldwide. The winner of five "Majors", three Opens and two Masters, Seve has a greater and more imaginative range of shots than anyone else in golf today.

BEN HOGAN

Hailing from Dublin, Texas, Ben Hogan became the dominant player in world golf in the immediate aftermath of the Second World War. His long game had an accuracy which has probably never been matched.

ARNOLD PALMER

One of the few men in sport who can boast an army, Arnold Palmer was the first golfer of the television age. Not one of golf's stylists, the pugnacious Pennsylvanian won the acclaim of the crowd for his whole-hearted commitment and his bold stroke play.

LEE TREVINO

Gloriously unorthodox, Lee Trevino was at his peak in the early 1970s. The wisecracking Mexican-American remains a highly successful and very popular performer on the Seniors Tour.

NICK FALDO

Though his sometimes unsmiling persona has not always endeared him to the media, Nick Faldo's single-minded dedication to his craft has ensured that he is frequently "the man to beat".

BOBBY JONES

In 1930 Bobby Jones came as close to achieving golfing invincibility as is humanly possible when he performed the Grand Slam. On retiring from championship golf, he built a course at Augusta, Georgia, and founded a golfing institution – the Masters

GARY PLAYER

A dedicated practiser and fitness fanatic, Gary Player had no rivals as golf's greatest world traveller. For much of the 1960s, the South African was one of the few overseas golfers to win regularly in the United States. His ninth major was the 1978 Masters.

THE TRIUMVIRATE

J. H. Taylor, Harry Vardon and James Braid were exact golfing contemporaries who together took no fewer than 16 of the Open championships between 1894 and 1914.

WALTER HAGEN

Ever a man to enjoy life, Walter Hagen won the US Open in 1914 and 1919 and was a relentless acquirer of trophies in the 1920s and '30s. His ability to extricate himself from the deepest trouble was his hallmark. He was also the first full-time tournament professional.

JACK NICKLAUS

An impetuous power-player who evolved into a cautious perfectionist, Jack Nicklaus was undoubtedly the world's greatest golfer in the 1960s and '70s, was still a leading contender in the 1980s and remains a doughty competitor in the 1990s.

GENE SARAZEN

A diminutive figure with an idiosyncratic style, Gene Sarazen's made a dramatic entrance into the golfing scene when he won the US Open and the US PGA as a 20-year-old. After a nine-year gap, he enjoyed a second purple patch, winning the British Open and US Open in 1932, the US PGA in 1933 and the Masters in 1935.

TOM WATSON

Tom Watson made his majestic mark on the game in the late 1970s and early 1980s with five British Open victories between 1975 and 1983, wresting away from Jack Nicklaus the crown of the world's greatest golfer.

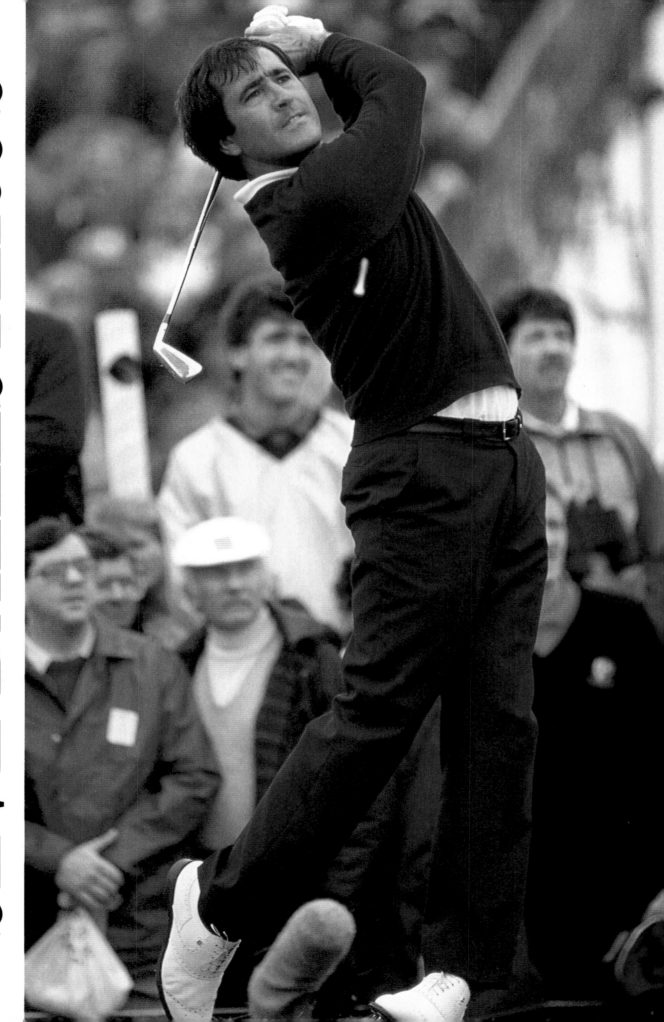

SEVE BALLESTEROS

THE NATURAL FROM SPAIN

Severiano Ballesteros makes the rest of a golf field look like a collection of cart-horses. The glory of his game is his golf swing and the poise and rhythm of the follow-through.

But there is a contradiction. Watch the man on a practice ground or playing a competitive round: he is all worry and rehearsal. He frequently remarks on his dislike of the state of his game and is seldom happy with the position of his club at the top of the backswing.

With the driver in particular he has often been crooked but long; now he is crooked and, by the standards of today, not particularly long. But other wizardries remain, not least his natural genius at those trouble shots – from deep rough, woodland or bushes – that his wayward driving forces him to play.

Ballesteros himself admits his short game isn't as good as when he first appeared on the golf scene in 1976. However, his putting abilities do not seem impaired. From long range he usually coasts the ball to the hole-side and seldom misses those decisive short putts. When he is bunkered beside a green, it is hardly worth watching – you know the ball will finish stone dead. From other trouble spots in this scoring zone, he has greater range of shot and imagination, still, than anyone else in the game.

Love in the press tent
It is no surprise that such a natural talent emerged young with his chal-

> ## 66 Seve's got shots the rest of us don't even know. 99
>
> *Ben Crenshaw*

lenge, at 19, for the 1976 Royal Birkdale Open. Few paid much attention when he tied for the first-round lead with a 69. Who was he? How did you pronounce his name? Interviewed in the press tent afterwards, Seve declared he might take 80 if the wind got up the next day. That remark may have been the beginning of the love affair that the Press have had with Ballesteros – particularly in Britain – throughout his career.

The next day, another 69 gave him a two-stroke lead. Could this very young unknown win? It was not to be, though he held the same margin over Miller after the third day's play. On the last day, however, Miller took the lead quickly while Ballesteros had more than his usual ration of wild tee shots. A late burst allowed him to finish second and he knew he was on his way.

It was only a matter of time before he won the Open, which he did at Lytham in 1979, cementing his growing fame for wild play in his final round by carving his drive into BBC vehicles and, of course, recording a birdie on the hole. When it was all over, his playing partner, Hale Irwin, remarked that he could not understand how anyone could finish as Open champion after so much bad driving.

Seve had still to prove himself in the USA. It didn't take him long: in the 1980 Masters his start of 66, 69, 68 gave him a seven-stroke lead going into the final round. At one

LYTHAM 1988 *Ballesteros played the round of his life*

point he increased that to ten before some embarrassing play from the 11th to 13th. Easing up, he won in some comfort.

There was the same four-stroke margin in 1983, this time largely because of a blistering start in his final round – birdie, eagle, par, birdie and out in 31. There were no real alarms and he finished by chipping in for a par on the last after roaring through the green with his second and then misjudging his third.

Going steady at St Andrews
The following year came his second Open title, at St Andrews. It saw some of the steadiest play the Spaniard has produced.

Through the rounds par followed par but birdies were few. By generally choosing to go left from the tee to avoid trouble he was leaving himself more difficult lines into the greens. On the 71st hole, he again went well left into the rough, giving himself little chance of hitting, let alone holding, the green. But that is what he did. A birdie putt at the relatively easy last hole then saw him home by two from Watson and Langer.

Career Milestones

1957 *Born Pedrena, northern Spain.*

1976 *Wins first Tour event, Dutch Open, aged 19.*

1979 *First Spaniard to win the British Open and first Continental European since Arnaud Massy in 1907.*

1980 *First European to win the Masters and, at 23, the youngest champion.*

1983 *A second Masters title.*

1984 *His second British Open title, distinguished by steady play.*

1988 *Third British Open title, defeating Nick Faldo and Nick Price with a final-round 65 – "the best round of my life".*

His last major came in 1988 with that classic last-round encounter with Nicks Price and Faldo. It is perhaps doubtful whether he will win another and he has thrown a few away over the years. Yet he still remains the most exciting player in world golf.

NICK FALDO

THE MODERN HOGAN

Nick Faldo, despite an already successful career, famously decided in the mid-1980s that he needed to totally remodel his swing, and went on to become the best golfer in the world.

Faldo first came into the public eye in 1975, when he won the British Youths' Open Amateur Championship and the English Amateur. He turned professional the following year and his first tournament win came in 1977. That year saw another boost to his career when he formed a good partnership with Peter Oosterhuis and also beat Tom Watson – a Watson still with the glow of the Masters and the Turnberry Open Championship about him – in the singles of the Ryder Cup at Royal Lytham and St Anne's.

Determined to be one of the great players of golf's history, and conscious that his swing was not sufficiently reliable under pressure, Faldo astutely chose David Leadbetter as his coach. The swing that emerged after much tutelage took time to work. Faldo won in 1984 but no more successes came his way until the Spanish Open of 1987, the year that saw his arrival as a world figure. Faldo's 68 in the first round of the British Open saw him very

> ❝ **This run doesn't have to end. If someone is going to beat me then I'm going to make sure they've worked for their victory. Let them come and get it from me.** ❞
>
> *Nick Faldo*

well placed, despite the fact that the Australian Rodger Davies held the lead with a 64. Few saw him as a real threat, but Faldo's second-round 69 brought him level. His 71 in the next round put him a short head behind leader Paul Azinger, just a stroke behind.

Faldo's final round is already part of the golfing legend for in misty, chilly weather he parred every single hole. In the end, he won because of Paul Azinger's failing. With a three-stroke lead and nine to play, he faltered with bogeys on the last two holes. Faldo did not, and his play on the difficult final hole was exemplary – a good drive, an excellent five-iron to the front of the green and two putts.

America is converted

However, his reputation wasn't yet made in the USA. Many thought all those 18 pars could hardly be inspirational golf. Winning the Masters in 1989 changed that, although he had an apparently disastrous third round when he took 77, which dropped him five strokes behind the leader Ben Crenshaw. His putting had been rather poor.

It was very different on the final day. On the 1st hole he got the ball in from about 20 yards and was on his way and reached the turn in 32. Birdies accumulated on the back nine on the 13th, 14th and 16th, where he holed a putt with an almost impossible amount of break. Another from long range followed on the 17th and he finished in 65 to tie with Scott Hoch, who then proceeded to assist Faldo to his second major win. On the first play-off hole

Hoch missed from about two feet and a grateful Faldo birdied the next for the title. When it was all over it seemed that Faldo had birdied almost everything in the final hours.

Millionaire golf

Faldo's best year was in 1990, when he came close to equalling Ben Hogan's 1953. First there was another Masters. After rounds of 71 and 72, a 66 then put him in third place, three shots adrift of Raymond Floyd, and a final round of 69 was good enough to force a playoff with the overnight leader. The second hole was again decisive as Floyd put his second shot into the water and that was that. Only Jack Nicklaus, in 1965–66, had won two straight Masters.

In the US Open that same year, he missed the play-off by one shot. Soon it was time to go to St Andrews, where he played his most devastating golf ever. Four majors in the record books. By now Faldo was a millionaire many times over, and his rise to pre-eminence had done much to win Leadbetter his reputation as the new guru of golf.

Muirfield in 1992 saw some silly betting, but Faldo did seem invincible. His 66, 64 start put him three ahead and the only crises came in the final round when he began to drop shots while John Cook went ahead – but not for long. Cook failed over the last two holes while Faldo steeled himself to "play the best four holes of my life". Two birdies gave him his fifth major title.

KEEPING IN LINE
Fanny Sunnesson helps Faldo read putts

Career Milestones

1957 *Born Welwyn Garden City, Hertfordshire.*
1977 *First professional tournament victory, the Skol Lager event.*
1987 *British Open champion at Muirfield.*
1989 *First Masters win.*
1990 *Repeats Masters victory and wins his second British Open title.*
1992 *Heads European money list; wins six tournaments, including his third British Open Championship.*

WALTER HAGEN

"EDDIE – HOLD THE FLAG, WILL YOU?"

Walter Hagen probably got more enjoyment from his career in top golf then any great player before or since – and only Jones and Nicklaus won more majors. The above remark came during a social round of golf with Edward, Prince of Wales, soon to be, briefly, Edward VIII. It shows how much Hagen felt at ease with everyone, from kings and presidents to ordinary followers of golf.

Hagen had come to the top very quickly. He played the 1912 Canadian Open and finished 11th. Asked at his home club how he had done, Hagen replied, "I lost." This was an early variation on his famous adage that no one remembers who finished second. He lost again in the 1913 US Open, finishing a stroke behind the play-off between Vardon, Ray and Ouimet. The following year, 1914, was better. He began the US Open with a record 68 and held on to win. He lost some of his career in the war years but won the US Open again in 1919. He was ready to spread his wings further afield and prove himself in the British Open.

Cocking a snook

Hagen arrived at Deal for the 1920 event. Since, as a professional, he was not allowed to enter the clubhouse, he hired a limousine, had his chauffeur park it in front of the clubhouse and enjoyed the contents of his hamper, quite likely prepared by the Ritz Hotel in London. It was a typically grand gesture from a man who enjoyed cocking a snook, but Hagen's play did not impress the spectators nearly as much. He came in 53rd of the 77 qualifiers.

He realized that, to compete more effectively on links courses, he must learn the pitch and run. Having done so, he enjoyed a great run in the British Open during the 1920s. After being sixth the following year, he won in 1922, was second the next year and won again in 1924. For his next entries through to 1929 he was third, first and first. With that last victory, he was nearly finished with the Open.

In the US Open, he was far less successful in

WALTER HAGEN
Matchless nerves

the 1920s, not adding to his two titles. The fact that Bobby Jones was always in the field had a great deal to do with this.

But Jones as an amateur was not eligible for the matchplay US PGA, and Hagen proceeded to compile perhaps the greatest run of success of anyone in a major championship. In 1916 he reached the semi-finals and next played in 1921, when he won. His next appearance was in 1923, when he lost a fiercely contested match to Gene Sarazen in the final. Then came his unparalleled run of four in a row, which involved 22 successive match wins.

Nerveless nipper and putter

The strength of his game was from, say, 100 yards in. He was a short pitcher of excellence, could nip the ball off the sand nervelessly when in a greenside bunker and was the best putter in the business. Hagen's long game was less impressive. Not particularly long off the tee, his swaying swing was perhaps the cause of wildness. However, when surveying a shot from wild country he had the sang-froid to be able to say: "Well, I put it there." And then his recovery shots were as fabled as those of Seve Ballesteros later.

By the end of the 1920s, Hagen had taken 11 major titles and was close to entering his 40s. His tally of majors could well have been higher: he did not have the chance to compete in the Masters, which began in 1934, until his best days lay well behind him. To some extent he may have lost his appetite for centre-stage and by this time his name was easily big enough for him to spend much time on exhibition tours world-wide where he could both enjoy himself and make the money he needed to support his luxurious

Career Milestones

1892 *Born Rochester, New York.*
1914 *Wins first US Open.*
1919 *Second US Open title.*
1921 *Begins a sequence of five US PGA titles from 1921 to 1927.*
1922 *First victory in the British Open Championship.*
1924 *Second victory in the British Open .*
1927 *Captain of the winning US Ryder Cup team in inaugural match against Britain.*
1928 *Third victory in the British Open.*
1929 *Fourth victory in the British Open and losing Ryder Cup Captain.*
1931 *Successful Ryder Cup Captain.*
1933 *Ryder Cup Captain for the fourth time, and second time on the losing side.*
1935 *Third victory as Ryder Cup Captain.*
1937 *Ryder Cup Captain for sixth time, first victory for away team.*

> **Never hurry, never worry, and don't forget to stop and smell the roses on the way.**
>
> *Walter Hagen*

lifestyle. Hagen had a great capacity for enjoyment and only a brief interest in family life, though he was much addicted to the company of attractive women and kept a little black book to record their phone numbers around the world.

He fulfilled his ambitions. Perhaps he didn't passionately desire the major and tournament titles he amassed over the years. They were the means to an end: enjoying life. As he used to say: "I didn't want to be a millionaire. I just wanted to live like one."

BEN HOGAN

LONG GAME, GRAND SLAM

Ben Hogan had a long game the accuracy of which has probably never been matched. The man's shots seemed always to home in on the flag. It then became almost a matter of the luck of the bounce if they stuck a little too short or skidded through a little too far. But, as legend has it, they were always on line.

In his peak years, Hogan was almost as accurate with the driver but never a supreme putter. His method was perhaps too mechanical so that he always lacked real delicacy of touch. But, like his nearest modern counterpart, Nick Faldo, he could stuff the ball into the hole from six feet and under.

At the outset, there were many years of failure, but Hogan was persistent. He first played the US Tour in 1931 and, from time to time, for several years afterwards. There was little if any sponsorship in those far-off years. Hogan would do odd jobs, save up the dollars and then play for as long as the money lasted. He won virtually no prize money. In 1937 he did win some money and, the following year, his first event, a four-ball. He was already 34 years old.

The legend is born
But 1940 saw the beginning of the Hogan legend. He won the North and South event over Pinehurst 2 and was on his way.

Then came the war, with Hogan becoming a dominant player, play-ing 39 events in 1941 and being only once out of the top five. The reasons for this astonishing improvement were that he had become a good short-range putter and had trained himself on the practice ground to shorten the length of his backswing, which had been absurdly beyond the horizontal. His long game immediately became more consistent.

After the war, he emerged as a supreme talent, with 21 wins in the first two seasons, which included the 1946 PGA Championship. He was by no means satisfied. Hogan was aiming at the consistency which leads to greatness. Over the winter of 1947–48 he worked on changing his low drawing hook into a slice. Although he succeeded, he lost much of his length. But the ball finished on the fairway, Hogan's main aim. That slice quite quickly became a slight fade. The length was little altered and the shape of shot was consistent. You rule out the trouble along the left and then have the whole of the fairway to aim at. Hogan won his first US Open.

From smash to slam
But Fate had a trick up its sleeve. Early in 1949, Hogan was very severely injured in a road accident. Many thought he would never play again and he was indeed out of the game for nearly a year. When he returned, walking was an agony and he had to restrict himself to just a few events. The majors became his aim though he had to exclude the US PGA, then a 36-hole match play event, because he knew his legs wouldn't take him around that many holes in a day.

Having missed the 1949 US

Open, Hogan took the title on three of his next four entries. His winning last-round 67 at the spectacularly difficult Oakland Hills course in 1951 was, he thought, the best round he ever played. His last US Open win came in 1953, his greatest year, when he also took his second Masters and won the British Open on his only entry to complete the modern Grand Slam.

It was thought at the time that Hogan would go on winning the majors as long as he wanted to. As Hogan himself said, desire was what counted. But he was wrong. Hogan kept both desire and will, but his putting stroke went. He developed what is variously called "the twitch", "the jerks" or "the yips". In one US Open, when still in contention on the final green, he was noticed apparently trying out a variety of putting methods on the edge of the green. A friend later commented on this. Hogan explained that he hadn't been trying to find a stroke that would hole a putt but one that would make missing look respectable.

After 1953, Hogan went into a slow decline, but remained a force to be reckoned with until towards the end of the 1960s.

> ❝ **"I'm glad to have brought this monster to its knees."** ❞

Ben Hogan after winning the US Open at Oakland Hills in 1951

TRIUMPH AT WENTWORTH *Ben Hogan in 1956*

BOBBY JONES

THE EMPEROR WHO HAD HAD ENOUGH

Bobby Jones achieved a success rate that was, and remains, beyond compare. In his whole quite brief career he played only 52 tournaments, either amateur or professional, and won 23 of them. Jones played just a handful of events a year and otherwise played his friendly club fourballs at weekends, took the winter of Atlanta off and then warmed up in the spring with some practice shots. On average, that was his golfing year. Yet on that very limited golfing diet he could quickly fire himself up and, usually, go out and win a major championship.

GRAND SLAM *Jones (left) with the four major trophies and his biographer*

By around the age of 20, Jones was already nearly the golfing phenomenon of the age and there could have been few who doubted that he would become the greatest golfer ever. In that decade up to 1930 he provided the proof. Then the question was "Who has a chance of beating Bobby?" In fact, quite a few did over the years – but no one ever beat him twice. Such a great player as Walter Hagen never won a British or US Open when Jones was competing.

It all took off in 1923 when he won his first major, the US Open. This despite completing his final round bogey, bogey, double bogey. It was probably nerves – or was there a flaw in Jones's armour in that he tended to let up when in a commanding position? He was clearly better when under the whip.

That came in the play-off against Bobby Cruickshank. At the last he had to risk all to win, needing to hit a long iron from a sandy lie over water to the green – or play short of the hazard for safety, with the likelihood of having to play another 18 holes. Jones went for the bold shot and played it to perfection.

With the knowledge that he had it in him to win a major, Jones was on his way. In the US Amateur, for instance, from 1924 to 1930, he won five of his seven entries and was runner-up once. In those days, moreover, there were no temptations from lucrative professional tours. There was no money there until much later. So amateurs kept their status and the strength of fields was much greater than today.

In the US Open, Jones's four victories still give him a share of the record. In the other years between 1922 and 1930 he finished 11th – a dismal failure in Jones's terms – was second twice, and lost two play-offs.

His record in the British Open was the most remarkable of all. He first appeared in 1921 when aged 19. After two rounds he was four behind the leaders but then had a disastrous 46 to the turn at St Andrews, double-bogeyed the next two holes – and tore up his card.

He did not appear again in a British Open until 1926. As it was a Walker Cup year, his travelling expenses were paid and the US team then went on to compete in the Amateur. Miffed at not winning, and wanting to show the British what he was made of, Jones decided to stay on for the Open at Royal Lytham and St Anne's. He won, in the end as a result of a cracking mid-iron to the heart of the 71st green from a sandy lie in the rough.

Though he couldn't really afford the trip, Jones felt he had to return for the St Andrews Open the following year. A champion owed it to the public to defend his title. He won comfortably this time with a record score and no theatricals necessary.

Transatlantic Double Whammy

His final Open appearance was at Hoylake in 1930. Again he won, despite once dropping eight shots in the space of three holes and, in his final round, once taking five more to get down when being just short of a par five in two. 1930 was the miracle year, with Jones winning the Amateur and Open Championships of both Britain and America. He had had a hunch that this might just be possible, and in the winter had taken the unusual step, for those days, of trying to keep fit.

Shortly after the completion of the never-to-be-repeated Grand Slam at Merion in 1930, Jones decided to retire. Alexander the Great always felt that his empire could be even bigger. Jones felt that there were no more fields left to conquer.

Instead, he designed some of the best iron clubheads ever, and was instrumental in the design of the Masters Tournament and of the Augusta course. With his amateur status gone, he also made a lot of money from his golf fame.

> **I'd run into Bobby, and he would absolutely annihilate me. You have no idea how good Bobby was.**
>
> *Francis Ouimet*

JACK NICKLAUS

THE COURSE MANAGER WHO CHANGED

Jack Nicklaus knew he was comfortably the best there was and, many would say, played too cautiously. If he had a weakness, it was arrogance. He knew he ought to win and didn't want to let the others in through playing bold shots which could have gone wrong. Safety was almost always his watchword.

That is, until the final round, with Nicklaus, say, a few strokes behind in a major championship and no longer anything to lose. Then, for his last-round tee shots, he would leave the long irons in the bag. At Muirfield in 1966, he manoeuvred his way around, mostly playing the irons from the tee for placement and avoiding the hayfields along the fairways. He won. Several years later, at the same course, he arrived as both Masters and US Open champion. To achieve the modern Grand Slam (Masters, US Open, British Open and US PGA in the same year) was a serious possibility.

Charge of the late brigade

Nicklaus, with a round to play, lay six strokes behind the leader, Lee Trevino. Now he would have to go for everything. For a while, it all came off. About two holes behind, Trevino and Jacklin heard the roars come back to them as the Nicklaus birdies mounted. He was out in 32 and then birdied the next two holes. Suddenly he was in the lead. But

> ## " Jack is playing an entirely different game, and one which I'm not even familiar with. "
>
> *Bobby Jones, watching Nicklaus win the 1965 Masters*

HIS LAST MAJOR? *Nicklaus after winning the 1986 Masters*

there were no more birdies and one dropped shot meant, in the end, that Nicklaus – despite his fine 66 – finished a shot behind Trevino's winning total. He had left it too late.

There were many of these magnificent last-round charges in both major championships and tournament play, but it makes one wonder how much greater his record might have been if he had attacked from the very first shot in the first round. Instead, Nicklaus usually played a cautious game. He analyzed a course and, particularly from the tee to the fairway, concentrated on placement. Even if the green was an open target, he would often not go for the flag but aim for a safer area of the green. From that point on he felt confident that the piston-like action

of his putting stroke would not let him down. Indeed he has been one of the most nerveless putters of all.

The wonder of the age

Like Jones about 40 years before, Nicklaus (with two US Amateurs under his belt and a near miss in the 1960 US Open) was quickly recognized as a rising star. He truly became one with his first professional season win in the 1962 US Open, which included the added drama of beating the great Arnold Palmer in an 18-hole play-off.

Despite the overwhelming popularity of Arnold Palmer, Nicklaus soon became the new wonder of the age and easily the dominant golfer on the world scene. In 1963, his potential stature was confirmed when he added both the Masters and the US PGA to his record.

When he won the 1965 Masters, breaking the Hogan scoring record by three strokes, winning by a record nine strokes and including a single round of 64, Bobby Jones was moved to remark that his performance was "the greatest in golf history".

Nicklaus had undoubtedly become the greatest golfer in the world, and his dominance lasted from the early 1960s until, you could say, 1977, when Tom Watson managed – just – to beat Nicklaus in both the Masters and the Open. He was the new Number 1.

Even so, Nicklaus was not to be out of the reckoning for a good many years to come. In 1980 he came back from his worst year to take both the US Open and the US PGA. In 1982 he came agonizingly close to adding a record-breaking fifth US Open to his record at Pebble Beach, only foiled by Watson's little pitch from greenside rough on

Career Milestones

1940 *Born Columbus, Ohio.*
1956 *Wins Ohio Amateur Championship at age 16.*
1959 *First US Amateur Championship at 19.*
1961 *US Amateur champion for second time.*
1962 *Wins first US Open, defeating Arnold Palmer in play-off at Oakmont.*
1963 *Two-time major winner, taking both the Masters and US PGA.*
1965 *Second victory in Masters.*
1966 *Completes Grand Slam of all four majors when he follows a third Masters victory with his first British Open.*
1967 *Second victory in US Open.*
1970 *British Open Champion for the second time.*
1971 *Second US PGA .*
1972 *Another two-major year with victories in the Masters and US Open.*
1973 *Wins his 15th major, a third US PGA title.*
1975 *His fourth two-major season, as in 1963, taking the Masters and US PGA.*
1978 *Becomes British Open Champion for the third time at St. Andrews*
1980 *His fifth two-major year: a fourth US Open win and fifth US PGA title.*
1983 *Winning Ryder Cup Captain.*
1986 *Aged 46, wins his record sixth Masters.*
1987 *Losing Ryder Cup Captain, as USA goes down 13–15 on the course he built.*

the 71st which astonishingly went into the hole. He had one more major in him, surging up the field over the last nine holes with one of his greatest charges to win the 1986 Masters. It may well be that he will never again put together four superb championship rounds to win – but he is still highly capable of shooting a 65 here and there.

ARNOLD PALMER

BATTLING ARNIE THRILLS HIS ARMY

Arnold Palmer had a style of play that was largely responsible for his unique charisma. He has always made the game seem a battle against the golf course. Spectators at an event and the television viewers at home loved to see him play and even today, when he is well into his 60s, many would rather see him open a soft drink can than others hole a full bunker shot.

Top players have mostly hit the ball very hard, but that has often been disguised by a rhythmic swing with the real acceleration coming only in the strike area, followed by a finish that is poised and sometimes elegant. Not so with Arnold. The takeaway is quite fast, and after impact the club is flung towards the sky. Sometimes it can look more like a boxer throwing a knock-out punch.

It may not look pretty, but it does look very forceful indeed – and it worked. Palmer is one of the best drivers of a golf ball the game has seen. The method worked equally well for the long and medium irons, usually full shots. However, Palmer was never up with the best when he had to play, for example, a finessed wedge or a gentle eight-iron. Giving the ball a good smash has always been his territory.

Attacking the hole

At his best, the same applied to his game around and on the greens. The aim wasn't to get the shot stone dead, but to hole it. This was especially true of his putting. Many concentrate on trying to achieve perfect pace, so that the ball gently drops into the hole. Not Palmer in the great years. He gave it a firm rap. If he missed, there was no problem with the return from four feet or so.

With the wear of the years, Palmer became less confident. Arguably his long game actually improved, but his putting in particular was increasingly cautious. Instead of aiming to bang it into the hole, he began to want to be sure of getting down in two. He also partly abandoned his policy of always going for the flag – and never mind the penalties for failure – in favour of more percentage shots.

A second important element of his appeal is his expressive face. Spectators always felt they could feel what Arnie was going through. Joy, amusement, anger, disappointment, amazement, ecstasy and even depression – all were on view.

Although Palmer had won two Masters by April 1960, his legend really began with the 1960 US Open in June. He went into the final round six strokes behind the leader, but thought that a 65 might still swing things his way. Out in 30, he parred his way home while his two closest rivals, the aging Ben Hogan and young Jack Nicklaus, faltered.

Instantly, he had the reputation of being the man who could mount a last-round charge to victory, and it remained with him throughout his main career, even though it was by no means entirely true. Palmer was probably better at seizing an early lead and then keeping his nerve right through to the finish.

Blazing a British trail

In Britain, he transformed the Open Championship almost overnight from a slightly parochial affair which interested few Americans (in 1960 the dominant force in world golf) into a major event on the world scene. He came second in that centenary Open and then won the next two years, producing his greatest major championship performance in the Troon Open of 1962. US entries gradually grew from that period onwards, and a great debt is owed to Palmer for the clear fact that the Open Championship field is far more representative of world talent than the other three majors.

The appeal of Arnold Palmer continues, even though it is over 30 years since he last won a major. On the US Senior Tour and on his occasional appearances elsewhere, Arnie still has his "Army", however far down the field he may be. And because of his appeal he is said to be the highest earner of them all.

Career Milestones

1929 Born Latrobe, Pennsylvania.
1954 US Amateur Champion, after which he turns professional.
1955 First professional win, the Canadian Open.
1958 Wins his first major, the Masters.
1960 Two majors in the year, the Masters and US Open.
1961 Wins British Open Championship.
1962 Two more majors, a third Masters and second British Open Championship.
1963 Becomes the last Ryder Cup Captain to play in the event, leading the USA to a 23–9 victory.
1964 Wins his fourth, and last, Masters.
1975 Ryder Cup Captain for the second time, this time in his home state.

> **“He comes onto a tee looking like a prize fighter climbing into the ring ready for a world championship bout.”**
>
> *Charles Price, US golf writer*

ARNOLD PALMER *The face always shows his feelings*

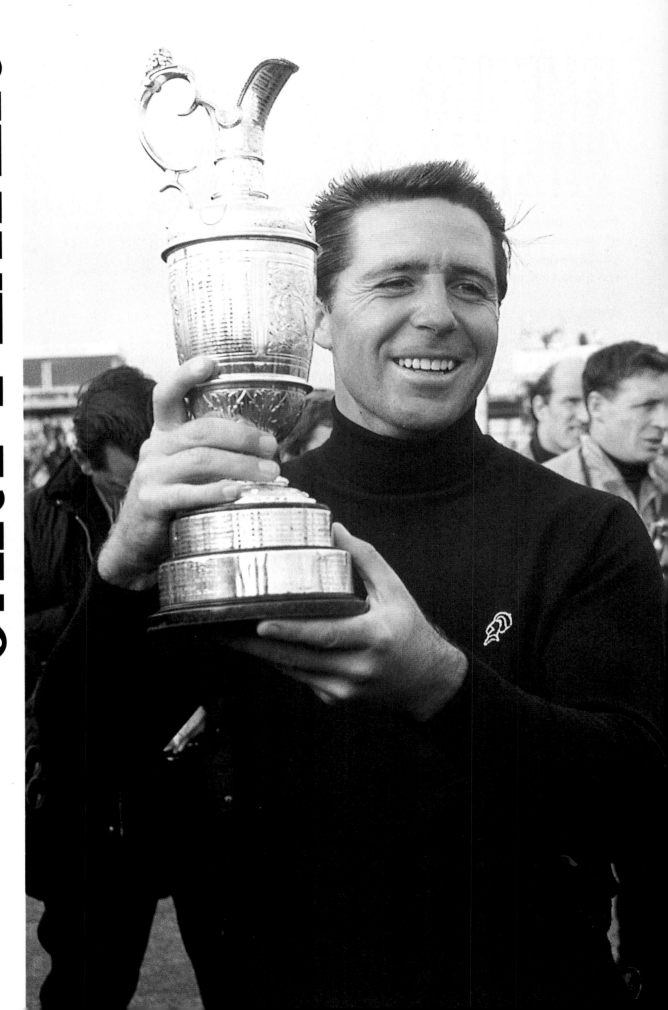

GARY PLAYER

THE GREAT PRACTISER

Gary Player could hole a chip or bunker shot or play a ball dead by the holeside. No fluke was involved. The results were achieved only with remorseless practice. For both these shots Player has a method which may be unique. The stroke is a downward stab.

His short game has remained Player's greatest strength over a career which has lasted about 40 years, more than 25 of those seeing him contend for and win major championships. Yet when he first arrived in Britain in the mid-1950s he was advised by professionals of the time to give up the game as a livelihood, go back to South Africa and just play for fun. Opinion was that Gary had a hooker's grip, that his swing was

> ❝ **You know, it's truly amazing. The more I practise, the luckier I get.** ❞
>
> *Player, answering taunts that he was a lucky golfer*

too flat and he lacked rhythm and feel for the game. Perhaps unnoticed was the effectiveness of that stab on the shot shorts. You could say he was the first great golfer to expect to get down in two more once he was near the green.

A regime for length

Another first for Player was the emphasis he put on physical fitness and diet. Before his time, most golfers considered that just playing the game was enough to keep you in trim. The same was largely true of eating and drinking. Moderation was good enough.

Player being a small man, one of the main aims of his fitness regime was to increase his length from the tee. Compared to a Nicklaus, hitting a wedge for his second shot on a long

par four, he found himself using a medium iron. Player once said he had gained about 25 yards from his healthy foods and strenuous exercise. Though those yards were undoubtedly important, far more significant was his will to win. As someone else said: "Gary just likes beating people."

He began doing that in the mid-1950s and by 1958 had become one of the rare overseas golfers to win in the USA. But his breakthrough to the status of a golfer to be reckoned with on the world scene came in 1959 when he won the Open Championship at Muirfield. Successes in the Masters and the US PGA followed in the early 1960s, and his victory in the 1965 US Open made him one of the happy band to complete the slam of all four majors. Even more, with Nicklaus and Palmer, he was a founder member of what came to be known as the Big Three. The advertising and sponsorship money poured in.

In his native South Africa, with the decline of Bobby Locke, Player was by far the dominant golfer. But he had to be an international golfer, and over the years has probably clocked up more air mileage than anyone else. The United States was his main arena, but he also made annual appearances in Britain and played in Australia often enough to take their Open seven times. In Britain he jointly holds the records

Career Milestones

1935 *Born Johannesburg, South Africa.*
1958 *Earns his first US Tour win.*
1959 *Wins his first major, the British Open Championship.*
1961 *Collects the Masters.*
1962 *Wins his third major, the US PGA.*
1965 *Takes the US Open to become only the fourth player to win all four majors.*
1968 *Wins his second British Open Championship.*
1972 *Wins his sixth major, the US PGA.*
1974 *Wins two majors in the year, the Masters and British Open Championship.*
1978 *Wins his ninth major, the Masters at age 42.*

of winning the World Matchplay Championship five times and the Open on three occasions. His 1959 success at Muirfield was perhaps a little lucky, as those in pursuit defeated themselves. At Carnoustie in 1968, however, he had to battle head-to-head with Jack Nicklaus. Six years later, at Royal Lytham and St Anne's, he gave one of his finest performances with much use of his one-iron in the strong wind.

Player masters green

Perhaps his finest hour, however, came at Augusta in 1978, when Player was becoming a figure of the past. Entering the final round of the Masters, he was seven behind leader Hubert Green. His outward nine in 34 was good but seemed unlikely to affect the outcome of the tournament. But his second half did. With six birdies, he was home in 30. Player's remarkable 64 – one of the greatest final rounds in major championship golf – gave him victory when Hubert Green missed a short putt on the last green.

Perhaps that was Player's last hurrah, but he is still competitive on the US Senior Tour and in recent years has represented South Africa on the nation's return to international team golf in the Alfred Dunhill Cup at St Andrews.

PUNCHING HIS WEIGHT *Gary Player at Muirfield in 1972*

GENE SARAZEN

THE SHORTEST CHAMPION

Gene Sarazen had a career that fell into two distinct and highly successful phases – the second culminating in the achievement of the first professional Grand Slam.

First came a change of name. Born of Italian immigrant stock, he decided that Eugene Saraceni, while fine for a violinist, didn't sound right for a 17-year-old who wanted to be a professional golfer. So he went into his career as Gene Sarazen.

By the time the 1922 US Open came around, though he had won a tournament, he was very little known – not surprising at 20 years and four months of age. At the end of that week at Skokie, Illinois, he'd become a national figure on the golf scene. Sarazen closed with a 68 to win – at the time the lowest final round recorded to win a championship .

In the same year, he also won the US PGA and beat Walter Hagen in a challenge match for the "The World Championship". In the following year, he again beat Hagen, this time in the final of the US PGA, then played as match play.

Getting to grips

Suddenly, Sarazen seemed to be the dominant player. However, Hagen was far from finished and Jones was emerging as the golfer who could beat them all. Sarazen also began to experience technical problems. His swing was compact and powerful (especially so for a man of only 5 feet 3 inches, the shortest of major champions) but his grip was laughable by modern teaching standards. With the left hand, he could see four knuckles and explained that there were advantages: the left wrist didn't break down when almost side on to the line of fire.

There was an even more weird feature of his grip: his left thumb played no part but flapped in the air. Sarazen also, like Jack Nicklaus, used the relatively rare interlocking grip, where the little finger of the left hand is fitted between the index and middle finger of the right.

The fast reactions of extreme youth, it could be argued, could cope with these unorthodoxies but, after the first flush of success, Sarazen did not maintain his pace. He could win tournaments from time to time, but the majors were beyond his grasp.

Inventing the sand wedge

He entered his second phase. By the late 1920s and early 1930s he was winning good tournament money, featuring often in the majors, and was only narrowly defeated, 1 down, in the final of the 1930 US PGA.

He was a potentially great player once again – and then also had a revolutionary idea. During this time even players of true excellence had trouble with bunker shots. Today most would prefer to have a good lie in a greenside bunker rather than a good grassy lie from the same distance. The lofted clubs of the day were not effective. Because they bit into the sand, the only way to use them was either to flick the ball off the surface or explode it out, hitting behind the ball and then down and through.

Sarazen decided that what was needed was a clubhead that would glide through the sand, slicing underneath the ball, instead of digging in. So he took a club with a broad sole and added lead solder to raise the height of the rear. After much experimenting and test driving he had cracked the problem. Future players would be able to aim at getting near the flag from a greenside bunker instead of just being content to get their ball out of the hazard.

Sarazen himself was on his way

RYDER CUP PRIDE *Sarazen was always at his best in match play*

> **Perhaps the reason why it all seemed so easy in 1922 was that I had no idea at the time how difficult the things I was accomplishing really were.**
>
> *Gene Sarazen*

to more major championships and had a glorious 1932, first winning the British Open at Prince's, Sandwich, in 1932 by five strokes and then, a fortnight after, the US Open.

A year later, he took the US PGA for the third time but his most mystical achievement came in the second – and his first – Masters. With no apparent chance of catching Craig Wood, he suddenly holed a four-wood second shot at the par-five 15th, in front of just a handful of spectators. Sarazen had drawn level and went on to win the play-off the next day.

In 1940 he lost a play-off for the US Open and continued to play on the US Tour. Much later he still had a couple of spectacular shots left. On day one of the 1973 Open at Troon he holed in one with a five-iron shot on the Postage Stamp hole (the 8th). The next day he missed the green and was bunkered. No great problem: he holed his shot from the sand.

LEE TREVINO

UNORTHODOX CAN WORK

Lee Trevino is an odd-looking golfer indeed, but at his peak around the early 1970s this effervescent Mexican-American could beat the best. Trevino's method centres on having a hooker's grip with his left hand and then doing a variety of things to ensure that he plays with a slice. It seems Trevino never was willing to change his grip and so he had to produce counter-measures to avoid a right-to-left shape of shot.

For a start, he takes up the classic slicer's stance, very open to his target line. The club is then taken away on an outside path, but eventually is inside to out in the impact area. To stop that clubhead being shut at impact, Trevino drives strongly with his legs and also pulls the club through with his left side and arm. But really there's more to it than that. Ben Hogan once remarked that he liked watching Trevino because he worked his hands so beautifully through the ball. Trevino is very controlled in the strike zone and has great feel for how his swing is working.

Even though his swing proved effective, no one praised it as he took centre stage. It was described as being that of a weekend hacker and "more suitable for scything grass with".

Difficult hacker to beat

In his 20s, Trevino served in the US armed forces overseas and returned to work in local golf. He did not attempt to qualify for the US Tour. However, he did play in the 1966 US Open. His 54th position made no headlines, but it was a respectable performance when he had previously done little more than win the Texas State Open, which was not a Tour event. The following year, he gave it another go and came in fifth. Again no headlines, but it gave Trevino the feeling of certainty that he could compete with the best.

He proved it at Oak Hill in 1968 when he destroyed Bert Yancey in head-to head play over the final round to win by four, the first man to break 70 in all four rounds of a US Open. Some thought this was a fluke win, that Trevino had happened to hit peak form for one week, and that this was his first and also his last tournament win. In fact he was off on a great career.

In retrospect, his peak years ran from his US Open victory to around the mid-1970s, though he remained a player to be reckoned with for long after that, his last major victory coming with the US PGA as late as 1984. Again, at Shoal Creek, all his rounds were below 70.

Partly through his consistency, Trevino always won very large amounts of money on the US Tour and never had a bad year. For a time he seemed a likely rival to Jack Nicklaus for world supremacy. After being leading money-winner on the US Tour in 1970, he went on to have an even better year in 1971. In the space of five weeks he took the US Open, the Canadian Open and the Open Championship. And in the US Open he had beaten Jack Nicklaus in a play-off. In 1972, he again beat Jack Nicklaus – and Tony Jacklin – for the British Open Championship. But Nicklaus continued on his winning ways while Trevino's peak years were already over. No threat to Nicklaus for supremacy in world golf, he continued to pile up tournament victories.

Office gossip – and a windfall

Trevino is unusual in his relationship with spectators. Most players look as if they are having rather a bad day at the office. Sometimes they are anguished, at other times distressed, pained or just plain bored. Trevino, uniquely, is always full of chat. He does quiet down when in contention, but not completely.

For a time during the 1980s he seemed to be losing interest in tournament golf. In the sunset of a great career he was perhaps thinking more of TV, company days and the like. But the Senior Tour came as a gift when he reached 50. Since then, he has been the most effective competitor, aided considerably by a Nicklaus who does not care to play often. But, as the money pours in, Trevino probably doesn't mind in the least.

Career Milestones

1939 *Born Dallas, Texas.*
1967 *Wins his first tournament, the Hawaiian Open.*
1968 *Wins US Open.*
1971 *Wins his second US Open and follows it with British Open Championship.*
1972 *Successfully defends British Open Championship.*
1974 *Wins his fifth major, the US PGA.*
1984 *Wins his second US PGA eight years after being seriously injured by a bolt of lightning at Western Open.*
1985 *Losing Ryder Cup Captain at the Belfry.*

> ❝ **You don't know the meaning of pressure until you play for five bucks with two bucks in your pocket.** ❞
>
> *Trevino*

LEE TREVINO *Always a wonderful player from sand*

THE TRIUMVIRATE

TWENTY YEARS OF DOMINANCE

J. H. Taylor, Harry Vardon and James Braid were exact golfing contemporaries who together, astonishingly, took no fewer than 16 of the Open Championships between 1894 and 1914.

J. H. Taylor emerged first, winning the Open in 1984 and 1985. For a brief spell, having set new standards, he was thought almost invincible. Taylor's style was to stand flat-footed and give the ball a thump, with most of the power appearing to come from his forearms. Two features which distinguished his play were low flight – which helped him to be a great player in high winds – and his ability to impart fizzing backspin with his mashie (about a five-iron). This enabled him to be perhaps the first player to go directly for the flag and stop the ball quickly. One wonders how he would have used modern wedges.

James Braid was a formidable golfer by the late 1890s; his first Open win, however, was a little overdue when it came in 1901. He then became the dominant member of the Triumvirate, his fifth success in the Open in 1910 putting him temporarily ahead of his two rivals and also making him the first man to win

> ❝ From 1894 to 1914, they were to rule the world of golf far more completely than did Arnold Palmer, Jack Nicklaus and Gary Player half a century later. ❞

John Hopkins, golf writer

IN HIS SUNDAY BEST *Taylor after his first British Open win*

five Opens. He then lost form to some extent. Of the three, Braid, in his best years, was very likely the best putter and the longest hitter, with a flailing lash of a swing.

Harry Vardon, technically, was the most revolutionary of the Triumvirate. He is sometimes supposed to have invented the "Vardon grip" – where the little finger of the right hand overlaps the index finder of the left. In fact, this method of holding the club had been used a few years earlier by the famous Scottish amateur Johnny Laidlay – and perhaps others. Both Taylor and Braid used the same grip, and it was named after Vardon simply because he became the most famous and the most imitated of the Triumvirate.

Vardon's swing was far more revolutionary than his grip. Compared with the conventional "St Andrews swing", which involved a wide stance and a flat path back and through, producing a low flight, Vardon's swing path was very much

higher, and the downswing was also naturally much steeper. The result was the high flight which made him consistent at holding fairways and greens and was particularly useful when the ground was hard. It was soon apparent that no one could equal Vardon when it came to playing wooden club shots to the flag, while his driving accuracy became legendary.

Harry Vardon arrived in 1896, first defeating Taylor by 8 and 7 in a match at Ganton and then defeating him for the Open title after a 36-hole play-off. For a few years Vardon was nearly invincible, and by 1903 he had won his fourth Open title.

Then he was afflicted by tuberculosis (and poor putting). He continued to be a great player, but the Open eluded him until 1911. In 1914 he won again, becoming the first and still the only man to win the Open Championship six times.

Today, the Open tallies are usually regarded as the measure of these great players. The other tournaments they played in the same period have become forgotten events. However, the results of recent research by Peter Lewis, director of the British Golf Museum, are revealing. In this period, Vardon won 52 events, 34 per cent of all those he entered, while he topped 50 per cent for first and second places. In his most dazzling period, he won 17 out of 22 tournaments and was second in the others! This is dominance of a kind that only Byron Nelson was able to achieve in later years.

Braid had 34 victories and Taylor 32, but they were a step below Vardon. In his best year, 1898, Vardon won ten times, whereas the other two never bettered four in any one year.

Career Milestones

JAMES BRAID
1870 *Born in Earlsferry, Fife.*
1901 *Wins his first British Open Championship.*
1905 *Collects his second British Open Championship.*
1906 *Successfully defends his British Open Championship.*
1908 *Takes his third British Open Championship in four years.*
1910 *After another year's gap, wins a record fifth British Open Championship.*

J. H. TAYLOR
1871 *Born in Northam, Devon.*
1894 *Wins his first British Open Championship.*
1895 *Successfully defends his British Open Championship.*
1900 *Wins his third British Open Championship.*
1909 *Wins his fourth British Open Championship.*
1913 *Equals the record of Braid and Vardon as he wins his fifth British Open.*
1933 *Captains Great Britain Ryder Cup team to victory.*

HARRY VARDON
1870 *Born in Grouville, Jersey.*
1896 *Wins his first British Open Championship.*
1898 *Collects his second British Open Championship.*
1899 *Successfully defends his British Open Championship.*
1900 *Goes to America and wins US Open.*
1903 *Emulates the record of three others with his fourth British Open Championship.*
1911 *Equals Braid 's record as he wins his fifth British Open Championship.*
1914 *Wins his record sixth British Open Championship.*

TOM WATSON

THE FRESH-FACED KID FROM KANSAS CITY

Tom Watson made his majestic mark on the game with five British Open victories in only nine entries, and wrested away from Jack Nicklaus the crown of the world's leading golfer.

Watson is no longer a kid but he is still fresh-faced and still lives in Kansas City. To remain faithful to roots is unusual among professional golfers. Americans tend to flock to the temperate climes of, say, Florida or California, but Tom Watson, on the other hand, has remained in his home area of Kansas, relishing the challenge of winter golf with his friends – usually not professional golfers.

Early in his career (he turned professional in 1971) Watson earned the reputation of being a "choker", a man who was found wanting when the pressure was on. That was first turned around when he won the 1974 Western Open, shortly after having "choked" in the US Open, blowing a one-stroke lead he held going into the final round with a disastrous 79.

The Open road

It was the British Open Championship that began to establish him as a force to be reckoned with. In 1975 he arrived unheralded at Carnoustie, having finished poorly in both the Masters and US Open, and without even the time to play a full practice round. Eyes were on others as Watson went quietly about his business. He was hardly noticed by the television cameras until he holed a long birdie putt on the final hole to set a target which no one could better. However, one matched it, Jack Newton, but Watson narrowly won the 18-hole play-off the following day.

This success sparked winning ways, and he soon became the dominant player on the US Tour, being five times leading money-winner in the period 1977 to 1984. It quickly came to seem that this might be the man who would dethrone Jack Nicklaus as World Number 1. Psychologically, that came in the 1977 British Open at Turnberry, when, playing the last two rounds head to head, Watson became champion when some great play brought a one-stroke margin over Nicklaus.

Watson was now the man to beat in this event. His next success was even more emphatic. He swept into a comfortable lead at Muirfield after a 64 in the third round and cruised home by four strokes.

Troon in 1982 saw tougher going for Watson. There were others, such as Nick Price and Bobby Clampett, who "ought" to have won. As he said: "I didn't win it. It was given to me." Even so, it was Watson who produced a steady final round and a firm few closing holes while the others faltered.

It was a different story at Royal Birkdale the following year. Several players subdued the course, which was not playing at its most difficult. In the final round Watson lost his narrow lead and didn't regain it until he birdied the 16th. He came to the last, a long four, needing a par to win. The way he achieved it was classic. First he banged a long drive down the middle and he followed up with a superb long iron to the heart of the green. That was that.

Elusive victory

With five Open Championships to his credit in only nine entries, Harry

DOMINANT FORCE *The Open trophy seemed a fixture in Watson's hands*

Career Milestones

1949 *Born Kansas City, Missouri.*
1974 *First US Tour win, the Western Open.*
1975 *Wins his first major, the British Open Championship.*
1977 *Wins two majors, the Masters and British Open Championship.*
1980 *Collects his third British Open Championship.*
1981 *Wins his second Masters title.*
1982 *Has another two-major year, the US Open and British Open Championship.*
1983 *Joins Peter Thomson as a five-time modern British Open Champion.*
1993 *Successful Ryder Cup Captain, as the US win at the Belfry.*

Vardon's record six victories were nearly in his grasp and he was ready to make that mark at St Andrews in 1984. However, a loose long iron to the 71st hole (the 17th) finally killed his chances.

Like Tony Jacklin after his 1972 Open disaster, Tom Watson has not been quite the same man since. However, he continues to feature prominently in the majors and other events, though he has not won on the US Tour since 1987.

His long game remains imperious but his short game – especially his putting – is not what it was. At his peak, Watson used to give the hole a chance, with a firm rap. If he went a few feet past he was confident he could hole the return. In more recent years he has been far more tentative. There are still the good days with low scoring but as he approaches the later 40s, he is less able to maintain his form through four rounds.

❝ I think we are paid far too much. We are not worth it. ❞

Tom Watson

THE GREAT GOLFERS

Every era produces its great golfers. These are the men and women who have captivated the gallery down the years not merely with their play but by their charisma. They drew spectators who may personally have had only the most rudimentary golfing talent, but who were awe-struck by the skills of their idols. Here is a selection of 200 of the greatest of them all.

A

Amy Alcott
Born: February 22, 1956
Kansas City, Mo, USA

At club level many women golfers take the club back much too far and then have to waste effort in lifting it back again to a horizontal position. Alcott is the reverse. The club goes back little beyond shoulder height and she then delivers a very firm blow indeed. The short back-swing, if not taken to extremes, can be an aid to consistency, and over a long professional career of about 20 years she has indeed always performed well from week to week, though her career may now be on the wane. In her first 15 years on the LPGA Tour, she was never worse than 18th on the money list and often did a great deal better than that, five times finishing in the top five. Her tournament wins are also impressive. Between 1975 and 1991 she amassed 29 wins, of which five rank as majors: three Dinah Shores,

one Peter Jackson plus the 1980 US Women's Open. Her best years were 1979, 1980 and 1984, with four wins in each of these years. Perhaps her outstanding achievement was her US Women's Open victory. Her 280 aggregate was then a record for the event and saw her home by a remarkable nine-stroke margin.

AMY ALCOTT *Short swing can work*

Peter Alliss
Born: February 28, 1931
Berlin, Germany

This is a man who likes talking, and does it incomparably well. Apparently it all began when a BBC producer heard him keeping his fellow tour players in uproar on a journey back to England from Ireland. An invitation followed for him to make a few comments on the air about a tournament round he had just completed and how the course was playing. In due course this led on to television commentary immediately after his main playing career ended in 1969. Peter is now regarded as comfortably the world's best golf commentator and has been voted, in Britain, the best sports commentator. As a professional golfer, he never quite fulfilled his potential, though he was very good indeed, winning some twenty important events during the 1950s and 1960s, including three successive events in Europe in 1958. He was selected for every Ryder Cup team bar one between 1953 and 1969, and also played ten times for England in the World Cup. Alliss was one of the longest and most consistent hitters in the game and was also very

tidy around the green. But his putting became his Achilles heel. He had begun with a highly unorthodox grip – but it worked. He was advised to change it, and did, never to be the same player again.

Willie Anderson
Born: circa 1880
North Berwick, Scotland

In the US Open, Anderson set two records that have still to be surpassed. In 1905 he won his fourth championship, a record since equalled only by Bobby Jones, Ben Hogan and Jack Nicklaus – but even they couldn't go on to a fifth title. Anderson also won three of his titles in a row, an achievement which might have been matched by Ben Hogan – winner in 1948, 1950 and 1951 – but for his severe car accident early in 1949. Anderson had a very high performance level in the US Open, for besides his victories he had one second place, one third, two fourths and three fifths. In a relatively short career – he died at the age of 30 – Anderson was nearly always in contention in this championship. He had numerous successes in local tournaments, most of which have disappeared into unrecorded history, as well as a remarkable four wins in the Western Open, which in those days ranked second only to the US Open. Anderson is unusual in that his victories came with two different kinds of ball, the gutta percha and the rubber core. He had a flat swing, with a good deal of bend in the left arm, and opponents thought his greatest strength was an unflappable temperament.

Isao Aoki
Born: August 31, 1942
Abiko, Chiba, Japan

Aoki is one of the most unlikely looking great players, for he uses a remarkably – now unfashionably wristy – technique for both full shots and the short game. In his putting stroke, where he is one of the best performers ever, he uses a centre-shaft putter with the toe of the club cocked high in the air – and raps it into the hole. He is one of the rare Japanese golfers to come close to winning a major championship. This is because the Japan Tour is very lucrative indeed, so few trouble themselves to play on other tours. Aoki does, and in 1994 he won well over $500,000 on the US Senior PGA Tour. He has been leading money winner in Japan five times and has won more than fifty times in both his home country and worldwide.

ISAO AOKI *Playing at St Andrews, 1990*

He is the only Japanese to have won on four different tours – Japan, Australia, Europe and the USA. Perhaps his greatest international success came in the 1980 US Open, where he broke the scoring record with rounds of 68, 68, 68, 70 and still finished a couple of strokes behind Nicklaus. He won the 1978 World Matchplay title at Wentworth and the 1983 European Open, while his third-round 63 in the 1980 Open Championship at Muirfield equalled the lowest ever shot in the event.

George Archer
Born: October 1, 1939,
San Francisco, Ca, USA

Archer is one of the players who must rejoice that the Senior Tour has become such a great commercial success. In the 1990–94 period, he has averaged over $750,000 per year and has twice got very near to the million mark. In just a few years he has piled up 15 victories, already a little better than he did on the main tour, with 12 wins between 1965 and 1984. One of these was a major, the 1969 Masters, where he began with a very good first round of 67 and held on to win by a single stroke. The greatest strength of his game is his putting, where he must surely be ranked in, say, the top half a dozen of modern times. From his great height of 6 feet 5½ inches he crouches low over the ball and then gets himself even nearer by gripping well down the handle of his putter. Besides his highly unusual set-up to the ball for putting, Archer likes to feel that he is guiding the putter with his left hand, while the right is what gives him feel for pace. Playing in the 1980 Heritage Classic he set a tour record by taking only 94 putts for the four rounds.

Tommy Armour
Born: September 24, 1895
Edinburgh, Scotland

Tommy Armour won three major championships. First came the US Open of 1927, when he holed a putt of 10 feet or so on the last hole to tie Harry Cooper and then beat him in a close-fought play-off. Armour's effort had been particularly fine because he had scattered shots in his

PAUL AZINGER *A crowd favourite at Kiawah Island in the 1993 Ryder Cup*

fourth round and needed an excellent last four holes to draw level. His next win was in the 1930 US PGA, where he had a narrow victory in the final over Gene Sarazen. But the prize he really sought was the British Open, and he won it, against the odds, at Carnoustie in 1931, producing a very good final round while others threw it away. By this time Armour was already on his way out, suffering from the putting "yips", a term he himself invented. When he retired from the game he became a very highly paid teacher and best-selling author of instruction books. Armour achieved the reputation of being a superb iron player. Tommy himself thought he was a better wooden club player and that it was his positioning from the tee which gave him easier shots into greens. Perhaps that is why the woods he is said to have originally designed are much sought after today. Tommy is also remembered for the immortal reply he gave when challenged about his notoriously slow play: "Whoever said golf was supposed to be played fast?"

Paul Azinger
Born: January 6, 1960
Holyoke, Ma, USA

"When you're 33 you don't expect anybody to tell you that you've got cancer. I was in my prime. I felt bullet-proof." Before 1993, Azinger was possibly the man in American golf thought most likely to become a superstar. In a seven-year winning run from 1987 on the US Tour he had four times been in the top four

money winners and never lower than 11th. In 1993 he took the US PGA Championship. Then, following the best season of his professional career, Azinger was informed that a troublesome problem in the shoulders was in fact lymphoma in the right shoulder-blade. Happily, good performances towards the end of 1994 seem to indicate both recovery from the disease and a return to golf form. However, he is not a dominant figure and may be influenced by the memory of his failure in the British Open at Muirfield in 1987. That is the one Nick Faldo won because Azinger dropped shots at both of the last two holes to let Faldo in. However he has also had plenty of successes. The most dramatic came in the 1993 Memorial Tournament, when he holed out from a greenside bunker to win by a stroke from Corey Pavin.

Ian Baker-Finch
Born: October 24, 1960,
Nambour, Australia

At Birkdale in the 1991 British Open, all the talk concerned whether or not Seve Ballesteros could perform on the final round and win. Meanwhile, no one was paying much attention to Baker-Finch. They soon were, after he birdied five of the first seven holes and played the first nine in 29, a very rare feat indeed. He finished with a 66, to win by two strokes. Much earlier he had looked a champion – at St Andrews in 1984, when rounds of 68 and 66 gave him a three-stroke lead. A 71 then left him tied for the lead with Tom Watson, but a disaster at the 1st hole in the final round damaged his confidence. Playing to the green, his ball twisted back into the Swilcan Burn which fronts it. And that was that. He managed to break 80, but only by a single stroke. His next real attempt at an Open title came in 1990 when a third-round 64 took him into a tie for second place, with Nick Faldo five strokes ahead. Faldo did not falter. Baker-Finch has been consistently successful in his homeland, Japan and Europe, but the US Tour is probably his main target. He won there, in 1989, the Southwestern Bell Colonial, and also had good years in 1990 and 1991. Since then, his form has sadly subsided.

John Ball

Born: December 24, 1861
Hoylake, England

This player has a very strong claim to be considered the greatest amateur of all time – as long as one excepts Bobby Jones. But even Jones did not win as many amateur championship titles in Britain and the United States as did Ball, who totalled eight in Britain between 1888 and 1912 and was also the beaten finalist twice. He did not compete at all in America. During his peak years in the 1890s he was fully capable of competing with the very best professionals. In 1890 he became the first Englishman to win the Open Championship, which he achieved at Prestwick as a result of extremely consistent play. In the next few years he was a man to watch out for, but was very likely far more interested in the Amateur Championship, as he may well have preferred the matchplay format and also the camaraderie of those he knew the best. Ball was not renowned as a putter, and his great strength was the accuracy of his long shots up to the flag. In this respect, he was a revolutionary player. Be-

BRIAN BARNES *Senior tour offer*

fore his great days, all had been content to aim for the green. Ball wanted to be close to the flag.

Severiano Ballesteros

see Legends pp 86–87

Miller Barber

Born: March 31, 1931
Shreveport, La, USA

Barber's money-winning achievements show how important the Senior US Tour can be. He has won close on $3¹/₂ million as one of the more effective performers, with 24 victories between 1982 and 1989. He twice led the money list and eight times finished inside the top 10. The end of 1994 saw him tieing with Lee Trevino with 24 wins, but Trevino will undoubtedly move far ahead. Barber was also extremely effective on the main US Tour, which he joined in 1959, going on to win 11 times. He played in two Ryder Cup matches, in 1969 and 1971. During the period from 1963 to 1978 he was never out of the top 40 money winners and was 12 times in the top 25. Barber seldom featured strongly in the major championships though he did equal the Masters record low round with a 64 in 1979. His best chance of victory in a major came in the 1969 US Open, which he led by three with the final round to play. However, he then fell away with a round of 78 to finish in only sixth position. Barber's swing is highly unorthodox but has worked well for him, as even a very eccentric swing can when the oddities have become more ingrained than the orthodox.

Brian Barnes

Born: June 3, 1945
Addington, England

Regarded as one of golf's eccentrics, Barnes has been known to wear shorts, smoke a pipe and drink copious quantities of canned beer when out playing a tournament. Some would say that this player's greatest achievements came in the Ryder Cup, where he was in every team from 1969 to 1979. In the 1975 event he beat Jack Nicklaus twice in singles in one day. He has also made many appearances for Scotland in both the World Cup and the Double Diamond event. The winner of nearly 29 professional tournaments, he probably had his finest hour in the 1981 Tournament Players' Championship when he had a last round of 62 which got him into a play-off, which he then won. He is a powerful player using a short backswing, followed by a lunge at the ball. He might have become a great player if he had won an Open Championship early in his career, when he had the potential. Now his main playing career has long seemed over, and he has appeared more interested in running a golf club, but he has been seen again in tournament play in recent years. Perhaps he has a Senior tour in mind.

Jim Barnes

Born: 1887
Lelant, England

Nicknamed "Long Jim" because of his 6 feet 3 inch height, Barnes emigrated from his native Cornwall in

1906 to San Francisco. In 1913 he tied for fourth place in the US Open and the following year achieved the first of three victories in the then very important Western Open. Even more significant was his victory in the first ever US PGA Championship of 1916. He also won the first post-war event in 1919, and was to reach two more finals, in 1921 and 1924, each time losing to Walter Hagen. His greatest triumph came in the 1921 US Open. His opening 69 gave him the lead and he drew away round by round, eventually finishing with what remains a record nine-stroke margin. Though Barnes became an American citizen, he still liked to return to Britain, where he tied for second place in the 1922 Open and won in 1925 in the infamous Prestwick event. It was thought that Macdonald Smith had been cheated of victory because of crowd disturbances during his final round. Barnes played in what some consider the first Ryder Cup in 1926, but was ruled out afterwards because he was not a native-born American.

Andy Bean

Born: March 13, 1953
Lafayette, USA

Is golf good for the health? In the case of professionals it's rather doubtful. Constant practice imposes stress on certain body parts, particularly the lower back and the left wrist. Andy Bean was once a real prospect for superstardom, and also physically strong enough to bite golf balls in half. He had enormous

ANDY BEAN *Could bite a golf ball in half, but his back is weaker than his jaw*

power and very good touch around the greens. In recent years, however, he has been plagued by medical problems and is now a member of the US Tour by reason of a "Special Medical Extension". His best years came in the period 1978 to 1986, when on five occasions he was in the top seven of US Tour money winners. In much the same period he accumulated all his 11 wins. Bean was a Ryder Cup player in 1987, when he had a notable victory against Ian Woosnam in his singles match. He had also played for the USA against Japan in 1984. Since those days, however, his game has declined sharply. In 1994 he entered 19 tournaments and only three times made money, finishing 253rd on the US money list, his worst ever placing. It could well be that he has it in him yet to make a come-back. If not, he has still won over $3 million.

Frank Beard

Born: May 1, 1939
Dallas, Tx, USA

Beard won 11 titles on the US Tour between 1963 and 1971 and was leading money winner in 1969. He once came close to a US Open title, in 1975, when he was in the lead after the third round but then finished disastrously. His 78, after he had finished with two bogeys, left him a stroke away from the play-off between John Mahaffey and Lou Graham. In his best years, Beard was always regarded as being somewhat colourless. Perhaps this was a reflection of his strictly businesslike attitude to the life of a professional golfer. However, Beard is also a man of other parts. His book *Pro*, published in 1970, is still the most perceptive account of what living on the US Tour is really like. When his competitive days on the tour came to an end, he continued to practise his writing skills, mainly as a columnist in a golf magazine. He produced a follow-up to *Pro* in 1992, in which he did the same job for the Senior Tour. On this tour he was quite successful, his best year coming in 1990, when he won over $300,000. However, having probably started to lose interest, he is now concentrating on television work.

Chip Beck

Born: September 12, 1956
Fayetteville, USA

Undoubtedly the highlight of Beck's career is the 59 he scored in the third round of the Las Vegas Invitational at Sunrise Golf Club in October 1991. That made him the second player, after Al Geiberger, to break the magic 60 in a US Tour event. He went out in 29, starting at the 10th, with seven birdies, and the other nine holes were just as eventful. The birdies continued to flow in, and at the last of his holes he fired in an eight-iron shot to about three feet and then completed the job. That meant a total of 13 birdies and no dropped shots – and a reward of $500,000. Beck had a quiet start to his US Tour career in 1979 and did not begin to make real money until 1983. His first big year was 1987, though he had still to win. In 1988 he rectified that with two victories. His closest approach to a major came in the 1993 Masters, when he finished second to Bernhard Langer but four strokes behind. Some observers considered that he had been mentally ready to settle for second place. However, in the Ryder Cup that same year he came from three down with five to play to defeat Barry Lane by one up.

CHIP BECK *At the 1991 Ryder Cup*

Deane Beman

Born: April 24, 1938
Washington, DC, USA

Beman succeeded Joseph Dey as commissioner of the PGA Tour in 1974 and held that position for twenty years. He earned a reputation for being an excellent administrator but also made a few enemies. Perhaps ready for a change after such a long time, he joined the Senior US Tour mid-way through the 1994 season, but made few entries and little impact. However, Beman had already shown potential by qualifying to play in the British Open and finished only a shot behind champion Gary Player in the Senior British Open at Turnberry in 1991. He had put himself through an energetic practice regime to get his game back into trim. His best golf was probably played as an amateur. He represented his country four times each in the Eisenhower Trophy and the Americas and Walker Cups. More significantly, he won the British Amateur in 1959 and the US Amateur twice – 1960 and 1963. Later he left a highly paid insurance brokerage job at the age of 29 to compete on the main US Tour from 1967 to 1974, when he won four events as well as finishing as runner-up in the 1969 US Open.

Patty Berg

Born: February 13, 1918
Minneapolis, Mn, USA

Berg reached the final of the US Women's Amateur on her first entry in 1935. She was there again two years later, but had to wait until 1938 for her first victory. A hugely successful amateur golfer, she won something like 40 events before turning professional just before the Second World War. Together with Babe Zaharias and Betty Jameson, she was one of the three founder members of the fledgling US Women's Tour, which took off properly in 1948, and in which she became a dominant force. In 1946, she had won the first Women's Open, then match play, and went on to win what was billed as the World Championship in 1953, 1954, 1955 and 1957. She was also leading money winner in 1954, 1955 and 1957. This meant that she was the first woman to pass $100,000 in career money winnings. Berg also set the low round record, 64, in 1952 which stood for 12 years until it was beaten by Mickey Wright. Having first won a professional tournament in 1941, she won her last more than 20 years later in 1962, bringing her total to 57. Her last entry came in 1980.

Tommy Bolt

Born: March 31, 1918
Haworth, USA

Bolt was a sublime striker of a golf ball and in his peak years was thought to have the most fluid golf swing in the game. However, he was a rather poor putter – the worst, he was known to claim, among his playing contemporaries. Temperamentally he could handle his bad putting, believing that the good putters were inferior players who didn't appreciate what the game of golf was all about – excellence in the shots through the green. Here Bolt excelled, but earned his "Thunderbolt" nickname through his quite frequent losses of temper when such a shot didn't come off. Clubs would be snapped over the knee or hurled to the heavens. Though already a professional for a few years, Bolt didn't join the US Tour until 1950, at the age of 32. However, he went on to win 11 tour events between 1953 and 1961, and four others of significance but not then regarded as official. His most important victory was in the 1958 US Open, which he took by four strokes from the very young Gary Player. Bolt also had a run at the Masters, in 1952, but his putting again let him down – he three-putted three of the last four greens and came in third.

Michael Bonallack

Born: December 31, 1934
Chigwell, England

Bonallack is one of just three candidates for the title of "Greatest British Amateur Ever", the others being John Ball and Harold Hilton. However, with his consecutive wins in 1968, 1969 and 1970 he achieved something that even they had not managed in the British Amateur. Bonallack had also won this event in both 1961 and 1965. Sometimes uncertain in the long shots, Bonallack was unexcelled even by his professional contemporaries at the short game in general and, particularly, at putting. Asked about his method in this department he declared that he "willed the ball into the hole". A more obvious feature was the way he spread his feet wide and crouched over the ball, a style uncommon nowadays but not earlier this century. Bonallack was indeed a master of the short game. During one of his five wins in the English Amateur Championship, one final came his way despite the fact that he missed 22 greens and still managed to get down in two more. Later, he went into golf administration, and since 1983 he has had one of the key roles in world golf as secretary of the R&A.

Julius Boros

Born: March 3, 1920
Fairfield, USA

Boros was one of those golfers who look more relaxed than they really are. Fearful of becoming locked over the ball, he evolved a method to avoid this. He would walk casually up to his ball, shuffle his feet into his stance – and then swing. It worked so well that people thought that this was the way the game should be played. Boros was a late developer, not

giving up accountancy for professional tournament play until the age of thirty. Then he immediately contended for the US Open in 1950 and was fourth the following year. In 1952 he bested the great Hogan comfortably, having trailed him by four strokes after 36 holes. If this was a surprise victory, his win in 1963 was something of a shock to Boros himself. His 76 in the third round did his chances little good, and a 72 in the afternoon round, leaving him nine over par, merely suggested he would get a reasonable pay-cheque in a very high-scoring event. But no one beat that score, and in the 18-hole play-off the following day Boros's 70 was good enough to beat Arnold Palmer by six and Jacky Cupit by three. His other major was the 1968 US PGA at the age of 48, which made him the oldest winner of a major championship.

Pat Bradley

Born: March 24, 1951
Westford, USA

Now probably a little past her best, Pat Bradley was for long one of the very top players on the US LPGA Tour. She first won in 1976, and her last victory to date came in 1991. From 1976 to 1991 she recorded 12 placings in the top six money winners and had just one bad

year, the result primarily of hyperthyroidism. She has won six LPGA events which count as majors – two du Maurier Classics, one Nabisco Dinah Shore, one Peter Jackson Classic, an LPGA Championship and the 1981 US Women's Open. Her greatest money-winning year came in 1991, when she took home more than $750,000 and was first on the money list. She had the same placing in 1986, but 1991 was easily her best year. She had four victories, increasing her total to 30, and thus earning a place in the US LPGA Hall of Fame. That same year she also won the Rolex Player of the Year award and the Vare Trophy (for best scoring average) for the second time in her career. Aided by the yearly increases in prize money, Bradley was the first woman golfer to surpass, in turn, career winnings of $2 million, $3 million and $4 million.

Harry Bradshaw

Born: October 9, 1913
Delgany, Ireland

In 1949 Bradshaw was playing the Open Championship in Sandwich and in contention after a first-round 68 and at the peak of his form. Playing the 5th in the second round, he found his ball resting against broken glass. He thought he was very likely entitled to a free drop, but was unsure. Nowadays any professional would automatically call for an official ruling. Bradshaw, however, decided to play the ball as it lay, was hit by flying glass and moved the ball less than twenty yards. He took six instead of the par four which had been likely. Worse, he was upset and his normally superb putting stroke was far less sure for the rest of his round of 77. The next day he had recovered his composure, and with rounds of 68 and 70 he went on to tie with South African Bobby Locke – only to be totally outplayed in the play-off. Bradshaw was never again to be in real contention for an Open. His greatest achievement, in partnership with Christie O'Connor, was to win the World Cup, in which, despite being affected by the high al-

PAT BRADLEY *A consistent performer*

titude, he was individually second. He made three Ryder Cup appearances, and among other successes recorded two wins in one of the most important tournaments of the day, the Dunlop Masters.

James Braid

see Legends pp 106–07

GORDON BRAND JNR *Mr Consistency*

Gordon Brand Junior

Born: August 19, 1958
Kirkcaldy, Scotland

Brand's outstanding amateur career was followed by more-or-less instant success as a professional golfer. In his first year on the European Tour, 1982, he won twice and finished seventh on the money list. However, he was unable to maintain his pace the following year. Some said he was striving for too much length on his tee shots when not naturally a long hitter. Perhaps he was listening to too much wise advice and becoming confused. Happily he was soon back on the winning path, and 1984 saw him win two more tournaments and again finish seventh on the money list. Perhaps he had stopped listening. Since then, Brand has been consistently successful on the European Tour: until the end of 1994 he has never been worse than 34th on the money list and has had eight placings in the top 12. He has played in three Ryder Cup teams – 1987, 1989 and 1993 – and represented Scotland eight times in the Dunhill Cup at St Andrews and six times in the World Cup. His most remarkable performance came during the 1993 season, when he led in the European Open at the East Sussex National from start to finish and sailed to victory by the unusual margin of seven strokes.

Jack Burke

Born: January 29, 1923
Fort Worth, Tx, USA

Winning a sequence of events on the US Tour – or indeed any other tour – is very difficult indeed. That is why the achievements of Byron Nelson are regarded as so phenomenal. Burke had his winning streak in 1952, when in just over three weeks he won four events. It wasn't the stuff of Byron Nelson, whose 11 wins in a row will surely never even be approached, but Burke was hailed as the wonder of the age. Was he going to be better than Nelson? Better than Hogan? The answer was certainly no, for Burke was never quite as good again. However, he had many high achievements ahead of him. The one that secured him a place in golfing legend was his victory in the 1956 Masters. As they entered the final round, amateur Ken Venturi was eight strokes better than Burke's aggregate but, in bad weather, Burke played a well-managed 71 while the amateur staggered in with an 80. Burke also won the US PGA that year and was voted Player of the Year. Burke won a total of 15 events on the US Tour and played on five Ryder Cup teams, captaining his country in both 1957 and 1973.

Dick Burton

Born: October 11, 1907
Darwen, England

Burton's greatest achievement came in the last Open Championship to be played before the Second World War. At St Andrews he had rounds of 70, 72, 77 and 71 to win by two strokes from the American Johnny Bulla. Burton's play on the final hole particularly impressed all who witnessed it. The 350-yard 18th on the Old Course must be one of the easiest climaxes in championship golf. The only real danger for the tee shot is to hit a hotel or golf clubhouse along the right and go out of bounds. Most players, in conditions where they think they have no chance of reaching the green, play safe and aim left. Burton, however, hit his drive tight along the railings to the right. Though dangerous, this gives the best line into the green. It was almost all over. He flicked a short iron to holeable distance and then, as his putt went on line, casually tossed the club to his caddie. Because of the war, he was Open champion for the longest spell of anyone – seven years. Alas, again because of the war, he made little money from his win. Burton had two other high placings in the championship, and set a record for tournament scoring with rounds of 68, 66, 64 and 68 – 266.

Mark Calcavecchia

Born: June 12, 1960,
Laurel, USA

This player's best years to date came between 1987 and 1990, when he was always in the top 10 on the US money list. In the same period he also had most of his six wins on that tour. However, a greater claim to fame is his victory in the 1989 British Open Championship at Royal Troon. Here, he was always in touch with the leaders but never looked a likely winner until, in his final round, he first holed a long putt on the 11th and then lobbed a shot from a bank into the hole on the next. His round brought him a play-off with Wayne Grady and Greg Norman, who had come storming through the field. In the four-hole play-off Norman took an early lead but dropped a shot on the penultimate hole. The last was a disaster for him as he first drove into a fairway bunker he believed he could not reach, and then went out of bounds through the green. Calcavecchia, on the other hand, hit a much poorer drive but into a reasonable position and then ripped a five iron to about seven feet and birdied for victory. This must have been a consolation for his defeat by Sandy Lyle in the Masters the previous year, when with Calcavecchia readying himself for a play-off, Lyle played his famous long bunker shot, holed the putt, and was champion.

Dorothy Campbell

Born: 1883
Edinburgh, Scotland

In the early years of this century, Dorothy Campbell was arguably the best woman golfer in the world. In 1909 she became the first woman to win both the British and US titles in the same year and remains one of only three to do so. Later she became the first woman to complete the Grand Slam of British, US and Canadian titles. A Scottish international, she also played twice for Britain against the USA and it is estimated that she won in excess of 750 prizes during her career. Early in her golfing career, Campbell won the Scottish Championship three times (1905, 1906 and 1908). Emigrating to Canada on her marriage, after winning the British Ladies title in 1909 and 1911, she won the Canadian in the three years 1910 to 1912 and added a third US championship in 1924. On moving to America at a time when British players were still the best in the world, she won numerous state and regional titles. It was there that a moment's inattention cost Dorothy Campbell (by then Hurd) her life. She was standing on a railway line when she failed to notice an oncoming train and was killed.

José-Maria Cañizares

Born: February 18, 1947
Madrid, Spain

Cañizares joined the European Tour in 1971. He recorded his first win in Italy in 1972, but no more until 1980, when he won twice. His peak years came in the 1980s, when he was six times amongst the top 11 on the money list and collected most of his seven wins on the European Tour. (He has also won significant events in Kenya and Spain.) Cañizares holds a share in the European Tour nine holes scoring record – 27 – while his lowest round is a 61. When he is hot, he is really hot. One of his most memorable moments came when he won a decisive Ryder Cup singles at the Belfry in 1989. Ironically, there is little doubt that captain Tony Jacklin had placed him in the middle of his singles line-up because he was thought likely to lose. (The strong men were positioned at the head and tail of the order.) He has played in four Ryder Cup teams and also won the individual prize in the 1984 World Cup. There are also four Dunhill Cup appearances on his record to add to his selection as one of the pair in eight World Cup finals. He remains an effective player in mainstream golf, but is no longer a likely winner unless everything goes his way one week.

JOSÉ MARIA CAÑIZARES *A very long career*

Joanne Carner

Born: April 4, 1939
Kirkland, USA

Nicknamed today "Big Momma" and earlier "The Great Gundy" (which referred to her maiden name of Gunderson), Carner compiled one of the great records in amateur golf. Starting with the USGA Girls title in 1956, she went on to win the US Amateur five times – 1957, 1960, 1962, 1966 and 1968 – and then turned professional after winning an LPGA event as an amateur in 1969. She was immediately successful, but her best years came in the period 1974 to 1984, when she was never worse than ninth on the money list, headed it three times and was second or third on another four occasions. She added the US Women's Open to her list of majors in 1971 and had a repeat victory in 1976. The first of these wins meant that she became – and remains – the only woman to win the USGA Girls title, the US Amateur and the US Open. On the US LPGA Tour, she won 42 times between 1970 and 1985, and though she is now in her mid-forties she has second-place finishes to her credit and is still a possible winner. She also wins her fair share of prize money despite a fairly limited playing schedule. In 1994 she was a very popular captain of the US Solheim Cup team – and a victorious one.

Joe Carr

Born: February 18, 1922
Dublin, Ireland

Carr is one of the greatest amateurs from the British Isles ever. With his vast hitting and tremendous recovery powers, he is also one of the few British players to prosper in the US Amateur, where he reached the semi-final stage in 1961. In his native Ireland his record was outstanding. Besides a host of regional successes he also won the Irish Closed Amateur Championship on six occasions and the Irish Open Amateur four times – 1946, 1950, 1954 and 1956. Even more significant were his performances in Britain and abroad. In the British Amateur he had a formidable record, winning in 1953, 1958 and 1960. On two occasions he beat leading American amateurs in the final at a time when they were normally superior. He played in every Walker Cup team from 1947 to 1965, captaining the side on the last occasion. He was then non-playing captain for the next match. Carr made a limited number of entries in professional tournaments and was second in the 1959 Dunlop Masters, which was then one of the most prestigious events in Europe. He also came quite close to the centenary British Open, entering the final round just two strokes behind the leader.

BILLY CASPER *An all-time great putter*

Billy Casper

Born: June 24, 1931
San Diego, Ca, USA

Casper was a phenomenally successful golfer on the US Tour, though somewhat prosaic in style compared with his charismatic contemporary Arnold Palmer. Casper's aim was to get his ball into the fairway and then find the green. Thereafter, he knew he was just about the best putter around, albeit an unusually wristy one. As a competitor in the majors, his most dramatic moments came in the 1966 US Open. With nine holes to play, Arnold Palmer held a seven-stroke lead. It was all over, it seemed; Billy Casper was merely playing for second place. But Palmer then began to cast strokes to the wind while Casper plodded methodically on. In the end Palmer had to hole a testing putt just to tie with Casper. It was a similar story in the 18-hole play-off. At the halfway point Palmer led by four but again collapsed, giving Casper his second US Open. His first in 1959 had also been remarkable: he used only 112 putts in his four rounds. Casper's other major victory came in the 1970 Masters, and he also took a total of 51 events on the US Tour. Only five players have won more.

Bob Charles

Born: March 14, 1936
Carterton, New Zealand

It is an oddity of golf history that the greatest left-handed golfer ever is naturally right-handed. He began playing left-handed purely because his parents played that way around and had some spare clubs. It took Bob Charles a long time to make up his mind to become a professional – six years after he won the 1954 New Zealand Open. Thereafter he was soon winning in both Europe and the USA. On the main US Tour he won five times and had eight wins in Europe. Putting excellence has always been central to his success and particularly led to his greatest triumph, the 1963 British Open Championship, when he averaged 30 putts per round. He then went on to destroy American Phil Rodgers in the 36-hole play-off. However, his peak success came as a senior golfer in the USA. From his debut year of 1986 until 1993 he was always at least in the top 10 money winners and topped the list in both 1988 and 1989. In 1993, while finishing second, he won over $1 million. He has over 20 victories on this tour and among other victories has twice taken the Senior British Open.

Howard Clark

Born: August 26, 1954
Leeds, England

Blessed with one of the best swings in British golf, Clark has probably not done his talents full justice, though he came back to form in 1994 and captained the England team in the Dunhill Cup. Before this his game appeared to be in decline, partly perhaps owing to an elbow injury. He had been a consistent performer from 1976 to 1989, with his best years being 1978 and the period 1984 to 1986. Clark has been very successful in team events, playing in five Ryder Cup teams from 1977 to 1989 and representing England in several World Cups. In 1985, he was the individual winner. He has also made five Dunhill Cup appearances. In addition, he has won 12 times on the European Tour, once winning two in a row. His most prestigious win was the PGA Championship at Wentworth in 1984. Clark has been known to be sharp with caddies at times, as he is also with photographers. In the late 1980s, interestingly, Fanny Sunesson, who has recently achieved near superstar status as caddie for Nick Faldo, did the same job for Howard Clark, but attracted less attention. To be a top caddie you must do a good job for a top golfer.

Neil Coles

Born: September 26, 1934
London, England

Coles turned professional at the age of 16. Seven years on, he started to make his mark, and from 1961 began a run of astonishing consistency. From then until 1980 he was never worse than 12th on the money list, was leader twice and second once. He finished in the top six on 12 occasions. But he was not merely a money winner. At a time when the tournament schedule was limited and based largely in Britain, he

HOWARD CLARK *A great swinger of the club, he could improve still*

racked up 28 wins. Coles is probably the best British player since the war never to have come really close to an British Open Championship title. However, he did very well on occasion, coming third as early as 1961. A relatively poor last round at Carnoustie in 1975 saw him fall away from strong contention. In 1973, by contrast, he played one of his best rounds, a 66, but had gone out too far behind to have any real chance. He tied second. Apart from his having played in the most Ryder Cup matches in his eight appearances, his proudest achievements are probably his victories in the Match Play Championship (three times), the Dunlop Masters and the PGA Championship. He has won eight times on the Senior Tour, still competes regularly, and is chairman of the board of directors for the PGA European Tour.

Glenna Collett (Vare)
Born: June 20, 1903
New Haven, Ct, USA

Glenna Collett was perhaps the greatest American woman amateur ever, her record of six victories in the US Amateur is approached only by Joanne Carner. Her wins in the US Amateur came in 1922, 1925, 1928, 1929, 1930 and 1935. She was runner-up in 1931 and 1932, and on four occasions was medallist (the leading stroke play qualifier for the match play stages). In her career, over a period of 18 years she won a total of 49 leading amateur events. These included the French title in 1925 and the Canadian in 1923 and 1924. Early on she was a keen baseball player, and this may have helped with her muscle development, for she hit her tee shots a very long way indeed. At the age of 18 she struck one drive which was measured at a little over 300 yards – and this with grace and precision rather than brute force. During her peak years, her only rival on the world scene was Joyce Wethered, who defeated her on two occasions in the British Amateur. The second of these matches was the final at St Andrews in 1929. Collett was out in 34 and seemed home and dry at five up. However, at lunchtime

after 18 holes, the lead had been cut to just two up and in the afternoon the English player pulled ahead to win by 3 and 1.

GLENNA COLLETT *Greatest US amateur?*

Archie Compston
Born: January 14, 1893
Penn, England

Compston was one of the most likely British hopes in the British Open Championship from the early 1920s to the 1930s, when Americans were largely carrying all before them. In 1925 he finished a stroke behind the winner, Jim Barnes, at Prestwick's last Open, and in 1930, Bobby Jones's Grand Slam year, he went into the final round one ahead of the great man. Compston had played a third-round 68 to eliminate his five-stroke deficit. On the final afternoon, Compston fell away completely with an 82. It is said that this one round permanently dented his confidence. In the 1928 Open he had suffered a disappointment of a different kind. Walter Hagen, favourite to win in the absence of Jones, had barely stepped off the boat from American when he went into a challenge match against Archie over 72 holes at Moor Park. Compston was at the top of his form, while Hagen had not yet found his "landlegs". The result was

outrageous. Compston won by 18 and 17, and went into the Open at Sandwich as the new favourite. Alas for Compston, Hagen had put in some fairly serious practice and won easily, with Compston well beaten in third place.

John Cook
Born: October 2, 1957
Toledo, Oh, USA

Since 1980, Cook has been a journeyman pro on the US Tour. His best year was 1992, when he finished third on the US money list. Otherwise, he has never been better than 16th, but has accumulated $4¹/₄ million and won six times. His moments of maximum exhilaration and despair probably came in the 1992 Open Championship at Muirfield. Cook opened with strong rounds of 66 and 67, which still left him three strokes behind Faldo's 66, 64. To the betting men it seemed to be all over when Faldo then produced a 69 to Cook's 70. But it is often said that a tournament is won and lost over the last nine holes. Cook started with a bogey on the first, but after six holes was only a stroke behind Faldo. He then dropped some strokes, but made an apparently decisive move when he birdied both the 15th and 16th. He was two strokes into the lead over the struggling Faldo, and apparently made the championship secure when he struck a three-iron to around 10 yards on the par five 17th. Another birdie here and he was almost there. Instead, having shaved the hole with his eagle attempt, he then took a couple more putts. He was still almost certain to win if he parred the difficult final hole. Having hit a poor second shot, he didn't.

Harry Cooper
Born: August 4, 1904
Leatherhead, England

Cooper, whose family emigrated to America when he was a child, is one of the best US Tour players not to win a major championship, though he came very close. He finished one stroke behind Horton Smith in the 1936 Masters after being in the lead going into the final round, and was second again two years later. His ex-

perience of close encounters with the US Open was probably even more disappointing. In 1927 he three-putted the last green while Tommy Armour holed a good one to earn a play-off, which Cooper lost. In 1936 he broke the scoring record for the same event, but the relatively unknown Tony Manero still came in two strokes better. However, Cooper, nicknamed "Light Horse Harry" because of his speed about the golf course, was an extremely successful tournament player. His total number of victories is not known but is probably about the 25 mark. His best year was 1937, when he took nine titles and was both leading money winner and holder of the new Vardon Trophy for the lowest stroke average. He is today almost a forgotten man. It's the major championships that earn immortality.

Henry Cotton
Born: January 26, 1907
Holmes Chapel, England

Cotton was the man who put the pride back into British golf, mainly by his achievements in the 1930s, when he took two of his three British Open Championship titles after a long period of American dominance in the event. Though he won the Open again in 1948, there can be little doubt that much of his golfing prime was lost to the war. Cotton was a first in British golf, a public schoolboy from a middle-class background who turned professional. The conventional course would have been to remain an amateur and do "something in the City", but Cotton wanted to be a great player to maximize his income. He succeeded in both aims. Always a prey to nerves, Cotton threw away chances of an Open title before his first victory at Sandwich in 1934. Even then, although he won comfortably enough in the end, he had a near disastrous last round of 79, having begun it with a nine-stroke lead thanks to his superb play earlier. His finest hour came in 1937, when he won the Open at Carnoustie with all the US Ryder Cup team in the field. Cotton was without doubt the greatest British player since the Triumvirate, but arguably he has found a rival recently in Nick Faldo.

Fred Couples
Born: October 3, 1959
Seattle, Wa, USA

Fred Couples first began to make a name for himself on the US Tour when he took the 1983 Kemper Open, and since then he has had 11 US Tour wins and six placings amongst the top 10 money winners. He was leading money winner in 1992, when he won three US events. The most important of these was the Masters, his only major to date, though he has often featured among contenders. He has also been a very effective player for the USA in team competition. In 1994, he and Davis Love III became the first pairing to win the World Cup three times in a row, on the last of these occasions with phenomenal scoring. Couples won the individual International Trophy by five strokes after rounds of 65, 63, 68 and 69. Seemingly a very relaxed golfer, Fred no doubt has his problems like anyone else. Putting is one of them. He has lost a few events through very poor holing out at crucial stages of tournaments and came to resort, for the time being at least, to the reverse-grip method. Fred's long game is extremely fluent and long, perhaps aided by what appear to be very loose shoulder joints. One of the world's leading players, he is still a prospect to be the world's number one.

FRED COUPLES *Long driver*

Bruce Crampton
Born: September 28, 1935
Sydney, Australia

Nicknamed "The Iron Man" because he used to play nearly all events on the main US Tour, Crampton has continued along the same path on the Senior Tour. Playing his first full season there in 1986, he won seven events and was leading money winner. Several good seasons followed, but his career, towards the mid-1990s, seems to be petering out. Up to the end of 1994, Crampton had a total of 19 Senior victories and had won over $3\frac{1}{2}$ million – more than twice the sum he won on the main tour. Crampton first came to the fore in 1956 when he won the Australian Open at the age of 20. Having joined the US Tour in 1957, he was very unsuccessful for a few years but had his first victory in 1961. More followed fairly regularly until he had totalled 14 by the end of 1975. Although he never won a major, he was twice second in the US PGA, once in the Masters and once in the US Open. In fact, in 1972, he was second in three of the four majors. After his good years his form fell away rapidly and his health gave way. He retired and went into the oil business, before making his triumphant return as a Senior.

Ben Crenshaw
Born: January 11, 1952
Austin, Tx, USA

Crenshaw was a youthful prodigy whose first success came on his debut as a PGA Tour member. In his early days he looked set to be an all-time great, but now that he is into his 40s, this no longer seems likely, though as he proved in the 1995 Masters he still had a major championship in him. Some swing analysts have thought that the weakness in his game is an overlong backswing, past the horizontal, which can mean a lack of control. Ben has certainly hit his share of fairly wild wooden club shots – as have most others. In contrast, his putting is extremely compact. Many regard him as the best putter in the game, especially after his biggest career victories, the 1984 and 1995 Masters. On the US Tour, Crenshaw has been extremely con-

sistent with only one bad year. He has seven times been in the top eight on the money list and has 18 career victories. Crenshaw is unusual amongst Tour professionals in having a strong interest in the history of the game. Like many players, he is also becoming involved in golf course architecture, where his knowledge of traditional values should prove useful.

Fred Daly
Born: October 11, 1911
Portrush, Northern Ireland

By the age of 30 Daly was becoming consistently successful on the Irish golf scene, but as tournament play in Britain and Europe was suspended during the war, he lost what might well have been several of his most productive years. As soon as the war was over, however, Daly began to enjoy his heyday, which lasted until 1952. The biggest victory of his career was the 1947 Open Championship, over Royal Liverpool's course at Hoylake. He began with rounds of 73 and 70 in testing conditions, then sagged to a 78 on the morning of the final day. In the afternoon, he played a good 72 in reasonable weather and set a target that none of the later starters, in worsening conditions, could match – he was champion by a stroke. The following year he was second and then third in 1950. In 1952 he was third again, having led after two rounds but fallen away fairly badly on the final day. He played every Ryder Cup match between 1947 and 1953, once winning his singles by 9 and 7, and a further eight important tournaments in the British Isles came his way.

John Daly
Born: April 28, 1966
Sacramento, Ca, USA

At golf tournaments there is sometimes a buzz of expectation and a rush of spectators – usually indicat-

ing that the leaders are approaching. The exception is John Daly. He can attract almost as big crowds even when positioned well to the bottom of the field. They enjoy gasping at the distance he can hit the ball. In recent US Tour statistics he *averages* about 290 yards – his longest blows go a good deal further than that. The length comes from natural power, aided by a huge shoulder turn and a backswing that is absurdly long by modern standards. He is also prepared to take risks and let fly from the tee with the driver when others might be thinking about a prudent three-iron. Daly first came to attention with his dramatic appearance in the 1991 US PGA Championship at Crooked Stick. Informed just before the start of the event that a late withdrawal had given him a place in the field, he drove there, his first look at the course being during his first round when he shot a 69 to be two behind the leader. His following series of 67, 69, 71 gave him a three-stroke victory over Bruce Lietzke. A star was born. Since then, Daly has had drinking and marital problems and has only won twice, and his potential remains difficult to assess.

Beth Daniel
Born: October 14, 1956
Charleston, SC, USA

Daniel had a short but outstanding amateur career, making two Curtis Cup appearances and winning the US Amateur title in 1975 and 1977. She was also a member of the World Cup team. When she began competing on the LPGA Tour in 1979, she was immediately successful. She had her first win and finished 10th on that year's money list. She was soon doing much better and threatening to replace Nancy Lopez as the wonder of the age. In both 1980 and 1981 she topped the money list and increased her tour victories to eight. However, she did not top the list again until 1990, her best year, when she won seven times – a feat rarely achieved in modern times – and her winnings of over $860,000 set a new record. So far she has seven times finished in the top eight money winners. By the end of the 1994 season

LAURA DAVIES *The world's best woman player in 1994*

she had racked up 31 tour wins, which ranks her 11th in the all-time listings. Oddly, only one of these is a major, the 1990 LPGA Championship. She has played in every Solheim Cup match to date.

Eamonn Darcy

Born: August 7, 1952
Delgany, Ireland

If quite a few Irish golfers have had stylistically entertaining swings, none have been odder than Darcy's. Perhaps the unorthodoxy accounts for his fluctuations in form. In 1975 and 1976 he seemed to be on the verge of becoming a major force in European golf with finishes of third and second on the money list. His

1975 results included a second place finish behind Arnold Palmer in the PGA Championship, in which he also reached a play-off the following year with Gary Player and Neil Coles, which the Englishman went on to win. He also had two wins in 1976, and another in 1977, but his overall level of performance fell away, a slump which continued until 1981. Then he finished ninth on the money list and earned his third Ryder Cup team place. His Cup record is poor, except for his fourth and final appearance, at Muirfield Village in 1987, when he came back memorably at Ben Crenshaw and holed a very missable putt for victory on the last hole. Darcy has six

European Tour wins on his record and six more overseas. He has also played seven World Cups, and was in the winning Irish team on one of his three appearances.

Laura Davies

Born: May 10, 1963
Coventry, England

In 1994, Laura Davies became the world's leading woman golfer. Despite playing a limited schedule, she topped the US money list and produced the remarkable feat – never achieved before by man or woman – of winning on five different tours. She won three times in the USA, twice in Europe and once each in Thailand, Japan and Australia. Earlier, her greatest success had been in winning the 1987 US Women's Open when not a member of the US LPGA Tour. This caused that organization to give her exemption, after amending its constitution, from the need to qualify for Tour membership. Davies has played with great success in the Curtis Cup and the Solheim Cup. In the latter she has been an inspiration for her team because, as with such male players as Seve Ballesteros and Nick Faldo in the Ryder Cup, she is a player much feared by her American opponents. She is renowned for her prodigious hitting, but her greatest strength, she herself thinks, lies in her crisp and accurate short game.

Rodger Davis

Born: May 18, 1951
Sydney, Australia

Many professional golfers like to identify themselves by their clothing. Davis has had two trademarks for long periods in his career: his long socks and plus-twos. He has been a strong contender in the British Open Championship. In Ballesteros's first year at Lytham in 1979, for instance, he held the lead with five holes left to play but, like a few others, fell back over the testing finish. At Muirfield in 1987 he started with a blistering 64, which gave him a three-stroke lead, but his following rounds of 73 and 74 took him out of strong contention. On the final day he never quite looked like

winning, but his 69 was eventually good enough to earn him a tie for second with Azinger, leaving Faldo victorious by a single stroke. Davis was a winner in Australia when he first decided to try his luck in Europe in 1977. He immediately made occasional impact, sometimes fading out of contention after good starts. His first win came in 1981 and he has had half a dozen more since then, the most important being the PGA Championship in 1986 and the Volvo Masters in 1991. He has won 20 times in Australia and New Zealand.

Jimmy Demaret

Born: May 10, 1910
Houston, Tx, USA

One of the greatest players not to have won a US Open, Demaret was the first to win the Masters three times. He did this in 1940, 1947 and 1950, once managing a 30 over the second nine at Augusta, Georgia. Despite his numerous tournament successes, Demaret was noted above all for his flamboyant clothes. Walter Hagen was probably the first golfer to attire himself in, for example, two-tone shoes, a bow-tie and matching slacks and top. Demaret went much further and might grace the golf courses of America topped by a tam-o'shanter, with vivid shirt and trousers, the ensemble completed from his vast collection of shoes. If Demaret was the Payne Stewart of his time, there is no evidence that he had a lucrative clothing contract, as do Stewart and so many other modern players. As a golfer, he was very influential in his shape of shot. Before him, most top professionals favoured a draw, because of the greater run on the ball. Demaret decided that the fade was better, as that side-spin held both fairways and greens more effectively.

Bruce Devlin

Born: October 10, 1937
Armidale, Australia

Devlin began to come to the fore in 1959, when he won the Australian Open and decided he was good enough to turn professional. He then played worldwide for a while before settling in the USA. Between 1964 and 1972 Devlin won eight events on the US Tour, but continued to make appearances in Europe, most notably in 1966 when he was leading money winner. Devlin was for long considered a likely winner of a major championship, though he never came particularly close. Perhaps his best performances were two fourth places in the Masters and two sixths in the US Open. One of the latter came at Pebble Beach, in his mid-forties, when he held a two-stroke lead after two rounds but dropped back to six strokes behind winner Tom Watson. He plays a limited schedule these days on the US Senior Tour, where he has had little success. However, from his Houston base, he has worked intensively in golf course design and produced some 140 since the mid 1960s.

BRUCE DEVLIN *Consistent money-winner around the world*

Leo Diegel
Born: April 27, 1899
Detroit, Mi, USA

"They keep trying to give me the championship, but I won't take it," said Leo Diegel after yet another title had been cast to the winds. But it might all have been so different. He contended strongly for the US Open as early as 1920. A win then might well have given him the self-assurance so much needed by a young player. Though blessed with a great talent, Diegel never quite fulfilled it. Perhaps his main problems were that he lacked composure and his nerve sometimes cracked at crisis points in the majors. In the 1933 British Open at St Andrews, for example, he needed only a par four at one of the easiest last holes in golf to tie, but his putting let him down. It often did, despite endless experiments with different putters and a revolutionary method. The latter involved crouching low over the ball, club grip almost touching his chin, and pointing both elbows outwards. He hoped this would take his jerky wrists out of the putting stroke. It was much imitated. Despite his failings, Diegel was still a formidable tournament player and is credited with some 30 victories. The most important of these were in the Canadian Open, which he won four times, and the US PGA Championships of 1928 and 1929, the first of which ended Walter Hagen's great run.

Flory van Donck
Born: June 23, 1912
Tervueren, Belgium

Easily the finest golfer Belgium has so far produced, van Donck was almost a dominant figure in continental Europe and highly effective in Great Britain. The extent of van Donck's dominance in his native land can be seen from his record in the Belgian Professional Championship. Between 1935 and 1968 he won it 16 times. In 1979, at the age of 67, he was still representing his country in the World Cup, an event in which he played regularly from 1954 to 1970 and was individual winner in 1960, when it was at a peak of its prestige. In continental European Opens van Donck was for years the man you had to beat. He won the Belgian and the Dutch five times each, the Italian four times, the Swiss and the German twice and the French three times. The toughest competition, however, was then to be found in the British Isles, where he won five events and had some close encounters with the Open Championship. For nearly a dozen years from 1949 he was very seldom out of the top 10 and twice finished in second place. Van Donck had a smooth and rhythmic swing but was less elegant on the greens: he liked to putt with the toe of his putter high.

George Duncan
Born: September 16, 1883
Methlick, Scotland

Duncan emerged young on the British golf scene, and was in the Scotland team by 1906. However, it was several years later, when he beat both Braid and Taylor in the News of the World Matchplay Championship, that he really became a name. In 1913 he beat Braid again, in the final. By this time he was just about on a level with the Great Triumvirate and Sandy Herd, and was much in demand for challenge and exhibition matches. After the war, much was expected of George Duncan and Abe Mitchell, but even they could not prevent the growing American dominance of the Open Championship. However, Duncan won at Deal in 1920, and an amazing victory it was. He began with a couple of 80s, which put him right out of contention. His driving had been the main problem, but after playing his second round he picked up a driver in the exhibition tent, had a few swishes with it – and money changed hands. His game was transformed. On the final day, he had rounds of 71 and 72 and was champion by a couple of strokes.

J. Douglas Edgar
Born: September 30, 1884
Newcastle-upon-Tyne, England

Although Tommy Armour said he was "the best golfer I ever saw", and Bobby Jones called him "a magician with a golf club", Edgar is now a largely forgotten figure in the history of golf. The reason he has been forgotten is that he died prematurely – and mysteriously – in Atlanta, Georgia, as a result of a small but deep wound in his thigh. He had bled to death. Was it a mugging? Perhaps murder for an unknown reason? Or was he simply the victim of a hit-and-run driver? There were headlines for a short time and then the story became a shadowy part of golf history. The crime was never solved. Edgar became a name to be reckoned with when he won the 1914 French Open by six strokes from Harry Vardon. Then came war, after which he emigrated to

STEVE ELKINGTON *Australian globe-trotter*

America. There his greatest achievement came quickly when he won the Canadian Open by 16 strokes from Bobby Jones and Jim Barnes, still the greatest margin ever in a national Open against a top-class field. He won the same event again the next year and also reached a US PGA final. He was killed in 1921. A revolutionary feature of Edgar's game was that, like many others, he had a very full shoulder turn but, unusually, a much more restricted hip movement. He always felt he would play his best when his hands felt "thin".

Lee Elder
Born: July 14, 1934
Dallas, Tx, USA

Lee Elder is famous above all as the first black golfer to play in the Masters. There is little or no doubt that those who used to rule at Augusta hoped that no black would compete. When it was a purely invitational event this was relatively easy to achieve – there were in any case few blacks in the USA playing to a really high standard. However, once it was decided to introduce a direct qualifying system, in addition to invitations, winners on the US Tour were allowed in. Thus in 1974, when Lee Elder won his first title, the Monsanto Open, beating Peter Oosterhuis in a play-off after a dramatic last round, he qualified

to play in the 1975 Masters. There, ironically, he failed to survive the half-way cut. Elder had three further wins on the main US Tour and played on the 1979 Ryder Cup team. Later on he was successful during the 1980s on the Senior PGA Tour. Between 1984 and 1988 his worst finish on the money list was 19th, and in his best year, 1985, he was second. During this period he had eight victories, in one of which he opened with a 61, a Senior Tour record.

Steve Elkington
Born: December 8, 1962
Inverell, Australia

Elkington first came to the fore in 1981, when he won the Australian Amateur Championship. The same year, while winning the Doug Sanders Junior World Championship, he was evaluated by the University of Houston golf coach and offered a "scholarship". Since then, Elkington has been mainly based in the USA. Success while at Houston showed that he was undoubtedly a promising prospect, and by 1987 he had qualified for the US Tour, immediately achieving some good results. In 1990 he won the Greater Greensboro Open, and his greatest success came the following year, when he won the Tournament Players Championship, after a tough fight with Fuzzy Zoeller. This is an event which ranks just below the four major championships. It earned him nearly $300,000 and 10-year exemption from having to qualify for the US Tour. In 1992 he won again on the US Tour and also took the Australian Open, another event just below major championship status. After another win in 1994, his money winnings in what is still a short career were over $3¼ million. He also represented the International team against the USA in the first President's Cup match, an event played between the USA and the rest of the non-European world, which it is hoped will emulate the success of the Ryder Cup.

ERNE ELS *On his way to the US Open*

Ernie Els
Born: October 17, 1969
Johannesburg, South Africa

In 1994 Els became the most talked-about player in professional golf, earning about £1.8 million on the various world tours. He also became easily the best young player in the game of golf and perhaps the world's best of any age. His achievements that year were rivalled only by those of Nick Price. He ended his year by winning the Johnnie Walker World Championship – but this, some would say, is not actually the championship of anything, just another tournament. The same could be said of the World Matchplay event at Wentworth in the autumn, which he also won. Far more significant was his play-off victory in the US Open the same year. Historically, the majors are what count in the end. Els first came to prominence in 1992, when he won the most significant titles in his homeland – the South African Open, the PGA and the Masters. This was the first

time such a hat trick had been achieved since Gary Player did it a dozen and more years earlier. Ernie Els's game seems as good as that of anyone in the world. He has great length off the tee, great feel for pace and line around the greens – and then there's always his putting. There's simply no one better.

Chick Evans
Born: July 18, 1890
Indianapolis, In, USA

The Western Amateur remains one of the top events on the American circuit. Evans won it eight times, including a sequence of four in a row. However, his main target was the US Amateur. It did not come easily. In 1909, 1910 and 1911 he was defeated at the semi-final stage. The next year he got as far as the final but was heavily defeated, 7 and 6, by Jerry Travers, after having been three up early on. But Evans was good enough to defeat the leading professionals of his time, taking the Western Open in 1910. Then came a trip abroad and a win in the French Amateur – and also a meeting with James Braid, which led him to switch to the Vardon grip. In 1914 he was nearly US Open champion, finishing just a stroke behind Walter Hagen. But he did it in 1916, and in a grand manner. His 286 total brought him in by two and set an aggregate record that was to last for 20 years. That year, he also took the US Amateur at last – apart from Jones, he remains the only man to win both titles in the same year. He won again in 1920 and also reached the 1922 and 1927 finals. He still qualified for the US Amateur as late as 1953.

Nick Faldo
see Legends pp 88–89

Johnny Farrell
Born: April 1, 1901
White Plains, NY, USA

Farrell is one of the very few who beat Bobby Jones when this great American was in his peak years. It happened at Olympia Fields in the 1928 US Open. The two tied on 294, and went into a 36-hole play-off, as was then the norm. Farrell, with a 70, was three better than Jones after the first round, but Jones came back at him in the afternoon. However, Farrell held on, and a seven-foot putt on the very last hole was good enough for a one-stroke victory. That was his only major victory, though he was second in 1929 in both the US PGA and the British Open Championship. He also finished one behind the Jones/Willie Macfarlane play-off in the 1925 US Open. In the period 1923–24, he made money in every tournament he entered, but an even better spell came early in 1927, when he won seven consecutive tournaments. He had eight wins in all that year, to follow his five the previous season. Farrell played in the first Ryder Cup team in 1927 and in the next two events also. The great strength of his game was his putting.

His long game was not among the most powerful, but his swing was elegant and he was very good at keeping the ball in play.

Max Faulkner
Born: July 29, 1916
Bexhill, England

Faulkner was one of the more eccentric players of modern times. In his search for putting perfection he assembled a vast collection of putters – making most of them himself – said to have reached a total of around three hundred. He must have experienced many disappointments! Faulkner was constantly experimenting with subtle variations of the other clubs too, and seems virtually never to have played with a full conventional set. All this was because Faulkner had great feel for the shape and flight of a shot and was one of the few players who found it easy to bend the lofted irons either way. His victory in the 1951 British Open Championship at Portrush was achieved with an extremely light putter with a pencil-like shaft and grip. Faulkner went into the event with his long game in a dreadful state. That gradually improved under the influence of all the unlikely putts that were dropping. He began the final round with a six-stroke lead and was scarcely troubled in winning by two. He was the last British golfer to win until Jacklin 18 years later. Faulkner was five times in the Ryder Cup team and had 16 wins in Britain and Europe.

David Feherty
Born: August 13, 1958
Bangor, Northern Ireland

"I think I can win. I've got nothing better to do this weekend." Feherty is certainly not the best player in the world, but he is probably the most quotable. This remark was made at the British Open Championship at Turnberry in 1994, when he was in hot contention until the closing stages. That year, he had made the slightly unusual decision to compete on the US Tour instead of on the European Tour, where he has been consistently successful since early in the 1980s, winning five titles between 1986 and 1992. His 1994 US

MAX FAULKNER *A colourful and eccentric figure, but a very successful golfer*

venture was a modest success, netting him nearly $200,000. Feherty has, like most but not all professionals, suffered the putting yips but, aided by a centre-shaft putter, may have conquered them. He was number one in the European Tour putting statistics in 1991, using just 28.5 putts per round, and is also one of the longer hitters in the game.

Jim Ferrier
Born: February 24, 1915
Sydney, Australia

Ferrier came into professional golf having dominated the Australian amateur scene for several years. He won the Australian Amateur title four times in the late 1930s. Also as an amateur he won the Australian Open twice, in 1938 and 1939, and at St Andrews in 1936, became the first Australian to reach a final of the Amateur Championship. He turned professional in 1940 and, deciding that Australian golf was rather a small pond, departed for

the USA the following year. He made money but no great impact on the US Tour until the mid-1940s, and scored his first win in 1944. His only major came in 1947 when he won the US PGA, then a match play event, defeating Chick Harbert in the final. Ferrier also finished second in the 1950 Masters to Jimmy Demaret – but he ought to have won. He only needed to score 38 on the final nine holes, but his game fell apart. At the 13th he hit into Rae's Creek and then dropped shot after shot for a while, eventually taking 41. However, as consolation that year, he was second on the money list. Altogether he had 21 wins on the US Tour, the last of these coming in 1961.

Dow Finsterwald
Born: September 6, 1929
Athens, Ga, USA

There was not much dash about Finsterwald's play. Although he was an excellent shot-maker, he always had safety in mind. Once on the green he knew his excellent putting would be the equalizer. As a result he was one of the most consistent scorers of his era. His lack of adventurousness meant he seldom had a bad round, and at one time he held the record for the most tournaments played without missing the half-way cut. He joined the US Tour in 1952 and had some very bad years, but it all went a great deal better from 1956, when he was second in the money list. The next year he won the Vardon Trophy for the lowest stroke average. He was a good performer in the majors though he won only one, the 1958 US PGA, the first year the event switched over to stroke play. He had been second, under the match play format, the year before. In 1962 he tied Arnold Palmer and Gary Player for the Masters but Palmer won the 18-hole play-off easily. Finsterwald won 12 events on the US Tour and played four Ryder Cups between 1957 and 1963. He was later non-playing captain.

Jack Fleck

Born: November 8, 1922
Bettendorf, Ia, USA

For an hour after Hogan had completed his four rounds in the 1955 US Open, he sat in the locker-room accepting the congratulations on a record-breaking fifth US Open. He was five strokes better than anyone who had finished, and there was only one still out on the course with a statistical chance: Jack Fleck, an unknown pro from a municipal course in Davenport, Iowa. He had once finished as high as sixth in a tour event and had also gone around the Olympic course in 87 in a practice round. But he was playing well enough now, and needing a birdie at the last to tie Hogan, he duly hit a very difficult approach shot to about eight feet and then holed the putt. Words failed him in the Press tent afterwards. As for Hogan, he was in peak form and no one, least of all the inexperienced Fleck, was going to beat him over 18 holes. But he did. Taking a one-stroke lead into the last hole, he took four while Hogan hooked into deep rough and took three to get back to the fairway. This was very easily

Fleck's finest hour. He did win a couple of tour events several years later, but little else, and the Senior Tour came a bit too late for him.

Raymond Floyd

Born: September 4, 1942
Fort Bragg, NC, USA

Today a successful Senior Tour competitor and arguably the best player in the world for his age, Floyd was chosen for the Ryder Cup team by captain Tom Watson as recently as 1993. His professional career began in 1963, and he won in his first season on the US Tour. In later years he has added a further 21 tour wins and has totalled more than $5 million in prize money. While Floyd has had his share of moderate seasons, he has seven times been among the top nine of money winners on the US Tour. His best years were 1981 and 1982: each time he was second on the money list and had three victories. Floyd has won four major championships, the first coming in 1969, the US PGA. Perhaps his next win was the best. He dominated the 1976 Masters throughout, winning by a record eight strokes and equalling Jack Nicklaus's record 271 aggregate. In 1982, aged 40, he took his second US PGA, having started with what he called "the best round of my life" – a 63. The US Open he so much desired came his way four years later at Shinnecock Hills after a last-round 66. At 44, he was the oldest player to win the championship.

RAY FLOYD *The agony of a missed putt*

Doug Ford

Born: August 6, 1922
West Haven, Ct, USA

Not many men hole a bunker shot to win a major, but Ford did so to take the 1957 Masters. It gave him a 66, and a three-stroke margin over Sam Snead. This was his second major championship, following his success in the 1955 US PGA. Ford's swing was quite short and ugly, and although he attacked with venom, he was by no means a long hitter. However, the short hitter has a better chance of keeping the ball on the fairway and leaving a precise shot to the green. Once there, Ford was right up among the best putters of his day. He came into the game as the son of a golf club professional and, from the age of 18, had a successful amateur career, mainly in his home area. His first professional victory came in the Houston Invitational and he joined the US Tour full-time in 1950. By the end of his main career, he had won 19 events and tied in seven others where he lost play-offs. His peak years were from 1951 to 1960, when he was never worse than 10th on the money list and was twice second. Ford was on every US Ryder Cup team between 1955 and 1961. The Senior Tour came rather too late for him, but he had some good results into his sixties.

David Frost

Born: September 11, 1959
Cape Town, South Africa

Frost turned professional in 1981 and tried to play the US Tour, but with no success. Instead he tried Europe and in his first full season, 1983, finished 32nd on the money list. The following year he rose to 10th place and also won the Compagnie de Chauffe Cannes Open. Frost then qualified for the US Tour and has played it more or less full-time since then from his Dallas base. He had a quiet first two seasons but won good money before leaping to 11th place on the money list in 1987. The following year he had two victories in the Southern and Tucson Opens and moved up to ninth. In 1989 came his best win to date in the World Series of Golf, which gave him a ten-year exemption from

having to qualify for US Tour events. His best tour season came in 1993, when he recorded consecutive victories in the Canadian Open and Hardee's Golf Classic. His aggregate of 259 in the latter event was just two strokes above the tour record for 72 holes. He topped $1 million for the year and was fifth on the money list. In 1994 Frost had wins in the USA (bringing his total to nine), Hong Kong and South Africa. He has also won the Sun City Challenge three times.

DAVID FROST *Will he win a major?*

Robert Gamez

Born: July 21, 1968
Las Vegas, Nv, USA

Turning professional in 1989, Gamez almost immediately became a potential star name when he won on his first entry on the US Tour – the Northern Telecom Open. He was then quiet for a couple of months before becoming one of the many who have given Greg Norman a jolt by holing an unlikely shot. This was no greenside chip. On the 72nd hole of the Nestlé Invitational at Bay Hill, with 176 yards to go to the flag, he holed a seven-iron shot for an eagle and a one-shot victory from nowhere over Norman. This unlikely feat, added to his earlier win, made Gamez a hot property, and at the end of the season, with money winnings of nearly $500,000, he was duly accorded Rookie of the Year honours. He was 27th on the money list. But Gamez has not maintained that pace, though he won around $250,000 in each of his next three seasons – not big money in the context of earnings on both the US and European tours. His other main achievements have been to lose to Fred Couples in a play-off for the 1993 Honda Classic, a first-round 61 and an eventual second-place finish in the 1991 Milwaukee Open and, in 1994, wins in the Pebble Peach Invitational (not a Tour event) and the important Casio World Open.

Al Geiberger
Born: September 1, 1937
Red Bluff, Ca, USA

Geiberger will always be remembered for being the first to break the magic 60 in a US Tour event, which he did on June 10, 1977, in the second round of the Danny Thomas-Memphis Classic. He went on to win, one of 11 successes on the main US Tour between 1962 and 1979. His most important victory came with the 1966 US PGA Championship, but others of almost equal significance were his wins in the 1975 Tournament of Champions and the Tournament Players Championship, both events which rank just below major championship status. Geiberger has always been plagued by stomach problems and found it helped him to eat little and often. His chosen snack on the golf course, famously, was the peanut butter sandwich, but even this couldn't contain the stomach problems and he has had to have several operations. When be became eligible for the Senior Tour at the age of 50, Geiberger immediately became one of the most effective competitors. Apart from being injured in 1994, he has always been among the top 20 money winners and, since 1987, has four times been in the top 10. He has won nine events. Geiberger was on the US Ryder Cup teams in 1967 and 1975.

Bob Goalby
Born: March 14, 1931
Belleville, USA

Goalby was involved in perhaps the most famous rules decision of all time. It happened at the end of the 1968 Masters. Roberto de Vicenzo having dropped a shot at the last, after a great round, glumly signed his card – marked by a fellow competitor. Alas, he had failed to notice that his score on the 17th was wrongly shown as a par, not a birdie. Roberto was not disqualified for his error, as he had merely signed for a higher score than he had actually achieved. But that score had to stand, and instead of de Vicenzo being in a play-off for the Masters, Goalby had won. This was very unfortunate – for both men. Goalby, after all, had finished with a great 66 and would anyway have tied de Vicenzo. He had played a great tournament and, as like as not, would have won the play-off. But what is remembered is that Roberto was the real winner but that someone or other else got the green jacket. Goalby had joined the US Tour in 1957, and in 1958 was named Rookie of the Year. Usually in the top 60, he won 11 tour events in his career and was second in both the 1961 US Open and the 1962 US PGA. With a lively temper and a pronounced in-to-out swing, his great problem was a draw which could become an uncontrollable hook. Despite this, he had his very hot streaks and once set a tour record with eight consecutive birdies.

Wayne Grady
Born: July 26, 1957
Brisbane, Australia

Though he didn't win, the Troon Open Championship of 1989 was perhaps Grady's finest hour. A 67, following a first-round 68, gave him a one-stroke lead. After the third round, Grady had retained his narrow lead of one – over Tom Watson. In the final round, Grady did little wrong, but some inspired golf from Greg Norman, who had started the day seven behind, and some very good, if occasionally lucky play by Mark Calcavecchia, produced a three-way tie – and a four-hole play-off, won by the American. For Grady, it was a rare encounter with the possibility of greatness. However, a major championship did come his way the very next year when he won the US PGA, playing very solid golf throughout. Grady had made his US Tour debut in 1985, finishing 41st on the money list. The next three years were less kind, but Grady broke through in 1989 when he won the Westchester Classic and was 27th on the money list. The following year he improved to 21st, mainly a result of his US PGA win, since when he has done relatively little. Twice Australian PGA Champion, Grady also won the 1984 German Open.

WAYNE GRADY *US PGA Champion*

David Graham
Born: May 23, 1946
Windsor, Australia

The Australian tour having limited seasons, Graham, like many of his countrymen, has had to make himself an international golfer. Indeed, he has won all over the world, though his principal efforts have been on the US Tour, where he has won eight times. He is now inactive on that tour, but if his putting remains good, he should be phenomenally successful on the Senior Tour. Putting has always been a very strong feature of his game. Graham has won two major championships. The first of these was the 1979 US PGA. This was the first success by an Australian in a major since Peter Thomson won the 1965 Open Championship. He started off four behind the leader in his final round, but got to the turn in 31 and had birdies at the next two holes. With the event in his hands, Graham then showed considerable clumsiness around the green on the last hole, and could only tie. However, he won the play-off against Ben Crenshaw with the aid of some truly remarkable putting. In 1981, he became the first Australian to win the US Open. He did it with a last-round 67, thanks largely to his precision through the green. He took 33 putts – but missed only one fairway and no greens.

Ralph Guldahl
Born: November 22, 1912
Dallas, Tx, USA

Guldahl may well be an example of a golfer ruined by writing a golf instruction book. It caused him to think about the way he himself played the game, which was extremely unorthodox. He had very little flow, with either legs or in foot roll, and compensated for a lack of cock in his right wrist action on the backswing by letting the club move in his grip. Thinking and writing about it may have ruined him, for he suffered a permanent loss of form. Guldahl himself had various other explanations, ranging from a bad back to the fact that he had done it all in competitive golf. The latter was certainly true – if only for a brief spell. He first hit the headlines in 1933 when he came within a four-foot putt of a tie for the US Open. Guldahl then disappeared for a few years but came back in 1936 as a the second highest money winner. The next spring he experienced his famous loss in the Masters, largely due to a disastrous 5, 6 sequence on the 12th and 13th holes. But his time was coming. Two months later he won the US Open and then had a rare repeat victory the following year. The Masters came his way the next year, partly because of those previously fatal holes. This time he played them 3, 3. And that was just about the end of it for Ralph Guldahl.

Walter Hagen

see Legends pp 90–91

Sandra Haynie

Born: June 4, 1943
Fort Worth, Tx, USA

Haynie is one of the great figures of the US LPGA Tour. In the period 1963 to 1975, her worst placing on the money list was ninth, and she had at least one victory every year. Usually, however, she was a multiple winner, 1974 being her most successful year. Then she won six times, including the LPGA Championship and the US Women's Open, two of the four majors she has won in a long career. No other player has achieved the feat of winning two majors in a single year, except for Mickey Wright (who went one better by winning three). Haynie was troubled by arthritis from the age of 33, and soon after her great years she became only an occasional competitor, playing just 17 tournaments in the space of the four years from 1977 to 1980. Yet 1982 saw her in peak form once more. She had two victories and finished second on the money list, one of the five times she has been in this position (while never being number 1). Once Haynie was into her forties she became a receding force, and has not competed since playing a full season in 1989 without any real success. Sandra Haynie was inducted into the Hall of Fame in 1977, and in 1970 won the Player of the Year award.

Clayton Heafner

Born: July 20, 1914
Charlotte, NC, USA

Displays of temper are now rare, but in earlier days on both the US and British tours, they were considered to show you had some competitive fire. One player who certainly had it was Heafner, who was quite easily upset by matters other than an unsatisfactory shot. He once stormed off the 1st tee to his car, hurled his club in, and drove off in a cloud of dust, having been angered by the announcer's introduction. Heafner just missed out on the great events. In 1942 he tied for the Tam o'Shanter, which was for some time the richest prize in American golf. He lost the play-off. In two US Opens he also came very close. At Medinah in 1949 he and Sam Snead tied for second place, just a stroke behind Cary Middlecoff's championship-winning score. Worse than this, perhaps, followed in 1951 at Oakland Hills, where most of the field were irate at Robert Trent Jones's all too successful attempt to toughen up the course. Heafner went into the last round tied with Ben Hogan and then produced a 69, which was one of only two scores below 70 throughout the championship. Alas for Heafner's chances, Hogan tamed the "monster" course with a 67, arguably the greatest round of his great career.

Sandy Herd

Born: April 22, 1868
St Andrews, Scotland

Always just a notch below the standards set by the Great Triumvirate of Vardon, Taylor, and Braid, Sandy Herd outlasted them all. His long professional career began in 1892 at Huddersfield Golf Club. The same year, he won three tournaments and made a good run at the Open Championship, being held for the first time at Muirfield, finishing tied for second place behind Harold Hilton. Herd was again second in 1895, this time at St Andrews, and looked likely to win at Muirfield the following year when he started with a 72 – five strokes better than anyone and 11 better than the eventual winner, Harry Vardon – before his form collapsed. His finest hour came at Hoylake in 1902, when he won the Open by a stroke from Vardon and Braid. He was the first champion to use the "modern" rubber core ball instead of the guttie. After Herd's win, the guttie was finished. It was to be many years before Herd was. He was second in the 1920 Open, having been in the lead with a round to go, and last played 1939, 54 years after his first appearance. In 1926 he upstaged even the Great Triumvirate with what is probably the greatest feat ever performed by an "old" golfer. At the age of 58, he took the News of the World Matchplay Championship, then ranked second only to the Open.

Dave Hill

Born: May 20, 1937
Jackson, Ms, USA

Like a Hogan or a Nelson, Dave Hill has always delighted in trying to achieve perfection in his lonely vigils. "You paint pictures out there," he said, "and each good shot is a deft stroke." During the 1960s, Hill earned an outstanding reputation as a ball striker and also for being more outspoken than various authorities liked. He was particularly rude about the Hazeltine National course, site of the 1970 US Open, in spite of the fact that he eventually finished second. "All the course needs," he declared, "is 80 acres of corn and four cows." This and similar comments brought him a $150 fine. Hill joined the US Tour in 1959, and from 1960 to 1975 was 11 times in the top 30 money winners. He achieved his best placing of second in 1969, his peak season, which included three wins. Altogether Hill won 13 times on the main tour and also made three Ryder Cup appearances. Eventually, he tired of tournament golf, particularly because he felt that success depended too much on putting. When he became eligible, however, he returned on the Senior Tour in 1987 and has recorded six wins. He has been as high as third and fifth on the money list, but his career now seems to be in decline.

SANDY HERD *Just a step behind the Great Triumvirate*

The Great Players

Mike Hill

Born: January 27, 1939
Jackson, Ms, USA

The Senior US Tour has provided ample evidence that some golfers who have been relatively unsuccessful in their prime may last better than their peers. Mike Hill is a clear example of this. On the main tour, although he did finish in the top 60 money winners several times and also won three tournaments in the 1970s, he was never better than 28th on the money list. Regarded then as considerably less talented than his brother Dave, Mike has outstripped him as an over-50 golfer. Having won not much more than $500,000 on the main US Tour throughout his career, he came reasonably close to that in his first year on the Senior Tour. In his next year, 1990, he won five events and finished second on the year's money list with winnings of close on $900,000. Even better times were to follow. In 1991 he again had five wins and became only the second man to top $1 million in a season on the Senior Tour. In the seasons 1992–94 he did not do quite as well, but did add more than $2 million to his winnings and advanced his Senior wins to 16. He currently equals Lee Trevino as having the longest winning streak – five tournaments – on the Senior Tour.

Harold Hilton

Born: January 12, 1869
West Kirkby, England

Hilton is generally ranked alongside his fellow Royal Liverpool club member John Ball as the greatest of British amateur golfers. He may have taken only four Amateur Championship titles to Ball's eight, but he won two Opens to Ball's single victory. He remains the only British amateur to have taken the Open twice and, perhaps surprisingly, the one British amateur to have taken the American title, when he succeeded at Apawamis in 1911. Hilton's first Open Championship victory came in 1892 at Muirfield. He had not intended to play and gave himself time only for a day's practice. His start wasn't promising, but his final rounds of 72 and 74 were

truly outstanding for the time. Five years later, on his home course of Hoylake, he did it again, beating James Braid by a stroke. Oddly, he found winning the Amateur Championship more of a problem, partly because his great rival, Freddie Tait, used to get the better of him. However, he won in 1900 and 1901 and then, during a revival shortly before the First World War, came two more victories.

SCOTT HOCH *Gave Faldo a Masters*

Scott Hoch

Born: November 24, 1955
Raleigh, NC, USA

Hoch came into professional golf after a good amateur career, perhaps his peak achievement being to reach the final of the 1978 US Amateur. On the US Tour since 1980, he has always made a good living, 12 times being 40th or better on the money list. On this Tour he has won five times and also been effective overseas with a Pacific Masters on his record and two Casio World Opens. Hoch was once robbed of a major victory by a putting aberration that may haunt him until his dying day. It happened in 1989, and the scene was the play-off for the Masters. He had tied with Nick Faldo and seemed to have had it won on the first play-off hole, Augusta's 10th. Faldo had hit his second shot into a bunker while Hoch was less than a dozen yards from the hole and on the green. Faldo

splashed out to about seven feet. Hoch coasted his putt almost stone dead. To stay alive, Faldo had to hole out for his bogey and did so. Hoch then had to complete the formalities, with a putt of perhaps a couple of feet – but missed. As he later said, "The message between my brain and my hands got crisscrossed." Faldo holed quite a long one on the next and was Masters champion. For Hoch, history may show that this was his closest encounter with a major. The chances don't come often.

Ben Hogan

See Legends pp 92–3

Tommy Horton

Born: June 16, 1941
St Helens, England

Horton's early career was boosted by a man called Ernest Butten, who had a passionate desire to see a British player win the Open Championship. The last to do so had been Max Faulkner at Portrush in 1951. The scheme was that Butten would put some money into grooming three players with the potential to become superstars. Faulkner would teach them how to swing the club, putt and have the mental toughness to be winners. As it turned out, none of them came really close to winning the Open, but Brian Barnes and Tommy Hor-

TOMMY HORTON *Success on Seniors Tour*

ton did become very considerable players. Horton was twice joint leading British player in the Open Championship – in 1976 and 1977. His finest hour was probably his victory in the 1978 Dunlop Masters, then very much a top tournament. Quite a small man, Horton was somewhat underpowered and often found himself having to hit long irons into greens when Brian Barnes, for example, might have needed just a firm wedge. So Tommy Horton became one of the best long-iron players in European golf. He had eight tournament wins in Europe, was second on the money list in 1967, had three victories overseas and was in the 1975 and 1977 Ryder Cup teams. He was PGA captain in 1978.

Bernard Hunt

Born: February 2, 1930
Atherstone, England

Seniors usually fade quietly away once past their mid-50s – but apparently not Hunt. As recently as 1994 he was competing in a senior event in Northumberland, and pulled his trolley throughout. The 64-year-old Hunt would have won the play-off, which lasted a remarkable six holes, but for a careless short putt. Hunt was one of those players who radically modified their golf swings. He began with a long backswing and was quite a wild driver at times. However, by his early 20s he had solved the problem and became a winner with a much shortened action. He was still best with the shorter irons, and was a very reliable putter. He broke through in 1953 when he won an amazing six events on what was then a very limited tour. Ironically, that year also saw Hunt's greatest disaster. Playing in the Ryder Cup at Wentworth, he needed to get down in two putts to tie the match. He failed. This was his first appearance, but in his next, at Lindrick in 1957, he beat his opponent by 6 and 5 and went on to be very effective in later matches until he bowed out in 1969. Hunt was nonplaying captain in 1973 and 1975. He thrice won the Vardon Trophy for the season's lowest stroke average and won 26 tournaments.

Jock Hutchison

Born: 1884
St Andrews, Scotland

Hutchison was one of many Scots who emigrated to America to find fame and fortune and mainly developed their game there. He began to make his mark around 1910, and was fifth in the US Open the following year. His best finishes in the event were two second places, in 1916 and 1920, and he was third on two other occasions. In 1916, he came close to winning his first major, the US PGA, but was beaten in the match play final by the Cornishman Jim Barnes. However, all was well in 1920 when he defeated another English export, J. Douglas Edgar, in the final of the same event. His greatest success came on home ground, in the 1921 British Open at St Andrews. After the four rounds, he was tied with the English amateur Roger Wethered, but easily won the 36-hole play-off. There was some controversy afterwards. Hutchison's clubs were heavily scored, and it was felt that it was this factor that enabled him to stop the ball so quickly on hard and fast greens. Such designs were later banned. Hutchison won an estimated eight events of significance on the fledgling US Tour.

Juli Inkster

Born: June 24, 1960
Los Altos, Ca, USA

Inkster had a glittering amateur career which has not quite been maintained as a professional. In the years 1980–82 she became one of only three women – the others being Glenna Collett and Virginia van Wie – to have won the US Women's Amateur title three years in a row. In her last amateur season she won both her Curtis Cup matches, heading the US team, by 7 and 6 and later on went on to take the individual prize in the Women's World Amateur Team Championship by a comfortable four strokes. She was, without doubt, the world's best woman amateur. After turning professional she quickly captured her first LPGA title. In 1984 she was named Rookie of the Year and won two majors, the Nabisco Dinah Shore and the du Maurier Classic. She was sixth on the money list and went on to have her best season in 1986, when she moved up to third, winning four times. Since then, she has not been quite as successful, partly because of the demands of motherhood, but the wins have continued to pile up, including a third major, the 1989 Nabisco Dinah Shore. Two major play-offs, in 1992, were lost. At the end of 1994 she had increased her total of tournament victories to 15. She played in the 1992 Solheim Cup team.

Hale Irwin

Born: June 3, 1945
Joplin, Mo, USA

In the 1990 US Open at Medinah, Irwin played one of the most dramatic shots in the history of golf. He holed a putt of about 60 feet on the last green to tie with Mike Donald. Again they were level after a further round and Irwin then holed a birdie putt in sudden death to win. At 45, he had become the oldest winner of the US Open. Irwin has two more US Opens on his record. His

first came over the very difficult Winged Foot course in 1974, where seven over par was good enough for a two-stroke victory. This win demonstrated one of Irwin's great strengths. He is by no means an outstanding putter or a genius at close range, but he does find most of the fairways and greens, so tough courses bring out the best in him. His second US Open win came in 1979 and included the shot of the year in his third round, a two-iron to a couple of feet or so. He has won 20 titles on the US Tour and over $5½ million, including over $800,000 in 1994 alone.

Tony Jacklin

Born: July 7, 1944
Scunthorpe, England

Not many players lead a major after every round, but Jacklin did this in the US Open at Hazeltine in 1970. He cruised home to win by seven strokes, becoming the first Englishman to win the US Open since Ted Ray in 1920. Jacklin had won the Open Championship the previous year and

for a month or so was one of the select few to hold both the national championships. He was a British national hero and seemed on the verge of becoming an all-time great, but thereafter the big prizes eluded him. Lee Trevino had much to do with this, holing some outrageous and very telling shots at Muirfield in 1972, when the pair were locked in combat for the Open Championship. Playing the penultimate hole, Jacklin had victory in his grasp as Trevino struggled, but he three-putted for a six. Later that same season he played brilliantly against Trevino in the World Matchplay Championship – but again it was the American who came out on top. Though Jacklin was to play other excellent tournaments, never again did he contend in a major championship. He was a brilliantly successful Ryder Cup captain during the 1980s.

Peter Jacobsen

Born: 1954
Portland, Or, USA

This player is one of those most in demand for US golf clinics and company days. The main reason is that he is a jovial fellow who enjoys communicating. Unlike some others, he is also good copy for press tent interviews. Overall, his career has been impeded by medical problems but he has seemed to be hitting top form

around the age of 40. Jacobsen likes to play internationally and it is appropriate that his first win came in the 1979 West Australian Open. The following year he won his first event on the US Tour, the Buick Open. Since then, up until the end of 1994, Jacobsen has only been an

TONY JACKLIN *Britsh hero*

occasional winner, though often a contender, medical problems being a factor. Jacobsen first broke through in 1980, when he won twice and was eighth on the US money list. This remains his highest position but he has three times more featured in the top 20. The strongest feature of his game is consistency through the green. He hits the fairways more than most and then goes on to find the greens. He is also thought to be the best there is at imitating the swings and mannerisms of other players.

Mark James

Born: October 28, 1953
Manchester, England

Watching Mark James play, you would think that playing professional golf is a very sad affair indeed. However, once he gets away from the office – the golf course – he is one of the most entertaining people in the international game. James had a very good amateur career, representing his country at all age levels in the first half of the 1970s, winning the English Amateur title in 1974 and reaching the final of the British Amateur the next year. In the same period he showed his toughness in match play, when he was involved in winning close on half the points the Great Britain and Ireland team won in the 1975 Walker Cup. He has shown the same qualities in the Ryder Cup, in which he has made the team six times between 1977 and 1993. Appropriately, his first pro-

LEE JANZEN *The surprise winner of the 1993 US Open*

fessional success came in the 1978 Sun Alliance Match Play Championship. Since then, tournament wins have come consistently and he has often seemed on the edge of becoming a great, rather than just a very successful, player. Up to the end of 1994, Mark James had won 16 events on the European Tour and three more elsewhere. He has been in the top 20 money winners 14 times, with a best placing of third.

Don January

Born: November 20, 1929
Plainview, USA

January has been an important figure in US golf since he joined the tour in 1956. He had his first victory that year and continued to win occasional tournaments until his victory in the Tournament of Champions in 1976. In this phase of his career he was always a consistent money winner and was 20 times in the top 60 money winners. This was despite the fact that he was not a hard worker in terms of tournament entries. Once he had won what he thought enough money for a year, Don would take things a great deal easier. In 1972, he decided to take things even easier and left pro golf to design golf courses. However, there was a slump in that business so he came back in 1975. The following year he finished ninth on the money list. January won ten times on the main tour, including the US PGA Championship in 1967, and has

22 successes as a Senior. The first golfer to benefit substantially from the take-off of the Senior PGA Tour, he was in the top four earners each year from 1981 to 1986 and was either first or second for the opening four years of the tour. Now a Super Senior, he can currently claim to be the best over-60s golfer in the world.

Lee Janzen

Born: August 1964
Austin, Tx, USA

There are not many people who have tied Jack Nicklaus for a record, but Janzen has. When he won the US Open in 1993 from Payne Stewart, his aggregate of 272 tied the record that Nicklaus had set back in 1980. Janzen first appeared in the US Open in 1990, but made little impact until he won his first event two years later. Then came his 1993 victories in both the Phoenix and US Opens. In 1994, he looked a good bet to repeat his US Open success, having taken the Buick Classic by three strokes over South African Ernie Els the week before. Alas for Jenzen, Els went on to win the US Open while Janzen missed the cut. Like many players, Janzen looks a little anonymous because he wears a sponsor's baseball cap. (They sometimes refuse to remove them because of a clause in their contracts.) During the 1993 British Open at Royal St George's he was politely but firmly told they were not permitted attire in the clubhouse.) Since his US Open win, Janzen has failed to reach superstar status, but as he is in his early 30s, the prime of many players, he still has time.

Bobby Jones

See Legends pp 94–5

Betsy King

Born: August 13, 1955
Reading, Pa, USA

Betsy King first attracted notice at the 1976 US Open, when she finished

in eighth place – a feat which has not been matched since by an amateur. However, after joining the US LPGA Tour in 1977, she found it all a very slow learning process, and her first successful season only came in 1983. That year she finished 14th on the money list, and she was on her way. From 1984 until 1994 her worst placing was ninth, and she has six times been in the top three. She was leading money winner in 1984, 1989 and 1993. Since her first success in Japan in 1981 the victories have piled up. Her first LPGA success came in 1984. Two others followed that same year, after which she did not have a winless year until 1994. In 1989 she set a new target (broken the next year) for a season's money winnings with over $650,000. She had won six times, including the US Women's Open. This was one of her five major titles to date, the others being the Dinah Shore in 1987 and 1990, the LPGA in 1992, and the increasingly rare feat of a second Women's Open in 1990, making it two in a row. King currently has 29 LPGA titles to her credit.

Sam King

Born: March 27, 1911
Sevenoaks, England

Sam King's career spanned the Second World War, and he made Ryder Cup appearances on either side of it. One of these was the disastrous first post-war match at Portland, Oregon, where Great Britain and Ireland lost every match – except Sam King's final singles. King often featured in the British Open, but had a tendency to fade in the final stages. His best performance was in the 1939 St Andrews Open when he finished third, four strokes behind champion Dick Burton. He had several other top six placings and made a very strong run as late as 1959 at Muirfield. After three rounds, he was four strokes ahead of the eventual champion, Gary Player, but his final 76 left him four behind. In 1961 and 1962 he won the British Seniors but lost to Paul Runyan in the World event. King performed well for so many years because he was not often off the fairway and had great skill with the mid to short irons. His putting was excellent in his youth, but less reliable in more mature years. He won three major events, and the Kent Championship a remarkable 12 times between 1932 and 1951 in spite of the wartime interruption.

TOM KITE *A great money winner*

Tom Kite

Born: December 9, 1949
Austin, Tx, USA

Tom appears a rather anonymous player, partly because his face is normally shielded by a very large pair of spectacles and hooded by a sponsor's eye shade. He is perhaps more famed for blowing major championships than winning them, but he is the biggest money-winner of them all, with over $9 million to his credit. Kite has achieved this by his consistency rather than by winning tournaments. After joining the US Tour in 1972, he had only three tournament victories to his credit ten years later. His strike rate, however, has greatly increased since then. He is not a long hitter but a master with the wedge, often carrying three to enable him to play a full shot more often, thanks to the choice of loft available to him. His peak year was 1989, when he set what was then the US Tour money-winning record at just under $1,400,000. However, having long been described as the best player never to have won a major championship, he was probably far more pleased by his victory in the 1992 US Open at Pebble Beach.

Catherine Lacoste

Born: June 27, 1945
Paris, France

For a while Lacoste was arguably the best woman player in the world. She also has a strong claim to be ranked as the greatest French player of either sex. She had a lot to live up to, coming from a very sporting family. Her father René had been a great tennis player; her mother the first overseas player to win the British Ladies Golf Championship. Catherine's finest achievement was her victory in the 1967 US Women's Open, when a few days past her 22nd birthday. She was the youngest player to win this event, the first and only amateur, and only the second overseas player. An even better year for her was 1969, when she became only the third player to win both the British and US Amateur titles the same year. Catherine would undoubtedly have become a highly effective player on the US LPGA Tour. Instead, she married a Spaniard and competed relatively little afterwards. She did, however, add two Spanish national titles to her record following four earlier victories in the French Open Amateur. The strength of her game was her unusual power with the long irons.

Ky Laffoon

Born: 1908
Zinc, USA

Laffoon was an excellent golfer, but better known for his eccentricities, not least in his behaviour towards his golf clubs. If his putter behaved well and a long one went down, he might stroke it lovingly, but when things went wrong he was less kindly. It is said that on one occasion he attempted to strangle it. When that didn't work, he tried to produce death by drowning – not hurling it into a lake, mind you, but holding it under water. However, he usually had more respect for his equipment and liked to work on it. He particu-

larly liked a sharp leading edge on his pitching clubs. So, while driving, he would grab a club, open his car door and grind it on the highway. You could often tell that Ky was on his way to the next tournament by the trail of sparks he left behind him. Laffoon made his main impact in the mid-1930s. In 1934 he won four times and also took the trophy for the year's low stroke average. This performance gave him a Ryder Cup place the following year. Perhaps a fiery temperament told against this part Native American, for his skills did not match his achievements, although he won several more tournaments and did well in both the US Open and the Masters.

BERNHARD LANGER *Most consistent*

Bernhard Langer

Born: August 27, 1957
Anhausen, Germany

No man has conquered a putting twitch as successfully as Langer, who is now at the peak of his career as regards all-around consistency. Even by his teens, Langer was renowned as a great approach putter but very ineffective from short range. Then he found a putter that worked, for a year or two, and later resorted to the left-hand-below-right grip. When this too failed him he had to invent another method to eliminate a convulsive breakdown, or twitch, in the left wrist. He has done so very effectively with the most weird method of putting yet seen. The left hand is placed well

down the grip with the shaft well up the inside of the left forearm. The right hand then clamps the shaft to the forearm. Langer's invention seems to work and has been imitated by other tournament players. Langer is the most consistent player on the European Tour by far. At the end of 1994 he had not missed a cut for 52 events and had recorded wins for 16 consecutive years. He has challenged for the British Open but would probably consider his two Masters victories in 1985 and 1993 his greatest achievements. He has 31 wins on the European Tour and a dozen others worldwide.

Cecil Leitch

Born: April 13, 1891
Silloth, England

Charlotte Cecilia Pitcairn Leitch was perhaps the first woman to give the golf ball an uninhibited thump. Her style was based on a broad stance and she used a palm grip with the right hand. For a few years, she was probably the best in the world – until the arrival of Joyce Wethered. Cecil won the British Ladies' Championship in 1914, 1920, 1921 and 1926. She first made a name for herself by reaching the semi-final stage of the 1908 British Ladies' and achieved her first major win, the French title, in 1912. By this time, she was recognized as a new breed of woman player and was a cause of much debate about the comparative abilities of male and female players. In 1910, she played a 72-hole challenge match against the best British amateur of the day, Harold Hilton. She won, though it should be mentioned that Hilton conceded her a stroke on alternate holes. Cecil's peak years spanned the First World War. Her most devastating victory came in the 1921 Canadian Championship. At lunch she was 14 up in the final and then won the first three holes afterwards.

Tony Lema

Born: 1934
Oakland, Ca, USA

Lema is remembered chiefly for two events in his career, one a triumph, the other perhaps the most remarkable defeat in the history of match play golf. In 1964, when the British Open still attracted only a few of the top US players, Lema decided to enter at St Andrews. Even so, he took it casually. He hardly knew the course, and mainly just tried to hit it where the caddie told him. Nevertheless, on his first appearance in the British Open, and with no previous experience of golf on linksland, he won by five strokes from Jack Nicklaus – and threw a champagne party, one of his trademarks after a win. If this was remarkable, his defeat by Gary Player the following year in the World Matchplay Championship at Wentworth was astonishing. Lema completed the first 18 holes six up and then won the first hole in the afternoon. Alas for Lema, Player then became inspired, drew level on the last hole and won the first play-off hole. That same year, Lema had been in sight of a second consecutive British Open – but Australian Peter Thomson had other ideas. From 1957 until his death in a plane crash in 1966, Lema won 16 events worldwide.

Bruce Lietzke
Born: 1951
Kansas City, Mo, USA

If Lietzke's ambitions had matched his undoubted talents he might have had a superstar. However, perhaps his limited golf workload suits his temperament. It may also have given him a longer career. He likes to spend as much time with his wife and two children as he can, to support the Dallas Cowboys and do "serious fishing". Lietzke was probably at his best when making his way up the ladder of success. His first very good year came in 1977, when for a time he played golf in a kind of trance. He didn't have any thoughts about the golf swing at all. As he put it, "I just stood over the ball and pulled the trigger." That year, he won his first two tournaments and finished fifth on the money list. The following year he was not as successful but won the Canadian, a win he repeated in 1982. This was as near as he has come to winning a major championship. But perhaps Bruce isn't much interested in the majors.

He is certainly one of the now few top Americans who apparently have no ambition to win a British Open. He has won 13 times on the US Tour, most recently in 1994, and seems to win as much money as he needs – nearly $5½ million in all.

Lawson Little
Born: June 23, 1910
Newport, RI, USA

This player was the first and last since the retirement of Bobby Jones who might have built a record – at least at amateur level – to have rivalled that of Jones himself. He came to the fore in 1933, reaching the semi-finals of the US Amateur and earning a Walker Cup place which took him to Britain the following year. In both his matches, the British opposition was overwhelmed, and Little moved on from St Andrews to Prestwick for the British Amateur. Having progressed smoothly to the final, he beat a strongly supported local man, by 14 and 13 after arguably the best stretch of golf ever produced by an amateur. He then went home and won the US Amateur, beating his opponent by 8 and 7. How do you follow that? Well, 1935 was nearly as good for Little. First he took the British Amateur, after a close fight with an English doctor, and then proceeded to win the US title again – the only time both championships have been won by the same man in two successive years. With four major championships under his belt, Little turned professional but failed to become the dominant force he was expected to be. He did, however, win the 1940 US Open, beating Gene Sarazen in the play-off.

Sally Little
Born: 1951
Cape Town, South Africa

Sally Little came to the LPGA after a successful career in South African amateur golf which included both the match play and stroke play titles. Having made a big impression in the

DAVIS LOVE III *A major breakthrough?*

1971 World Amateur Team Championship, she joined the LPGA Tour. It was not until 1976, however, that she had her first victory, when she holed out from a bunker for a birdie on the final hole. After this success, she established herself as one of the leading LPGA players from 1977 to 1982 and was never out of the top 10 money winners. The last of these years was her most successful season because, as well as coming third on the money list, she had four victories. Altogether she has won 15 titles and three of them have been majors: the 1980 LPGA Championship, the 1982 Dinah Shore and the 1988 du Maurier Classic. Ill health cut her down in her prime, for in 1983 she had both abdominal and arthroscopic knee surgery and was only able to play a handful of events. She tumbled down to 139th on the money list and, despite her 1988 win, has never really regained the same form.

Gene Littler
Born: July 21, 1930
San Diego, Ca, USA

"Here's a kid with a perfect swing like Sam Snead's …only better." This was a comment from Gene Sarazen when Littler was a young man. The player also earned the nickname "Gene the Machine", because he made the golf swing look so effortless and the results were so predictably perfect. With his near perfect swing, really excellent putting and precision short-iron play, it is surprising that Littler did not become a superstar. Lack of a driving passion to be the best might have been the reason. He sometimes seemed content to make a good start to the season and then take things relatively easily. He first emerged in 1953, by winning the US Amateur, and his profile became more distinct the very next year when he won a US Tour event as an amateur – a very rare feat indeed. On turning professional, he continued to be successful, winning four events in his first full season, 1955. His best year was probably 1959, when he won five times. In 1961 he took the US Open and later lost play-offs for the 1970 Masters and the 1977 US PGA. He won 29 times on the US Tour, eight times on the Senior Tour, and also made seven Ryder Cup appearances.

Bobby Locke
Born: November 20, 1917
Germiston, South Africa

Locke was the first golfer to dominate golf on three continents – America,

Europe and his native South Africa. Some of this came about because Sam Snead won the 1946 Open Championship. Locke suggested an exhibition tour of singles match play in South Africa and Snead accepted – to his eventual regret. Locke won 12 of the 16 matches and Snead two. The American had been putted to death by a man who, to Snead, just seemed to hole everything. This success against just about the greatest player of the time persuaded Locke to try his luck in the USA, where Snead had told him he ought to be very successful. Locke won event after event and in a short 1947 season was placed second on the US money list. The following year he won three times. He then fell foul of the tour administration and afterwards played far more of his golf in the British Isles and Europe. His career as a winner of Open Championships now began to flourish. He won in 1949 at Sandwich, the following year at Troon and at Lytham in 1952. Though Locke continued to win tournaments he then ceased to take the Open until 1957, when he had his fourth and final victory at St Andrews.

Nancy Lopez
Born: January 6, 1957
Torrance, Ca, USA

Lopez once seemed destined to be regarded as the greatest woman player ever, but it didn't quite happen. Why? One reason could be her liking for family life. Another is faulty technique – her backswing finishes in a very shut position at the top. Most of the time, however, she has it all adjusted by the time she gets the clubhead into the strike zone. She is also an outstanding putter. It was in 1978 that she set the US LPGA Tour on fire. Then she had five straight wins, which seemed to triple the gate money at US women's tournaments. Of course, it could not go on for ever, but she won nine times that year and the publicity ensured that the US LPGA has never looked back. She was also highly successful the following year with eight wins, but thereafter lost her absolute dominance. You cannot maintain an av-

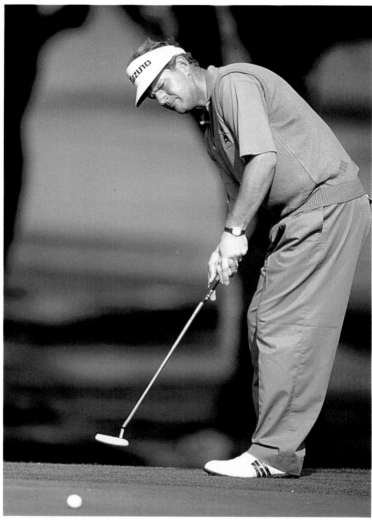

SANDY LYLE *Time for a change of fortune?*

erage, unless you are Bobby Jones, of winning 17 of the 50 events you enter. She remains a formidable competitor, having won 47 events and headed the US money list three times. In only three years since her debut in 1977 has she failed to win a tournament.

Davis Love III
Born: 1964
Charlotte, NC, USA

Love ranks a little below John Daly in sheer distance – about half a dozen yards according to 1994 US Tour statistics. He does it in a much more controlled fashion, which makes the whole performance less exciting to the eye, but the results are usually more predictable. With his enormous distance, Love is many people's bet to go on to be one of the great players towards the end of

this century, when not a few of today's superstars will inevitably begin to fade. He joined the US Tour in 1986 and had a respectable first season. In 1987 he had his first tournament win, the Heritage Classic. After one more victory in the intervening years, he won the same event for the second time in 1991 and also had his first high placing on the US money list – eighth, with nearly $700,000 banked. It was in 1992 that he first emerged as a major figure in world golf. Once again he won the Heritage as well as the Greater Greensboro Open and the Players Championship. The following year he won twice, including the Tournament of Champions, another event of high prestige. Playing with Fred Couples he has won three World Cups, and he has also represented the United States in the

Walker, Dunhill and Ryder Cups. In 1995 he was runner-up to Ben Crenshaw in the Masters.

Sandy Lyle
Born: February 9, 1958
Shrewsbury, England

The first of Lyle's two supreme achievements came at Sandwich in 1985, when he won the Open Championship, helped somewhat by Bernhard Langer and David Graham falling away. Even on the final day Lyle made no dramatic move until he had successive birdies on the 14th and 15th, to move into the joint lead. Disaster loomed at the 18th, when a little pitch shot from rough at the edge of the green almost came back to his feet. However, he got his bogey five and that was good enough. Lyle's greatest year was 1988. Having won the Phoenix Open and the Greater Greensboro, he enjoyed his finest hour at the Masters. He began with a 71 in high winds and then moved two strokes ahead of the field with a 67. A third-round 72 was good enough to keep that advantage. On the final day, he began to pull well away from the field but faltered on the second nine. At the last he put his tee shot into a fairway bunker along the left, but nipped a seven-iron off the sand past the flag, and his ball drifted back to about three yards. The putt went down and he was champion. Later the same year, he won the Dunhill Masters and the World Match Play. Lyle has won only three times since, and his glory days seem to be behind him. But things can change.

Mark McCumber
Born: September 7, 1951
Jacksonville, Fl, USA

McCumber seems to be one of those golfers who only occasionally emerge from anonymity, but even so he has a good and long-standing career record. US Tour earnings of nearly $4½ million attest to that. He turned professional in the mid-1970s and had little success until 1979, when he won his first tournament. It was not until 1983, however, when he won two events and finished eighth in the money list, that he was established as a player to be reckoned with. He still seems to be an up-and-down player, but when he's good, he's very very good, and he has won ten times on the US Tour, including the important Players Championship in 1988 and the Tour Championship in 1994. This last year was comfortably his best in golf. He won three times, quite a rare achievement, and was placed third on the US Tour money list, having decided to concentrate more on golf. He and his brothers have a variety of business interests, including golf-course design. McCumber played in the 1989 Ryder Cup team and has also twice been in the United States World Cup pairing, winning in 1988.

Johnny McDermott
Born: 1891
Philadelphia, Pa, USA

In 1911 MacDermott became the first native-born American to win the US Open. He had already come very close to victory the previous year, aged 19, losing a play-off to Alex Smith. He was again in a play-off situation in 1911, this time opposed to George Simpson and Mike Brady, both formidable players destined never to win their national championship. With his victory, McDermott became the youngest player, then or now, to win a major championship. The following year he won again with scores of 74, 75, 74, 71, making him still one of the select few to have achieved consecutive victories. In 1913, he proved in a US tournament that he could beat the best of the British. Harry Vardon and Ted Ray, who were until then all-conquering on a tour of the United States consisting mainly of exhibition matches, were left miles behind. Much encouraged, McDermott crossed the Atlantic to see if he could win the British Open, and came in fifth. A long and bril-

liant career seemed ahead of him, but instead he had a mental breakdown in 1915 and that was that.

C. B. Macdonald
Born: 1856
Niagara Falls, NY, USA

Macdonald is arguably the least great golfer in this book but, nevertheless, one of the game's most influential figures. He became fascinated by golf while a student at St Andrews University from 1872, and learned to play on the Old Course. He is said to have played against all the well-known players, including Young Tom Morris. When he returned to the United States, he had to do without golf for a few years because there were no courses. Eventually, in 1893, he solved the problem himself by designing the first 18-hole course in the country at Chicago. His monument, however, is the National Golf Links of America, where, with magnificent terrain at his disposal, he also drew on his memories of golf in Britain to design a proportion of the holes. In the meantime, Macdonald had, in fact, found open spaces where he could knock golf balls around and was reasonably well primed as competitive golf at national level began in the USA. He won the first US Amateur in 1895, by 12 and 11 in the final, having reputedly not gone to bed until five in the morning. He then played the remaining holes with a spectator friend.

Mark McNulty
Born: October 25, 1953
Bindwa, Zimbabwe

McNulty has been almost as successful over the years as his school friend Nick Price, only a major championship eluding him – though he's come close with a second place in the British Open. McNulty is underpowered by modern standards though his smooth measured swing ensures that he seldom has a bad round. The strengths of his game, however, are on and around the greens, his skill with his centre-shafted putter being legendary. Since the 1980s McNulty has been one of the leading performers on the South African circuit, where his wins include the 1987 South African Open and the Million Dollar Challenge the same year. In the two years 1986 and 1987 he had a formidable 13 wins, eight of them in 1986. In Europe too he has been a much respected competitor, with 13 tournaments to his credit between 1979 and 1994. He had three wins there in 1987, with the Dunhill British Masters being his biggest. Currently based at Sunningdale in England, in future McNulty may devote more time to the US Tour.

Lloyd Mangrum
Born: 1914
Trenton, NJ, USA

With his centre parting, thin moustache and an ever-present cigarette between his lips, Mangrum had something of the air of a Mississip-

pi river boat gambler. He was indeed a hard man, hard enough to win two Purple Hearts while under the command of General Patton during the 1944 Battle of the Bulge. Apparently undeterred by his wounds, he went off to recuperate at St Andrews and won a GI tournament there before returning to the USA for the 1946 golf season. He had already made his mark there, and had in fact caused a sensation in 1940 by setting what was then an Augusta record with a first-round score of 64 in that year's Masters. In the end, he finished second to Jimmy Demaret. In 1946, he won his only major championship, a marathon US Open. He tied with Byron Nelson and Vic Ghezzi, and in the 18-hole play-off all three had 72s. So out they went again for another 18 holes. This time, Mangrum's 72 was enough for a one-stroke victory. This was the beginning of his great years, when he twice won the Vardon Trophy, topped the money list and was always up there near the top. Tournament wins piled up and he is credited with 34 on the US Tour.

Graham Marsh
Born: January 14, 1944
Kalgoorlie, Australia

This Australian is a truly international golfer who has won all over the world, from Switzerland to Malaya. He never made a prolonged assault on the US Tour, though he did win the important Heritage Classic in 1977. Elsewhere, he has won at least 56 significant events worldwide, including 24 in Japan. Marsh qualified by age for the US Senior Tour in 1994 and showed that he maintained his very consistent game by being only once out of the top 25 in 22 events. His best performance was to finish in second place in the US Senior Open. It seems inevitable that he will be a great success on the Senior Tour – if he continues to compete. However, as he paid relatively little attention to the main US Tour when at his peak as a player, this may be unlikely. The gap in Marsh's record is that he failed to win a major championship, though he has won both the European Open

MARK McNULTY *Consistency is the name of his game*

and the World Matchplay. Marsh is always meticulous in his preparations before playing a shot, particularly making sure that all the right parts are in precise alignment with the target. He then strikes neatly and with enough power and always seems to finish well balanced. He also controls his emotions and avoids histrionics, unlike his brother Rodney, the cricketer.

Phil Mickelson

Born: 1970, San Diego, Ca, USA

Harry Vardon was once asked who was the best left-hander he had ever seen and is said to have replied that he had never seen one worth a damn. There was some justice in this, because Bob Charles is the only left-hander ever to win a major championship. But Mickelson is widely predicted to be the next. Like Charles, he is a superb putter, and his long game is perhaps even more impressive. He may also have learned that skiing is not conducive to good golf, having broken his left femur and cracked his right ankle early in the 1994 season. Mickelson seems to have most things going for him, especially as bones heal better when you are young. In 1990, he won the US Amateur (the only left-hander to do so) and that same year became the only amateur, except for Jack Nicklaus, to win both that title and the NCAA in the same year. He played in the Walker Cup in both 1989 and 1991. In the latter year, he was also one of the few amateurs ever to win a full US Tour event. As a professional, he won twice in 1993 and once in 1994, when he also finished third in the US PGA Championship.

Cary Middlecoff

Born: January 6, 1921
Halls, USA

Middlecoff was one of the players who helped to turn golf into the slow game it is today. He took a great deal of time to align himself to the ball, and even the very uncritical Bobby Jones was moved to remark that it was not a visually attractive process. A serious analyst of the golf swing, Middlecoff was among the first to grasp how important the set-

up can be. Another of his theories concerned getting the clubhead in the right position at the top of the backswing, where he would bring it to a careful halt before initiating the downswing. Such was his slowness, by the standards of the times, that in the play-off for the 1957 US Open his opponent, Dick Mayer, took out a camping stool on which to perch himself while Middlecoff took his time. If this was a psychological ploy it may have worked. Middlecoff went around in 79; Mayer won rather comfortably with his 72. Even so, Middlecoff's overall record was far superior. He won the US Open twice, in 1949 and 1956, and the Masters in 1955. He was also the leading US Tour player during the 1950s with a total of 37 victories, which puts him well up the all-time list. The end of his career came, as with so many great players, because of a twitch on the short putts.

JOHNNY MILLER *Brief spell at the top*

Johnny Miller

Born: April 29, 1947
San Francisco, Ca, USA

For a short span of time Miller played golf as well as it has ever been played. He was undeniably the best golfer in the world in 1974, when he headed the US Tour money list, but his peak years lasted only from 1973, when he won the US Open, to his victory in the 1976 British Open at Royal Birkdale. At Oakmont Country Club in the US Open, Miller was six strokes behind the leaders when the final round

began, but a start of four birdies immediately brought him into contention. There were more birdies to come and Miller finished with a 63, at the time the lowest score ever recorded in championship golf. His putting had by no means been phenomenal. It was the supreme quality of his iron play that counted the most. In 1974 he had no fewer than eight victories on the US Tour, followed the next year by four more and a close encounter with the Masters. His 1976 British Open triumph marked the end of his great run. He lost form dramatically but did make a come-back during the early 1980s. Remarkably he won again early in 1994, having made no money in the previous year, then hardly bothered to play again.

Abe Mitchell

Born: 1887
East Grinstead, England

The Great Triumvirate of James Braid, J. H. Taylor and Harry Vardon certainly set standards that no British trio have achieved since. With the end of the First World War, the Victorian greats were all well past their prime, and the question of their successors arose. The two more obvious candidates were George Duncan and Abe Mitchell, although the latter had not established himself to the same extent. Duncan was to win a British Open; Mitchell did not. Perhaps he never quite recovered from his disappointment at Deal in 1920, when he was 13 strokes ahead of the eventual winner, Duncan, after two rounds and then three-putted the first three greens, had a seven on his card, and finished in 84. As Byron Nelson once said: "Winners are a different breed of cat." However, Mitchell was still the most effective British golfer through the 1920s and a little beyond, and had a formidable record in match play, winning the championship three times. He was also the man Americans feared most in the Ryder Cup, where, either in singles or with partners, he had such winning scores as 8 and 7, and 9 and 8 to his credit and overall took seven points out of a possible ten.

LARRY MIZE *140-foot chip won a major*

Larry Mize

Born: September 23, 1958
Augusta, Ga, USA

Mize had his finest hour in the 1987 Masters, where his birdie at the final hole produced a tie with Seve Ballesteros and Greg Norman. A play-off began in which death was indeed sudden – Seve departing in despair after just one hole. On the next Norman played a good safe shot, away from the water on the left, to the right side of the green. If he could get down in two, he looked sure to be the champion, for Mize was well off the green further right. However, from 140 feet away he played a good running pitch that seemed just a touch too strong – but down it went and that was that. It was a fluke, of course, but a highly popular one in the town of Mize's birth. The rest of his career has been less spectacular though he has been a good journeyman since he joined the US Tour in 1982. His first win came the following year, and he has added three more Tour wins. His other great achievement was his fine winning performance in the 1993 Johnnie Walker World Championship in Jamaica – worth over \$1.2 million.

Dottie Mochrie

Born: August 17, 1965
Saratoga Springs, NY, USA

Mochrie joined the LPGA Tour in 1988 and was an immediate success, winning over \$130,000 in her first season and her first event the following year. Her first three years on the Tour were very respectable, for she totalled about $500,000 in money winnings. Then her career really began to take off. In 1991 she won no tournament but was extremely consistent, rising to third on the money list and establishing herself as a leading name in American women's golf. Since then her status has remained much the same as she continued to be in the top four up to the end of 1994. Her best year was 1992, when she had four wins, of which the most important was the Dinah Shore, so far her only major championship. She was also that year's leading money winner, with close on $700,000 to her credit. A very tough competitor indeed, Mochrie is well known for what some think over-aggressive demonstrations during the Solheim Cup, in which she has played three times.

Colin Montgomerie

Born: June 23, 1963
Glasgow, Scotland

There's that saying that you drive for show and putt for dough. However, if you can't hit the ball quite long and fairly consistently straight from the tee, you will putt in vain. Montgomerie's game is strong in both these departments. He is a long hitter who can usually be confident that his fade will "take". This means that he can rule out trouble along the left, aim more-or-less at it, and leave himself the whole width of the fairway to play with. Thereafter, he

is one of the best putters in the world. One achievement that has so far eluded Montgomerie is a win in a major championship, but he has performed very well in the US Open. In 1992 he seemed a likely winner when he completed his final round, but he ended up in third place. He came closer in 1994, when he tied for second after playing poorly in an 18-hole play-off with Loren Roberts and the eventual champion, Ernie Els. On the European Tour he has become a dominant figure, leading the money list in 1993 and 1994 and making a strong start in 1995. As a tournament winner he is less prominent with seven European Tour wins up to the end of 1994.

Gil Morgan

Born: 1946
Wewaka, Ok, USA

Most American golfers have been to university and some emerge with prefixes to their names. One example is Cary Middlecoff, who qualified as a dentist but found that golf paid even better and paid no further attention to teeth. In 1972 Morgan graduated with his doctorate from the Southern College of Optometry and fixed his eyes firmly on the US Tour, which he first qualified to play in 1973. His first big year came in 1977, when he won his first tournament, but 1978 was better still. Winning twice and finishing second on the US Tour money list, he seemed

to have established himself as a name player. That has not quite happened, but he has continued to perform well: by the end of 1994 he was approaching $5 million in money winnings, had won seven times on the US Tour, and played in two Ryder Cup teams in 1979 and 1983. His greatest triumphs and disasters, however, came in one particular event, the 1992 US Open. Here he became the first golfer to reach ten under par, and even improved that by another two – only to subside dramatically to tie for 13th place.

Tom Morris Senior

Born: June 16, 1821
St Andrews, Scotland

Winner of the first truly Open Championship in 1861 (the first the previous year was not open to amateurs), Old Tom Morris went on to further victories in 1862, 1864 and 1867. He began playing over the Old Course at St Andrews when he was about six, and became apprenticed to Allan Robertson for the making of both clubs and feathery balls. The pair then became a formidable partnership in foursomes challenge matches for large sums of money. However they fell out when Robertson spotted Old Tom playing with a gutta percha ball at a time when these were rapidly replacing the feathery from 1848 onwards. Robertson felt they would kill his trade. Morris set up his own workshop, but in 1851 moved away to become professional and keeper of the green at the new Prestwick Golf Club. Returning later to his home town to take over a similar role, he became a revered and much-loved figure in golf. He did the original designs for many courses in the British Isles.

Tom Morris Junior

Born: April 20, 1851
St Andrews, Scotland

"Young Tommie", as he was usually called, was a brief comet on the golf scene, dying at the age of 24, just a few months after his wife in 1875. However, if only for a few years, he was the dominant player of his time. Indeed, like several players in succeeding generations, he changed the whole notion of how well the game

could be played. A long hitter, he was also excellent in his recovery shots from bad lies in the rough, and his iron shots to greens were revolutionary. Where earlier players had tended to use short-shafted lofted woods, he used a rut iron. This was a small-headed club, originally intended to enable players to, literally, escape from ruts. Young Tommie used it to gain far greater backspin in his short approaches. He won the British Open for the first time in 1868, in succession to his father, at the age of 17, and retained it the next two years. Then a problem arose. The original trophy was a morocco leather belt, presented with the proviso that anyone who won three titles in a row got to keep it. With no trophy to hand, no championship was held in 1871. The following year, Tommie won the replacement, a claret cup. He remains the only man to have won four Open Championships in a row.

Kel Nagle

Born: December 21, 1920
Sydney, Australia

Nagle was one of the late developers in golf. Although he first won a tournament in his late twenties, he then almost totally disappeared from view for several years. When he again became a factor in tournament golf his game had been transformed. Formerly a long but wild hitter and a relatively poor putter, he was now shortish but one of the steadiest from the tee and a very sound putter indeed. However, he continued to be primarily an Australasia-based golfer. As he approached the age of 40 he had won the Open Championships of Australia and New Zealand, while elsewhere his record was unimpressive. Then came the British Open at St Andrews in 1960. The new hero was Arnold Palmer, making his first Open appearance, but although he played well he was left five strokes

DOTTIE MOCHRIE *A fierce competitor, especially in the Solheim Cup*

behind Nagle after two rounds. Nagle had gone round in 69 and 67 but was still given little chance. The climax came in the final round. Palmer holed out for a birdie on the last while Nagle faced a par putt on the treacherous 17th of some seven feet. He got it and went on to par the last for a one-stroke victory. After this success his confidence blossomed, and some 25 titles followed.

TOMMY NAKAJIMA *Likes to play abroad*

Tsuneyuki Nakajima

Born: October 20, 1954
Gunma, Japan

Unless "Tommy" Nakajima can manage yet to achieve international glory, it may be his sad fate to be remembered chiefly for two disasters which befell him in one year – 1978. Qualifying to play in the Masters, he managed to run up a score of 13 on the 13th hole at Augusta, where most players are thinking about eagles or at least birdies. Three months later, at St Andrews in the British Open, he earned a cruel kind of immortality. The famous Road bunker, hard by the 17th green on the Old Course at St Andrews, has almost, but not quite, been renamed "The Sands of Nakajima" following his toils there while in close contention for the championship. Nakajima was and is a superb sand player, but the shot was exceptionally demanding, with the flag close by and a narrow thread of green beyond and then the road. Trying for a delicate shot which

would just clear the steep face of the bunker and gently settle on the green, poor Nakajima took four attempts to succeed, and a nine eventually went down on his card. In Japan, however, he has been prodigiously successful, with four Opens, three PGAs and three Matchplays to his credit, and has won more than 50 events.

Byron Nelson

Born: February 4, 1912
Fort Worth, Tx, USA

Between 1944 and 1946 Nelson was the greatest golfer ever. In 1944 he won seven times, but reckoned that occasional lapses of concentration were costing him something like a stroke a round. The following year he knocked a stroke and a half off his average per round. This resulted in easily the greatest winning streak ever. From March to August he played 11 tournaments and won them all. He went on to win another seven. Oddly, some might think, he was nearly burned out by the effort. In 1946 he won five more times and then, at the age of 34, announced his retirement. It is likely that there were several reasons. He disliked all the travelling involved and the constant appearances demanded of him for publicity and with sponsors. It is also claimed that competitive play made him feel physically sick. In the majors, he did not give himself enough time to build an outstanding record. Even so, he won the 1937 and 1942 Masters, the 1939 US Open and the US PGA in 1940 and 1945. Doubtless he would also have completed the professional Grand Slam had he entered the British Open more often. He played only twice, and never during his greatest years.

Larry Nelson

Born: September 10, 1947
Fort Payne, Al, USA

In terms of money winnings, Larry was only outstanding between 1979 and 1981, particularly in 1979 when he was second on the US money list. However, he has occasionally played superbly in the major championships when, after none too good a year, he has had moments of in-

LARRY NELSON *You don't hear from him – then suddenly he wins*

spiration. The greatest of these came in 1983 when he won the US Open at Oakmont. He had been having a poor season and was seven strokes off the lead after two rounds. However, a 65 then brought him into contention and in the final round play was suspended because of thunderstorms with the contest really being between Watson and Nelson, who restarted on the 16th, a par three of 226 yards. He found the green and then holed out from about 20 yards. It proved the decisive shot of the championship. Nelson has also won the US PGA on two occasions, 1981 and 1987.

Liselotte Neumann

Born: May 20, 1966
Finspang, Sweden

"Lotta" Neumann has been a key part of the surge in Swedish golf which could some day see them become the dominant force in Europe. This is all the more remarkable in a country which has such a short playing season. Neumann first made her mark in the early 1980s, when she twice won her country's Amateur Championship, as well as the Matchplay Championship, and represented Sweden in international events. On turning professional she achieved immediate success in Europe with wins in such events as the German Open (three times) and the European and French Opens. Her really big breakthrough, however,

came in 1988, when she won the US Women's Open during her first season on the LPGA Tour. That year she won nearly $200,000 and, not surprisingly, gained the Rookie of the Year award. Since then she has been consistently successful, especially so in 1994. She was third on the money list, with just over $500,000, and had three wins. One of these was in the Women's British Open, which now rates as an official LPGA event. She also finished in third place in three of the LPGA major championships.

Jack Newton

Born: January 30, 1950
Sydney, Australia

Newton's finest hours came in two major championships. In 1980 he came second to Seve Ballesteros in the Masters. Five years earlier he had come tantalizingly close to victory in the British Open at Carnoustie. He began with rounds of 69 and 71, and a 65 then brought him up to within a single stroke of the leader, Bobby Cole. In the final round he looked to be doing even better. With the leading pack faltering, only Newton was playing consistently. Then, two strokes ahead on the leader board with four holes to play, he began to make his own errors. After dropping a shot at the difficult 17th, he needed to birdie the last to win – and couldn't quite do it. He had, however, tied with the then little known

GREG NORMAN *He has lost more majors than anyone*

Tom Watson. In the 18-hole play-off the next day, the pair were level after 17. However, Newton bunkered his shot to the green and didn't get his recovery close. Newton won in America, Australasia, Africa and Europe, but his career ended abruptly when he walked into a airplane propeller in the dark and was very seriously injured and disabled.

Jack Nicklaus

See Legends pp 96–7

Norman von Nida

Born: 1914
Strathfield, Australia

Australian golf was a very small world when von Nida arrived on the scene. During the 1930s he had to content himself mainly with winning state titles and money games with wealthy amateurs. Having tried the Far East Tour, then in its infancy, and finished as runner-up in the 1939 Australian Open, he decided to try his luck in the United States. However, the outbreak of the Second World War put a stop to that project. It was in 1946 that he really emerged as an international golfer. He turned up in Britain with total reserves of £17 but immediately began winning money. The following year he dominated the tournament scene, taking four of the first six events. By the end of the season he had won or tied for first place seven times and was leading money winner with over £3,000. That year he

had also shared the lead in the Open Championship after three rounds but faded on the final afternoon. He was never to repeat the success of 1947, but remained a force to be reckoned with for a few more years. He won the Australian PGA four times and the Australian Open three times.

Greg Norman

Born: February 10, 1955
Mount Isa, Australia

Norman must be considered one of the unluckiest golfers ever. Several major championships have slipped through his fingers. Sometimes it has been the result of lucky shots by other players at critical moments; at other times he has brought about his own downfall. By the mid-1990s Norman could have had anything up to a dozen major championships to his credit. Instead he has just his two Open Championships. Both were memorable occasions. At Turnberry in 1986 he began with a good 74 in very difficult conditions, and then on day two equalled the championship record with a 63, despite three-putting the last green. In the final round, he was never even threatened. At Royal St George's he produced one of his trademarks, a blazing final round. Often this has happened when Norman is virtually out of contention owing to the fact that his early rounds have perhaps been over-cautious: like Nicklaus, he knows that he is always a potential winner and wants a steady start. In the 1995 US

Open, however, leading at five under, he shot 74, 73, and finished two behind Corey Pavin. Although he has the dubious distinction of losing play-offs in all four majors, Norman is a prodigious winner of tournaments, with victories in no fewer than 13 countries, and is likely to be the favourite in any event he plays.

Andy North

Born: March 9, 1950
Thorp, USA

Of the 16 golfers to have won more than one US Open, North is perhaps the least distinguished. Oddly he has won only one other tournament on the US Tour, the 1977 Westchester Classic, and has never finished higher than 14th on the money list. Plagued by injuries, he competes rarely on the US Tour, and is able to do so only because of his exemption as a former US Open champion. His first US Open came at Cherry Hills, Denver, in 1978, where he had a four-stroke lead with five holes to play but rather staggered home. Needing a bogey five at the last to win, he only just did it. Short of the green in two, he then played his short pitch into a bunker but came out fairly close and was relieved to hole the putt. After a series of poor years he re-emerged to win the 1985 US Open by a stroke. That was a surprising year, for the runners-up too were hardly great names – T. C. Chen, Dave Barr and Denis Watson. North then disappeared again but, as Walter Hagen said: "Anyone can win one US Open, but it takes a great player to win two."

Christy O'Connor Senior

Born: December 21, 1924
Galway, Ireland

Many Irish players are unorthodox, and O'Connor, nicknamed "wristy Christy", was no exception. Nevertheless, he was not only one of the greatest Irish golfers ever but was

also at the top of British golf for many years. He came very close to the British Open in 1958, when his start of 67, 68 was the best since Henry Cotton's 67, 65 back in 1934. Thereafter he faltered a little, but came to the last hole at Lytham needing a par to tie. On this difficult hole, he did not quite manage it, and it was Peter Thomson who went on to win, beating Dave Thomas in the play-off. O'Connor was third, a position he repeated in 1961, and in 1965 he was second. It is tempting to speculate on what he might have achieved had his putting stroke been more solid and far less wristy. He played in every Ryder Cup match from 1955 to 1973 and also represented Ireland 15 times in the World Cup, partnering Harry Bradshaw in the winning team in Mexico City in 1958. More important for him was probably the fact that he won 24 European tournaments and dominated domestic golf in Ireland.

Christy O'Connor Junior

Born: August 19, 1948
Galway, Ireland

O'Connor turned professional in 1967 and first played on the European Tour in 1970. In 1975 he won the Irish Open and the Martini International. In 1976 and 1978 he also won the Sumrie-Bournemouth Better-ball in partnership with Eamonn Darcy. However, it was at the 1976 British Open that he really hit the headlines, sharing the first-round lead with Seve Ballesteros, then far less well known than O'Connor. Both went round Birkdale in 69, but the Irishman's score was the more remarkable, for it included an eight. In trouble, with his ball resting against a root, he had hit a branch on his backswing and played an airshot. A far more famous shot came years later in the 1989 Ryder Cup. His singles opponent, Fred Couples, had hit a marvellous drive along the final fairway and was left with little more than a lob to the final green. However, O'Connor then produced a cracking two-iron shot which won him the hole. O'Connor has not been a frequent winner. There have been two successes in Africa, four in Ireland and six in Europe, the most important being the 1992 Dunhill British Masters.

José-Maria Olazabal

Born: February 5, 1966
Fuenterrabia, Spain

Olazabal has long been many people's choice to become the world's greatest player. After a brilliant amateur career, he joined the European Tour in 1986, finishing second on the money list in his first year. He was already a star and on his way, with two professional victories already to his credit. Olazabal was soon hitting the ball longer, having refused to listen to the advice he was being given to change his grip. He knew that, for him, it worked and that many new professionals have been ruined by too much advice. No one gave him much advice about his short game, for it was as

good as anyone's in the world. On the European Tour, though he has had his moderate years, he has always been a consistent money winner and is always among the pre-tournament favourites – even when he proclaims he is playing very badly. He has also been high in the betting for all the major championships, but none came his way until his 1994 Masters victory, achieved with three rounds under 70 after an opening round of 74. Despite this win, his most dazzling performance came in the 1990 World Series of Golf, which he won by an almost laughable 12 strokes.

Mark O'Meara

Born: January 13, 1957
Goldsboro, NC, USA

O'Meara is something of a Pebble Beach specialist, having won over the course four times in US Tour

events. Though he is a little underpowered compared with many players, it is likely that this great course suits him because it demands precision and imagination in shot-making. O'Meara has both of these qualities. His game is varied, and when he is playing his best he prefers to draw his wooden club shots, for extra distance, but to fade his irons, for more control on the ball when it hits the green. Turning professional in 1981, it took him three years to make his mark, but he then went on to number two position on the money list in 1984, when he had his first US Tour win. That year he also had five second places and the most top ten finishes on the US Tour. Since then he has won another seven times and has also lost three play-offs. O'Meara has had his moments in the majors and has won the US Amateur, which he did in 1979. A US Ryder Cup player in 1985, 1989 and 1991, he likes competing internationally and has won in Japan, England and Australia.

Peter Oosterhuis

Born: May 3, 1948
London, England

This player had a meteoric rise to the top of European golf but, alas, his descent was almost as rapid. In 1966 he first began winning amateur events of significance, played in the Walker Cup team and then turned professional. For four years from 1971 he topped the Order of Merit and was easily the dominant player in Europe. However, Oosterhuis wanted to be a great player and decided that could only happen if he moved to the US Tour. He did so, particularly encouraged by his success in the 1973 Masters, where he headed the field by three strokes after the third round but dropped back to come in third, then the best finish achieved by a British player. When he left Britain he had played 200 tournaments, been in the top ten in more than half of them, won 20 and been second 26 times. In the USA he had a reasonable first year but the rest was mostly downhill. He had some high placings and eventually won a tournament, the 1981 Canadian Open. His nearest ap-

proaches to a major championship came with high finishes in the Opens of 1974, 1978 and 1982. Oosterhuis's greatest strengths were on and around the greens. When his shot in missed, he always seemed able to get down in two more. His weakness was a tendency to block his long shots out to the right.

PETER OOSTERHUIS *Meteoric rise and fall*

Francis Ouimet

Born: May 8, 1893
Brookline, Ma, USA

Ouimet became a national hero overnight when he beat the great Harry Vardon and recent Open champion Ted Ray in an 18-hole play-off for the 1913 US Open close by his home town. Oddly, it seems his victory the next year in the US Amateur Championship gave him more pleasure. Perhaps that was because his performances had earlier been poor. In his four previous entries he had three times failed to qualify and had once been knocked out in the second round. Much later, in 1931, he was to win this title again, but that was after Bobby Jones was safely retired. Despite his working-class background, Ouimet never considered turning professional. Nevertheless, he did lose his amateur status for a few years when the USGA decided he was profiting from his golfing fame by opening a sports shop in Boston. There was an ironic sequel in 1951, when the R&A decided to choose their first American captain. The

CHRISTY O'CONNOR JUNIOR *Nephew of a more famous player*

obvious choice was perhaps the greatest golfer of all time, Bobby Jones, who had not broken the rules of playing golf as an amateur, but who had certainly made a great deal of money after his retirement. Yet it was Ouimet who was invited, and he performed his tasks with both grace and diplomatic skill.

Masashi Ozaki

Born: January 24, 1947
Tokushima, Japan

Japanese players seem unwilling to display their talents on the world stage. It is difficult to know why, because there is so much talent on their home tour. Perhaps, because of the language barrier abroad and the rich pickings to be had at home, there is simply little incentive to travel to places where they can be made to feel somewhat alien. "Jumbo" Ozaki is a prime example. If he turns up at, say, the British or US Open, few spectators are much interested in him, and some may even not have heard his name before – although he is the biggest tournament money winner ever. A comparison with Tom Kite is interesting. Kite's consistency in achieving high placings, even if not a large number of tournament wins, has earned him the reputation of being the highest money winner ever. So he is in terms of US and European golf – but Ozaki is miles ahead. At the end of 1994 his winnings, mostly from Japanese golf, totalled more than £8 million. In financial terms he is the most successful player in golf history and, even though in his late 40s, he seems to be getting better and better and hitting the ball further and further. In 1994, he became the first player to win more than $2 million on the Japan Tour, and his number of victories went to more than 60.

JUMBO OZAKI *Gets better with age*

P

Alf Padgham

Born: 1906
Caterham, England

There are many ways of putting and, for at least a while, Padgham found an unusual answer to his putting problems. Instead of keeping his eye over the ball, he lined up with it very much further away from his body. Padgham decided on this method because it helped him to imitate his excellent chipping stroke. The extended arm action worked for him, and for a while he carried all before him. Of course, Padgham didn't do it all on putting alone. He had one of the best swings in the British game. Vardon thought it perfect and his contemporary Dai Rees considered it the equal of Sam Snead's. In the few tournaments of his time Padgham set a record, between 1935 and 1936, of winning four consecutive tournaments. He was also very effective in match play, taking the *News of the World* event twice and reaching the final on another occasion. he won his only Open Championship, in 1936, after breaking into a pro's shop – at Hoylake. Arriving early in the morning to begin the day's final 36 holes, he found it shut and resorted to smashing the window with a brick in order to collect his clubs.

Arnold Palmer

See Legends pp 98–9

Willie Park Senior

Born: 1833
Musselburgh, Scotland

Willie Park Senior has the distinction of being the first winner of the Open Championship, in 1860. He went on to win three more times – in 1863, 1866 and 1875. For a good many years, the principal players of their time were Park and Tom Morris Senior, both eventually eclipsed by the genius of Tom Morris Junior. Park first came to notice in the mid-1850s when he challenged all and sundry to play for £100 a side, very large stakes indeed for the time. Most tended to avoid confrontation with him because he was a very long driver indeed and also an excellent putter – a difficult combination of talents to beat. Perhaps it came from his upbringing as a golfer when he used just one club for both these parts of the game of golf. Besides this, he would sometimes challenge club golfers, offering to play them standing on one leg and using just one hand. Legend has it that he lost just once.

Willie Park Junior

Born: February 4, 1864
Musselburgh, Scotland

Although golf professionals had previously been makers of clubs and balls as much as expert players, William Park Junior can be called the first businessman golfer. His success as an Open Championship winner in 1887 and 1889 (the third member of the family to win, after his father and uncle Mungo) gave him the prestige to branch out into other fields, almost certainly to the detriment of his golf. He too went into club-making but was soon tending to employ other craftsmen rather than doing the work himself as his predecessors generally had. Park had shops in both London and New York, but this business faded gradually with the development of mass manufacture. A man of imagination and energy, he then made himself the first great golf architect. He worked intensively in design and construction in Britain, continental Europe and, in his later years, North America, but Sunningdale Old is probably his masterpiece.

Craig Parry

Born: January 12, 1966
Sunshine, Australia

Nicknamed "Popeye" because of his powerful forearms, Parry began to emerge in the late 1980s. In 1987 he won both the New South Wales Open and the Canadian Tournament Players Championship; two years later, he also won in Japan. A successful competitor on the European Tour, in 1989 he took two events, the Four Stars Pro-Celebrity and the German Open, and finished third on the money list. In 1991, he won the Italian and Scottish Opens and finished fifth. Having already competed a little in the USA, he decided to increase his appearances there, but so far has been less successful than in Europe. His best results on the US Tour have been second place in the 1994 Honda Classic and third in the 1993 US Open after sharing the lead in the first round. In 1992 he was in strong contention for the Masters, holding the lead after the third round before subsiding to a 78 and a position well down the field. That same year he also contended for the Players Championship. In Australia he has twice won the Australian Masters – in 1992 and 1994.

Jerry Pate

Born: September 16, 1953
Macon, Ga, USA

Golf is a more stressful game, physically, than many might think. Professionals often practise for hours on end, with the clubhead frequently crunching into the turf, and the results are a variety of injuries, mainly to wrists, elbows and shoulders, while the lower back suffers from the twisting motion of the golf swing. Pate seemed set to become one of the modern greats, but shoulder problems killed him off after a brilliant early career. In 1974 he won the US Amateur and also tied for the individual prize in the World Amateur Team Championship. Off he went to the US Tour qualifying school and was medalist in 1975. What better can you do than win the US Open the very next year in your first season as a professional? That is what Jerry Pate did, also hitting what many would say was the shot of the season. This was a five-iron from the rough, over water, and to a tight pin position. Pate got his ball to about two feet. He was US Open champion. That year, and until 1982, Pate was a big money winner, and at the age of 27 became the youngest player to achieve career winnings of $1 million. Then came injury.

Billy Joe Patton

Born: 1922, USA

"Hell, it ain't like losing a leg." So said Billy Joe in the press tent about his feelings after blowing the 1954 Mas-

ters, and this after arguably the best performance by an amateur in a major championship for decades. Patton, playing in his first Masters, went into the lead after two rounds – but who cared? Obviously Hogan or Snead or another great name would win. Sure enough, Patton then shot a 75 to fall five behind. But a hole in one can help, and after 12 holes on the final round the unimaginable had happened. He was back at the top of the leader board. The last nine holes at Augusta are legendary, particularly because of the shots over water, where contenders have the difficult task of judging the distance precisely and clearing the water barriers by no more than a few feet. Patton had no problem with length from the tee. He swung the club back just about faster than his downswing and was likely to win any long-driving competition. Obviously, after a dubious drive along the par five 13th, he went for the green over the creek. He took seven and soon after had a six on the par five 15th – to lose to Hogan and Snead by a stroke.

Corey Pavin

Born: November 16, 1959
Oxnard, Ca, USA

Pavin had an excellent amateur career in regional golf and made the 1981 Walker Cup team. Turning professional the following year, he had to wait until 1984 for his first title on the US Tour. He won the 1995 US Open at treacherous Shinnecock Hills, his final score of level-par 280 being a testament to solid play. Until his US Open victory, Pavin had been recognized as the best golfer to never to win a major. He had come close at Royal St George's in the 1993 British Open when, after tying Nick Faldo for the lead after three rounds, his final 70 would was overshadowed by Greg Norman's blistering 64 and Pavin finished fourth. That year he won the World Matchplay Championship. In 1994 he was eighth in the Masters and second in the US PGA. He has 12 successes to his credit on the US Tour. All this has been achieved despite not having a powerful drive. Pavin averages around 250 yards, but is accurate, and he is one of the best putters and

sand players in the business. His lack of power also means that he is inventive in his shot-making. Where others will be thinking of cracking a mid-iron directly at the flag, Pavin may draw or fade a wood into the green, perfectly illustrated by the magical second shot he played to four feet in the final round to ensure his US Open victory.

Calvin Peete

Born: July 18, 1943
Detroit, Mi, USA

Peete had an unusual introduction to golf. One of 19 children, he did not take up the game until the age of 23, and even then was hampered by a broken left elbow, which means he cannot straighten that arm. At his peak, Peete had superb balance through the strike area which helps to account for his legendary accuracy from the tee. For 10 years in a row he topped the US Tour averages for finding the fairway. Perhaps more important, he was also among the most consistent at hitting greens in regulation figures. Alas, for some time his putting did not equal his other abilities, but he broke through in 1979 to win his first tournament. Peete's top years were 1982 to 1985, when he won nine events on the US Tour and was three times in the top four money winners. After 1986, his success rate dropped rapidly, partly as a result of shoulder and lower back problems. His last two victories came in the Tournament of Champions and the USF&G Classic in 1986,

MANUEL PIÑERO *Small but very effective*

which brought his total of tour events to 12. Nowadays he has virtually stopped competing on the main tour but is active among the Seniors.

Henry Picard

Born: 1907
Plymouth, Ma, USA

Picard once performed the remarkable feat of beating Walter Hagen in a play-off. He must have had great character to resist the master golfing psychologist. Picard was essentially a 1930s golfer and well up among the most successful of that era. He might, for instance, have won the first Augusta National Invitational (later to become known as the Masters) and came close the second year with a 67, 68 start which put him four ahead of the eventual winner, Gene Sarazen. He put that right three years later in 1938 by producing four very consistent rounds of 71, 72, 72, 70 to win by two strokes from Harry Cooper and Ralph Guldahl. Picard won the US PGA Championship in 1939, beating Byron Nelson by 1 up in the final. Picard first became a tournament winner in 1934 and remained extremely successful until around the beginning of the Second World War when ill health virtually halted his career. By that time he had won 27 tournaments and had been leading money winner – with a little over $10,000!

Manuel Piñero

Born: September 1, 1952
Puebla de la Calzada, Spain

Piñero has always been among the best putters on the European Tour. At about 5ft 7in, it is not surprising that he is not a long hitter, but his all-round short game has made up for that. He reached the top 30 in both 1974 and 1975 and went on to produce a year of remarkable consistency in 1976 when he was never out of the top 11 and won the Swiss Open. He also made his second World Cup appearance and, with Seve Ballesteros, won the title for Spain. Piñero has appeared nine times in that event, and in 1982 he won the individual event and team prize with José-Maria Canizares. Otherwise Manuel Piñero's biggest wins came in the 1977 European PGA Championship and the 1982

European Open. He has won nine times on the European Tour and, between 1976 and 1982, was four times in the top five on the money list. Perhaps his proudest moment was playing number one in the 1985 Ryder Cup and winning his singles.

Gary Player
See Legends pp 100–01

Nick Price
Born: January 28, 1957
Durban, South Africa

In 1994 Price won six times and soared to the top of the Sony rankings. Perhaps most importantly, he won two major championships back to back, the British Open and the US PGA. With his five wins in the United States it is hardly surprising that he finished as leading money winner with just under $1½ million – roughly a repeat of his position in 1993. Though Price won the World Series of Golf as long ago as 1983 and has been a name player since 1982 he did not become a really major figure on the world stage until very much later. His performance in the 1982 British Open at Troon did cause a stir, however, and for years he probably lived with the memory of the major he should have won – but for a few lost strokes over the closing holes. Price was to lose another British Open, at Lytham in 1988, but this time through inspired play from Seve Ballesteros rather than his own failings. His breakthrough came with two US wins in 1991 and then the US PGA Championship the next year. After that he added another 16 wins around the world by the end of 1994.

Ronan Rafferty
Born: January 13, 1964
Newry, Northern Ireland

Rafferty was a youthful prodigy who in 1981, having already played for Ireland as a full international, became the youngest Walker Cup player ever. He turned profession-

NICK PRICE *Lines up a putt at the Turnberry Open, one of his two majors in 1994*

al that year and qualified to play the European Tour by virtue of good performances in South Africa. He immediately made some impact, and in both 1986 and 1988 was 9th on the money list. He had previously been successful in other parts of the world, his first win coming in the 1982 Venezuelan Open. Rafferty has proved to be particularly successful in Australia, where he has four wins to his credit including the 1988 Australian Matchplay Championship. He has also won in New Zealand. In Europe, 1989 was his best year. He had three wins – the Italian Open, the Scandinavian Enterprise Open and that grand finale to the season, the Volvo Masters. He finished top of the money list, was the best at hitting greens in regulation figures and won the Vardon Trophy. He also played in the Ryder Cup that year and won his singles match against Mark Calcavecchia.

Since then, he has been a little less successful, partly because of putting problems.

Judy Rankin
Born: February 18, 1945
St Louis, Mo, USA

Judy Rankin was a very early developer, winning the Missouri state title at the age of 14 and going on to finish low amateur in the US Women's Open the following year. By the age of 17 she was playing the LPGA Tour, though with very modest success – $701 in her first season. However, she made good progress and was ninth on the money list by 1965. In 1968 her stroke average came down substantially and she also had her first victory. Judy Rankin was on her way, and over the next ten years the victories piled up. In both 1976 and 1977, when she had six and five wins respectively, she was leading money

winner on the LPGA Tour. From 1969 to 1979, her worst placing was 15th, and she was nine times ninth or better. By the end of 1979 she had 26 tournament wins in the USA, but that was more or less it. Rankin had a very strong left hand grip, which tends to put stress on both the left wrist and can lead to an increased twisting movement of the lower spine. Within a few years, she had retired from tournament golf because of back problems.

Betsy Rawls
Born: May 4, 1928
Spartanburg, SC, USA

Rawls did not begin playing golf until her late teens but was soon winning her the Texas state title and the more important Trans-National and Broadmoor Invitational. While still an amateur, she finished second in the US Women's Open. From 1951, she played as a professional and her first win was in the US Women's Open, the most important of women's titles, which she won again in 1953, 1957 and 1960. She also won the Western and the LPGA Championship twice each. Her total of 55 LPGA victories ranks her behind only Kathy Whitworth, Mickey Wright and Patty Berg. As a money winner, she was in her prime from the mid-1950s (for which records are incomplete) until 1970. She was leading money winner in 1959 when she won a truly remarkable 10 times, and was never worse than 16th in a 14-year period. Yet in those years women's golf did not attract high prize winnings. The most she won in a season was only about $26,000. Rawls went on to become Tournament Director of the LPGA Tour during a period of rapid growth in the last half of the 1970s.

Ted Ray
Born: March 28, 1877
Jersey, Channel Islands

European success is now a common occurrence in the Masters, but not in the US Open. Only three British players, for instance, have managed to add this title to a win in the British Open: Harry Vardon (when, to be frank, it didn't matter very much), Ted Ray in 1920, when Americans were on the verge of dominance of world golf, and Tony Jacklin in 1970. Ray first really announced himself in British golf by reaching the 1903 final of the News of the World Matchplay Championship and losing to James Braid, then at the height of his powers. Ray began to contend for the British Open but had to cope with the stiffest competition from Vardon, Taylor and Braid. He finally broke through in 1912 at Muirfield, beating Vardon into second place by a comfortable four strokes. Ray was a dramatic player to watch because of his prodigious power. Even Bobby Jones was in some awe of him while watching him on a US exhibition tour. The power showed to good effect when Ray took his US Open title. On one par four hole he managed a long carry of some 280 yards over a ravine and birdied the hole in all four rounds. He excelled at thrashing the ball out of bad lies, but also had a delicate touch on the greens.

Dai Rees

Born: March 31, 1913
Barry, Wales

Rees's greatest achievement came at Lindrick in the 1957 Ryder Cup. He was in the only winning pairing on the Great Britain and Ireland side, of which he was captain, and on the second day trounced his opponent, 1954 US Open champion Ed Furgol, by 7 and 6. Equally notable was his failure to win a British Open, well though he played. Either he or Abe Mitchell must be the best British player not to win. Rees first began to make some impact in the event towards the end of the 1930s but became a really significant factor after the Second World War. He might well have won in 1946, when he had the lowest round of the championship, a 67, and went into the final round tied with the eventual winner, Sam Snead. Alas, he then had a disastrous start and could only partially recover. He was fourth. In 1950 and 1953, he outscored the eventual champions for two rounds, but they lasted better. In 1954, he needed a par on the last to tie, but his ball skipped through the green. Rees thought it

had hit a small stone. His last chance came at the age of 48, when he was one behind. In compensation, he was a most consistent tournament winner with 28 to his credit.

Mike Reid

Born: July 1, 1954
Bainbridge, USA

After a strong amateur career, which included being leading amateur in the US Open, Reid has proved to be rather a journeyman pro. He wins money but not many tournaments. So far they are the important Casio World Open in Japan in 1990, the 1987 Tucson Open and the 1988 World Series of Golf, the event which gave him considerable TV exposure and which he won in a play-off with Tom Watson. Reid is one of the US Tour's shorter hitters, currently averaging something like 250 yards. This may not be as great a disadvantage as some might think, because it has made him a master with a fairway wood, and he is no worse at hitting greens than most of his fellow competitors. Perhaps his worst moments came in the 1989 US PGA Championship. After three rounds, he held a three-stroke lead and was still in the same position after 69 holes. He bogeyed the next hole and played the 71st disastrously. On this par three his ball ran just through the green into quite a dense lie. From there he took a lob and three putts to get down. Afterwards he said in the press tent: "Where can you go around here to have a good cry?"

José Rivero

Born: September 20, 1955
Madrid, Spain

Rivero started in life as a caddie and in his late teens became a club professional in Madrid. Though many good players are content with the life, most players of quality, whether amateur or professional, want to see how well they can compete against the best. So, rather late in the day, Rivero decided to attempt to qualify for the European Tour in 1980 and eventually made it. The Spanish Golf Federation gave him a loan of about £2,500 ($3,800) to enable him to compete and, after a modest

year in 1983, he came through the next year with a win in the Lawrence Batley International and finished 11th on the money list. Since then he has won the 1987 French Open, the 1988 Monte Carlo Open and the 1992 Open Catalonia. This is perhaps not a great career record, but Rivero is very consistent, usually finishing well up the field, and by the end of 1994 had earned more than £1½ million. He would probably have done far better but for occasional failures with the putter. Rivero has often represented Spain in the Alfred Dunhill Cup and the World Cup, winning the team event once. He also played in both the 1985 and 1987 Ryder Cup matches.

Allan Robertson

Born: 1815
St Andrews, Scotland

Allan Robertson may have been the reason for the founding of the Open

Championship. Correctly or not, he was reputed to be the best golfer in Scotland, which, in the 1850s, virtually meant the world. When he died in 1859 it was decided that a successor should be found, and Prestwick Golf Club began its rudimentary organization of the Open Championship the following year.

As his career took place in the early days of photography, no visual evidence of his style exists. However, contemporary accounts of his playing abilities stress his accuracy, especially for shots up to the flag. For these he used an iron far more than his contemporaries, especially once the feathery ball had been displaced by the gutty – much to his disgust because of the excellent trade in the earlier ball. Robertson is the earliest known golf course architect. He was influential in the development of the Old Course at St Andrews and is

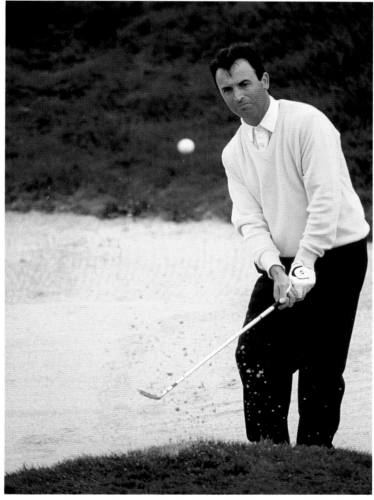

JOSÉ RIVERO *All Spaniards are in the shadow of Ballesteros and Olazabal*

believed to have designed the famous Road Hole (17th) with its wickedly difficult approach.

Chi-Chi Rodriguez

Born: October 13, 1935
Rio Piedras, Puerto Rico

Rodriguez is an even more talkative player than Lee Trevino, and in his younger days on the US Tour was known to many as "the clown prince of the Tour". Others, who disliked his chatter and on-course antics, called him "the four-stroke penalty". They felt that was about the number of strokes he cost them with his distracting behaviour. Such august figures as Arnold Palmer and Jack Nicklaus told him to moderate it, and he did so, while still remaining exuberant. Rodriguez had

a successful career on the US Tour between the beginning of the 1960s and the early 1980s. His first win came in 1963, his last in 1979, and he totalled eight in all. However, he has prospered far more as a Senior since 1985 and has been one of the most prolific winners ever. In 1986 he won three times and the next year took seven events, including the PGA Seniors. That year he also managed the feat of birdies on eight holes in a row, a record, which helped him to his record fourth straight win in a single season. He continued to take a title every year until the end of 1993. Rodriguez was a member of the US Ryder Cup team in 1973 and played for Puerto Rico in 12 World Cup teams.

Bill Rogers

Born: September 10, 1951
Waco, Tx, USA

Rogers worked his way gradually to the top and then subsided rapidly. As an amateur, he made the 1973 Walker Cup team. He then turned professional and first made a real impact by winning the 1977 Pacific Masters. The following year he took the Bob Hope Desert Classic, the first of his eventual five victories on the US Tour. In Britain, Rogers attracted much attention when he won the 1979 World Matchplay Championship at Wentworth. By this time, the strengths of his game were becoming apparent. Not long off the tee, he was very accurate and his scoring average was always good. His putting, excellent, involved an

action with relatively stiff arms, the stroke coming from the shoulders. In 1981, he reached his peak. He won three times on the US Tour and was named Player of the Year. More importantly, he took the British Open at Royal St George's, going into the last round with a five-stroke lead. That year he had a five wins in six entries, worldwide. Since then he has only won once, in 1983. "Then I had a very positive attitude," he said recently. "It was never the same after that."

Douglas Rolland

Born: 1860
Earlsferry, Scotland

Douglas Rolland was probably the best striker of a golf ball from the early 1880s to the mid 1890s. Many

CHI-CHI RODRIGUEZ *The crowds love his chatter; he's a big star on the Seniors Tour*

EDUARDO ROMERO *Argentina's best player, he has improved with age*

were the tales of his great length from the tee, though his putting was held in much lower regard. Although the Open Championship was quite well established by the time of Rolland's peak years, he seldom competed in the event. One reason is said to be that he faced prosecution, or a divorce case, if he returned to his native Scotland. He spent most of his life in England, where he held several golf club jobs. His fame during his best years mainly depended on his success in exhibition and challenge matches. He played the championship very little indeed but finished 13th in 1882, 10th the following year and, in 1884 tied for second place. Did this inspire him to greater efforts? Apparently not. As far as we know, he played just one more time, finishing second to J. H. Taylor in 1894. It seems his game declined shortly afterwards, perhaps because of a riotous lifestyle.

Eduardo Romero

Born: July 12, 1954
Cordoba, Argentina

Since the early 1980s, Romero has been Argentina's best player. He first won his own country's PGA back in 1983, and has repeated that success twice. The Argentine Open, however, eluded him until 1989, but he has also won the Chile Open twice. Golf in South America, however, is on a somewhat small scale and players have to make their names and earn their fortunes abroad. Romero plays mainly in Europe, with excursions to the USA and elsewhere. He began his European career in 1984 and started to make real progress in 1988 when he reached the top 50. Since then he has done a great deal better, his first big season coming in 1989 when he moved up to 13th on the money list and also won the Lancome Trophy, which has a select field. He won the Open di Firenze in 1990, and had two successes in 1991 – the Spanish Open and the French Open. These meant that he was comfortably in the top 20 money winners in the years 1989–91. In 1994, he took the Italian Open and the European Masters, earning more than £250,000/ $375,000 in the season.

Doug Sanders

Born: July 24, 1933
Cedartown, Ga, USA

Doug Sanders won 19 times on the US Tour between 1956 and 1972, and had five wins in 1961, but his fame rests on one never-to-be forgotten shot. Unfortunately for him it was a missed putt, which cost him the 1970 British Open. By then past his prime, Sanders had had to prequalify, but he was a master of improvised shots and St Andrews was his ideal arena. He came to the last two holes needing a couple of pars to win the championship. It was not easy, because the 17th is just about the most difficult hole in world golf. With the aid of an exquisite bunker shot, Sanders got his par four. The Open then seemed to be his, for the last hole at St Andrews is as easy a finishing hole as you can find. Sanders hit a good enough drive, slightly thinned his approach so that he ended up to the back of the green, putted up to four feet or less and then contemplated that putt for the championship. You have to make up your mind. Sanders did, but then noticed a mark along the line. He paused to remove it and then did not go through the usual routine – and missed. He then lost the 18-hole play-off with Jack Nicklaus by a stroke. Never mind, he is still better remembered for that missed putt than many are for a dramatic winning shot. If you ask Doug today if it preys on his mind he is likely to reply, "No, sometimes I don't think about it for five minutes."

Gene Sarazen

See Legends pp 102–03

Peter Senior

Born: July 31, 1959
Narangba, Australia

Almost all professional golfers seem to develop a putting twitch in the end – from Vardon, through Snead and Hogan, to Watson. Today, how-

PETER SENIOR *An ungainly hitter and putter ... but his methods work*

ever, solutions of a kind are to be found. The weird method of Bernhard Langer is being copied by some tour players, while others have found that the long putter has rejuvenated their game. Peter Senior is one of these. He had some disastrous years, largely caused by his putting problems, but then a fellow sufferer, Sam Torrance, gave him a long putter. This method, which involves tucking the club under the chin and then swinging it pendulum style, thus making demands on a different set of small muscles and nerves, has enabled him to be competitive again. His full swing shots are unusual, as he lifts up on the ball just after impact, whereas most players aim to maintain a low path into and after impact. Senior was first on

the Australasia money list in 1987, 1989 and 1993. His first win came in the 1979 South Australian Open and he has 20 victories worldwide. Most of these have come in Australia, where in 1989 he won both the Australian Open and the Australian PGA Championship. Outside Australia, his most important win was probably the European Open.

Patty Sheehan

Born: October 27, 1956
Middlebury, USA

As an amateur, Sheehan won a string of state titles and climaxed her career with a win in the 1980 AIAW National Championship. She played in the Curtis Cup that same year and won all her matches. Turning professional late on that year, it was not long before she made an impression, her first win coming the following year in the Mazda Japan Classic. In the USA she first won in 1982 and had two other victories that same year. She was already a star and has remained so. Her money list placing has always been high – never worse than 13th between 1981 and 1994. In the intervening years, eighth has been her worst placing and she has five times finished second on the money list, a formidable achievement. The tournament victories have piled up to a total at the end of 1994 of 32 (plus a Women's British Open in 1992). These have earned her, in addition to nearly 4^{1/2}$ million, membership of the LPGA Hall of Fame. She has won five major championships (or six if you include the British Women's Open, which will surely become one now that it is an official LPGA event). These are the LPGA three times and the US Women's Open twice.

Denny Shute

Born: October 25, 1904
Cleveland, Oh, USA

There was little money on the fledgling US Tour of the 1930s, so Shute had to devote much of his time to his club professional's job. Even so his achievements were very considerable, notably his victory in the 1933 British Open at St Andrews. The course was playing very short, which does not mean easily, because the greens were not holding and that puts a premium on precise judgment of the pitch and run. Shute had the odd result of four rounds of 73, which gave him a total one lower than Syd Easterbrook and a tie with Craig Wood. He went on to win the play-off. Easterbrook had already featured in Shute's year at Southport and Ainsdale in the Ryder Cup. There, at the climax of the match, Shute had three-putted the last green to lose to Easterbrook, and the USA went down. Revenge was very likely sweet. In the previous Ryder Cup matches in the USA, Shute had been a great deal more successful. He and Walter Hagen won their foursomes by 10 and 9, and Shute his singles by 8 and 6. Shute won two major championships

in his own country, the 1936 and 1937 PGAs, the last player to win two in a row. He was elected to the PGA Hall of Fame in 1957.

Scott Simpson

Born: September 17, 1955
San Diego, Ca, USA

After a successful amateur career, which included Walker Cup status, Simpson twice failed to qualify for the US Tour but made it in 1979. Since then, he has always made reasonable money but tends to disappear from the public view for quite long periods. His greatest season was 1987, when he finished fourth on the US money list but, much more important, won the US Open after a very close confrontation with

Tom Watson. He came through by a stroke with Watson narrowly missing a long putt. All this took place at the difficult Olympic Club. Since then, Simpson has seemed a US Open specialist, though he has not won again. He tied for sixth place in 1988 and 1989, and for first place in 1991, where he lost a play-off with Payne Stewart. Simpson is regarded by some as a journeyman professional, but he is much more accurate than many from the tee, which can give him an advantage when players are confronted by the tight drive zones and dense rough that are normally part of a US Open set-up. Besides his US Open he has won five events on the US Tour and four important events overseas.

PATTY SHEEHAN *One of the most consistent players on the US LPGA Tour*

Vijay Singh

Born: February 22, 1963
Lautoka, Fiji

Singh is the only golfer of world class that Fiji has produced. Given the amount of travelling he has had to do, because there is so little competition, relatively, in his homeland, his achievements have been enormous. First he settled in Malaysia, and after successes there decided to compete more widely. He was particularly successful in Africa, where he won three events in 1989 and has played the European Tour since his first appearances in 1988. He was soon a winner, taking the Volvo Open in 1989. By the end of 1994 he had taken his total of victories to six, perhaps the most important being the Trophée Lancôme, which has a select field. Singh has the reputation of practising more than just about anyone else, and his results reflect this kind of dedication. In a short European career he has won more than £1$^{1/2}$ million/2^{3/4}$ million. His best year was 1994, when he won about £450,000/$675,000 and rose to sixth on the money list. Singh currently spends more of his time in the USA, where he won the 1993 Buick Classic and two other titles in 1995, with earnings close to $2 million.

Jeff Sluman

Born: September 11, 1957
Rochester, NY, USA

Sluman's greatest achievement to date came at the Oak Tree Golf Club in the 1988 US PGA Championship. There he went into the final day three strokes behind the leader, Paul Azinger, but reversed that position with a closing 65. Surprisingly, that PGA still remains his only career victory – but, as they say, one crowded hour is worth an age without a name. Despite not winning, Sluman makes a good living and gets himself into good positions. He has lost three play-offs, and in 1994 he held the lead in the BC Open for three rounds, having opened with a 63, but even a steady enough 72 saw him finish four shots behind the winner. Sluman seems to have some knack of competing well in major championships. In 1992, at the tough Pebble Peach, he came second in the

VIJAY SINGH *Fijian on the verge of greatness*

US Open after a 71 in his final round, one of only four below par that day, and tied for the lead in the Masters after an opening 65, when he also became the first player to have a hole in one on the 4th. Sluman finished the event tied for fourth place. He has won about $3¼ million on the US Tour, his best year being 1992, when he earned over $700,000.

Horton Smith

Born: May 22, 1908
Springfield, USA

Being the first to win an event gives you a better chance of entering the history books – if only because yours is the first name on the trophy. Horton Smith won the First Augusta National Invitational in 1934, the tournament which was soon to become known as the Masters. The event aroused great interest, mainly because Bobby Jones, who had retired from all competitive golf four years before, was making a reappearance in "his" tournament. But Jones never repeated his previous form in any of the Masters he played. Smith won this first event by a stroke from the ever unfortunate Craig Wood. He repeated that success a couple of years later, this time by one from Harry Cooper, another player who seemed to be able to win anything – except a major. Smith had first burst on the scene in the 1928–29 winter, when he won eight out of nine events. He was the new

wonder of the age. Of course he could not maintain that phenomenal success rate and was in fact never again as devastating a force. Those two Masters were his only majors, but he was third twice in the US Open and once in the British. He played on three Ryder Cup teams and won some 30 tournaments.

Macdonald Smith

Born: 1890
Carnoustie, Scotland

Bing Crosby, himself a low handicap golfer, watched most of the greats over nearly half a century and considered that Smith had the best-looking swing of the lot. However, although he won over 30 times in the USA, Smith is often rated the best player not to have won a major. But how close he came. As early as 1910, for example, when only 20, he tied for the US Open and lost the play-off. He was never to come quite as close to a major again. By far the most famous failure came at Prestwick in 1925, after he took an almost impregnable five-stroke lead into the final round. The Scots turned out in their thousands to see their man from Carnoustie win. Crowd control was very poor on a course that presents difficulties in this respect. Smith sometimes had to wait too long to play his shots and occasionally, it is said, had to fire blind over spectators. As it turned out, a 76 would have been good

enough but, alas, he took 82. In the majors Smith had a tendency to produce a weak last round when in contention, keeping his brilliant ones for when it didn't matter very much.

Jesse Snead

Born: October 14, 1941
Hot Springs, Va, USA

Jesse, or J. C., Snead is a nephew of the great Sam Snead. Both were born and brought up in Hot Springs, Virginia; both still live there. Jesse did not decide on golf as a career until well into his 20s. This was because he was a good baseball player as a youngster and became a professional on the Washington Senators farm system. When golf eventually won the day, it took him four years to qualify for the US Tour, which he managed in 1968. Success eluded him at first, but in 1971 he suddenly won the Tucson and Doral-Eastern Opens in two weeks. These and other good performances won him a Ryder Cup place that year; he also appeared in 1973 and 1975. In that first year he had an outstanding record, winning a foursomes, two fourballs and narrowly defeating the British number one, Tony Jacklin. Snead's highest placing on the US Tour money list is sixth, which he achieved in both 1974 and 1976. He had eight wins on the US Tour, the last coming in 1987, when he beat Seve Ballesteros in a play-off. He has also won the Australian Open. He is now a big money winner on the Senior Tour, though he has won just once.

Sam Snead

Born: May 27, 1912
Hot Springs, Va, USA

Whereas some would argue that Ben Hogan had the most technically effective swing of all time, Snead declared that he would take care never to watch Hogan swing. He thought the whole performance too quick and snatchy, and didn't want to be infected by the same rhythm. And rhythm was certainly what Snead had, to an almost unrivalled degree, combined with great acceleration into the ball. One of the greatest tournament winners of them all, Snead never did win the US Open, though he several times came close,

sometimes agonizingly so. However, he won all the other majors. He was US PGA champion in 1942, 1949 and 1951, and took three Masters titles in 1949, 1952 and 1954. Reluctantly Snead also competed in the 1946 British Open at St Andrews, where he expressed his disgust with the course, his caddie, the accommodation and the food. "Whenever you leave the USA, you're just camping out", was his comment. In spite of all this he did become Open champion, but did not care to play in the event again until long past his best. Snead is probably the most prodigious tournament winner of them all. He is credited with 81 victories on the US Tour, and his worldwide total has been put at 135, though he claims to have won 165.

Mike Souchak

Born: May 10, 1927
Berwick, Pa, USA

How is this for nine holes of golf – 2, 4, 4, 3, 3, 3, 3, 3, 2? That was how Souchak played the second nine at Brackenridge Park during the 1955 Texas Open, for a total of 27. If he hadn't gone out in a relatively "poor" 33 he would have broken the magic 60. However, he was inspired that week, and rounds of 60, 68, 64, 65 gave him an aggregate of 257 which stood as a record low in tournament play until 1981, when Peter Tupling beat it over a 6,000-yard course. On the US Tour, only Al Geiberger and Chip Beck have bettered that first-round 60. However, it should be said that Souchak's score was achieved on a fairly easy course, while Tupling's involved putting on sand greens, which are easier than grass. Souchak played on the 1959 and 1961 Ryder Cup teams and won 16 times on the US Tour. He was in the top 10 of money winners four times – in 1956, 1959, 1960 and 1964. During this period he was a prominent performer in the US Open, achieving three third-place finishes. In 1960 he looked a likely winner after the splendid start of 68, 67, and a third-round 73 had him still comfortably placed. However, this was the year of Arnold Palmer's great charge, and while Palmer finished with a 65, Souchak could only manage a 75.

CRAIG STADLER *Will the Walrus return to the top*

Craig Stadler

Born: June 2, 1953
San Diego, Ca, USA

Nicknamed "The Walrus" on account of his profuse moustache and a 210-pound outline, Stadler is one of the most recognizable figures in world golf. He had a strong amateur career, during which he won the 1971 World Junior title and the 1973 US Amateur, and played on the 1975 Walker Cup team. After a slow start as a professional, he recorded his first two victories in 1980 and shot up the money list from 55th to 8th, a position he repeated in 1981. The following year he finished as leading money winner, with close on $500,000. More importantly, he also won four times in the USA. The most significant of his victories was undoubtedly the Masters, though that was a trying experience for him. After 11 holes of the final round he held a five-stroke lead, but then dropped shots on the 12th, 14th and 16th. He came up the last hole needing a par for victory, but three-putted to tie with Dan Pohl. However, he parred the first play-off hole and that was good enough. Stadler has played two Ryder Cups, won 11 times on the US Tour (with over $5½ million in money winnings) and has also had wins in Europe, South America and Japan.

Jan Stephenson

Born: December 22, 1951
Sydney, Australia

Like Laura Baugh, Jan Stephenson has sometimes received more attention for her sex appeal than her golf. She has turned down offers to pose for both *Playboy* and *Penthouse*, but has appeared topless in a French magazine. "I'm not ashamed of my body," she said, "and I'll flaunt it if I want to." In her teens, Stephenson was phenomenally successful in Australia, winning a host of girls' and junior titles and then, after turning professional in 1973, dominating what there was of an Australian Tour. Her future obviously lay in the United States and she began to play the LPGA Tour in 1974, winning good money and being named Rookie of the Year. Her first win came in 1976, since when she has taken 16 titles on the US Tour plus two Australian Opens, the 1981 World Ladies, the French Open, and a Japanese event. Her peak years in the USA were between 1976 and 1988, when she was only once out of the top 20. She has won three major titles on the LPGA Tour: the 1981 Peter Jackson Classic, the 1982 LPGA Championship and the 1983 US Women's Open.

Marlene Stewart

Born: March 9, 1934
Cereal, Canada

Stewart is probably the best golfer, male or female, that Canada has produced. She won her national closed championship nine times, and the total would have been higher had the event not sometimes been cancelled. The Canadian Open Amateur provided her with another record – and is a more significant gauge of her abilities, because it obviously attracted a higher class field. Starting in 1951, she won this championship eleven times up to 1973. One of her final opponents, a Miss M. Gay, must have been particularly unhappy. She played Marlene Stewart three times and lost by 9 and 8, 11 and 9, and 8 and 6. Outside her native land, Marlene did not, of course, pile up the wins as prolifically. However, in the USA she won the prestigious North and South and the US Women's in 1956, beating the great Joanne Gunderson (later Carner) in the final. She met the same opponent again ten years later, again in the final, and this time lost on the 41st hole – at least setting a record for the longest match. The British Ladies used to be a prime target for all amateurs of stature. Marlene won it in 1953, as usual trouncing her final opponent.

Payne Stewart

Born: January 30, 1957
Springfield, USA

Even in the distance, Stewart is instantly recognizable by his flamboyant attire, based on American football team clothing. He wears it supposedly to publicize the sport, and is no doubt paid hugely for doing so. He certainly attracts a great deal of attention, though it is not quite the gear to be wearing if you have to back into a gorse bush to play a shot. Stewart may well find himself in occasional gorse bushes, because he is one of the few Americans who are fond of playing outside the US. His first professional wins came in India and Indonesia during 1981, and another followed in Australia the following year. He won in the US in both 1982 and 1983, but thereafter found it easier to win large amounts of money than tournaments. In 1993, for instance, he set a US Tour season record for money winnings – nearly $1 million – without scoring a victory. His first major event came in 1989 in the US PGA. Two years later came the US Open after an 18-hole play-off with Scott Simpson, a formidable championship player, at Hazeltine National. Stewart has won eight times on the US Tour winning over $6½ million.

Dave Stockton

Born: November 2, 1941
San Bernardino, Ca, USA

Stockton is one of those players whose greatest achievements have been in over-50s golf. In a long career on the US Tour, which basically lasted from 1964 to 1980, he won 11 times. This may seem a modest total, but it did include two major wins, both in the PGA Championship. In the 1970 event Arnold Palmer was one of the players he forced into second place; in 1976 Raymond Floyd and Don January were the two who came in second after Stockton holed a putt to win from several yards. Putting was, and is, the main strength of his game. He had a severe back injury in his early teens, and since then has never been able to hit full out. He himself has claimed that he merely guides the clubhead through the ball – but he still drives 250 yards or so. Stockton twice played on the US Ryder Cup team – in 1971 and 1977 – but will be best remembered for his captaincy of the winning team in 1991, when Berhard Langer's famous missed putt allowed Hale Irwin and the United States off the hook. Stockton was rewarded by his team tossing him into the Atlantic. On the Senior Tour he has already won nine times, earned well over $3 million, and has twice been leading money winner – in 1993 and 1994.

Frank Stranahan

Born: August 5, 1922
Toledo, Oh, USA

Stranahan, an amateur, was one of the first golfers to introduce the idea that extreme physical fitness might be important for golf. Earlier it had been thought that no excessive consumption of food, alcohol and nicotine was all you had to aim at. Stranahan caused a sensation when, shortly after the Second World War, he arrived at a famous British hotel with his weight-lifting kit. Whether or not it did his golf much good is open to question, for in golf the ability to accelerate a light clubhead counts for a great deal more than the musculature to shift inert weights. In Britain, if not America, the methods earned him the nickname "Muscles". His ideas of fitness apart, Frank was one of the great amateurs of the immediate post-war years. He won a host of US regional titles, though he never did better than reach the final of the US Amateur, when he lost on the 39th. In Britain he was much more formidable, winning the Amateur comfortably in both 1948 and 1950 and reaching the 1952 final. He was a very frequent competitor in the British Open and tied for second place in 1947 and 1953, when he was the world's best amateur.

Curtis Strange

Born: January 30, 1955
Norfolk, Va, USA

In 1988 and 1989, Strange became the first man since Ben Hogan to win consecutive US Opens. 1988 also saw him become the first to pass $1 million in a year's US Tour earnings, as well as achieving the rare feat of winning four times. If Strange's proudest achievements are his US Open victories, which are in the record books for ever, there is another that certainly won't be in the future. That is his 62 over the Old Course at St Andrews in the 1987 Dunhill Cup. This achievement is slightly devalued because the event is played as stroke match play, and over the closing holes, Strange would have been under little real pressure. Strange has had an up-and-down career, and since 1990 has not really featured as a major player. His first outstanding year was 1980, when he emerged as a significant force and finished third on the US money list. He then subsided a little before being top money winner in 1985, 1987 and 1988. Altogether he has won 17 events on the US Tour, and about $6½ million. In his early profession-al days he earned the reputation of being far better at winning money than tournaments, but later became known as an "iron man" when in contention.

Louise Suggs

Born: September 7, 1923
Atlanta, Ga, USA

Louise Suggs ranks as one of the greatest of women players. As an amateur, she won numerous state and regional titles and capped that part of her career in some style. She won the US Women's title in 1947 and followed up by capturing the British in 1948 and playing in the Curtis Cup. She then turned professional, being a founder member of the US LPGA. As a professional, she had a great record in what were then ranked as major championships. She won the 1957 LPGA Championship, the US Women's Open in 1949 and 1952, the Title-holders in 1954, 1956 and 1959 and the Western Open in 1949 and 1953.

The most remarkable of these was her first US Open victory, which she won by a record 14 strokes from Babe Zaharias. In these early years of the LPGA tournaments there were really only three players usu-ally in contention – herself, Patty Berg and Zaharias. Suggs later said it was like watching three cats fight-ing over a plate of fish! Louise fought very well. In her best years she was always among the top money winners and won consis-tently. Her last success came in 1962. It was her 50th.

Hal Sutton

Born: April 28, 1958
Shreveport, La, USA

Sutton was a player who seemed destined to become one of the stars of the modern game. He had made a big impression as an amateur, making the Walker Cup team, win-ning several regional events and tak-ing the 1980 US Amateur. At Pinehurst he was the individual win-

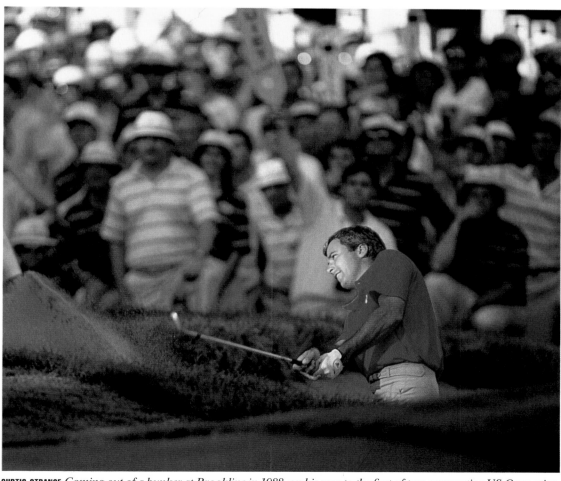

CURTIS STRANGE *Coming out of a bunker at Brookline in 1988, on his way to the first of two consecutive US Open wins*

ner in the World Amateur team championship, winning by nine strokes while his 276 total set a record for the event at 12 under par. In 1981, he was leading amateur in the British Open and again played in the Walker Cup team. Following a very good first professional season, crowned by victory in the last event, the Disney Open, 1983 was even better. He led the US PGA from start to finish, beating Jack Nicklaus by a stroke. He also won the Tournament Players Championship. These and other results made him leading money winner for the year and saw him elected PGA Player of the Year, a title also given him by the Golf Writers of America. His results fell away considerably in 1984, but he won twice in each of the next two seasons, when he was seventh and sixth on the money list. Since then nothing much has gone right, although there were signs of a return to form in 1994.

T

Freddie Tait
Born: January 11, 1870
Edinburgh, Scotland

Winner of the Amateur Championship in both 1896 and 1898, Tait was only beaten on the 37th hole of the 1899 final. It was fitting that his conqueror was an even finer amateur, John Ball. He was also a highly effective competitor in the Open Championship, being leading amateur three times in the 1890s and third overall twice. However, his forte was probably match play, in which, together with John Ball and Harold Hilton, he formed an amateur triumvirate. Tait was a prodigious hitter and also famed for his recovery play. He always seemed able to rip the ball out of the rough for great distances – highly disconcerting for a match play opponent. Harold Hilton, for instance, may well have been a greater player but he could seldom handle Tait. A lieutenant in the

DAVE THOMAS *Another vast hit*

Black Watch, Tait seems to have been allowed plenty of time to play golf, but his profession was the death of him. He was killed in 1900, leading a charge in the Boer War.

Dave Thomas
Born: August 16, 1934
Newcastle-upon-Tyne, England

For a good spell Thomas deserved his reputation for being the longest straight driver in the world. Thomas twice came close to winning the British Open, perhaps most noticeably in 1958 as a young man. Several players came to the last hole at Royal Lytham and St Anne's with a chance to win, but only Thomas and the Australian Peter Thomson survived in par. Thomas had already missed his chance to win on the previous hole, the long and difficult par four 17th. Having hit a huge drive, he then did the unforgivable and missed the green with a short iron. A 36-hole play-off followed the next day. Few could beat Thomson in a play-off of any length, and so it proved this time, though Thomas put up a good fight. A new star seemed to have arrived, but his results were not as good as expected, partly as a result of a weakness in his game he was never able to cure – the short pitch. Perhaps it was because Thomas was at his best on the full shot, whereas this one demands delicacy of touch and confidence. He was again second in an Open in 1966, to Nicklaus, and had 16 career wins.

He is now a very well-known course architect.

Peter Thomson
Born: August 23, 1929
Melbourne, Australia

Thomson was probably the ultimate master of running the ball over linksland turf. These skills made him one of the greatest competitors ever in the Open Championship, which he won five times – in 1954, 1955, 1956, 1958 and 1965. During the 1950s his only serious rival was the South African, Bobby Locke. Both had a similar approach to golf: get your tee shot on the fairway and the next one on the green, and then don't three-putt. From the beginning of the 1950s until the late 1960s Thomson was the man you had to beat in Europe, Australasia and the Far East. He was less formidable in the USA. He did not much enjoy playing there, nor many of the courses on that tour. They tended to suit long, high-flying driving, and

the man who putted best in a particular week was too often the winner. However, when long retired from competitive golf and more concerned with golf architecture, Thomson decided to try the Senior PGA Tour. In 1985 he was the supreme performer, breaking all the money-winning records. Then, having done what he wanted to do, he returned to golf architecture – and writing. He may be the best professional golfer writer ever.

Sam Torrance
Born: August 24, 1953
Largs, Scotland

Torrance's long and largely successful career is a testament to his long hitting and rhythm as much as anything. For a time, a twitching putter looked likely to bring his career to a premature end. Then he decided to experiment with a long putter. An avid snooker player, he practised with it on his table and the balls started to go in without that fatal tremor. He is

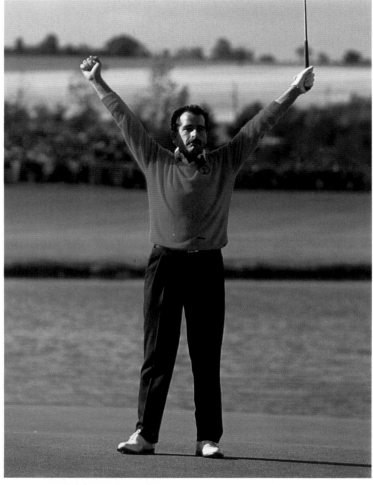

SAM TORRANCE *Celebrates his and Europe's winning putt at the 1985 Ryder Cup*

now probably a better performer on the greens than ever. He first played the European Tour in 1971 and made moderate progress until 1976, when he won twice and was third on the money list. Since then, Torrance has had only two fairly poor years on the European Tour, and is often up near the top of the money list. His highest position was second, in 1984, and he has nine times been in the top 10. His best period was 1981 to 1985, and he continues to be a very strong performer, though not at his best in major championships. He has won 18 times on the European Tour as well as four other tournaments. His career money winnings approach £2½ million.

Jerry Travers

Born: May 19, 1887
New York, NY, USA

There was a time when players carried far fewer clubs than they do today – one British Open champion carried just seven! Travers was rather a different case, however. He was seldom happy with woods, and may have been the first golfer of high ability to prefer an iron off the tee. But if Travers suffered the severe problem of being erratic with his woods, he usually made up for it with his brilliance on and around the greens. He was one of the first to concentrate on this, while others thought more of excellence through the green. His putting was particularly outstanding. Travers worked on various methods to see what worked best for him. He settled on an upright stance, keeping the body still throughout the stroke and making the head of the putter follow along the line – all conventional ideas today. What made Travers unusual in his day was his emphasis on an upright stance: many used to crouch low over the ball, with legs splayed wide. Travers won four US Amateurs – more than anyone except Bobby Jones. He won the US Open in 1915 – and never played in it again!

Walter Travis

Born: January 10, 1867
Maldon, Australia

Travis, who left his native land as a youngster, did not take up golf until his mid-30s, but made up for it with the intensity of his efforts. A very reliable wooden club player, Travis compensated for his shortness off the tee by hitting accurate woods to the greens. His putting was deadly. Undoubtedly his greatest claim to fame was his performance in the 1904 British Amateur at Sandwich. In practice, Travis found his putting had deserted him, but then he was offered a Schenectady, a centre-shafted putter with a mallet-type head. Suddenly his skills came back and the putts started rattling in once again. Travis cruised through round after round to meet Edward Blackwell in the final. There were great contrasts in their play. Blackwell drove the ball way past Travis, but the American had the equalizer on the greens and won by 4 and 3. He was the first overseas player to win the title. It was not a popular success with the British, and the Schenectady putter was later banned. In the US, Travis won three US Amateurs and was second in the 1902 US Open. Later he founded *The American Golfer* and became a distinguished golf course architect.

Lee Trevino

See Legends pp 104–05

Bob Tway

Born: May 4, 1959
Oklahoma City, Ok, USA

In 1986 Tway hit one of the most famous shots in modern golf. It came on the final hole of the US PGA Championship at Inverness. After the opening two rounds, Tway lay no fewer than nine strokes behind Greg Norman, but a third-round 64 reduced the gap to four. In the final round, Tway pulled level, and then came the drama of the final hole. Norman hit a good approach which spun back into the semi-rough around the green. Tway bunkered his approach and was left with a very difficult shot to make his par. A touch too strong, and his ball would run off the green; if he came up short, he would be left with a nasty downhill putt. He played a perfect shot, the ball pitching about 20 feet short of the hole – and running in. Norman then needed to hole his chip to tie and, not surprisingly, failed. This

KEN VENTURI *Came back from despair to win the 1964 US Open*

was Tway's fourth victory of the season in his second year on the US Tour. He finished second on the money list, with some $650,000, and was named PGA Player of the Year. Since then he has had two more victories on the tour, but from 1992 to 1994 was never better than 109th on the money list.

Harry Vardon

See Legends pp 106–07

Ken Venturi

Born: May 15, 1931
San Francisco, Ca, USA

Venturi will never forget the Congressional and the 1964 US Open. He had suffered a disastrous slump in form and had qualified to play the championship for the first time in four years. Earlier his career had been as promising as anyone's. While still an amateur in 1956 he had come very close to winning the Masters after beginning with rounds of 66 and 69, followed by a 75 in poor weather. Alas, in the final round he took 80, but had still been in the lead with two holes to play. Another Masters disaster followed in 1960. With two holes left, he had a one-stroke lead over Arnold Palmer. But the great man was unkind enough to birdie the last two holes and that was that. Even so, at this stage Venturi had the consolation of 10 wins on the US Tour, including four in 1958. Thereafter his consistency went, and he also suffered problems with his hands. In 1964, his game began to come back and he made a sound start to that US Open, followed by a 66 on the final morning. In extreme heat, he had to be accompanied by a doctor on the final afternoon but managed to make it through to victory. That was the happy end to Venturi's story, for his game soon to faded because of poor health.

Roberto de Vicenzo

Born: April 14, 1923
Buenos Aires, Argentina

The greatest South American golfer ever, de Vicenzo is still probably best known for an error in checking his score card on the last day of the 1968 Masters, which also happened to be his birthday. He played the round of his life, a 65. But he failed to notice that his playing partner had marked him down for a par four on the penultimate hole, which Roberto had birdied. He was a little distracted by his bogey five on the last hole of all. He thought he had lost the event by his errors there, but it was the calligraphy on the 17th that cost him the chance of a play-off. "What a stupid I am," he said. He was less stupid at Hoylake the previous year in the Open Championship. A third-round 67 gave him a two-stroke lead over Gary Player and a three-stroke advantage over the defending champion, Jack Nicklaus. He held on to win, his round climaxed by three superb tee shots. At 44 years and 93 days he was the oldest Open champion of modern times. De Vicenzo won over 30 national titles around the world. His overall total of wins is not known, but at well over 200, he may be the most prolific of all time. Roberto, a very easy-going character, has very likely not kept count.

Lanny Wadkins

Born: December 5, 1949
Richmond, Va, USA

Wadkins plays brilliantly when the inspiration flows. Almost as quick a player as there is, he goes for the flag rather than safe parts of the

green. Sometimes everything comes off; sometimes it doesn't. Perhaps this accounts for his fluctuating results in money winnings on the US Tour since his career began in 1971. He has eight times been in the top 10, but also 10 times out of the top 50. His best placings are second, once, and third, twice. His iron shots at the flag are probably the strongest part of his game, while his putting has been more variable. When his game is on song, Wadkins seizes his chances and he wants to win rather than just finish well up the field and pocket a respectable cheque. As a result, he has been a frequent winner on the US Tour and totalled an impressive 21 victories by the end of 1994. At the same stage he had won just short of $6 million. He has played on seven Ryder Cup teams, in the World Cup three times and twice in the Walker Cup. His captaincy of the 1995 Ryder Cup team at Oak Hill will be interesting – he is certain to fire his men up.

Tom Watson

See Legends pp 108–09

Tom Weiskopf

Born: November 9, 1942
Massillon, Oh, USA

Nicknamed "Terrible Tom" by the Press, Weiskopf was sometimes his own worst enemy. A perfectionist, gifted with a magnificent swing, he didn't feel it was "proper golf" to miss greens and scramble pars by means of a chip and single putt. His play in the 1969 Masters was characteristic. He missed only four greens in the tournament but still managed to finish only second, having three-putted 13 times. More dramatic was his play in the 1980 Masters. This time he came to the par three 12th having played competent golf. This shot to the green must be exact for distance: just a touch short and you are in Rae's Creek; a little long and it's difficult to salvage a par. Tom sent ball after ball into the creek and emerged with a 13.

LANNY WADKINS *Emotions always show*

TOM WEISKOPF *Elegant swing remains*

After his round he declared: "If you think I'm composed, you're badly mistaken." His great period was quite short. Towards the end of 1972 he won the World Matchplay Championship. He went on the following year to take four US Tour events and, more significantly, won the Open Championship at Troon in generally unpleasant weather. He was never headed at the end of any round and equalled the record aggregate. Thereafter Tom remained a fine performer but never again threatened to be the best in the world.

Joyce Wethered

Born: November 17, 1901
London, England

Bobby Jones declared that Joyce Wethered was the best player of either sex he had ever seen and she may well have been the greatest woman player of all time. All a player can do is defeat the best of the day – and she certainly did that. Joyce first came to public notice at the 1920 English Ladies' Championship at Sheringham in Norfolk. She had entered mainly to keep a friend company. The friend was soon knocked out, but Joyce went through to the final where she beat the greatest player of the day, Cecil Leitch, after being well behind. She went on to win the event in her next four entries and apparently thought that was enough. She did not compete again. Her record in the far more international British Ladies' Championship was almost as good. She won in 1922, 1924, 1925 and 1929. In this period she lost only two matches and missed out the years 1926–28. She did not much enjoy championship golf and returned in 1929 mainly because the event was being held at St Andrews. This time she beat the great American Glenna Collett in the final. For Joyce Wethered that was the end of championship golf. There were no more fields left to conquer.

Kathy Whitworth
Born: September 27, 1939
Monahans, Tx, USA

Whitworth played the LPGA Tour from 1959 until 1991, and was consistently successful between 1962 and 1985. Her money-winning achievements were truly remarkable. She was leading money winner eight times and on another 10 occasions finished no worse than ninth. By the end she had racked up a total of 88 victories on the LPGA Tour. This beat Mickey Wright's record of 82 and also is more victories than a man has achieved on the US Tour. Whitworth was named Player of the Year seven times and also won the Vare Trophy (for stroke average) on the same number of occasions. Her first really big year was 1963, when she had eight wins, a feat she repeated in 1965, before going one better the following year. In 1968 she won 11 times. The flow of victories continued until she began to tail off in the late 1970s, though remaining a very competent performer. She did well in the majors but was less dominant than in normal tournament play. She took the Titleholders twice, the Western once and the LPGA three times. Despite all those triumphs, she missed out on the US Women's Open.

Craig Wood
Born: November 11, 1901
Lake Placid, NY, USA

Craig Wood earned a reputation as a man who always just missed out on major championships. Easily the most famous one was the second Masters in 1935. Wood was in the clubhouse and no one on the course

had a chance of catching him, unless you counted Gene Sarazen, who had to birdie three of the last four holes to tie. No one has done that in a major before or since. Playing that perilous second shot over water at the 15th, Sarazen let fly with a 4-wood – and holed out for a double eagle. Not surprisingly, Wood lost the 36-hole play-off by a wide margin – 5 strokes – the next day. By this time he had also lost the first Masters by a stroke to Horton Smith and had a close encounter with the 1933 US Open. That same year he tied Denny Shute for the British Open and, of course, lost the play-off. The

US PGA in 1934 wasn't any kinder to him: he lost the final on the 38th hole, his massive driving overcome by short-game expert Paul Runyan. Wood later lost the 1939 US Open to Byron Nelson, again in a play-off but this time Wood tied the Texan after 18, so they went round again. The man seemed doomed never to win a major, but he turned the tables with a vengeance in 1941. First he won the Masters. Then, at the US Open, having decided to withdraw after playing a few holes because of bad play and an even worse back, he was persuaded to carry on for the time being – and won comfortably.

Ian Woosnam
Born: March 2, 1958
Oswestry, England

Only 5 ft 4¹/₂ in tall, Woosnam is probably the longest-hitting short man ever. A superb striker of the ball, he hits a right-to-left shape of shot, his one pronounced weakness being with the putter. However, even on the greens he is often very good indeed – no one can have his kind of tournament-winning record without a very considerable putting talent. Woosnam has not performed as well in the major championships as his abilities would suggest. His single triumph has been in the 1991

IAN WOOSNAM *Emotional reaction to winning the 1991 US Masters, but will this be the Welshman's only major?*

Masters, though he has also come close to a US Open win. His most consistent performances have come on the European Tour, with 28 victories by the end of 1994, and he has also won in Africa and the Far East. Woosnam was European number one in 1987 and 1990 and every year since 1981 he has been in the top 12 money winners. He won the World Match Play in both 1987 and 1990. He has also been a Ryder Cup ever-present since 1983, though with a weak record until 1993, when he had two foursomes and two fourball wins and halved his singles. This made him Europe's top performer.

Lew Worsham
Born: October 5, 1917
Alta Vista, Va, USA

There are just a few shots which enter golfing legend. Worsham was involved in two of them, even if one was actually Sam Snead's rather than his. In 1947 the great Sam Snead holed a sizable putt to tie Worsham over 72 holes. In the 18-hole play-off, the pair were level as they played the 18th. Both then had quite short putts to lose or win – or carry on. Snead saw he was further from the hole and settled down to putt. Worsham, as he was quite entitled to do, questioned the distances and asked for measurements to be made. They were; Snead was right; he putted first – and missed. Worsham then holed out to be US Open champion. They say that no one remembers who finished second, and this is almost invariably true, but Snead's miss is far more a part of golfing legend than Worsham's US Open victory. A few years later, in 1953, Worsham produced an authentic great shot of his own. He was playing in the Tam o'Shanter World Championship, and approached the 18th needing to get down in two from about 100 yards to tie Chandler Harper. He holed his approach. The win was worth a fortune in both prize money and the exhibition fees which resulted.

Mickey Wright
Born: February 14, 1935
San Diego, Ca, USA

There are few real candidates for the title of greatest woman golfer ever. Joyce Wethered, Babe Zaharias, Nancy Lopez and Mickey Wright all spring to mind, but if the quality of the swing is taken into account, then only Wethered and Wright contend. Wright proved to be as long off the tee as Zaharias and was perhaps the best long iron player of all the women, striking with as crisp an action as very good men players. She first began to come to the fore in the mid-1950s and in 1958 won five times, taking her first US Women's Open and LPGA. The next year she again won the Open and three other events. It was 1960, however, that saw her become a great player, with six wins, including the LPGA. Then she began to fly. There were 10 wins in both 1961 and 1962, 13 in 1963 and 11 in 1964. At the end of that last season she had already taken 63 events, including the Open and the LPGA four times each. Her 13 wins in a season is still the record, and her 11 the second best. At this point, Mickey Wright began to have trouble with an arthritic wrist, and also foot problems, but she continued to be a winner, if more occasionally, until the early 1970s.

Babe Zaharias
Born: June 26, 1914
Port Arthur, Tx, USA

The Babe was not the greatest woman golfer of all time but possibly the greatest athlete. Just before the 1932 Olympics she entered eight events in the US National Championships and won six of them – and all this in well under three hours. At the Los Angeles Olympics she won the 80 metres hurdles, setting a new world record, and the javelin and was second in the high jump. With her supreme athletic abilities it is not surprising that, when she took to golf a couple of years later, the Babe was soon hitting the ball a very long way. However, there is a great deal more to golf than just long hitting. It took

her many years to master the game, and for some of that time she was something of a freak show in exhibitions. She began to peak about 1946, winning 16 consecutive amateur tournaments. This sequence included the US Women's, and she went on to take the British equivalent in 1947. Turning professional, she won about a third of all the events she entered, including the US Women's Open in 1948, 1950 and 1954 and was also leading money winner for four years consecutively. She died of cancer at the age of 41.

Fuzzy Zoeller
Born: November 11, 1951
New Albany, In, USA

Fuzzy Zoeller is one of the few professionals who look as if they are enjoying their day's work on the golf course. Despite playing for much of his career with severe back problems deriving from a basketball injury, he always has a jaunty lilt to his

stride up the fairways and is often whistling. He must also spend less time over the ball than any other significant figure in world golf. He takes his stance quickly, glances towards his target and swings. If only there were more like him! On the US Tour, Zoeller was a consistent performer from the mid-1970s but seemed to be on his way out towards the end of the 1980s. However, he came back strongly in 1993 and 1994, in the latter year contending for the British Open Championship. His greatest achievements were his two major victories, both after play-offs. The first of these came in the 1979 Masters, the first time Zoeller had qualified to play. After a slow start, Fuzzy found himself in a play-off with Ed Sneed and Tom Watson. He birdied the second extra hole to win. His play-off win in the 1984 US Open was very different, with Zoeller cruising round in 67 to Greg Norman's 75.

FUZZY ZOELLER *His name derives from his initials, Fred Urban Zoeller*

THE GREAT HEAD-TO-HEADS

Golf creates its most compelling moments of suspense when the relentless discipline of stroke play and the cut and thrust of match play come together at the climax of a major championship. Sometimes the contenders are paired together and the opposition is just a handshake away, on other occasions the enemy can only be anxiously glimpsed from ahead or behind. The struggle becomes intensely personal, a naked battle of wills, a matter of who blinks first.

Ouimet vs Vardon vs Ray (US Open, 1913)
Palmer vs Nicklaus (US Open, 1960)
Nagle vs Palmer (British Open, 1960)
Casper vs Palmer (US Open, 1966)
Trevino vs Jacklin (British Open, 1972)
Nicklaus vs Miller vs Weiskopf (Masters, 1975)
Watson vs Nicklaus (British Open, 1977)
Watson vs Nicklaus (US Open, 1982)
Ballesteros vs Price (British Open, 1988)
Price vs Parnevik (British Open, 1994)

TURNBERRY TURNABOUT *Nick Price consoles Jesper Parnevik after the Open*

OUIMET VS VARDON VS RAY
US Open, 1913

Francis de Sales Ouimet deserves to head the Great Head-to-Heads in anyone's book. He was the first amateur to become US Open Champion, snatching the title in 1913 from the master golfer of the era, Harry Vardon, and another mature and powerful British professional in Ted Ray.

Ouimet's play-off victory got golf on to the front page, at least in Boston, where the Open ended on September 20 at The Country Club, Brookline.

His triumph against all the odds had *Boys' Own Paper* romance about it, and sent the American golf juggernaut surging forward as the story of slim young Yankee upset-ting invading giants sank in with the US sporting public, who, like the English, love the underdog.

Besides, Ouimet was no rich country club member, and worked in a sports shop. He had begun his golf in the fields around his home not far from Brookline's splendid clubhouse, and his credentials as the underdog were impeccable.

Though he lived close to The Country Club, he entered for the Open as a Woodland club member. Shortly before it began he had lost in the second round of the Amateur Championship to the eventual winner, Jerome Travers.

Vardon had done it all, winning the British Open five times, and the US Open with his only previous attempt. Ray had won the British Open the year before.

It was only as recently as 1911 that a native born American, J. J. McDermott, had managed to end the British-born golfers' monopoly of the US Open. He won again in 1912, so was the main hope to repel the English experts.

Ouimet, with a 77, was six strokes behind the first-round leaders, both Scots, Macdonald Smith and Alec Ross, who fell from grace on the second day, when the English pair made their move. Ray returned 70, the lowest score of the entire Championship, and Vardon, 72. Ouimet had a 74, but another 74 on the third day brought him level with Vardon and Ray, who did not fare well on the outward half of the final round.

Other players, notably Walter Hagen, had chances to catch Vardon and Ray, but only Ouimet did, playing the last four holes in one under the par of 15. He chipped dead at the 15th to get his par four, chipped and putted for his par three at the next, and got the essential birdie at the 360-yard 16th, sinking at 12-footer across and down a slope: "a masterstroke", said Ray. Another good chip and a seven-footer at the 18th meant a total 304, level with Vardon and Ray.

The crowd for the play-off was estimated at 10,000; they endured heavy rain gladly as an upset developed... but a surprising one.

The local boy, using the less usual interlocking grip rather than the overlapping one that Vardon had made almost obligatory, most closely resembled the established pro, playing steadily from tee to green. His putting style worked well also: feet together, club swinging pendulum style from the shoulder. His opponents fell into one error after another, the clincher coming one hole from home where Vardon bunkered his drive and took five. Ouimet birdied, as he had the day before, and finished in 72, beating Vardon by five and Ray by six.

The *New York Times* awarded Ouimet the title "World's Golf Champion". Hagen, who like Ouimet was 20, shared fourth place with Long Jim Barnes, Macdonald Smith and Louis Tellier, from France.

Ouimet's caddie, Eddie Lowery, aged 10, had fought off any suggestion that he should step down in favour of an older caddie in the play-off. The logo designed for the 100th US Open of 1995 at Brookline is based on a silhouette taken from a 1913 photograph of little Lowery beside Ouimet.

Results	US Open, 1913 Brookline, MA		
	Pos.	Name	Score
	1	F. Ouimet	77, 74, 74, 79 – 304
	2	H. Vardon (GB)	75, 72, 78, 79 – 304
	3	T. Ray (GB)	79, 70, 76, 79 – 304
	Ouimet won play-off 72 to 77 to 78		

PALMER VS NICKLAUS
US Open, 1960

Arnold Palmer had already won the American Amateur Championship and the Masters twice when, at Cherry Hills, Denver, on June 18, 1960, he had a slight disagreement with a Press acquaintance as he took a snack lunch, with Ken Venturi among those present, between the two final rounds of the 60th US Open Championship.

Palmer was seven strokes behind Mike Souchak, five behind Ben Hogan. Not only that, but he was four behind a large blond amateur, aged 20, from Columbus, Ohio, one J.W. Nicklaus, holder of the US Amateur Championship.

The journalist, Bob Drum, thought that Palmer was too far back, and was dismissive of Palmer's contention that if he shot 65, six under par, he could win, for it would give him a total of 280. Hogan and Mike Souchak, the holder of the world tournament nine-hole record with 27, had both managed 67s in the second round at Cherry Hills, so Palmer decided on a fast start. "280s win Opens", he told the doubters.

At 31, he was a mature golfer, and confident of his strength as a competitor, for had he not won his second Masters in the spring by slipping past Ken Venturi with birdies at the two closing holes? He had

CONGRATS *Harry Vardon, Francis Ouimet and Ted Ray at the 1913 US Open*

been trying to drive the first hole, a par four, all week, and got off to exactly the start he needed by at last reaching the putting surface off the tee, despite the obstacle in front of the green of a strip of long grass. His ball just made it, stopping 20 feet from the hole, and setting up a two-putt birdie; the eagle he missed by a whisker. Fireworks continued as he holed a chip for another birdie at the next hole, and he was within a foot with his wedge approach for his third in a row. An 18-footer at the fourth saved another shot, so that Souchak's seven-shot lead had been reduced to three.

Nicklaus and Hogan were playing partners well behind Palmer, now two under par. Nicklaus led briefly, until his putter let him down twice on the back nine, and Souchak was frittering away even more shots.

The news of Palmer's meteoric progress acted like a magnet for the galleries: "Arnie's Army" was becoming a numerous, if not always disciplined, force, and their commander did not fail them, for he inserted a long, twisting birdie putt on the 6th, and a six-footer at the 7th, reaching the turn in 30.

More sedate progress followed, but there was no loss of position, as he made good his declared intention: 65 for the round, and a winning 280 for the Championship, winning because Nicklaus could not make any impression on par, while Hogan, with a splendid chance of outflanking Palmer's charge, and capturing a record fifth Open, played over-aggressive shots on both the 17th and 18th, twice hitting into water hazards: he finished 6, 7. That relegated Hogan to ninth place. So ended his chances of a 10th major championship, and his first since his trio of majors in 1953.

Palmer's 65 was the lowest final round by a US champion, beaten only by Johnny Miller's 63 in 1973 at Oakmont. His outward 30 equalled the record set by amateur James McHale in 1947. Nicklaus's feat of recording the lowest total ever returned by an amateur in the

CUP WINNER ARNIE *Palmer at Portmarnock in 1960*

Open, so beating every pro except Palmer, had to be regarded as a warning of things to come.

The Championship itself was setting records. Ouimet's Open had an entry of 165, so that the first qualifying round had to be staged. For Palmer's round the entry reached 2,453, necessitating 56 district and 13 sectional qualifying competitions. It also attracted a record gallery of more than 40,000, which enabled the prize money to be raised to more than $60,000, of which Palmer's share amounted to the sum of $14,400.

WARM WELCOME *Kel Nagle greets his wife in Sydney with the trophy*

Results

US Open, 1960 Cherry Hills, CO		
Pos. Name		Score
1	A. Palmer (US)	71, 72, 72, 65 – 280
2	J. Nicklaus (US)	71, 71, 69, 71 – 282
3	D. Harrison, J. Boros, M. Souchak, T. Kroll, J. Fleck and D. Finsterwald (all US)	– 283

NAGLE vs PALMER
British Open, 1960

Apart from Kel Nagle and his friends and relations at home in North Sydney, the people most delighted by his win in the 1960 Centenary Open at St Andrews were the bookmakers, for Arnold Palmer was heavily backed, and came thrillingly close to crowning a third successive title charge in a major championship.

However, at least one bookmaker took a heavy hit, the one who accepted Peter Thomson's wager on his fellow Australian at long odds. Thomson had registered a first and a second in the Open at St Andrews, and did his best fully to inform Nagle of its intricacies.

Nagle had won the Australian

Championship the previous year, to begin something of a come-back though fast approaching his 40th year. He had amended his game from long-hitter to straighter but shorter hitter, and unlike most he became a better putter with age.

His long game in the Open seldom faltered, and his idiosyncratic method of addressing the ball, with club head set inside the ball, became a familiar sight.

He faced in Arnold Palmer a player who was enjoying his hottest year as a pro. He had started out with three consecutive wins on the PGA winter tour, and travelled to Scotland to create a little history at the Centenary Open, for he was burning to equal Ben Hogan's unprecedented treble of seven years earlier, when he took the Masters, and both Opens…the British at his first attempt, as Palmer was now intent on doing.

The leader after the first round was Roberto de Vicenzo, who was 32 (four under par) for the outward nine, coming back in 35 to lead by two from Nagle and Fidel de Luca, another Argentine, with Palmer nicely placed one behind these two.

There was no catching de Vicenzo in the second round either, though Nagle was but two shots behind overall, for both men scored 67. Palmer seemed to be sliding out of the picture with a 71, for he had three putts on the Road Hole, and dropped another shot at the 18th, looked upon in reasonable weather conditions as a definite birdie chance. Palmer was now seven adrift of de Vicenzo, and five of Nagle.

While de Vicenzo blew up with a 75 in the third round, Palmer crept closer to Nagle, scoring 70 against the Australian's 71. He was two behind de Vicenzo now and, in company with Syd Scott, only four behind leader Nagle.

Then followed a frustrating interlude, for rain persisted, and forced a Saturday finish. This, it soon became clear, was to involve Nagle and Palmer, as their closest rivals began to slide down the leader board. Nagle was behind Palmer on the course, but a match play situation now began to develop. Both men were two under after nine holes, but Palmer birdied the 13th, while Nagle's indifferent approach at the 15th cost him a stroke, and cut his lead to two.

Nagle's nerves stood the grinding test of a seven-foot putt to save par at the 17th. Holing this was crucial, as Palmer persuaded the gallery of his coolness in a crisis by holing a birdie putt at the last. Nagle needed a par there, and got it safely enough, taking the Open trophy and a replica to celebrate the Centenary, together with a record first prize of £1,250. He had won by a shot with a total of 278, scoring a final 71 against Palmer's splendid but fruitless 68.

Nevertheless, this was Palmer's finest year, for he added six other tournaments to his two major victories. For British golf, his presence at the Open was to reverse the postwar trend of lack of interest by American golfers, a process his wins in the next two Opens at Birkdale and Troon were rapidly to intensify.

RAP ARTIST *Billy Casper's firm way with a putt earns an 11th hole birdie and equality with Palmer*

Results

British Open, 1960
St Andrews, Scotland

Pos.	Name	Score
1	K. Nagle (AUS)	69, 67, 71, 71 – 278
2	A. Palmer (US)	70, 71, 70, 68 – 279
3	B. J. Hunt (GB), H. Henning (SA) and R. de Vicenzo (ARG) – 282	

CASPER
vs
PALMER
US Open, 1966

The 1966 US Open at the Olympic Club, San Francisco, was a two-horse race. The also-rans, led by Jack Nicklaus, seven shots adrift, had no more than a distant view of the events that led to the Billy Casper vs. Arnold Palmer play-off.

The Olympic Club was an athletic and football club before members turned to golf. But it was an appropriate setting for a head-to-head contest: Gentleman Jim Corbett beat John L. Sullivan here in a battle for the world heavyweight boxing championship 74 years earlier.

The straight left is no good on the club's championship course, named Lakeside: nearly all the fairways bend to the right, so fade it and you've made it – with an important exception of which more later.

The greens are small, and though the yardage is little more than 6,700, the fairways are narrow, and lined with aggressive, ball-retentive trees.

Casper began with 69, Palmer with 71. Palmer was out in 32 next day, came back in 34 and took the lead – with Casper, who scored 68.

Palmer took a firm grip on Saturday, when he set out in company with Casper on the first hole of the 54 they were to play together. Casper missed fairways and greens and hit bunkers for a useful 73. Palmer, his Army keyed up, finished the round three ahead of Casper: 207 plays 210.

Palmer was out in 32 again on Sunday, which meant he was nine ahead of Nicklaus and seven ahead of Casper. He has not hidden the fact that at this point he thought the Open was his again, and that his target should now be the record score of 276 set by Ben Hogan in 1948.

He was still six up with six to play, and Nicklaus was heading for a 74. Palmer was calculating that level par would break the record, so in typically bravura fashion he went for a birdie to make sure. Instead, he missed the green at two short holes, which cost him a shot each time. At the second of these, the 15th, Casper got a birdie, bringing him to the relative luxury of three down with three to go.

The 16th was the exception to the Lakeside norm of left to right. It curved left, but Palmer overdid it into deep rough. His next blow, with a long iron, did not extricate his ball. A wedge did the trick, but his next was in sand, and though Palmer got up and down from there, Casper holed his birdie putt: one down.

Casper was soon level, for his celebrated, aggressive, wristy putting stroke was serving him well, saving his par at the 17th: no such luck for Palmer, who did well not to lose the day outright at the 18th, where he tried an iron from the tee, but again

missed the short grass. He recovered staunchly, leaving a tough 10-yard putt, followed at once, because of the new continuous putting rule, by a six-footer. The rule, intended to speed play, added to the tension for Palmer, since Casper had not yet started to putt. Palmer got his par, but so did Casper. Taking no chances, he lagged up carefully for a two-putt four. It may have been running through his mind that golfers who have successfully played catch-up, especially long-haul catch-up, don't usually lose play-offs.

In this one Palmer was three ahead at the turn. Most of this advantage evaporated in a two-stroke swing on the 11th, he let go three more strokes in the next four holes, and lost 73 to 69, Casper keeping his

Results	US Open, 1966 Olympic, CA		
	Pos. Name		Score
	1	W. Casper (US)	69, 68, 73, 68 – 278
	2	A. Palmer (US)	71, 66, 70, 71 – 278
	3	J. Nicklaus (US)	71, 71, 67, 74 – 285
	Casper won play-off 69 to 73		

nerve as the long-delayed crux was reached. Over the last nine holes on the last two days of the Open, Casper had taken 13 fewer shots than Palmer, who thereby suffered his third Open play-off defeat in five years. He never got as close again.

TREVINO vs JACKLIN
British Open, 1972

Lee Trevino's reputation as joker and miracle worker, especially in the pitching, chipping and putting departments, was well established when he arrived at Muirfield in 1972 for the Open. Yet only five years before he had drawn his first significant cheque, £6,000 for fifth place behind Jack Nicklaus in the US Open at Baltusrol.

Not only had he never won so much money, he had never *seen* so much, said Supermex: but then he had as many one-liners as any stand-up comedian about his family's poverty back in Dallas.

So Trevino knew "poor" and, after four years in the Marines, he

also knew "tough". But since 1967 he had been getting to know "rich", with two Open victories in America and one in Britain, by a whisker at Birkdale from the Taiwanese Mr Lu, and by two from the 1969 champion, Tony Jacklin.

The favourite at Muirfield was none of these, but the recent winner of both the Masters and the US Open, Jack Nicklaus. Like Arnold Palmer 12 years before, Nicklaus was burning to land the treble Ben Hogan had, uniquely, achieved in 1953. Besides, he knew how to win at Muirfield, having done so both as an amateur and in the 1966 Open, which he dominated with the length and accuracy of his iron play.

This deserted him on the first day, and the shape of things to come was heralded at the end of round two, when Trevino and Jacklin led, a stroke clear of Nicklaus, Johnny Miller, Peter Townsend and Peter Tupling.

Trevino's third round was slow to catch fire, but patience paid off with a quartet of birdies from the 14th to 17th. He holed lengthy putts for the first two. The third, at the short 16th, was a platinum-plated fluke. He thinned his shot from a greenside trap, and his ball was scooting speedily for no one knows where until it struck the flagstick, and vanished quick as a wink.

His 66 gave him a one-stroke lead going into the final round over Jacklin, whose 67 had been distinguished by sterling play from tee to green. When Jacklin and Trevino set out last together on the final day, Nicklaus, struggling six behind the leader, gambled with his driver and was out in 32, briefly disturbing the private duel the final pair were fighting out behind him, but faltering with a bogey at the 16th and failure to birdie the long 17th.

The Trevino-Jacklin plot did not so much thicken as curdle at the 17th, where a long, well-placed drive must be followed by a second of pinpoint accuracy between the sandhills guarding the green. Jacklin was 20 yards short in two. Trevino wandered untidily from side to side, and the closest he could get with his fourth shot was on a bank of fluffy

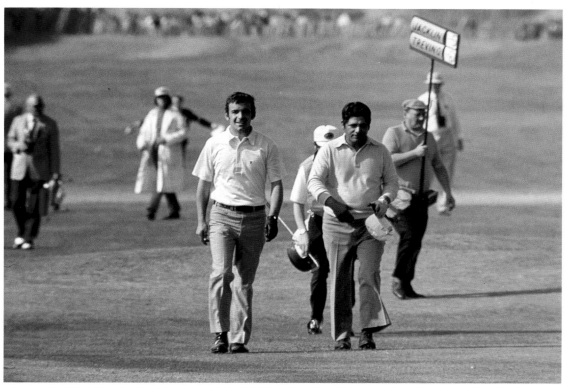

PRIVATE EVENT *Tony Jacklin and Lee Trevino battle it out at Muirfield*

rough behind the pin. Jacklin chipped on, not very expertly.

Trevino's chip ran smartly into the hole. He compared it afterwards with the last straw that broke ... and so it seemed as Jacklin three-putted. Another bogey on the last compounded British gloom, and gave Trevino his second Open by a stroke from Nicklaus, who, like Arnold Palmer in 1960, missed his treble by a stroke, and with exactly the same total, 279.

Jacklin was third, a shattering descent after the security of 99 per cent of his play. "They" said of this reverse of Jacklin's, as they had of Palmer's defeat at Olympic by Billy Casper, that he was never the same again.

The bottom line in Trevino's victory was the bottom line – 278 for four circuits of Muirfield, held by many to be a classic without peer. His total was a record, four shots fewer than Nicklaus took in 1966. No wonder Trevino reckoned Muirfield in particular, and Scottish links in general, his preferred golf terrain.

TURNBERRY TITANS *Nicklaus sinks his "miracle" birdie on the 72nd – but Watson has a tap in for victory*

Results		
British Open, 1972		
Muirfield, Scotland		
Pos. Name		**Score**
1	L. Trevino (US)	71, 70, 66, 71 – 278
2	J. Nicklaus (US)	70, 72, 71, 66 – 279
3	A. Jacklin (GB)	69, 72, 67, 72 – 280

NICKLAUS
VS
MILLER
VS
WEISKOPF
Masters, 1975

The outcome of the 1975 Masters tournament at Augusta depended on what might be called a two-way head-to-head. It involved Jack Nicklaus, looking for a fifth green jacket, Johnny Miller and Tom Weiskopf.

Neither Miller nor Weiskopf had

OPPOSITE: 5 GREEN JACKETS *Jack Nicklaus on his way to the Masters title*

won at Augusta, but both were particularly dangerous opponents. Weiskopf had been second three times, twice in the last three years; Miller had been shooting awesomely low scores on the PGA winter Tour, including 24 under par (Phoenix) and 25 under (Tucson).

There was no luck for the tournament's first black golfer, Lee Elder but plenty for the galleries, who saw what Masters regulars still recall as the most exciting finish of them all, perhaps because it concerned three golfers with a penchant for the spectacular.

Miller, seven behind Nicklaus on the opening day with 75, improved to 71 and then 65 on the third, with six birdies in a row from the second hole. That left him still three behind Nicklaus, whose grip had been loosened by his third-round 73, and four behind Weiskopf, he of the huge and stately swing arc, who had moved ahead on 207 thanks to a majestic third round of 66. Miller was in much the same course-burning vein on the final day, and close on the heels of his rivals, who were level at the turn.

The odd putt was clearly going to decide it. That seemed to have been achieved by Weiskopf, for he

birdied the 14th. Now Nicklaus hears the commotion behind him, and gets down to the problem of fashioning a birdie, quick. He is standing on the fairway of the par five 15th, 242 yards from the hole. It is reachable with a wood, but Nicklaus decides to use the club he trusts best, his one iron. His ball tears straight at the pin, rolls close by the hole, but 20 feet past. He is to rate this one of the "three finest maximum pressure one irons" of his career. His two-putt birdie is timely, because Weiskopf birdies the 15th too and moves ahead. Miller almost eagles the 15th.

Both stand on the 16th tee watching Nicklaus putt for a two. Nicklaus is playing with Tom Watson, who has put two balls in the lake that makes this 170-yard hole almost all carry. Watson, three months away from his first major, the Open at Carnoustie, putts first, on the same line as the 45-footer Nicklaus faces.

Nicklaus takes in the huge swing on Watson's putt, is convinced he can see the right line with crystal clarity, and strikes firmly up the slope ... and holes out for his two, celebrating with an atypical (for Nicklaus) golfer's gavotte. This is

not only a positive move for Nicklaus, but has a negative effect upon Weiskopf, who three-putts the 16th.

A roar from the 17th checks Nicklaus as he shapes up to his birdie putt on the 18th. He is anxious to know who has saved the shot there, and relieved to know it is Miller. So he lags his putt for a safe par four. His cool analysis of the situation gives a clue as to why he kept winning over so many years. Now he can only wait by the 18th green.

Both Weiskopf and Miller drive superbly. Their second shots leave Miller a 15-footer, Weiskopf an eight-footer. The putts are roughly on the same line, but Miller misses left, Weiskopf right. He is second for the fourth time, and this pressure cooker of a Masters provides Nicklaus with his fifth triumph.

Results		
Masters, 1975		
Augusta, GA		
Pos. Name		**Score**
1	J. Nicklaus (US)	68, 67, 73, 68 – 276
2	J. Miller (US)	75, 71, 65, 66 – 277
3	T. Weiskopf (US)	69, 72, 66, 70 – 277

WATSON vs NICKLAUS
British Open, 1977

The Royal and Ancient took a long time to move the Open to the Ailsa course at Turnberry, and when at last they did, in 1977, this most scenic of courses on the west coast of Scotland rewarded them with a duel between the two leading players of the day, Jack Nicklaus and Tom Watson, that for persistent quality and tension is unlikely ever to be surpassed.

Over the last two rounds, the pair were playing partners, moving further and further away from any challengers. Hubert Green robbed Lee Trevino of third place with 279 – but Green was 12 shots short of victory. For the 1977 Open produced the purest head-to-head that can be imagined in a stroke-play competition, the winner breaking the 72-hole record total by seven.

The Championship was played for the first three days in hot, humid conditions, which followed more than a month of dry weather, so the rough was not up to usual Scottish standards. The wind died away at lunch-time on the first day, so scores were low, though not until well into the gloaming did the leader come in, with 66 . . . John Schroeder, son of lawn tennis champion Ted. Nicklaus, Watson and Trevino had much earlier all gone round in 68 to share second place.

Mark Hayes, from Oklahoma, broke the Open 18-hole record next day. His 63, 13 better than his first round, included a bogey at the 18th. But Roger Maltbie's 66 for a total of 139 gave him the lead, one ahead of Green, Trevino, Nicklaus and Watson.

This latter pair, aged 37 and 27 respectively, set off on their third rounds on what might be called Furious Friday, for they both gave the course, 6,875 yards, par 70 (35=35), a severe pounding. By the 10th, Nicklaus was two ahead with 31 strokes to 33 by Watson, who was level again by the long but eminently reachable 17th, where a birdie each was disappointing for Nicklaus. He had hit his second to three feet. Six birdies and one bogey apiece left the duo level on 203 and all their rivals gasping. The Nicklaus-Watson scores were identical: 68, 70, 65.

Saturday began with more assaults on par, Nicklaus finishing off, with a birdie from 10 feet, a marvellous recovery from an awkward lie with the ball above his feet in the rough at the 2nd.

Watson dropped a shot, and fell three behind when Nicklaus reduced the well-named Woe be Tide short hole to a two from 10 yards. Watson came back at him, saving a shot at the 5th, another at the long 7th, with two drivers and two putts, and yet another at the 8th, only to reach the turn one behind when he could not get his par at Bruce's Castle, Turnberry's Lighthouse hole. Nicklaus out in 33, Watson 34.

Nicklaus stole two shots ahead on the 12th, with a sizeable putt. Watson pulled one back on the 13th, and the other with a two on the 15th from 20 yards: level again, and the form of both men holding up miraculously . . . until Nicklaus hit his four-iron approach to the 17th (500 yards) fat. He pitched up to little over a yard, but missed the putt, a tiny nod expressing his frustration. Watson's birdie put him one up.

Still the Turnberry tale had a twist: Watson's drive at the last was a cautious, straight, one-iron. Nicklaus gambled, but his driver left him in gorse. Watson, playing first, pitched almost to gimme distance. Nicklaus ripped through the gorse and left himself, improbably, a birdie putt of about 12 yards. Even more improbably, he holed it.

Watson, brisk as ever in his tempo at this searching moment, tapped his ball underground for his second Open.

CHEEKY CHIP *Watson dances with delight as his chip goes in at the 71st hole of the 1982 US Open*

WATSON vs NICKLAUS
US Open, 1982

Tom Watson approached the US Open at Pebble Beach in 1982 with three British Opens and two Masters to his credit, but as yet no US Open title. Jack Nicklaus's thoughts were that his unmatched career record would touch even further heights of achievement if he could win a fifth Open and move one ahead of his fellow record-holders, Willie Anderson, Bobby Jones and Ben Hogan; and his hopes were high when he considered that he had won the only previous Open held at Pebble Beach ten years earlier. Even for Nicklaus, now 42, time was running out.

Bruce Devlin shared the lead with the 1981 British Open champion, Bill Rogers, on the first day, but headed the field by two shots with a 69 for 139 at 36 holes.

Watson and Nicklaus were like prudent mountaineers, quietly working themselves into position for a dart at the summit. Watson was steadiest, though his putter had been his saviour in the first round, when his golf through the green had not been his best. But 72, 72, 68 = 212 earned him a share of the lead at 54 holes with Rogers. Devlin had faded to a 75 and stood on 214 along with George Burns, Scott Simpson and reigning champion David Graham.

Nicklaus was one under par for the Championship, a stroke behind this quartet. By the 9th in the final round on another gloomy day only Rogers was ahead of him, by a stroke: and he had caught Watson. Nicklaus bogeyed the 1st and parred the 2nd, then had five birdies in a row, including twos at the 5th and 7th, though another bogey at the 8th cut his advantage against par to four.

Behind him Watson could make no impression on par over the first half of the course, though the first six holes offer the best chance of birdies. He started back with a par that must have seemed like a birdie, for his second shot to the 10th might have bounced down on to the beach, but instead fell into spiky kikuyu grass below the green. His sand wedge left him a good eight paces from the hole, but down went the putt. A birdie from more than 20 feet at the 11th put him ahead, because his playing partner Rogers bogeyed it.

A poor bunker shot at the 12th cost him a shot, but for the moment he was one ahead of Nicklaus. Watson's birdie putt at the 13th missed by a fraction, while Nicklaus was saving a shot at the 15th, and they were level. A 35-foot putt at the long 14th was, Watson considered, the putt that won him the title.

Rogers fell away, but Watson missed a birdie chance at the 15th, and was happy, in the circumstances, with a bogey at the next. There, thanks to falling foul of a newly fortified bunker, his fourth shot was perforce a 50-foot putt with a 10-foot break. Watson managed to get it stone dead.

Relieved, he went to the 17th level with Nicklaus, who was just coming off the last green with a round of 69 and a total of 284. When he saw Watson pull his tee shot at the 209-yard 17th into thick rough 20 feet left of the flag, the odds against Nicklaus winning his fifth US Open were suddenly consider-

ably shorter. Now Watson played the *chip* that won him the title. The sun came out, his ball was on top of the grass, and he easily sank his chip with a sand iron, landing it just on the green, a foot to the right to allow for the break.

He calmed down after a little jumping about and rejoicing, laid up cautiously at the long 18th, but pitched and putted for a final birdie for a 70, beating Nicklaus by two. No wonder Watson was the author of that definitive book on the short game, *Getting Up and Down*.

BALLESTEROS vs PRICE
British Open, 1988

Spectators were relatively few and thus indisputably lucky as the duel between Severiano Ballesteros, from Spain, and Zimbabwean Nick Price reached its climax in the 1988 Open Championship at Royal Lytham and St Anne's on the Lancashire coast.

Smaller galleries were ensured when rain wiped out the third round, pushing the final round over to the Monday. The fortunate 15,000 had a close and uncluttered view, in greatly improved conditions, of classic stroke play. The second day's gate of 43,101 was a record for one day, and the extra day brought an overall record of 205,857.

The Saturday wash-out was a sur-

QUIET, PLEASE *Seve Ballesteros begs for silence to let his 1988 Open Championship victim Nick Price putt out for second place*

prise to all on the early holes where most of the leaders were playing. Greens 9 to 12 were worst affected by rain, two weather systems having apparently collided over the course.

The collision between Ballesteros and Price did not develop fully until Monday. Price led Ballesteros by a stroke at the half-way stage, and after his delayed third round of 69 he led Ballesteros and Nick Faldo by two. The three of them were to play together as the last group for the final 18, with Sandy Lyle, a further stroke adrift in fourth place, in the penultimate threesome with Edwardo Romero of Argentina and Larry Nelson of the USA.

Price had been in a more dominant position (three ahead with six holes to play) at Troon in 1982, when he admits he was convinced he was going to win his first major title. Tom Watson got the trophy, though, after spending nearly an hour in the clubhouse watching one player after another fail to match his total of 284, with Price proving the most fallible of his pursuers.

Two of the champions now pressing Price, Faldo and Lyle, soon found the Spanish/South African pace too hot. Lyle took 40 to the turn, and although Faldo's five at the long seventh does not sound damaging, his companions had an eagle apiece there. So the battle became a duel between Ballesteros, with two Opens and two Masters behind him, and Price, armed only with determination to avoid another Troon.

Battle was unrelenting, Ballesteros saving six shots on holes 7 to 12, with single-putt birdies on holes 8 to 11. Price had lost his two-shot lead after nine holes, having bogeyed the 2nd and failed to match the Spaniard's three at the 8th. Standing on the 10th tee, Ballesteros had taken 31 strokes, four under par. Price was two under.

They were still level on the 16th tee. Though Price dropped a shot at the 11th, so did Ballesteros as his tee shot fell short at the 198-yard 12th. Price looked good for the lead at the 13th, where he pitched close. His opponent didn't, but still got a birdie

to stay level. Price missed a great chance at the 14th, where both players missed the green. Price pulled his par putt from four feet after seeing Ballesteros chip on and miss *his* par putt.

Condign punishment followed at once for this untimely lapse, Ballesteros pitching dead with a nine-iron at the 16th. Price's fighting qualities were undiminished at the 17th, where he played the bravest of recoveries from the right rough, but he was still one behind.

Chipper extraordinary Ballesteros almost holed from the back of the final green, leaving Price with a putt to tie. He was too strong, missed the one back, and lost by two.

Ballesteros's 65 was the lowest winning final round yet – "the best of my life", he said. Price's final 69 made him the only player who had broken par every round. None could say this was a chance wasted, as at Troon. He had not lost: Ballesteros had won, and never spoke a truer word than when he told Price: "Keep playing like you did today and your turn will come."

Results

**British Open, 1988
Royal Lytham & St Anne's, Lancs**

Pos.	Name	Score
1	S. Ballesteros (SP)	67, 71, 70, 65 – 273
2	N. Price (ZIM)	70, 67, 69, 69 – 275
3	N. Faldo (GB)	71, 69, 68, 71 – 279

PRICE
VS
PARNEVIK
British Open, 1994

This is the age of the Information Superhighway, but a crucial message failed to get through to a young Swede who lived as if in a dream of golfing glory for 71 holes at the 1994 Turnberry Open. To start with, Jesper Parnevik, 29, played throughout in exalted company: two rounds with Jack Nicklaus, then two with

Tom Watson, winners of eight British Opens between them.

As the 123rd Open came down to the nervous nine that settles every title, some of the Tom Watson/Jack Nicklaus power had obviously rubbed off on Parnevik. But Nicklaus failed to qualify, and Watson flattered only to deceive. Though the wind blew every day but the

third, scoring was low, two players, Parnevik and Nick Price from Zimbabwe, equalling the record set by Ernie Els (South Africa) and Australia's Greg Norman at Sandwich the year before, returning four scores in the 60s.

Jesper Bo Parnevik had only won a single European Tour event, but he had eight top 10 finishes in 1993.

Price, 12 years older than Parnevik, was, thanks partly to David Leadbetter's coaching, a different player from the one who had blundered at Troon in 1982, and excelled in defeat at Lytham in 1988. Based in Florida, he now had a major championship to his name, the 1992 US PGA, and had headed the 1993 US Tour money list.

At Turnberry, Price moved gradually into a more threatening position day by day, closing to one behind Fuzzy Zoeller and Brad Faxon with a round to go, in company with Ronan Rafferty, Watson and Parnevik.

Following Parnevik, and with the final green almost in his sights, Price had still not managed to gain any advantage over Parnevik, whose ability to direct his long irons huge distances down the fairways was a marvel to behold. Indeed, in the first 10 holes, Price twice dropped a stroke, only to regain it to stand level with Parnevik at eight under. Zoeller and Faxon both fell away: Watson double bogeyed the 8th and 9th, and was gone.

Parnevik, distinctive in his white baseball cap with the peak pushed up, fanned hopes of a first Swedish win, keeping the leader board busy with birdies on holes 11, 12 and 13 to move two clear of Price. It was one clear after a bogey by the Swede at the 15th. Then he birdied the 16th – but so did Price. Parnevik birdied the 498-yard 17th too, and set off up the last in possession of a seemingly gold-plated two-stroke lead.

He had stuck to the old adage of playing the course, not his opponents, and said afterwards he had not watched the leader boards. He attacked the flag at the 18th, nestling behind a little hump, because cheers behind him suggested he needed another birdie.

His wedge shot fell into most threatening rough, from which his recovery finished three yards from the flag. The missed putt saddled him with only his second bogey of the day in a round of 67 – total 269.

Behind him on the 17th, Price did not know of that final bogey, still thought himself two behind, and looked hard at his 50-foot eagle putt. He did not hurry, but his putt did, moving right at the death and going underground at a fair rate of knots. After Price had danced an energetic war dance, he saw Parnevik had faltered at the last.

Would the 25-year-old Price have played the 18th at Turnberry with the same cool professionalism that 37-year-old Price now demonstrated—three-iron, seven-iron, two putts, for a winning par?

Price thought not, but reflected: "In 1982 I had my left hand on the trophy. In 1988 I had my right hand on it. Now, finally, I have both hands on it."

Results	**British Open, 1994** **Turnberry, Scotland**		
	Pos	**Name**	**Score**
	1	N. Price (ZIM)	69, 66, 67, 66 – 268
	2	J. Parnevik (SWE)	68, 66, 68, 67 – 269
	3	F. Zoeller (US)	71, 66, 64, 70 – 271

IN FULL CRY *Nick Price drives off in pursuit of Jesper Parnevik*

THE FAMOUS COURSES

An integral part of golf's unique charm is that the game is played in such imposing settings. The golfing landscape encompasses Florida swamplands, Arizona desert, Scottish Highland moors, English country estate parklands and the bare dunescapes of so many links courses around Britain. The most famous links course of all may be the Old Course at St Andrews, pictured below, where the R&A clubhouse stands behind the 18th green.

AUGUSTA NATIONAL

Augusta, Georgia, USA
Opened: *1933*
Designers: *Alister Mackenzie, Bobby Jones*
Yardage: *6,925* **Par:** *72*
Major events: *Masters 1934-1942, 1946-*

Not many people could tell you what the first nine holes look like. But from the 10th onwards the Augusta National is by far the world's best known course. Every hole on that last nine has become etched on the retinas of keen golf followers.

It hardly needs saying that this is because the Masters is the only major championship that keeps to the same venue every year, and Augusta the only course which hosts a major championship every year. The potent images return again and again as the contenders battle for the Masters title – not least on the crucial stretch known as Amen Corner. Will he go for a perilous flag set close to water at the left of the 11th? What will happen when the leader tries to judge the swirl of the wind above the tops of the trees on the short 12th? And then at the 13th, quite a short par five, he must surely go for the green with an eagle a possibility and a birdie almost certain if he carries the creek which fronts it… Yet many have found that creek and then been unable to get enough bite on their fourth shot.

Perhaps the most effective golf shot of all time was played at Augusta in 1935, in only the second year of what was then the Augusta Annual Invitational Tournament. With four holes to play, Gene Sarazen needed three birdies to tie Craig Wood, home and dry in the clubhouse. At the par five 15th, Sarazen hit a good drive and then let it rip with his four wood. His ball hit the bank beyond the water hazard and from there ran on and on, and into the hole for a double eagle. With that one shot he had caught Wood. Only a handful of spectators saw

the shot, but among them was Robert Tyre Jones Junior, who had taken a stroll from the clubhouse to see how his old opponents, Gene Sarazen and his playing partner Walter Hagen, were finishing off their rounds – and how the course was playing. As well as being arguably the greatest golfer of all time, Bobby Jones was also highly influential in the creation of one of the world's great courses. But Jones was a modest man. Incontestably the greatest player of the 1920s, he didn't think this in the least

qualified him to design a golf course. That was a job for a specialist. However, when Jones was first taken to see the Augusta property by an investment banker, Clifford Roberts (who would become the mainstay of Masters organization until his death in the late 1970s), he immediately grasped the potential, and together they called in the British course architect Alister Mackenzie, whose work at Cypress Point in California had much impressed Jones, when he had played there in 1929.

Opinions differ as to how much Augusta owes to Jones, Mackenzie, course superintendents and later architects who were called in to undertake revisions. What is beyond dispute, however, is that Mackenzie produced the original design in consultation with Jones. In particular, Jones hit hundreds of shots to help show how a hole would play for players of high quality. Between them, they came up with a course where a club player might play to his handicap. The fairways are broad, the rough is almost non-existent, and the greens are not too fearsome until cut to Masters pace. It's this last factor, together with often fiendish pin placements, which make Augusta a terror in Masters week.

AUGUSTA 16TH *Where Jack Nicklaus holed one of his greatest putts to beat Miller and Weiskopf for the 1975 Masters*

BALLYBUNION, OLD COURSE

Ballybunion, County Kerry, Ireland
Opened: *1896*
Designer: *Anon*
Yardage: *6,503* **Par:** *71*
Major events: *None*

This course is unlikely to hold major events because, like Dornoch, it is so remote, but with the New course as well, you have here perhaps the best 36 holes of links golf in the world. The Old, by itself, ranks very high on everyone's list of greats. As Tom Watson said during a visit: "Ballybunion is a course on which many golf architects should live and play before they build golf courses."

If the 1st hole is a comfortable enough start with a drive to a wide fairway, and downhill at that, the 2nd is more testing by far. You have to miss bunkers from the tee but also have to be long to have much chance of making it up to the green. The 3rd is 220 yards but plays downhill to a severely undulating green. At the 6th, after two relatively easy par fives, you head for the Atlantic Ocean. It is not a long par four – 364 yards – but the wind can play havoc. At the next two holes you play directly from the cliff edge and have a glorious view along the Atlantic shore, but at the 8th playing away from it with a following wind. This is no great help, as the hole is a short par three and the green will be more difficult to hold because of the reduced backspin. Apparently, on one visit Tom Watson played the hole four times and didn't once succeed in keeping his ball on the green. At the 9th, the drive is between sandhills but can be helped onwards by a couple of steps in the fairway. There is a central bunker short of the green and a steep rise to the putting surface.

This has already been outstanding golf, but many believe most of the real Ballybunion comes on the second nine. The 10th heads back towards the Ocean, bending leftwards through a valley, and at the 11th tee it is worth stopping to take in the view. Then a downhill shot confronts the player – but not an easy one. There is the beach one side and sandhills the other. Even a good shot can get into difficulties on the severely undulating fairway. If all has gone well with the tee shot, the second must be well aimed between the sandhills which protect the green.

The 12th, a par three of 192 yards, usually plays into the wind and, because the green is in the sandhills and is quite steeply sloping at the front, needs a full carry on the shot. The 13th, 484 yards, is not in the least a long par five but does demand caution. For those going for the green in two there is a stream perhaps 80 yards short. Then come two par three holes, of which the second presents an extremely testing shot to a well protected, two-tiered green.

The 17th has the most spectacular tee shot on the course, high up with dunes on either side. You are also heading straight for the United States of America. There is a sharp dog-leg left.

If the last hole is a bit of a disappointment, you can at least be sure of a warm welcome in the clubhouse.

DRAMATIC VIEW *The 7th at Ballybunion has the Atlantic Ocean crashing into the cliffs all down the right side and the prevailing wind in the players' faces*

BALTUSROL

Springfield, New Jersey, USA
Opened: *1895*
Designer: *Albert W. Tillinghast*
Yardage: *7,022* **Par:** *70*
Major events: *US Open 1903, 1915, 1936, 1954, 1967, 1980, 1993. US Women's Open 1961, 1985. US Amateur 1904, 1926, 1946. US Women's Amateur 1901, 1911*

Baltusrol's history had a somewhat macabre beginning. The club derives its name from Mr Baltus Roll, a wealthy farmer of Dutch extraction, who in 1831 was murdered in front of his wife by two thieves who believed he had a fortune hidden in his house.

The Baltusrol property eventually came to Louis Keller, a gentleman farmer and socialite, who decided to build his own course in the early 1890s. His first professional was Willie Anderson, the Scot who won four US Opens between 1901 and 1905, one of those over that original course at Baltusrol. Today there are two courses, the Upper and Lower, neither of which bears any resemblance to their predecessor. Albert Tillinghast was brought in to handle the design around 1922, at a time when golf was experiencing another boom.

While the Upper occupies the high ground, it is the Lower that has been the venue for a host of major championships, including five US Opens. Far from picturesque, it makes up for it in the challenge it presents to golfers of all standards. It is long, varied and something of an architectural anomaly in that it has only two par-fives and they are the 17th and 18th, thereby providing a sting in the tail. The 17th measures a monstrous 630 yards, which is a three-shot hole even for the long hitters. Just a few have covered the distance in two lusty blows. In the last US Open, in 1993, many were expecting John Daly to provide the fireworks, and he didn't disappoint, but Sandy Lyle did it first with aplomb.

Long before you reach the 17th there are other mountains to conquer, starting with the dog-leg par four 3rd at a cool 466 yards. Around the landing area, the fairway turns left and slopes downhill towards a creek that cuts across just in front of the green. The green is big but undulating and one of the most difficult to putt on because of its subtle rolls.

The short 4th can measure between 150 and 200 yards depending on the placement of the tee, and requires just a solid iron shot across a lake to a green that slopes left-to-right and back-to-front. When the hole was redesigned by Robert Trent Jones, members complained that it was too tough. Jones disagreed and, together with three other bigwigs, went out to test it. When it was his turn to play, he stepped up and hit a superb shot that pitched short of the flag and gently rolled into the cup for a hole-in-one. "As you can see, Gentlemen," said Jones, shrugging, "this hole is not too tough."

The straight 6th and the dog-leg 11th, both well over 400 yards and requiring two solid blows, can easily see shots surrendered, as can the 401-yard 13th, where the drive must carry the ditch which runs parallel to the fairway after crossing it. After the ultra-long 17th, the 542-yard 18th is played from an elevated tee down into the fairway then over a creek up to an elevated green protected by four bunkers at the front, left and right.

Baltusrol's US Opens have produced some famous winners as well as some daring deeds. In 1954, Ed Furgol, hooked his drive on the final hole, then played his second through the trees on to a fairway of the Upper course before playing back to the 18th green to win. In 1967 and 1980 Jack Nicklaus emerged victorious. On the first occasion he carded a closing 65 to beat Arnold Palmer by four strokes. In 1980 he opened with a record-equalling 63, matched by Tom Weiskopf, then went on to win his fourth US Open with a record aggregate of 272. This was matched by Lee Janzen at Baltusrol in the 1993 Open.

NO MARGIN FOR ERROR *With water guarding the green and almost no fringe, laying up is a safe option at challenging Baltusrol*

CARNOUSTIE

Angus, Scotland
Opened: *1842*
Designer: *Allan Robertson*
Yardage: *7,272* **Par:** *72*
Major events: *Open Championship 1931, 1937, 1953, 1968, 1975. Amateur Championship 1947, 1966, 1971, 1992. British Women's Amateur 1961, 1973*

When the Royal and Ancient Golf Club announced that the 1999 Open Championship would be held at Carnoustie, a huge sigh of relief seemed to permeate the whole of golf. The return of the world's most prestigious championship to these great links was long overdue. Also rejoicing will be the ghosts of all those past champions who have sampled the links, as well as the many sons of Carnoustie who, in years long past, went out to spread the golfing gospel around the world.

Carnoustie's spell in golf's backwaters had nothing to do with the quality of the course; more with what is required off it. The lack of a suitably large hotel in the town was given as the main reason, difficulty of access as another. The growth in popularity of the Open has made these important considerations, but a lengthy, concerted effort by the good folk of Angus and golf fans in general plus a new hotel scheme will see the world's top golfers back where they belong in 1999.

Carnoustie's history seems to have begun in 1842, when a large tract of land was bought from the Earl of Dalhousie and a 10-hole links was laid out by Allan Robertson. This was extended to 18 holes in 1867 by Tom Morris; Willie Park Junior made further alterations, but it was James Braid who remodelled the links in 1926 to what we recognize as today's supreme test.

Carnoustie has neither the deep-seated traditions of St Andrews or Muirfield, nor the breathtaking beauty of Royal County Down or Turn-berry. But what it does is throw down the gauntlet, and a glance at its Open Championship roll of honour proves that only a real champion successfully takes it up. Tommy Armour, Henry Cotton, Ben Hogan, Gary Player and Tom Watson are as good a quintet as you could find and each one etched his style into Carnoustie's folklore.

Armour, one of many Scots who left for America, triumphed in 1931 at the expense of Macdonald Smith. Cotton's win in 1937, the second of his three Opens, was gained against the victorious American Ryder Cup team. Hogan's victory in 1953 on his only Open appearance was, many feel, the greatest seen at Carnoustie. Each of his four rounds was lower than the one before, and he finished with 68. Player completed his second Open success there in 1968 when the course measured 7,252 yards, the longest in Open history. The 1975 contest brought a young Watson to the attention of golf fans as he beat Jack Newton of Australia in an 18-hole play-off. Since then these giant links have seen no Open action. Happily, 1999 will change all that and provide golf with another truly great champion.

Carnoustie is basically a flat course, but don't let that fool you. It is rugged and can be brutal if you stray from its fairways. It also has some famous features which set it apart from its rivals. It has only three short holes, all far from easy, and three par fives, one of which, the 14th, is named Spectacles after the twin bunkers that stand guard in the face of the ridge that runs across the fairway less than 100 yards from the green.

Yet it is the finishing stretch that poses the greatest threat. It begins with the long 14th, then comes the 461-yard 15th, whose green is set into an attractive bowl, followed by the 250-yard 16th, a tough par three that has a well-guarded plateau green.

The Barry Burn crosses the 17th fairway three times, putting a premium on precise shot-making; and if you negotiate this par four safely, you have to do it all again on the return trip, with the Burn lying in wait ahead of the tee and the green on this 486-yard home hole. A finish to be feared.

DON'T GET BURNED *Barry Burn must be crossed several times before reaching the haven of Carnoustie's 18th green*

GLENEAGLES, KING'S COURSE

Auchterarder, Perthshire, Scotland
Opened: *1919*
Designer: *James Braid*
Yardage: *6,452* **Par:** *70*
Major events: *Curtis Cup 1936*

One of the world's greatest golf complexes, Gleneagles has its origins in the development of the railways. As the system grew, and people were able to get to fairly remote areas, many courses were opened. To encourage business, the railway companies offered reduced fares, and sometimes built hotels, as, for example, at Cruden Bay, Turnberry – and Gleneagles.

The general manager of the Caledonian Railway, Donald Matheson, was well aware of the success of the Turnberry venture. One day, the train on which he was travelling broke down at Crieff, so he went for a walk to kill time. At what was to become known as Gleneagles he looked around him and was entranced by the landscape, with the Grampians, the Ochil Hills and the Trossachs offering magnificent views. If Turnberry was an ideal links site, Matheson had now found an ideal inland setting.

At the time, Harry Colt and James Braid were the leading golf architects, and it was appropriate that the Scottish Braid was asked to design the King's Course. Braid did not set out to design a so-called "championship" course of great length – though the King's can be stretched to around 6,800 yards. His task was to produce a course that would be enjoyable for a golfing holiday. He certainly succeeded. The course is one of his greatest triumphs. You begin with an easy enough opening hole of 360 yards to a wide fairway, and then play to a flag on the skyline where judgement of distance is important. It is quite possible to hit a shot which spins back towards you from the green. The 2nd offers a temptation

GLENEAGLES HOTEL *Offers excellent facilities on the inside, and a marvellous golfing challenge on the outside*

to let fly from the tee, as it is downhill, but you are playing to a narrow fairway flanked on either side by gorse, bracken and heather. The 3rd has many slopes to throw the ball where you don't want it, and the second shot to a two-tiered green demands both good judgement and an exact strike. Because of the lie of the ground it can seem a long way.

Most think the 5th the best of the par threes. Basically you aim at a mound with a levelled top which is quite severely bunkered. The 6th, perhaps the easiest hole on the

course, offers a good chance of a birdie; at the 7th you face a sharp dog-leg, though the shape of the ground should help golfers keep on the fairway. The 10th is the most difficult hole for most at 450 yards. It is rated at stroke index 1 and, besides its length, also has a small green. It is followed by a difficult par three of well over 200 yards.

The closing holes are generally not a particularly severe test, though the 13th, Braid's Brawest, is one of the most interesting holes, with a tee shot across an angled ridge set with

large bunkers. At 240 yards the 14th is a very short par four indeed, but for good hitters offers the prospect of getting home in two. The setting of the green is magnificent.

The last is an apparently weak hole. It is a par five where, if you clear the ridge, your ball may well run a long way. Tom Watson once drove over 480 yards and was then left with just a little pitch to the green.

At Gleneagles, the holes may not always be particularly difficult, but it is quite simply one of the most marvellous places to be.

MERION

Ardmore, Philadelphia, Pennsylvania, USA
Opened: *1912*
Designer: *Hugh Wilson*
Yardage: *6,544* **Par:** *70*
Major events: *US Open 1934, 1950, 1971, 1981. US Amateur 1916, 1924, 1930, 1966, 1989. US Women's Amateur 1904, 1909, 1926, 1949. Curtis Cup 1954. World Amateur Team Championship 1960*

The original Merion course, in the 1890s, was squeezed into 100 acres, formerly used for cricket, on the outskirts of Philadelphia. When the rubber-cored ball soon made it obsolete, the club had to look further afield.

Soon a plot of 127 acres of old farmland together with a stone quarry was bought, and the club assigned a group of young members to handle the designing. Among them was Hugh Wilson, an insurance salesman and first-class golfer. But before any work was carried out, Wilson spent seven months travelling around Britain, learning the fundamentals of constructing outstanding golf holes. On his return he set to work with the assistance of Richard Francis to build the new course at Ardmore, opened in 1912. He continued to refine the course for another dozen years, but unfortunately, it was the only complete layout to bear his name as he died prematurely in 1925 at the age of 46.

Merion is noted above all for its greens. They come in all shapes and sizes, beautifully shaped, cleverly contoured, sometimes on two levels, sometimes shelved into a shoulder of a hill, sometimes sloping away to the back. But each is protected by a bunker, a creek or a heavy rough.

A curiosity of the course is that, instead of flags, Wilson decided to mark the holes with a wicker basket atop the flagsticks. He is believed to have got the idea from Scotland where it used to be the practice to place lobster pots as markers.

Another feature of Merion is the infinite variety of its holes. There are long par fours and short par fours, two par fives, one of 600 yards, the 4th, while the short holes measure between 129 yards and 224 yards. There are right-hand dog-legs and left-hand dog-legs, while the final three holes provide what many feel is the toughest finish of any of America's US Open courses.

The 16th is the celebrated Quarry Hole of 430 yards, where the approach must carry the old quarry workings to a plateau green. The 17th is a 224-yard par three from an elevated tee back across the quarry to a green encircled by bunkers. The 458-yard 18th requires a blind drive across the quarry once again, then a medium or long iron often from a downhill lie to a green flanked right and left by bunkers. Golfers who manage par figures over that trio and can count themselves good players.

One of Merion's first claims to fame was in 1930 when it was the scene of the final act of Bobby Jones's Grand Slam. On its famous 11th, a hole of only 370 yards, the drive is down a slight valley, followed by a crucial second shot up over a brook to a green flanked on one side by the same ribbon of water and a bunker on the other.

Jones, who was eight up on Gene Homans in the final of the US Amateur, drove safely, hit the green with his second and two-putted for par and a half to win 8 and 7, adding his national title to the British Amateur won at St Andrews, the British Open at Hoylake, and the US Open at Interlachen.

Merion has staged many of America's national championships. Its first US Open came in 1934 when Olin Dutra won. The 1950 event saw Ben Hogan, hardly recovered from his horrific road accident a year earlier, tie with Lloyd Mangrum and George Fazio, then win the 18-hole play-off by four strokes. In 1971, Jack Nicklaus finished tied with Lee Trevino but it was the latter who prevailed in the play-off, 68 to 71. The most recent US Open saw the title go overseas, when Australian David Graham won with a near-perfect final round 67, not missing a fairway or a green throughout the 18 holes.

SANDY WASTES *The 10th hole is typical of the nightmare that awaits an errant shot at treacherous Merion*

TENTED VILLAGE *Corporate sponsorship (at Muirfield in 1980) and other entertainment for spectators mean that players now have competition for fans' attention*

MUIRFIELD

Gullane, East Lothian, Scotland
Opened: *1891*
Designers: *Old Tom Morris, Harry Colt*
Yardage: *6,941* **Par:** *72*
Major events: *Open Championship 1892, 1896, 1901, 1906, 1912, 1929, 1935, 1948, 1959, 1966, 1972, 1980, 1987, 1992. British Amateur 1897, 1903, 1909, 1920, 1926, 1932, 1954, 1974, 1990. Ryder Cup 1973. Walker Cup 1959, 1979. Curtis Cup 1952, 1984*

It is often said that Muirfield was designed by Old Tom Morris, and he did indeed lay out the first course. However, his original design was by no means ideal, and little more than the site of one green seems to have survived. The Muirfield of today is largely the work of Harry Colt during the mid-1920s. It was Colt, for instance, not Morris, who produced the two loops of nine holes, each ending at the clubhouse. Since Colt's time the course seems to have little changed, which is not surprising, for Colt was an architect of genius, whereas Morris certainly wasn't.

Some say that all courses ought to begin with a hole that causes worry; others that there should be a comfortable start and that the really testing stuff should come at the end. The 1st hole at Muirfield is one that all the competitors in a British Open are very glad to leave with a par four written on their card. It is long and has threatening bunkers, but overall the most difficult holes are the par threes, each offering a tight target to a raised green, with the fall-away often being to deep bunkers, where it can be necessary to play out sideways or even backwards.

One of the best holes is the 9th, a par five. It is reachable for modern professionals in two, but there are dangers. Out of bounds lurks along the left, which seemed to have destroyed John Cook's chances in the 1992 Open when he produced a snap hook over the wall, but he then played superbly – only to throw it all away on the last two holes of the championship. On this hole, Tom Simpson, the noted architect, placed a bunker more or less in mid-fairway short of the green. It is now known as "Simpson's Folly" but greatly affects the character of the shot in.

Muirfield is one of the most popular links courses for British Open competitors. The movement of the ground is gentle, which generally means that there are very few blind shots indeed. In a press tent interview at the 1992 Open, Jack Nicklaus described the course as "just a flat field". Seriously, however, he had liked it well enough to name his most prized design in the USA "Muirfield Village", though this may partly have been due to his wish to commemorate his first British Open win here in 1966.

That year, the course was extremely testing, with the rough allowed to grow so long that Doug Sanders remarked that he didn't mind about the championship but would like to have the hay concession. Nicklaus won largely by keeping out of the rough and choosing to play irons off the tees – and at that time he was perhaps the best long-iron player in the world.

Another memorable Open came in 1972, when Nicklaus played a thunderous last round, coming from behind, while the main battle was fought out between Tony Jacklin and Lee Trevino.

As late as the 71st hole, Jacklin appeared to have the title in his grasp before he pitched a little weakly and three-putted. In the space of a very few minutes the title was Trevino's after he chipped in on the same hole.

The course is the property of the Honourable Company of Edinburgh Golfers. Founded in 1744, they initially played at Leith Links, and later at Musselburgh, before they moved to what is certainly their final home at Muirfield. Their clubhouse contains some fine paintings, a silver club and a copy of Thomas Mathison's *The Goff*, the first publication devoted solely to golf.

PEBBLE BEACH

Monterey Peninsula, California, USA
Opened: *1919*
Designer: *Jack Neville*
Yardage: *6,799* **Par:** *72*
Major events: *US Open 1972, 1982, 1992. US PGA 1977. US Amateur 1947, 1961*

Most great golf courses have been designed by acknowledged great architects. But there are exceptions, the most famous being the Old Course at St Andrews, where local golfers evolved a route through the linksland over the years. Pebble Beach was also an amateur creation, but came from the creativity of one man, Jack Neville. He was an amateur golfer of great local distinction, winner of the California Amateur on five occasions and a choice for the 1923 US Walker Cup team. The property developer Sam Morse thought he was the man to design him a golf course. It was a decision which worked out.

In later years, Neville said: "The golf course was there all the time. All I did was find the holes." And what holes they are.

Though nearby Cypress Point has been described as the Sistine Chapel of golf, and also as "the dream of an artist who had been drinking gin and sobering up on absinthe", the Pacific holes at Pebble Beach are no less dramatic.

The drama begins at the 4th, which is a short par four, usually playing at about 325 yards but with the cliffs threatening any approach shot that drifts right. The 5th, like so many par fives, is not particularly difficult and, if the golf is not going well, there is at least the reward of a splendid view along to the 10th green. The 7th is apparently an easy par three at 120 yards, but the green is set at an angle to the line of play.

Then comes one of the toughest par fours in world golf. The tee shot is blind but the real problem is that it must be precisely weighted to fall short of a chasm, but not too short, as the shot to the green will then be longer than most will prefer. Nicklaus has called this "the finest second shot on any course I have seen". The next two holes are well over 400 yards, play into the prevailing wind and call for tee shots close to the cliff edge to ease the shots to the greens.

The 17th, particularly at the close of a championship, is a very demanding par three, close on 220 yards, with a green set across the line of play and tightly bunkered. It was here, in the final round of the 1983 US Open, that one of the truly momentous shots in golf history was struck. Tom Watson had just dropped a shot at the 16th to be only level with Jack Nicklaus. Here his tee shot missed the green, leaving him a little pitch shot from the rough which seemed doomed to race past the hole. But Watson thought positively. He tried to hole it, and did so. He was back in the lead and needed only to par the final hole to win. In fact, he birdied it, to win his first and only US Open, and to deprive Jack Nicklaus of his fifth.

That spectacular last hole presents a classic tee shot situation. The bold line is along the cliff edge, having carried an inlet. To the right is less dangerous but a pine can then block the second shot. This is one of very few par 5s that have been seldom reached in two. Perhaps it has not settled many championships, but those who win have been brave.

GREAT SHORT HOLE *The Pacific Ocean crashes on to rocks behind the 7th green at Pebble Beach, where the wind may demand a five-iron for the 120-yard tee shot*

PINE VALLEY

Clementon, New Jersey, USA
Opened: *1919*
Designer: *George Crump*
Yardage: *6,765* **Par:** *70*
Major events: *Walker Cup 1936, 1985*

A beautiful monster is how Pine Valley has been described. Laid out on a huge 184-acre bunker, with forests of pine, larch and oak trees, a generous amount of water and thick, dense undergrowth, it is the most terrifying course in golf. There are no continuous fairways, just islands of green amid the never-ending sandy wasteland, plus tees and greens which can be regarded as refuges to which the golfer inevitably struggles out of the mire.

Pine Valley is the work of Philadelphia hotelier George Crump, the leader of a band of golfers from the Philadelphia Country Club who made occasional trips to play at Atlantic City. One day on their journey by train, Crump spotted a piece of land which he felt would be ideal for golf, and on investigation found virgin forest, swamps, and impenetrable bush, but all on a sandy soil.

After spending some days at the site, Crump persuaded 18 of his friends to contribute $1,000 each, and the land, reported to be the highest ground in southern New Jersey, was bought in 1912. The course took seven years to build, and Crump took to living in a small bungalow on the site, directing the felling of trees, the building of dams to form lakes, the lay-out of holes and the positioning of greens.

However, in January 1918, Crump suddenly died with only 14 holes completed. He had spent $250,000 of his own money, but there was enough left in his estate to complete the remaining four holes. Hugh Wilson, the creator of Merion, and his brother Allen were called in to direct the remaining work.

The end product drew plaudits from course designers and leading players alike. But there have been thousands of ordinary golfers who have been shattered by Pine Valley's penal qualities.

It is not so much the problems that lie in wait in the apparently endless sand as the pressure that builds up in the mind through having to hit from one green oasis to the next, with little room for error, and the increasing sense of desperation with each disaster.

The story goes that club members have a standing bet that first-timers at Pine Valley never break 80. One who did was Arnold Palmer, who went there in 1954 as US Amateur champion. As he was about to get married, he took all the bets he could find, knowing that if he had lost he couldn't afford to pay them. In the event he shot 68 and left with a sizeable wedding present.

Then there was the late Woody Platt, a good amateur, who knew Pine Valley well and started with a birdie three at the 1st, where the drive is over the inevitable sandy wasteland, followed by a dog-leg right to a green that steeply drops away. The 2nd is just 367 yards, but again the tee shot must carry 180 yards of sand, then a second to an elevated green surrounded by even more sandy wastes, Platt left nothing to chance and holed a seven iron for an eagle.

On the short 3rd, there is nothing between the tee and green but 185 yards of sand. Platt went for it and holed-in-one. The 4th measures 461 yards with a blind tee shot over more sand to an island fairway which turns right. Even more sand must be carried to the green, and Platt hit driver, four wood then holed from 30 feet for a birdie to be six under. As the 4th returns to the clubhouse, he retired to contemplate the next 14 holes, especially the 226-yard 5th across a lake. He fortified himself with a drink and never came back out.

Despite its fame and reputation, Pine Valley has never staged, nor sought to stage, a major championship, its layout being unsuitable for large crowds. Perhaps it is just as well, as it could damage many a reputation.

THE SANDMAN COMETH *The 8th hole at Pine Valley typifies the whole layout with acres of penal sandy waste everywhere*

PINEHURST COUNTRY CLUB

Pinehurst, North Carolina, USA
Opened: *1895*
Designer: *Donald Ross*
Yardage: *7,020* **Par:** *72*
Major events: *USPGA Championship 1936. Tour Championship 1991, 1992. US Amateur 1962. US Women's Amateur 1989. World Amateur Team Championship1980*

Paradise can be a somewhat overused word when linked to golf courses, but in the case of Pinehurst it fits the bill perfectly. There are more than 35 courses in a 30-mile radius, and the club has seven of its own, designed by the likes of Ross, Fazio, Trent Jones and Maples. Little wonder that the great Bobby Jones dubbed Pinehurst the "St Andrews of United States golf".

Like so many top courses around the world, Pinehurst is situated among sandhills, thus affording magnificent terrain and, as the name implies, acres of towering pines that form majestic avenues for every hole.

Pinehurst was the brainchild of a Boston soda fountain magnate, James W. Tufts, whose idea was to set up a resort in the south where New Englanders could avoid the harsh winters in their home state. He eventually found what was then a desolate area of North Carolina. There was a natural progression to golf in the latter part of the nineteenth century, and a club was formed in 1895.

In 1900, Harry Vardon is reported to have played the original 18 holes and later that year a Scot, Donald Ross, who had been professional and greenkeeper at his local club, Royal Dornoch, was appointed as club professional.

Within a year of arriving in North Carolina, Ross started to build a second course. Opened in 1907, Pinehurst No. 2 has become the signature lay-out and has staged a number of top championships. Ross also redesigned the original course, then

UNUSUAL SIGHT *The only water hazard at Pinehurst No. 2 is at the 16th, where the tee shot must carry a small pond*

went on to build No. 3 (1910) and No. 4 (1919) during a 48-year stay at the resort. More recently, Ellis Maples was the creator of a fifth course (1961), Tom Fazio added a sixth (1979), and the seventh and latest was completed in 1986 by Rees Jones. But that isn't the end of the story. An eighth course, The Centennial, is being designed by Tom Fazio and will add yet another jewel to Pinehurst's glistening crown.

But it is Pinehurst No. 2 that evokes such delight and nostalgia. Ross called it "the fairest test of championship golf I have ever designed". The great Sam Snead said he rated it as his "number one course" because it constantly challenges the player. "You have to be alert and sharp for 18 consecutive holes; otherwise it will jump up and bite you. I guess that's why the experts rate No. 2 as one of the 10 greatest courses in the world." It has staged a number of major events over the years, from the US PGA and the Tour Championship to the US Amateur, Women's Amateur and the Ryder Cup. The US Open is scheduled to make its debut at Pinehurst in 1999.

It is a course where you have to drive the ball well, hit your long irons well, and, most of all, have a razor-sharp short game. The greens are small by modern standards because they fall off around the edges, allowing balls to run off into dips and swales.

Getting on to No. 2 is not easy, but it becomes a lot easier if you stay at the luxurious Pinehurst Resort Hotel, known at the Queen of the South, as tee times are reserved for guests. Access to the other courses is much easier, while staying at the New England-style village is an exercise in quiet and pristine living. Here you can enjoy wandering the sandy path from the resort to the village's quaint shops and boutiques, stocking everything from sportswear to antiques, fine wines and every gift imaginable for the golfer.

In every way, Pinehurst is, indeed, a golfer's paradise.

OAKMONT

Oakmont, Pennsylvania, USA
Opened: *1904*
Designer: *Henry C. Fownes*
Yardage: *6,921* **Par:** *71*
Major events: *US Open 1927, 1935, 1953, 1962, 1973, 1983, 1994. US Amateur 1919, 1925, 1938, 1969. US Women's Open 1992*

Oakmont, on the outskirts of Pittsburgh, is arguably the most penal lay-out in America, with hard, slick greens, bunkers everywhere, narrow fairways with thick rough, and a length of almost 7,000 yards. It begrudges low scores and these are almost impossible when it comes to major championships.

The club has also been renowned for doing its own thing, especially when it comes to staging US Opens. The 1953 and 1962 championships were marked by heated disputes between the USGA and the club over how the bunkers should be raked. This was because the rakes used at Oakmont were oversize and left wide furrows into which the ball would drop. It led to a famous remark by Jimmy Demaret, who said: "You could have combed North Africa with that rake, and Rommel wouldn't have got past Casablanca."

In 1983 there was another disagreement with the USGA – about the length of the rough. In the event, the players were greeted by thick, dense grass, some nine inches high in places, and could only hack the ball back on to the fairway. The dispute lasted two days of the championship before the mowers were summoned.

Oakmont is not the most beautiful course in the world. It was built on a stretch of flatlands at the foothills of the Alleghenies by a steel magnate, Henry C. Fownes in 1903. In those days the course was split by a railway line which curved through a gorge. In 1952 the Pennsylvania Turnpike was constructed, but as it followed the path of the railway the damage to the course was minimal.

Fownes certainly knew how to get things done. Work began in September 1903 with 150 workers and 25 teams of horses, and 12 holes were finished in six weeks; the other six holes in the spring. The whole lay-out opened that autumn with a "bogey" of 80, eight par fives, a par six, and a total of 220 bunkers. A year later it boasted no fewer than 350. Bunkers were something of a fixation with Fownes and the 8th underlines this. The hole is a par three of 244 yards but contains the Sahara bunker, which is 75 yards long and 35 yards wide and required 11 lorry loads of sand to fill it.

While the bunkers may dominate the course, it is the greens which visitors remember most. They have taken an awful toll of the top names over the years. In Oakmont's first US Open in 1927, Tommy Armour, the Silver Scot, won with 301, 13 over par; then in 1935, Sam Parks, a Pittsburgh man who knew the course like the back of his hand, won with 299, the only player to break 300.

After the Second World War, it was agreed to make Oakmont less intimidating. Some fairways were widened in the driving area and the number of bunkers was reduced to fewer than 200. In 1953, Ben Hogan came to Oakmont as Masters champion and spreadeagled the field with an opening 67. He won by six from Sam Snead and his awesome shotmaking was illustrated by his covering the final four holes in 13 strokes against a par of 15.

In 1962, Jack Nicklaus won the first of his four US Opens at Oakmont, beating Arnold Palmer in a play-off; then Johnny Miller took the title at Oakmont in 1973 with a closing 63 which was no doubt helped by very wet greens. After Larry Nelson's win at Oakmont in 1983, the 1994 event promised a possible British victory when Colin Montgomerie tied with Ernie Els and Loren Roberts. But, in the three-way play-off, Els clinched his first major success after he and Roberts had tied again with 74s, four ahead of the fast-fading Scot.

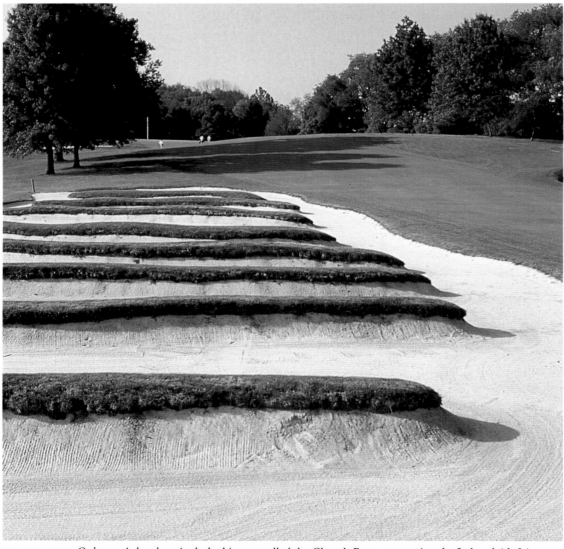

WING AND A PRAYER *Oakmont's bunkers include this row called the Church Pews, separating the 3rd and 4th fairways*

ROYAL COUNTY DOWN

Newcastle, County Down, Northern Ireland

Opened: *1889*
Designer: *Tom Morris*
Yards: *6,968* **Par:** *72*
Major events: *British Amateur 1970. British Women's Amateur 1899, 1907, 1920, 1927, 1935, 1950, 1963. Curtis Cup 1968*

In comparison to today's staggering construction fees, the cost of the course at Royal County Down was very reasonable. Back in 1889, the club's provisional committee convened in the hall of Mr Lawrence's Dining Rooms, and agreed to invite Tom Morris over from St Andrews to lay out a course "at an expense not to exceed £4".

There were already nine holes in existence, which Old Tom played, and he left recommendations for an 18-hole lay-out which was soon completed. The "outlandish outlay" probably represented his fee, but if such a magnificent piece of land became available today, many of the modern designers would arguably settle for a modest pay day.

Those who have had the good fortune to play this gem some 30 miles south of Belfast will have been enchanted by the sheer beauty of the place, never mind the splendour of the links themselves with their abundance of gorse. This is where, as it says in the song, the Mountains of Mourne sweep down to the sea, and, dominated by Slieve Donard, the highest peak in the range, they form a perfect backdrop, plunging some 3,000 feet sheer, almost to the edge of Dundrum Bay. Surrounded by such beauty, it is easy to be distracted – a grave mistake given County Down's tough reputation. In those early days, the club used the nearby railway station facilities, but by 1897 it had opened its first clubhouse. A year later, the club was affluent enough to put up a 100 guinea prize for a professional tournament between Harry Vardon, J. H. Taylor,

Ben Sayers, Andrew Kirkaldy, Sandy Herd, and Willie Fernie, which culminated in Vardon beating Taylor by 12 and 11 in the final.

The course has witnessed several changes in its first century. In 1904 the then professional, Seymour Dunn, suggested some changes; Vardon did the same in 1908, the year the club was granted its Royal Charter; but its current magnificence can be traced back to Harry Colt, who made the last significant changes in 1926.

Unlike many links courses which go out and back, County Down has two nine-hole loops of different character, courtesy of George Combe, a founder member and captain in 1895–96, who spent many years as chairman of the greens com-

mittee. Its other great virtue is that each hole is separate, occupying its own valley between the sandhills, with rarely a view of the next or the adjacent hole.

The front nine, or sea nine, is uncompromising. The premium is on long, straight shot-making which means those who can handle a driver will be at a distinct advantage. Those who stray from the often narrow fairways find themselves tangling with the dunes, wild roses and heavy bunkering.

On the landward or back nine, the problems are heavy rough in the form of seaside grass, heather and gorse, while many of the greens are small, with subtle slopes and hollows that highlight the merest blemish in a putting stroke.

There are those who criticize Royal County Down because the golfer is required to play a number of blind shots, but that is a minor irritant when there is so much to admire. Best of all is the view from the 9th tee, with the Mourne Mountains towering above the rooftops of Newcastle.

Big events have tended to bypass the club. It has staged only one Amateur Championship, in 1970 when Michael Bonallack won his fifth title, and his third on the trot, romping home 8 and 7 against American Bill Hyndman after being one down at lunch. But the women have been more frequent visitors, the British Women's Amateur having been held here seven times between 1899 and 1963.

ROYAL DORNOCH

Dornoch, Sutherland, Scotland
Opened: *Unknown*
Designer: *Anon*
Yardage: *6,577* **Par:** *70*
Major events: *British Amateur 1985*

If it were not so remote, 60 miles north of Inverness, Dornoch would undoubtedly be a British Open venue. It is one of the most beautiful courses anywhere, as well as one of the oldest. Indeed it may even have a claim to be the birthplace of the game.

No one knows when golf was played here, but it was known by 1630 when Sir Robert Gordon wrote: "About this town along the sea coast are the fairest and largest links or green fields of any pairt of Scotland. Fitt for archery, golfing, ryding and all other exercises, they doe surpass the fields of Montrose or St Andrews."

There is even an earlier reference to this cathedral city which, in size, is little more than a village. A 1616 account book of the Earl of Sutherland notes expenditure on archery, golf balls and clubs. Such evidence is rare, for golf was not regarded as important, so it was seldom recorded, and we are unlikely ever to find out where golf began. Dornoch undoubtedly remains a candidate, even though the club itself was not founded until 1877. Not that this is unusual: people had wandered the linksland of Britain hitting golf balls long before any clubs were formed, and the dates of many courses are guesswork.

The whole setting of the Dornoch course is magnificent, so much so that some of those from England who "discovered" the course did not mention it for fear that too many others would hear about it and spoil the tranquillity. Dornoch remained relatively un-known until it was very highly praised by the great American golf writer, Herbert Warren Wind, in the 1960s. Since then it has been visited and played by the likes of Ben Crenshaw, Tom Watson and Greg Norman, who might well prefer to play here rather than most of the British Open sites.

The course begins comfortably enough and in fact is never a really severe test on any particular hole. Instead, it is a steady challenge all the way. The layout is the once traditional one of out from the clubhouse and then back again. The sea is in view almost all the time. The 1st is a gentle introduction, a short par four of around 330 yards, but it is followed by a more testing par three of 180 yards which features a typical Dornoch green with fall-aways on either side. Many think the 5th the first really testing hole. It is played from an elevated tee, with a mound to be carried, and the second shot is to a long but narrow green, well guarded by bunkers. By this time one is well aware of the vast bank of gorse which runs along the left but does not significantly affect play. After the 6th, a very natural looking hole, you climb up the bankside to the 7th on a ridge and play between the gorse bushes and then drive off from a height along the 8th, which features a plunge in the fairway about 200 yards out.

The homeward journey begins with the 9th, a par five of close on 500 yards which follows the curve of the bay, as do the next several holes. In this stretch many find "Foxy", the 14th, the most memorable. It demonstrates that a golf hole doesn't need bunkers, mainly because the plateau green demands both a long and precise second shot.

Every hole, however, is a delight, and even if you are playing badly there ought to be consolation in the views of the Dornoch Firth and the hills of Sutherland. At the end, there is the welcome of a very pleasant modern clubhouse.

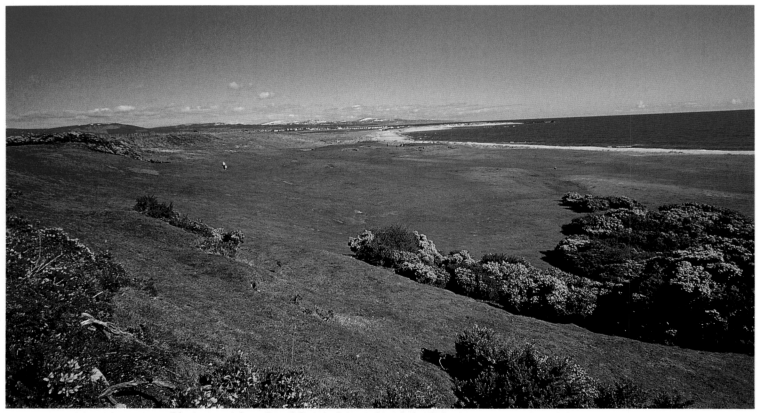

BETWEEN THE DEVIL AND THE DEEP BLUE SEA *Playing straight at Royal Dornoch is vital, with devilish gorse on one side and the Firth of Dornoch on the other*

ROYAL LIVERPOOL (HOYLAKE)

Hoylake, Merseyside, England
Opened: *1869*
Designer: *Anon*
Yardage: *6,780* **Par:** *72*
Major events: *Open Championship 1897, 1902, 1907, 1913, 1924, 1930, 1936, 1947, 1956, 1967. British Amateur 1885, 1887, 1890, 1894, 1898, 1902, 1906, 1910, 1921, 1927, 1933, 1939, 1953, 1962, 1975. Walker Cup 1983. Curtis Cup 1992*

Hoylake is considered to be one of the toughest tests in British golf, and can be stretched to around 7,000 yards. This is largely why the Open has ten times been held here. In 1897 it was only the second English course to be used (after Royal St George's, Sandwich). Here, in 1902, Sandy Herd became the first champion to use a wound ball, and in 1924 Walter Hagen took the second of his four British Open titles. However, easily the most momentous Open came in 1930, when Bobby Jones had his third British Open win in just four entries and completed the English swing of his eventual Grand Slam of all four British and US Amateur and Open titles. The last British Open was played here in 1967, when Roberto de Vicenzo memorably outplayed Jack Nicklaus and Gary Player over the last two rounds. Hoylake is very unlikely ever to host a British Open again, for the simple reason that there isn't enough room for today's Open crowds, particularly on the closing holes. However, the course is still used for top amateur events – the Curtis Cup, Walker Cup and British Amateur, which will return for the centenary of that initial Open. It also hosts European Tour events.

The course is extremely variable in appearance. On arrival, the impression is of a flat expanse with some undulating ground in the far distance by the Dee Estuary. That bit looks the most dramatic, but in fact many players find that the flat-ter holes are the most testing, while the stretch from the 8th to the 11th has the most visual appeal.

The 1st is one of the flat holes but is a frightener. You have to try to keep your tee shot as close as you dare to the practice ground along the right – but that is out of bounds. You are not in much trouble going left until you play the second shot. Then you have to contend with firing directly towards the out of bounds. The 7th also used to cause much fear. There was a turf bank just to the left of the green and be-yond was out of bounds. That penalty has now been removed. Judgement of distance and quality of strike, however, are just as vital as they ever were. As the course occupies a small area, out of bounds is an almost constant threat.

The course is beautifully maintained, the greens sometimes the best in Britain, and the clubhouse is full of interest, including what amounts to a museum of golf in the entrance hall.

Hoylake has seen quite a few firsts. In 1885, the club had the idea of staging a big amateur tournament, which was won by Allan Macfie. A generation later, this was recognized as the first British Amateur Championship. In 1921 the first golf international of any kind between British and American men was played over the course, and it was a forewarning of imminent American dominance that the British were trounced. In 1925 the English Amateur was inaugurated at Hoylake and, quite appropriately, was won by a Royal Liverpool member, T. F. Ellison.

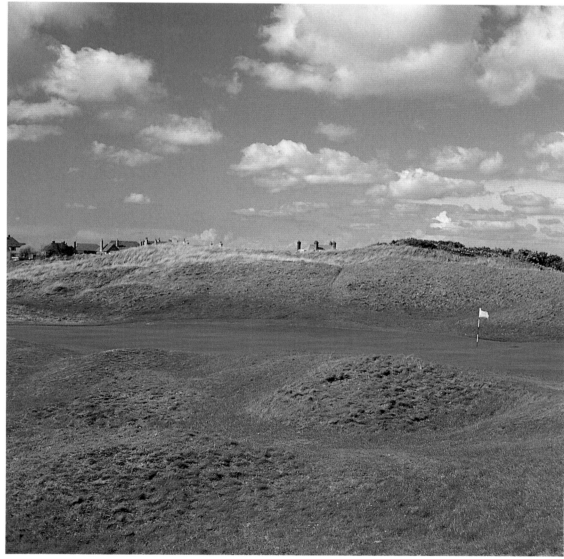

TIGHT FIT *Although no longer an Open venue, Hoylake still offers one of the supreme challenges in British golf*

179

ROYAL MELBOURNE

Melbourne, Victoria, Australia
Opened: *1931*
Designers: *Alister Mackenzie and Alex Russell*
Yardage: *6,946* **Par:** *71*
Major events: *Australian Open 1905, 1907, 1909, 1912, 1913, 1921, 1924, 1927, 1933, 1939, 1953, 1963, 1984, 1985, 1987, 1991. World Amateur Team Championship 1968. World Cup 1988*

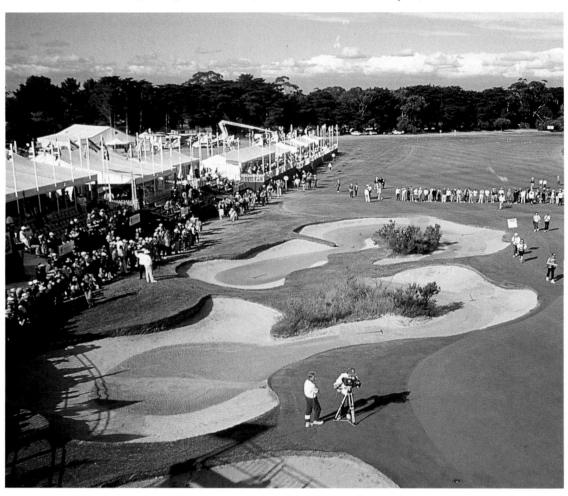

Sandy subsoils are the ideal ingredients to support golf courses as can be seen with the various Surrey clubs, those on the Lancashire coast and in many parts of Scotland. The same applies in Australia and especially in Melbourne, whose southern confines contain a 25 square mile area known as the Sand Belt. Here, the rolling terrain containing fine grasses and indigenous trees, reeds, heather and bracken, was considered the ideal site for the Royal Melbourne club to move to in the late 1920s.

The club had been founded as long ago as 1891, making it the oldest in Australia, but it had two other locations before eventually moving to its present site and building its reputation as one of the world's finest courses. The prime land was acquired in 1924, and club officials were in no doubt that they wanted "the best expert advice", irrespective of cost.

That advice was provided by Alister Mackenzie, the Scot who was later to go on to design Augusta National as well as many other top courses throughout the world. He began work in 1926 together with Alex Russell, the 1924 Australian Open champion, and the result was the West course, which many feel is a masterpiece.

While Mackenzie's name is synonymous with the course, Russell played a major role, and it was perhaps fitting that he should design and construct the neighbouring East course a little later. For champi-

onship purposes, a composite of the two courses is used, six holes of Russell's East linked with 12 from Mackenzie's West. The result is a lay-out of almost 7,000 yards and a tough par of 71.

Aesthetically Royal Melbourne leaves something to be desired because, over the years, the city's development has seen it surrounded by roads while houses back on to parts of the playing area. However, closer inspection reveals its true quality, notably in the thoughtful arrangements of humps and ridges, adding character, not to mention the odd hazard.

Apart from the overall design, another significant feature of Royal Melbourne is the large greens, which are usually extremely fast. The cred-

it for this belongs to the former head greenkeeper Claude Crockford, who was taken on to the staff in 1934. Such were his skills and devotion to duty that there are no truer or faster greens to be found anywhere; consequently, it takes the visitor some time to acclimatize and feel at home.

Crockford also carried out some redesign work, particularly with regard to the short 7th, which Mackenzie built with an elevated green that the members felt was a blind shot. They wanted it altered, so Crockford obliged by lowering it to where it could be seen. Even now, at just 148 yards, it is no pushover, with several very deep bunkers lying in wait for the wayward shot. In fact, bunkers were Mackenzie's signa-

ture, and there are 114 of various shapes, sizes and depths to be confronted or avoided if you are to come away with a decent score.

The 11th is generally regarded as the toughest hole on the course. From an elevated tee, this 455-yard par four presents a difficult drive to the elbow of the left-hand dog-leg, the fairway sloping left towards two large, luring traps. Turning left, the approach to a sloping green also requires accuracy to avoid a gaping bunker to the right of the putting surface.

Such has been Royal Melbourne's pedigree down the years that it has been a frequent host for the Australian Open and PGA Championships. It was also the venue for the World Cup in 1988, won by the Ozaki brothers from Japan.

ROYAL NORTH DEVON

Westward Ho!, Devon, England
Opened: *1864*
Designer: *Tom Morris*
Yardage: *6,662* **Par:** *71*
Major events: *British Amateur 1912, 1925, 1931. Women's British Amateur 1900, 1910*

The Royal North Devon club, situated on the north bank of the estuary of the River Torridge, is not only the oldest club in England, still played over its original land, but can claim to possess the finest natural golfing terrain anywhere. Golf began at Westward Ho!, which took its name from Charles Kingsley's famous novel, in 1853 on common land known as Northam or Appledore Burrows, and the first club was formed in 1864. Four years earlier, Old Tom Morris had travelled down from St Andrews to advise, and when he returned in 1864, he designed two courses, one of 17 holes and another of 22. There was another significant move in 1868, when the North Devon Ladies' Club was formed, which had its own nine-hole course adjacent to the men's. In 1908 the course was totally redesigned by W. Herbert Fowler. He had earned rave reviews for his creation of Walton Heath a few years earlier, but his work on this traditional linksland lay-out was also acclaimed.

RND has another jewel in its illustrious history. John Henry Taylor, who was to win the Open Championship five times, was born at Northam in March 1871 and joined the Westward Ho! greenstaff at the age of 17. After two years as a caddie he turned professional and became greenkeeper at Burnham. He was just 23 when he won his first Open at Sandwich in 1894, the first non-Scot to do so, retaining the title at St Andrews the following year. As well as being one of golf's Great Triumvirate Taylor was also instrumental in forming the Professional Golfers' Association in 1901 and generally raising the status of the professional. He spent most of his career as pro at Royal Mid Surrey, but when he retired back to Northam in 1957, RND made him their president.

In keeping with a club steeped in history, RND has been graced by some odd customs. When Horace Hutchinson won the club medal in 1875 at the age of 16, he was automatically elected captain while taking the chair at the annual meeting. It was a custom that existed for many years, but while that has been amended, the rights of locals to graze their sheep and cattle on the course hasn't, which provides the golfer with an additional hazard.

Looking over the wild, barren landscape from the wooden clubhouse, Westward Ho! provides a slow start, but the real fun begins on the par four 4th, where your drive must carry the huge Cape bunker at around 170 yards. The 5th is the first short hole towards the sandhills before two more par fours that demand good driving. The 8th is a par three of 197 yards on the edge of the estuary at the furthest part of the course before you turn back with the long 9th that, like many holes from here on, features the famous rushes that stand like huge shaving brushes waiting to snare every shot.

The back nine starts with four more par fours, the 13th, at 440 yards being the longest on the course. The par three 14th and 16th are played in almost the same direction, while the final two holes provide a tricky finish. The 17th, the Road Hole, is usually played into a wind, and at 548 yards that can prove quite a task. The road crosses just short of the green, while a ditch must also be crossed in front of the putting surface. If that wasn't enough trouble, at the par four 18th you have two burns to contend with. Par figures at these two final holes can have you singing the praises of Westward Ho! no matter what has gone before.

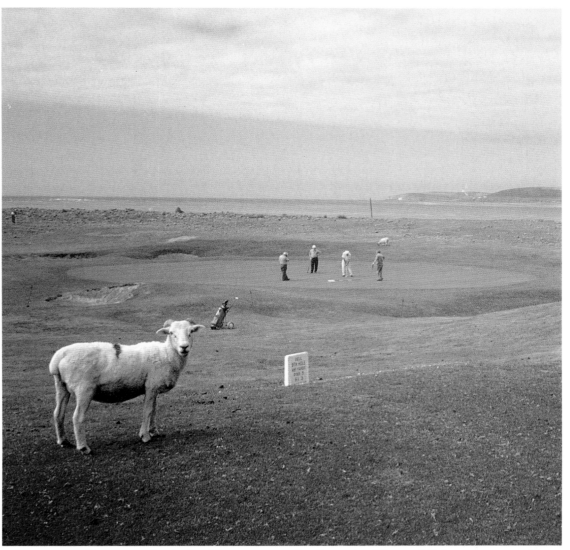

DON'T BLEAT ABOUT IT *The custom allowing local famers to graze their livestock at Westward Ho! creates extra problems*

ROYAL ST DAVID'S

Harlech, Gwynedd, Wales
Opened: *1894*
Designer: *Harold Finch-Hatton*
Yardage: *6,427* **Par:** *69*
Major events: *British Women's Amateur 1926, 1949, 1960, 1967, 1987*

The Royal St David's club, which celebrated its centenary in 1994, rejoices in the most splendid surroundings you can imagine. Flanked by the Irish Sea on one side, the whole scene is dominated by the ancient Harlech Castle, which sits with medieval dignity atop its hill, no doubt surveying with a certain amount of disdain the often futile antics being played out on the links below. Beyond, the mountains of Snowdonia provide a backdrop that completes a vista of almost unrivalled beauty.

The club was established in a somewhat curious way. The story goes, although it may well have been embroidered down the years, that in 1893 a young man by the name of Harold Finch-Hatton, just returned from Australia, was out on the low-lying grazing land known as Morfa, displaying his skills with a boomerang. He was spotted from near the castle battlements by a W. H. More, who climbed down and engaged him in conversation.

Some days later they met again, while Finch-Hatton was trying out some strange implements to play a game that was all the rage across the borders in Scotland and England. "This would be a great place for a golf links," said Finch-Hatton, or words to that effect. "Let's lay one out." More knew nothing about golf, but was not about to admit the fact as they set about positioning tees and greens. Soon the club was formed and More became its secretary, a post he was to hold for 40 years.

At that early meeting, they decided to prepare 18 holes in time for an autumn competition which, despite heavy rain, was won by the famous John Ball with a score of 152 – quite a feat on a course that couldn't have been in great shape. Four years earlier Ball had captured the Open Championship and that year won the Amateur for the fourth time.

So the St David's club was established, and it is among the oldest in Wales. Among its early patrons was Edward VII, then Prince of Wales, which prompted some proud members, somewhat prematurely, to assume the Royal prefix. Fortunately, that error was rectified in August 1908 when the King sanctioned the present title. The royal connection was reinforced later when the Duke of Windsor, while himself Prince of Wales, captained the club.

The course itself is generally flat, but always has the feel of being natural. That has a lot to do with the great sandhills, and achieving a good score requires long driving as half of the holes measure 427 yards or more. But at least there is the assurance that the ultimate destinations are fine, large greens.

After starting with three successive par fours, you come to the first of five challenging short holes; the second of these completes the front nine after the only par fives, the 7th and 8th. The return is towards the sea, while the final five holes present the best part of all as they head into the hills.

The beginning of the end comes with perhaps the best of the par threes, the 14th which at 218 yards involves quite a carry from the tee to a target encircled by dunes. The 427-yard 15th is a long two-shotter, while the tee at the par four 16th provides the only view of the sea during the round. Decision time comes at the 427-yard 17th – whether to carry the cross bunker in front of the green – while the home hole is another 200-yard par three.

Once you have played Royal St David's you are hooked, whatever the season; but perhaps the time to see the links at their best is June, when you can enjoy many wild flowers in bloom and the call of a host of birds overhead.

SPLENDID SCENERY *Ancient Harlech castle, the Irish Sea and the mountains of Snowdonia make Royal St David's one of Britain's most picturesque courses*

ROYAL ST GEORGE'S

Sandwich, Kent, England
Opened: *1887*
Designer: *Dr W. Laidlaw Purves*
Yardage: *6,857* **Par:** *70*
Major events: *Open Championship 1894, 1899, 1904, 1911, 1922, 1928, 1934, 1938, 1949, 1981, 1985, 1993. Amateur Championship 1892, 1896, 1900, 1904, 1908, 1914, 1929, 1937, 1948, 1959, 1972. British Women's Amateur 1922, 1964. Walker Cup 1930, 1967. Curtis Cup 1988*

Royal St George's, on the shores of Pegwell Bay, is a great links course with an illustrious history. In 1894 it staged the first Open Championship outside Scotland, which produced the first English winner in J. H. Taylor. It also produced the first foreign winner of the Amateur Championship, Walter Travis from Australia, who won at Royal St George's in 1904, and the first American winner of the Open, Walter Hagen in 1922. Another significant first was when Tony Jacklin holed-in-one at the short 16th during a final-round 64 on his way to winning the 1967 Dunlop Masters. It was the first time such a feat was captured on television.

Royal St George's was founded in 1887, when Dr Laidlaw Purves and some 50 friends formed a syndicate called the Sandwich Golf Association, obtained a lease on the links and turned them over to the club. The story goes that Purves spotted the land from a church tower in Sandwich after a long search for such a site.

Purves is credited with the original lay-out, but Royal St George's has seen some remodelling over the years, first by Alister Mackenzie, and more recently by Frank Pennink. It has long had a reputation as a driver's course, and indeed the last two Opens there were won by Sandy Lyle and Greg Norman, two of the longest hitters the game has seen. However, it also provides some of the most testing second shots found anywhere, starting with the opening two holes, both par fours.

The 3rd is the first short hole of 214 yards, before the course progresses among the expanse of dunes along fairways that rise and fall continually to heavily guarded greens. At the 4th, a par four of 470 yards, you drive over a cavernous bunker, while the green at the 422-yard 5th is reached between two hills.

The first par five comes at the 7th, which has a slight dog-leg, while the 8th, another par four, has a belt of mounds and rough dividing the fairway from the green. After the 9th and 10th – two more par fours played in opposite directions – the 11th is another short hole of 216 yards before the dog-leg 12th around a sandy ridge heralds a loop of three holes skirting the neighbouring Prince's course.

At the 13th you have to manoeuvre between a maze of bunkers, while the par five 14th requires straight driving to avoid the out of bounds before crossing the famous Suez Canal midway down the fairway. After another testing par four at 15 comes the short 16th which, depending on the wind, can play anything from a two to an eight iron to a green encircled with traps.

The closing holes, two more par fours, again call for accurate driving and sound second shots. At 18, the front of the green is guarded by bunkers right and left which are to be avoided, but so is Duncan's Hollow, named after George Duncan, the British pro who failed to get down in two from there to catch Walter Hagen in the 1922 Open, an area of thick grass below a steep bank that is a magnet for many shots.

The 1949 Open, won by Bobby Locke, from an unlucky Harry Bradshaw, who chose – some say unnecessarily – to play his ball out of a broken bottle, was the last Open at Royal St George's for 32 years. Despite its pedigree as a course, it was felt to be unsuitable to stage the ever-expanding event, but thanks to the building of a by-pass around the old town and other improvements, its long exile ended in 1981. In 1985 Sandy Lyle became the first British winner since Jacklin in 1969. As the only Open venue south of Lancashire, and with its close proximity to London, it is unlikely to be out on a limb again.

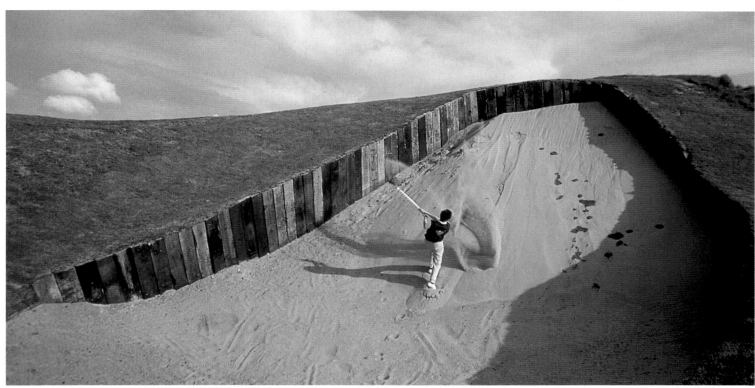

HIT AND HOPE *Anybody driving into the enormous and steep bunker on the long 4th hole will do well to make only a bogey*

ST ANDREWS, OLD COURSE

St Andrews, Fife, Scotland

Opened: *Unknown*
Designer: *Anon*
Yardage: *6,933* **Par:** *72*
Major events: *Open Championship 1873, 1876, 1879, 1882, 1885, 1888, 1891, 1895, 1900, 1905, 1910, 1921, 1927, 1933, 1939, 1946, 1955, 1957, 1964, 1960, 1970, 1978, 1984, 1990. British Amateur 1886, 1889, 1891, 1895, 1901, 1907, 1913, 1924, 1930, 1936, 1950, 1958, 1963, 1976, 1981. Walker Cup 1923, 1926, 1934, 1938, 1947, 1955, 1971, 1975*

This is one of the world's oldest and most revered golf courses and is deservedly known as "the home of golf". It is a favourite course of many top professionals and amateurs, perhaps because it is by no means fearsome in still air but always demands good strategy and shot-making, though some of the first ten holes are easy in the extreme.

The first exciting hole is the 5th, where you need to be a little left because of a cluster of bunkers along the right. There is a steep upslope, set with more bunkers; on hard ground, with a following wind, Craig Wood drove into one of them during the 1933 British Open. The distance is about 430 yards! Even so, most professionals see this as a clear birdie chance.

The 6th is a typical links hole. When you stand on the tee, you may wonder what has happened to the golf course. Most players simply aim at the marker post, but even if all goes well that far, the second shot is difficult. There is a rise before the green, and the putting surface then slopes away from the player. The 7th is the only dog-leg on the course, and even then only a slight one. It is best to be right rather than left, because Shell bunker is on line for an approach from the left, and the green slopes from left to right.

The real tests at St Andrews come on the route back to the clubhouse. The 11th, for instance, is one of the best par threes in world golf, feared because of the deep Hill bunker to the left of the green and Strath to the front on the right.

The 13th, 425 yards, has been ranked one of the great par fours, enhanced by the skyline of St Andrews. The second shot has to be played over a heathery bank to a flag which seems to be perched on the top. Another great hole is the 14th, where the tee shot is menaced by out of bounds along the right and bunkers known as "The Beardies" to the left. If you succeed and get your shot down the middle, the large Hell bunker lies directly in your path to the green. For long hitters this 567-yard hole is a birdie opportunity, but few manage to get the ball close to the hole, and to be just short leaves a difficult putt or chip.

By this time, many will begin to worry about the 17th, a devilish par four of 461 yards. The tee shot needs to be nearly out of bounds along the right, because from the left it is extremely difficult to hit and hold the narrow, angled green. Hardly any British Open competitors get past this challenge with four pars. In 1885 David Ayton took an 11 to lose by two strokes!

This is not true of the last, one of the weakest finishing holes in all of championship golf – though Doug Sanders memorably lost the 1970 Open by taking five!

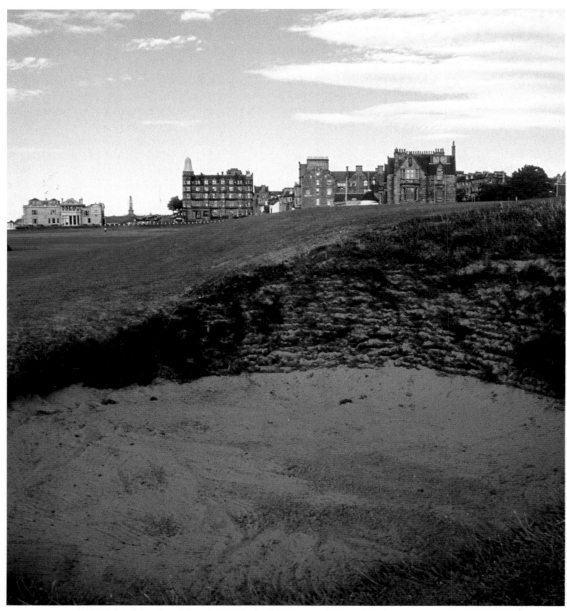

NIGHTMARE SCENARIO *A visit to the Road Bunker at St Andrews is to dice with a double-figure score at the 17th hole*

SUNNINGDALE

Sunningdale, Surrey, England
Opened: *1901*
Designer: *Willie Park*
Yardage: *6,566* **Par:** *72*
Major events: *Walker Cup 1987. Women's British Amateur 1956*

Sunningdale, like its neighbour Wentworth, is a gorgeous course on the Surrey sand belt. Originally three farms surrounded by heather, gorse and pine trees, the land was owned by St John's College, Cambridge, who around the turn of the century were persuaded by their agent T. A. Roberts that the land should be turned over to golf and residential development. A committee was formed and Willie Park, twice Open champion, was commissioned to design the Old course at a fee of £3,800.

Much of the site at that time was open country with few trees. The familiar wooded outlook we know today followed a general redesign by Harry Colt, who was Sunningdale secretary for 17 years before transferring his skills to full-time course architecture.

As a result each hole is self-contained, while nature's work over the years has been instrumental in seeing Sunningdale develop into one of the great inland courses.

Colt also found time to design a second 18 holes, the New course of 6,202 yards, par 68, which opened in 1922. The two courses, both tough lay-outs, complement each other and together make Sunningdale a delight to play.

Oddly enough, the Old course starts with two par fives, but the 1st, at 494 yards and slightly downhill, can be reached in two shots during a dry summer, while the 2nd, just 10 yards shorter, is another good birdie chance with accurate shotmaking. The 3rd, a short par four, also presents the chance of picking up a shot, but the 4th, the first short hole, requires a solid shot up to a well-protected green. The next short hole,

the 8th, which follows three par fours, is somewhat similar, while the 267-yard 9th is eminently drivable.

The 10th tee, at the highest part of the course, provides stunning views over the countryside. On this par five you drive down into a broad valley with bunkers to the right and left, leaving a long second shot to a receptive green. The 11th is another short par four with a drive over sand hills, and providing you avoid the trees and ditch on the right, only a short pitch is required to find the green.

The 12th is another testing par four, and after two teasing par threes and the final par five come three par fours that provide a daunting finish. The 18th is a superb finishing hole. Here, a long uphill drive is required avoiding large bunkers right and left, then a long second shot towards the big oak tree that is the club's symbol and stands between the clubhouse and green.

On the tournament side, Sunningdale has long staged its early-season Foursomes event for both amateurs and professionals, women being admitted in recent years, while it has also been a venue for the Ladies British Amateur, the Golf Illustrated Gold Vase and in 1987 the Walker Cup.

One of the greatest feats in Sunningdale's history was the famous round of 66 produced by Bobby Jones in a qualifying round for the Open Championship in 1926. It has often been described as the perfect round, because he covered each nine in 33 strokes, and he had 33 shots and 33 putts. Jones's score was also made up entirely of threes and fours, and he hit every green, except one, in regulation and was bunkered only once. He followed it with a 68, then claimed that he had peaked too early. He hadn't, of course, and he proved it by moving on to Royal Lytham and winning the title by two strokes from fellow American Al Watrous.

Sunningdale has long had a royal connection. The Prince of Wales, later Edward VIII, and the Duke of York, later King George VI, were both captains while over the years the club has become a mecca for the great and famous.

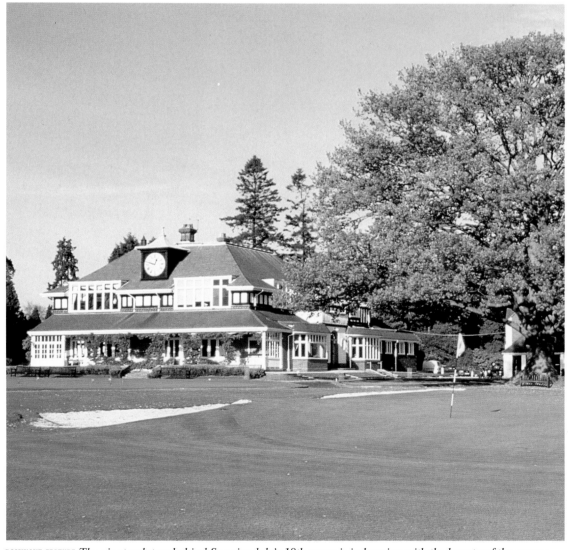

DOMINANT FEATURE *The giant oak tree behind Sunningdale's 18th green is in keeping with the beauty of the course*

TURNBERRY

Ayrshire, Scotland
Opened: *1903*
Designer: *Willie Fernie*
Yardage: *6,950* **Par:** *70*
Major events: *Open Championship 1977, 1986, 1994. Amateur Championship 1961, 1984. Walker Cup 1963. British Women's Amateur 1912, 1921, 1937*

Turnberry is one of Scotland's major golf centres. It has two fine courses – the Ailsa and the Arran – a modern clubhouse incorporating every facility, and an impressive hotel set high on a hill overlooking the complete lay-out, with the Firth of Clyde and the granite dome of Ailsa Craig beyond.

The original links course was the work of former Open champion Willie Fernie, while Turnberry, like several other resorts early this century, owed its development mainly to the coming of the railways. The line being pushed south down the Ayrshire coast required the building of a top-class hotel, and both were opened in 1906. Soon Turnberry became a mecca for the rich, and a second links course, the Arran, was opened in 1912.

However, the First World War put paid to golf. The area was used as a training ground for Royal Flying Corps pilots, while the hotel became the officers' mess. Much the same occurred in the Second World War, Turnberry becoming a base for RAF Coastal Command with much of the courses disappearing under concrete runways, hangars and other buildings.

In 1946 the then owners, British Transport Hotels, set about using the compensation from the War Office to restore the courses to their former glory. Philip Mackenzie Ross was brought in to redesign the lay-out, and the Ailsa course, most of which had to be returfed, reopened in 1951. It occupies undulating terrain, threading its way among the sand dunes along the seashore in a general north-south direction. However, the first six holes of the back nine are more east-west, which means the golfer, having got used to the wind direction, has to readjust.

Like all links courses, Turnberry's character changes with the prevailing conditions, which can vary between the docile and the stormy. It is said locally: "If you can see Ailsa Craig it's going to rain. If you can't see it, it's raining." Depending on the direction of the on-shore wind, some greens can enjoy a sheltered aspect, while others can be buffeted as if in a wind tunnel.

Apart from its majestic hotel, Turnberry's best-known feature is the lighthouse. This stands adjacent to the par four 9th hole, where the tee is built on a rocky outcrop of the cliff, requiring a drive across an inlet to the safety of the fairway beyond. The other signature hole is the 16th, another par four which presents few problems until you consider your second shot to a green perched on a knoll, below which bubble the waters of the Wee Burn. The number of shots which have found a watery grave here and the number of ruined cards are legion – for even hitting the putting surface is no guarantee of safety.

The Arran course lies inland from the Ailsa on more gently rolling terrain, but can be equally challenging, especially in the wind.

Despite Turnberry's long-established qualities, big-time golf only arrived with the Amateur Championship in 1961 and then the Walker Cup in 1963, when the home side crashed to a 12–8 defeat after leading 6–3 after day one.

But Turnberry's finest hour came in 1977 with the first of its three Open Championships. The links were at their most benign, the sun shone for all four days, and the low scoring reflected this, right up to the classic final day shoot-out between Tom Watson and Jack Nicklaus. Watson won by a stroke on 268, the lowest 72-hole aggregate in the event's history.

Conditions were almost the reverse in 1986, when Greg Norman defied wind and rain to secure his first Open; then in 1994 it was Nick Price's turn to gain his first Open after several near misses.

BLAZING SUNSET *The sky looks on fire as the sun sets over Turnberry's Ailsa course with the lighthouse silhouetted*

VALDERRAMA

Sotogrande, Cadiz, Spain
Opened: *1975*
Designer: *Robert Trent Jones*
Yardage: *6,819* **Par:** *72*
Major events: *None*

The list of courses that bear the name of Robert Trent Jones is long and impressive, while his workmanship has become familiar throughout the world. When he designed Los Aves, in a spectacular location in the hills above Sotogrande in southern Spain, it wasn't regarded as particularly newsworthy. Most people were more familiar with Sotogrande Old, his also, and even when Los Aves became Sotogrande New, there was barely a ripple on the surface of the game. But in 1985, when a Bolivian tin millionaire and golf fanatic by the name of Jaime Ortiz-Patino, and seven of his golfing friends, acquired and improved the club, changing its name again to

Valderrama, it was to have a far-reaching influence on the game, not only in Spain but in Europe and around the world.

Trent Jones was brought back in to remodel the lay-out, describing it at the time as "polishing the diamond to improve the shot values in some areas". Since then, Ortiz-Patino has made other changes on the way to making Valderrama into what he calls 'The Augusta of Europe'.

There is no disputing now that Valderrama is a magnificent course in every sense of the word. Its quality is of the highest order, and such has been the refining that it has become a severe test of even the best players, while its elevation into the nearest thing to Augusta in Europe has seen it become the permanent venue for the end-of-season European tour event, the Volvo Masters. Even more stunning was the awarding to Valderrama of the

1997 Ryder Cup matches, the first time the contest will have been held outside Britain when Europe has been the host.

Thanks to its quality, its reputation for being a tough examination, and its agreeable climate, many national teams take the opportunity of going there to tune up for the season ahead. Some of Europe's leading tour professionals also use the course to hone their games, including Seve Ballesteros, one of its biggest fans, who used the facilities at Valderrama to warm up for one of his US Masters successes.

Europe's pros, almost to a man, admit that Valderrama is probably more difficult than any other course in Europe. The scoring certainly reflects that, and while its selection for the Ryder Cup was criticized in many quarters, there is little doubt that it will prove a more than suitable battleground for the best from Europe and America.

Most of the holes are memorable for one reason or another but among the most memorable is the short 3rd, which measures around 170 yards but requires a solid shot to a severely bunkered green let into a hillside.

Then there is the par five 11th, where Trent Jones's redesign has left a sloping fairway with a nest of bunkers at the landing area followed by an uphill approach to the green which is difficult to judge accurately. Another testing par three is the 12th, which measures around 220 yards and is played from an elevated tee to a green set among cork trees. Anything off target is almost bound to catch one of the fearsome bunkers, while the green itself slopes from front to back and has many subtle undulations.

The 17th has also seen some changes in recent years, but this time Patino called in Ballesteros, and what used to be a long uphill par five, now has a lake guarding the front of the green. Anything short finds a watery grave, while anything too strong can leave you in clinging grass on the banking that surrounds the putting surface.

What is certain at Valderrama is that if something needs changing or improving, no expense is spared to see that it is done, so you can bet that everything will be pristine when the Ryder Cup arrives in September 1997.

RYDER CUP HOST *Valderrama will host the 1997 Ryder Cup and each hole will prove a memorable challenge the finest golfers from Europe and America*

WENTWORTH

Virginia Water, Surrey, England
Opened: *1924*
Designer: *Harry Colt*
Yardage: *6,945* **Par:** *72*
Major events: *Ryder Cup 1953. Curtis Cup 1932 (East course). World Cup 1956. Women's British Open 1980*

In the days after the First World War, developer Walter George Tarrant, who realized the potential for such facilities, and had gained considerable success in producing quality housing around a golf course at St George's Hill in Surrey, was looking for a similar site to repeat the exercise. At Wentworth he found and eventually secured 1,750 acres of prime countryside, just 21 miles southwest of London. While Tarrant set about developing the property, complete with swimming pool, tennis courts and a ballroom, his friend Harry Colt laid out two courses.

Colt was delighted with the land at his disposal. The Surrey sandbelt, with its heather, soaring pine trees, silver birch, and, in more recent times, huge banks of rhododendrons, lends itself ideally to golf courses. His handiwork has attracted worldwide acclaim, while everyone who plays Wentworth knows he faces quite a test. The East course, at 6,176 yards, par 68, is demanding in its own way. However, it is the West, completed two years later and better known now as the Burma Road, which is the more familiar, as more of the top professional events are played on it.

The West, which has always demanded accurate driving, features highly among the tour professionals' choice of top venues. Few of the holes can be seen from any other, while the conditions are seldom less than first class even in the darkest days of an English winter.

The back nine is regarded as the tougher half, and this is confirmed by the yardage and the par, 37 against the outward half of 35. The homeward run begins with a testing par three and a comfortable par four, after which the long 12th gives a chance of a birdie, if not an eagle for the leading players. But it is easy to give those shots back at the 441-yard 13th, where the line is down the right in order to open up the green to the approach. The uphill par three 14th plays every inch of its 179 yards to a two-tiered green, while the 466-yard 15th, with its diagonal ditch, requires strategy as well as a straight, long drive.

The par four 16th provides a lull before the storm which starts with the dog-leg 17th, one of the great par fives of British golf. The 571 yards is downhill from the tee for about 300 yards and the best line is to hug the trees down the left if you don't want your ball to spill off the sloping fairway into the right rough. Then the hole turns left uphill before descending to a generous green, but beware the private gardens down the left which are out-of-bounds. The pros hope to pick up a shot here, as they do at the 18th, another par five, but this time a dog-leg right. Here the drive should be to the elbow of the dog-leg, thereby providing another long shot to a green well guarded by bunkers at the front.

Although a comparatively young course, Wentworth has played its part in golfing history. It was here in 1926 that an informal match was played between the professionals of Great Britain and those of America, which the British won comfortably. This was to prove the forerunner of the Ryder Cup which began a year later.

In 1953 Wentworth played host to the Ryder Cup, with the United States scraping home by a single point, then three years later the Canada Cup, now the World Cup. The occasion provided Ben Hogan with his one and only appearance in England. He and Sam Snead carried off the trophy by a massive 14 strokes, both players shooting final round 68s. The World Match Play Championship has been played at Wentworth every year since its inception in 1964, and the Volvo PGA Championship has been resident at Wentworth since 1984.

In 1978 Wentworth acquired another 150 acres of land so it was decided to build a third 18-hole course, the South. The design of John Jacobs, with Gary Player and Wentworth professional Bernard Gallacher, it opened in July 1990 and was renamed the Edinburgh, in honour of the Duke, who performed the opening ceremony.

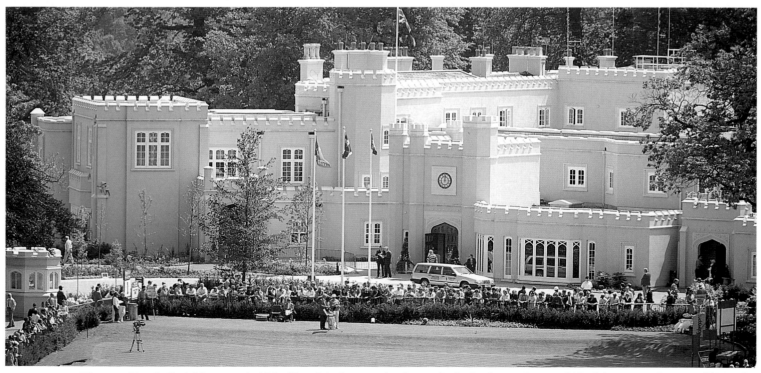

A GREAT COLT COURSE *Wentworth's rebuilt clubhouse, refurbished in original turretted style, overlooks the first tee, but would look just as good on a wedding cake*

WINGED FOOT

Mamaroneck, New York, USA
Opened: *1923*
Designer: *Albert W. Tillinghast*
Yardage: *6,980* **Par:** *70*
Major events: *US Open 1929, 1959, 1974, 1984. Walker Cup 1949. US Women's Open 1957, 1972. US Amateur 1940*

When Albert Tillinghast was commissioned to design a new lay-out in Westchester County, not far from New York City, he was tersely instructed: "Give us a man-sized course." The message was delivered by the gentlemen of the New York Athletic Club, from whose emblem the golf club takes its name, and the end result was the best golf course in Westchester County.

To create his masterpiece, Tillinghast had to move 7,200 tons of rock and cut down almost 8,000 trees. In fact, he created two courses, but it is the longer and more treacherous West course which has played host to four US Opens.

The key to Winged Foot is its 12 gruelling par fours, 10 of which measure 400 yards or more. These require long, straight driving, then a controlled second shot, often with a long iron, to greens that are fiercely contoured and guarded by deep bunkers.

Tillinghast's thinking was that "a controlled shot to a closely guarded green is the surest test of any man's golf". By the standards of some of America's top courses, Winged Foot's total of 60 bunkers is on the conservative side, until you consider that every green has at least two deep ones.

The club has not only produced a lot of low handicap players with excellent bunker skills; it has also had more than its fair share of national champions. At one time in the early 1940s it had both the US Open and Amateur champions in Craig Wood and Dick Chapman. Claude Harmon, who became pro six years later, won the US Masters in 1948; his assistants included Jack Burke and Dave Marr, both major winners, while Dick Mayer, the US Open champion in 1957, was a Winged Foot member before turning professional.

Winged Foot comprises two nine-hole loops, extending like two parallel arms. There are two 400-yard-plus holes to start followed by the 216-yard 3rd to a green flanked by two bunkers that run the length of the putting surface. Another long par four heralds the first of two par fives, the dog-leg 5th of 515 yards that is again heavily trapped near the green. After a shortish par four and a moderate par three, the front nine finishes with two more long par fours completing an outward 3,446 yards. The back nine starts with the par three towards a house, prompting Ben Hogan to describe it as "the 3-iron into some guy's bedroom", and finishes testingly with five successive par fours, all over 420 yards.

Bearing that in mind, it isn't surprising that of the four US Opens held there, only one has seen a winning score under the par of 280 for four rounds. Bobby Jones won the first US Open there in 1929. He tied with Al Espinosa on 294, then won the 36-hole play-off by a stunning 23-stroke margin.

The championship didn't return for 30 years, but in 1959 Billy Casper took the title with 282, single-putting 31 greens in the process. In 1974 Hale Irwin won with 287; then in 1984 came the memorable tie between Fuzzy Zoeller and Greg Norman. The Australian produced some amazing recovery shots over the final four holes, including holing a 30-foot par putt on the last, to finish on 276, four under par. Zoeller, waiting down the 18th fairway, thought the putt was for birdie and waved a white towel in surrender. Moments later he holed out for the same score. In the following day's 18-hole play-off, Zoeller won comfortably by eight shots.

That championship, perhaps more than any other, proved that Tillinghast did indeed produce a man-sized course.

FOUR IS NOT ENOUGH *Greg Norman lost to Fuzzy Zoeller in the 1985 US Open after tying on a Winged Foot record 276*

THE GOLF INDUSTRY

Golf is big business. The top professionals are among the wealthiest sportsmen and women in the world, at the head of an immensely rich industry. If money talks, then golf is indubitably the most loquacious of sports.

Big bucks for a growing sport

Four distinct periods can be discerned in the growth of US and British golf. First came the pioneer days of the 1890s, a decade which began with a handful of clubs and finished with hundreds in both countries. The second period of growth following the First World War was inspired by amateur and tour stars, notably Bobby Jones, Walter Hagen and Gene Sarazen; the third wave, after the Second World War, by Byron Nelson, Ben Hogan and Sam Snead. Both post-war surges were in any case periods of rapid economic growth and great wealth.

The fourth wave arrived and golf became a mass market – the global estimate is 40 million – once television hypnotized the stay-at-homes, seized the attention of the sponsors, and pushed tournament prize funds into seven figures. Ryder Cup star Chip Beck had a "bad" year in 1994, slumping to 68th on the US money list – with $281,131 (£181,375).

Yet the prize money offered is only part of the total cost of staging a tournament. It is generally accepted, that on top of the cash to be earned by the players, the tournament sponsors have to budget additionally for at least the same amount for controlling the event, preparing the course, and providing score boards, catering facilities, transport, media, medical staff, fitness centres, and even crèches.

The bigger the event, the greater the attendance, the bigger the on-costs, and for some tournaments the operating costs swell to far more than double the total purse.

The main US Tour, together with the "feeder" secondary tour (now the Nike Tour, but which started under Hogan's name in 1990) and the Senior Tour, put on around 118 tournaments in a year and offered nearly $100 million (£64.5 million) in prize money in the last full year for which figures are available. So it cannot be long at the present rate of progress (bearing in mind that the Senior PGA Tour took only 14 years to grow from two events in 1980 to more than 43 events in the mid-1990s) before the tours cost $250 million (£160 million). This does not include the Ladies Professional Golf Association Tour prize budget, which recently surpassed $20 million.

The European Tour's purses of better than £24 million ($37 million) suggest cash needs of twice that amount. The Japanese Tour also pays out huge winning dividends, with first prizes well up to standards in the West, and total purses in excess of $20 million.

On the professional tours worldwide, there are now approximately 400 events (men, women and seniors), with purses totalling in the region of $250 million (£160 million). There are more than 200 men's tournaments, paying out in excess of $150 million, and nearly 80 per cent of that goes to the top 300 golfers. Senior golfers in the US have already passed $5 million. All these figures are approximate, and they do not include extras such as skins games, shoot-outs and the like.

A magazine study of a week in 1994 when there were five major events (on the American and European PGA Tours, the US Senior, the American and European Women's tours) showed the total purse money was £1.47 million ($2.28 million), and combined attendance 240,728.

Tour finances are not concerned simply with the running of tournaments. The capital projects of the US PGA are spread far and wide. Their Golf Course Properties include more than a dozen Tournaments Players Clubs, and more are planned. During the 21 years Deane Beman was Tour Commissioner, the assets of the US PGA grew from $730,000 to more than $200 million.

The most extraordinary aspect of these Players Clubs is that they have enabled American tour players to become the only professional sportsmen in the world who own the stadiums upon which they play. Fans who can't make the tournaments have the benefit of the videos and TV magazine programmes from PGA Tour Productions.

The tour's charitable achievements are impressive too, for $250 million was disbursed country-wide between 1938 and the end of 1994.

PROS' PERKS *While amateurs insure themselves against a hole-in-one, for pros they can be very lucrative*

The Golf Industry

Footing the bill

American Express safeguarded the future of the Women Professional Golfers European Tour (WPGET) with a three-year deal worth at least $3 million, starting in 1995. So "Amex" become the headline tour sponsors … this after the company rejected approaches from the men's tour as "not value for money", which, in relation to the sort of treatment women all too often suffer in the game of golf, amounts to reverse discrimination. Soccer and a symphony orchestra fared no better in getting Amex money. Tour chief executive Terry Coates expects a £10 million prize fund by the end of the decade. No wonder the tour, with a 19-event 1995 programme, holds a qualifying school, from which there is no better chance that one in three of gaining a tour card.

WPGET's growing reputation was demonstrated at their first qualifying school at La Manga in Spain by the presence of the 1993 US Amateur Champion, Jill McGill. The tour had many uncertain early years, mainly owing to the damning bottom line that the players were not good enough to attract public or sponsors. Rapid improvements took place, with Laura Davies leading the way as the win-anywhere star and first Briton to reach the top of the

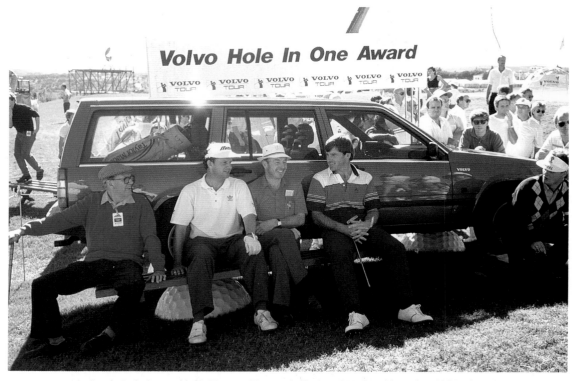

PRODUCT AND PLAYERS *Sandy Lyle (second left), Tommy Horton (in hat) and Nick Faldo at the 1989 Volvo Masters in Spain*

Ping world rankings. Yet the tour would not have survived at one point without a £50,000 subsidy from the R&A, nor would it be in its present buoyant state without the Solheim Cup win of 1992 which demonstrated a remarkable enthusiasm for European togetherness among players and fans.

The sources of the wealth funding the US men's tour, which since 1983 includes a pension fund for players, began with a few thousand dollars put in by the "Jaycees" (junior chambers of commerce) in southern US resorts back in the 1920s, the formative years of the US Tour; in Britain it all started with events set up after the foundation of the PGA, with prize money donated by club members. The Jaycees still do put on golf for local causes, but in the world of big-time pro golf millions flow in now from the modern headline or corporate sponsors of a tour, as with the Swedish carmakers Volvo and their major role in the European Tour.

It is a counsel of perfection for sponsors that they should never plunge into sport just because the board chairman or the chief executive is a 15-handicapper who would like to treat customers (and himself) to a few days out with the stars. It sometimes happens, though, and there are other ways in which a sponsorship proves to be flawed, as when a tobacco company found their event secured good UK publicity, but their main market was in Africa. Equally wrong-headed is any at-

tempt to alter the format of a sporting event to suit sponsor and guests. In other words, the performance in the market-place of the sponsorship should be the primary concern.

Sponsorship is not necessarily support of a single event, as we have seen with Volvo, whose satisfaction with their sponsorship was demonstrated when they added a three-year extension to the five-year corporate sponsor's agreement they struck with the European Tour starting in 1988. Their total involvement is £20 million ($31 million), based on Volvo's belief that golf is growing throughout Europe and that their cars suit the profile of golf's followers … the ABC1 groups of consumers.

Sponsors' Eastern promise

Volvo have quite different reasons for sponsoring the China Tour, which begins with only six Chinese touring pros, in a five-year deal centred on the China Open in Beijing. The field will consist mainly of Asian and Australian players, plus whoever Volvo can tempt away from Europe and the US. Volvo can as yet sell few cars in China, but many elsewhere on the Pacific Rim: be-

US RECRUIT *Jill McGill, WPGET card-seeker, on 1994 Curtis Cup duty* sides, no one can afford to ignore trade openings in such a fast-growing economy.

Golf has proved a useful marketing tool for companies who wish to establish a new service or product or, as in the case of the financial management company NM, a business which has changed its name, and needed to increase public awareness of the fact quickly. NM sponsored the English Open for three years for that purpose.

Johnnie Walker Scotch is another major sponsor, injecting £10 million a year ($15.5 million) into golf. United Distillers, the parent company, certainly cannot be accused of sponsorship on a chairperson's whim; theirs preferred yachting. Distillers' products are sold world-wide, so that the qualifying for their World Championship, going on in many different countries, and the speculation surrounding the selection of their other major event, the Ryder Cup, goes on for most of the year.

Performance of sponsorships is carefully monitored. Television exposure is the key, plus how many mentions the event wins in the other

media. The bottom line must be what happens to group sales.

The US Tour also has marketing contracts with multinationals such as soft drink makers and airlines. Any number of products can be adopted and their manufacturers endorsed as tour suppliers.

A point consistently agreed by the game's rulers and sponsors is that golf is seen as a clean sport: not too many spectator seats are thrown at tour or amateur events, and those who throw clubs in anger may find the practice expensive. It is well known that Volvo withdrew from tennis sponsorship because they considered the players got too much money and behaved badly.

Finally there are the fees for television rights, for this medium and the cash it raises are the key to the threefold rise in prize-money in a decade (200 per cent in seven years in Europe), and the knock-on effects enthusing newcomers to golf and consequent course construction.

Tapping the global market

The virility of the game is well demonstrated by the fact that since

BEAUTY IN DEMAND *Jan Stephenson*

the first exhibition of golf merchandise at the close of the 1920s, the attendance has always increased year by year, so much so in America that it is necessary to hold one show on the East Coast, and one on the West. When the show was staged at the Orange County Convention Centre in Orlando, Florida, it was attended by more than 800 companies and 35,000 potential customers. Exhibits could be seen on the PGA cable TV ser-

vice in Orlando hotel bedrooms.

Held out of season, the show permitted, or rather demanded, the presence of tour stars from many lands, who were required to back up in person the endorsements they make of their sponsors' products, in the design of which many of them have played a part. Gary Player, Ian Baker-Finch and Tom Kite were among those present, along with the coach David Leadbetter and, needless to say, attractive LPGA members such as Michelle McGann and Jan Stephenson. Europe's trade show brought in a record 6,013 to see the 300 stands, 60 of them new entries. Nearly 2,000 professionals attended.

The effort and expense put into these shows, replicated in every major golfing nation, is explained by the extent of the global market, with its target of an estimated 40 million players world-wide. Yet clearly, on the basis of the US figures which show that half the nearly 25 million American golfers do not play at all regularly, it is reasonable to suppose that many players get by with the minimum of equipment, or rent, borrow or share clubs.

How many have full sets of clubs is a matter for pure guesswork. If one takes the 20 per cent who are believed to play 80 per cent of the rounds in America each year (about five million golfers) and allows them an extremely conservative $500 dollars of equipment each, that would indicate an expenditure of $2.5 billion (£1.45 billion). Which makes one estimate of the golf market at £3 billion world-wide look suspect.

Persuading golfers to part with rather more than the minimum necessary to propel a ball around the local nine-holer requires a proof that the new product will genuinely help the customer's game. The use of space-age materials, the unending search for a bigger "sweet spot" on the face of the club so as to make a not quite perfect shot into a reasonable one, and production of a ball that flies furthest, are all part of the trade's effort. Temptation has to be strong, however, when a set of graphite shafted irons – and this applies to goods of pro-

BAHT MILLIONAIRE *Mats Lanner's 1992 hole-in-one in Bangkok paid him £25,250/$39,000 or 1 million baht*

shop quality, not the specialized equipment used by many top pros – can cost £1,300 ($2,000), and still leave the purchaser in need of a putter and woods.

Yet since the manufacturers must abide by the restrictions imposed by the USGA and R&A on the liveliness of the ball, and they do in the vast majority of cases, it is still the nature of the ball which rules the golfing roost, as it always has.

Recent moves by the golf industry's boffins have concentrated on the sweet spot, and occasionally a manufacturer will get a sales-swelling boost thanks to an heroic exploit or two.

When part-time tour player Johnny Miller, aged 46, won the AT&T National Pro-Am at Pebble Beach at the beginning of 1994, his first Tour win since taking the same prize seven years earlier, he did it in rough weather with the aid of Callaway's new big-headed driver.

Shortly before the company's new irons were officially launched the following year, Colin Montgomerie, the Scottish Order of Merit winner of the previous two years, began his defence of top spot on the European Tour in the Emirates, Dubai, and scored 68, 63 in his first two competitive rounds with the new clubs.

There is mighty competition for Callaway, whose sales have risen from $364,000 to $250 million in little over a decade, but who, according to their own figures, lag behind Taylor-made in driver use by PGA Tour pros, 17.53 per cent to 26.39 per cent. Callaway claim, however, that if all four major US tours are taken into account they are ahead in use of the driver.

Customer loyalty is strong, however. Kar-sten Solheim's original putter concept of weighting the heel and toe of the club has adherents without number, to the extent that the original series is collectable and examples reportedly command four-figure prices.

Arnold Palmer's meat packers

Arnold Palmer gets more popular with every passing year, and his farewell appearances, while not nearly as frequent as those of some singers one could mention, are widely discussed with regretful sighs. There are frequently jokes among the fans, like the one about the spectator who was booed because he made a poor throw sneaking Palmer's ball back on to the fairway.

Anyone that popular, whose dogged army of supporters was forming up while he was still in his twenties, has to be among the most marketable professional sportsmen of all time.

Yet Mark McCormack, at one time manager of the big three, Palmer, Player and Jack Nicklaus, who so dominated the 1960s, had to wait a long time before he was able to turn Palmer's promise into wads of dollars. This was because Palmer could not break free of a contract he signed with Wilson Sporting Goods Co. soon after becoming a professional in 1954.

The representatives of golf gear makers are ever on the look-out for the player who is one day going to pay off in huge endorsements and autograph club-making deals for all the golf balls, clubs and assistance put his way while in the apprentice stage. A good many amateurs are accorded much the same treatment, which in many cases is illegal but not too easy to check. Most of the reps' guesses are wrong, but Wilson was right about Palmer and certainly loath to let him go, definitely not after his second Masters win in 1960.

As a rookie on the tour he could not reasonably hope to appear as a good catch to the parents of his girlfriend Winnie Walzer, so he eloped with her and, as McCormack says, no doubt found the $5,000 a year he was getting from Wilson very useful. Moreover

BIG AND BEAUTIFUL? *Johnny Miller's AT&T trophy and $225,000/ £145,000 cheque at Pebble Beach in 1994 were a testament to big clubs*

in 1957 he had, rashly in McCormack's view, renewed the contract he signed in 1954. By 1958 he was winning nearly six times as much as in his first year ($7,958). McCormack's difficulty in selling Palmer's name, which was soon, figuratively speaking, blazing up there in lights, derived from the fact that he could do so only where Wilson's products were sold: not, for example, in Australia. Added to this, the royalties for Palmer's Wilson autograph clubs were not generous.

In 1960 it became clear that Wilson, a subsidiary of a meat packing company that had initially gone into the sports business using animal gut for tennis rackets, was not going to release Palmer from a clause in the 1957 contract that gave them an automatic renewal option until 1963. This was a disappointment to Palmer, who believed that he had shaken hands with Wilson executives on a promise that they would not want to keep him if he was unhappy. So, no release ... but almost at once Palmer mounted his most famous charge and won the US Open. He became, in his manager's phrase, "an immortal in alligator shoes."

After long negotiations with Wilson, whom Palmer was still loath to abandon, a 10-year contract was drawn up which suited everyone, though it fell far short of McCormack's marketing projections for Palmer. Everyone, that is, except, Judge James D. Cooney, head of Wilson. He said no deal, because no Wilson executive had a deferred-income plan or an insurance policy as stipulated in the contract.

McCormack wrote to Wilson to the effect that its decision would end up being the most expensive it had ever taken. However, Wilson even rejected Palmer's offer to pay back all monies he had earned from them, and buy out unsold Palmer clubs to a total of half a million dollars. So he and McCormack had to wait out the final days of the contract in 1963.

Ten years after his unfortunate renewal in 1957 of the original Wilson contract, Palmer's annual earnings were into six figures, and products from insurance to dry cleaning, as well as his own-firm autograph clubs, were

TOP MANAGER *Mark McCormack at the 1991 World Match Play at Wentworth; his first client, Arnold Palmer, won in 1961*

bringing in sales of $15 million a year. Later NBC paid millions for a piece of the Palmer enterprises.

The Palmer-McCormack bond has proved unbreakable to date. Not so McCormack's management of Nicklaus, who began in the marketing stakes with a grave disadvantage. He was bulky, and upon his crew cut descended all manner of imprecations because he beat Palmer. After leaving McCormack in 1971, he became a rep's delight, looking slimmer in build, with his fair hair profiting from a new, softer haircut. He became more comfortable in his relations with the Press. His "Golden Bear" motif fitted, and his businesses boomed, including an increasing involvement in golf architecture when, at long last, he stopped winning tournaments. Then he started winning again, on the Senior Tour.

The same magic was worked on John Miller, a Mormon who was induced to become Johnny Miller, though he preferred John. One wonders how much this can have helped the marketability of a player who had it all: huge distance off the tee,

steepling mid-irons, plus a tall athletic figure, blond hair and rugged good looks.

McCormack's International Management Group (IMG) looks after a large number of sports stars, and finds ways of advising event organizers, right up to R&A/USGA level, of mutual profitability. The R&A Open logo, which is registered throughout the world, is sold on sweaters and other products, and brings in much revenue, was an IMG notion.

Perhaps the most marketable golfer in the world today is that rare bird, a left-hander – tall, personable Phil Mickelson, who performed an even rarer feat – winning a professional tournament, the 1991 Northern Telecom Open at Tucson, while still an amateur. Mickelson had first come to international notice in the 1989 US Walker Cup team. That team lost, but in 1991 Mickelson, with three points out of four, played a strong role in the US team that snatched the Cup back. One of the men who has helped Greg Norman to profit from his golfing skill and powerful charis-

ma, watched Mickelson at the Masters giving out balls to children whose fathers he addressed as "Sir". This marketing man's opinion was: "You couldn't sit down with a blank piece of paper and create something better. He will make millions". As well as being the PR man's dream, Mickelson is the only golfer to equal Jack Nicklaus's record of winning four times on the US Tour before reaching the age of 24.

Fuzzy Zoeller, the rich runner-up

Few sporting contests allow the 100th finisher to pull up with $178,501 (£115,162) as his reward, but such was the luck of the Irish in the list of official money winners at the end of the 1994 US Tour. David Feherty's first year on the tour also left him in secure possession of his player's card for 1995.

Even more remarkable in a year awash with dollars was Fuzzy Zoeller's unprecedented feat of earning more than a million dollars – without ever winning a tournament. One is reminded that Jack Nicklaus has been heard to criticize

US golfers for being less than focused on winning, and being content with earning a good living … a possible source of Ryder Cup failures.

This accusation can scarcely be brought against Zoeller. He had been squeezed into second place four times before coming to the Tour finale at the demanding 7,005-yard Olympic club course at San Francisco. He finished 10 under the par of 284, returning three scores in the 60s, yet was second again. It required a 40-foot putt by Mark McCumber on the first hole of their play-off to beat Zoeller for the Tour Championship, total purse $3 million (£1,935,484). That's how hard McCumber was focused on winning the $540,000 (£348,387) first prize, and why Zoeller ended the season still winless since 1986.

Nothing is likely to block the flow of cash going to banner events like the Tour Championship, but the recession born in the 1980s is still having its effects on sponsorship. Torrey Pines, near San Diego, was in the days of the Andy Williams Open a magnet for southern Californians, and had an attractive showbiz touch lent by the singer.

Many changes of sponsorship followed, and a decline in the condition of the two courses cast a shadow, before Buick came to the rescue. Both North and South Courses have now been brought up to scratch, and the venue's future seems assured.

Sponsorship in Scotland, despite its standing as the home of golf, is a problem for both the men's and women's tours. Only six months before the male and female versions of the 1995 Scottish Open neither tour had found a backer.

The determining factor is usually television, without which sponsors are loath to invest. Yet offers were slow in coming in Scotland, despite the fact that the women's Open had three days of BBC coverage promised: the men would have to rely on satellite coverage.

Sponsors were there none when championship golf got under way in 1860, apart from the Prestwick Club and their Championship Belt. No money was offered in the Open until

1863, when Willie Park Senior got £10, a not inconsiderable sum in those days.

Prize money was forced past the £100 mark by the Musselburgh "revolt" of 1892. It went down to £100 the following year, and took another half century to get into four figures. But from £10,000 in 1965, it took only 28 years to reach £1 million, at the 122nd Open. US prize

cash has usually kept a step ahead.

Today prize money is but a minor part of the story. The opportunity to profit from endorsements runs a long way down the money list, and at the top level the rewards are spectacular. A second Masters for Bernhard Langer in 1993 earned him an immediate $306,000 (£197,420), but like Palmer he is in the financial care of Mc-

Cormack and his International Management Group. The endorsements IMG had gathered for him already included Adidas shoes, the American Express card, Hugo Boss clothing, Ebel watches, Lufthansa Airlines, Mercedes-Benz, and Palmer's erstwhile associates, Wilson. As a good-looking family man Langer is a commercial treasure, especially at home in Germany.

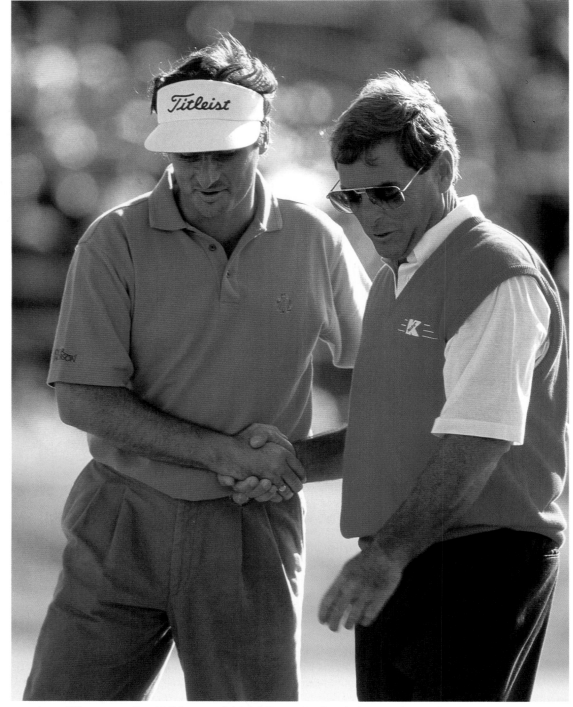

OPEN MEETING *US tour men David Feherty and (right) Fuzzy Zoeller shake it on during the Open at Turnberry*

Guesses at what all this means in cash terms go as high as $3 million.

Greg Norman is reputed to do even better, his second Open at Sandwich bringing additions to his list of endorsement contracts that had reputedly already been worth $12 million, thanks in particular to Australian, Japanese, and US admirers of his dashing style – and the fact that, as was once said of Palmer, it is often more thrilling to see Norman lose than to see others win. He has a winning way of losing.

The emancipation of the pro

The leading pros of the late Victorian/Edwardian generation, led by Harry Vardon, J. H. Taylor and James Braid, the tall Scot who came down to London in the role of a club-maker, can have pocketed less than £2,000 between them all told for their 16 Open wins. But they ascended to the dignity of the complete playing professional: indeed, while admitting that on hot days in America he had taken off his coat, Taylor adds, a trifle stuffily to our ears: "In England it is only the novice who plays in the style."

The golf boom of the 1890s had, in Taylor's words, disproved the erroneous impression that the task of manufacturing golf club heads by means of machinery would be an impossible one. Club pros were slowly being freed from the toil of club-making, though the pro incapable of rewhipping or regripping a club is very much the product of the era of the touring pro in the second half of the twentieth century.

"For today [1902] it is the simplest of simple matters to turn out heads to any required model in the course of a few minutes," Taylor added. He particularly dwelt on the excellence of the machine-made clubs he saw in America – "far the neatest in finish".

Taylor clearly had no high opinion of American home-bred professionals and felt that caddies there were not encouraged sufficiently with facilities to practise. Golf was more expensive in America than in Britain, and members did not like their fairways to be cut up or clogged up by youngsters. For

FAMILY VALUES *Marketable Master golfer Bernhard Langer, with his wife and children at Augusta in 1993*

all that, his prescient conclusion was that "ere long American players will be able to hold their own in the best company."

Even Taylor must have been surprised by the speed at which his prediction came true, culminating in golfers who win nothing but a million dollars.

Kindly transatlantic tyrants

It is a moot point whether the authorities administering golf do or do not make a better job of it than their counterparts in other sports. However, they certainly make less noise and fewer compromises.

What success they have managed is rooted in two achievements. Firstly, despite the odd tiff over the years, the major powers, the USGA and the Royal & Ancient, have produced between them a body of rules which, for once in a sport, is more honoured in the observance than the breach.

Secondly, they have come close to rigid control of the form of the clubs and the performance of the balls with which the game is played.

The degree to which they have managed to control professionalism

and keep the pure flame of amateurism burning bright is rather less clear. The distinction between the two is sharper in golf than in most other sports, for some of whom the term "shamateur" was mockingly invented. Among these are most notably athletics, lawn tennis, swimming and soccer, in former times, and rugby union now.

The USGA, which is almost exactly a hundred years older than this book, was founded to some degree because of Charlie Macdonald's impatience with the inadequate attempts made in 1894 to stage championships. He had a vested interest in this, for he had failed to become champion in these events which he condemned, if not in so many words, as not proper golf – and he had seen proper golf, in Fife. For all that, he and the other USGA pioneers brought a spirit of selfless service to the task of furthering golf.

Not only did Macdonald refuse to profit from his work in course design; he told Coburn Haskell, when the inventor of the rubber-cored ball offered him an interest in the project, that he had made it a principle

never to receive any profit from his association with the game.

As we have seen elsewhere, the USGA could raise hackles with the Draconian punishments it inflicted at the first hint of a violation of the letter of the amateur status law. It should never be forgotten, however, that the amateur game far outweighed the professional in importance well into the present century, and that the modern Olympic movement, which held its first Summer Games a few months after the USGA's inaugural championships, had similar attitudes.

The temptation to depart from the rules set forth by the R&A was not always resisted in America, on the grounds that differing conditions demanded change. Macdonald the traditionalist did resist a suggestion by USGA president R. H. Robertson that the rules should be Americanized, though as first chairman of the Rules Committee he did suggest minor departures from R&A orthodoxy.

Transatlantic journeys began to codify the rules. An early attempt at defining an acceptable club held that it should have a plain shaft and a head with no mechanical devices, such as springs. Relations ebbed and flowed across the ocean, co-operation becoming ever closer after the great coming together of the 1951 rules conference. A joint committee regularly reviews the rules, striving to make them proof against technological advance and changing conditions of play across the globe.

An enduring difference between golf in the old country and the new is the American love of pencil and card golf, that is, stroke play, at all levels of expertise, contrasted with the British focus on match play. This US obsession rules most professional events, and acceptance is general of the American practice, long since sanctified by rule, of picking up, marking and (horrors) *cleaning* balls on the green. This is anathema to the old school, which abhorred touching the ball from tee to holing out – except with a club.

When the USGA was barely seven years old, and with the start-up of the US PGA still 14 years in the future, J. H. Taylor, who had just playing a leading part in the creation of British PGA, declared that "Americans have thrown themselves into the pursuit of the game with such determination and goodwill that at the present time they know more about the game than we do ourselves" ... this in 1902!

Which is why America has forced the pace in the development of the game, never afraid to make a profit from it, and never afraid to follow and finance new ideas. The USGA has had to steer a middle course, identifying and restraining excess, encouraging research, as with their Green Section, begun in 1920. Both USGA and R&A have been much empowered by television revenues.

Their policeman's role, as every sporting administrator knows, is a walk on a knife-edge. Though the USGA started bravely with respect to the admission of black players to competition, they did not always maintain that stance; and they had governed for very nearly a century before a woman, Judy Bell, was allowed to play a part in the inner

STAR SILHOUETTES *Francis Ouimet (left) and Glenna Collett mark Centennial*

councils of the Association.

No issue has divided the R&A and USGA, and in recent years united them, as much as the legality or otherwise of club manufacture. We have seen how the centre-shafted putter was a metallic bone of contention for the early part of this century. There was considerable British disquiet about the R&A ruling against it, a decision opposed among others by Vardon, Hilton and Herd, and in any case a centre-shafted mid-iron made by Anderson of Edinburgh about 1870 had not been banned.

A united front was the watchword after the atmosphere at a cel-

ebration dinner attended by USGA and R&A members was somewhat chilled when both organizations were served with writs from Karsten Solheim. His Ping Eye 2 irons with square grooves instead of the usual V-shaped grooves had been ruled illegal. The Ping Eye 2, it was held, offered unfair advantages, at least to the expert player.

An American judgment in 1990 that an Arizona court had no jurisdiction over the R&A let Michael Bonallack, the secretary, off the hook. Caution was the watchword for the USGA, who had recently had to pay out several million dollars to a ball manufacturer. In the

end they and Karsten Manufacturing settled out of court. Compromise was reached on the crucial issue: existing Ping Eye 2 irons might be used, but clubs henceforward must conform to USGA specifications. In the long term, the USGA and R&A retain control of the tools of the trade.

Taming the landscape

Nearly a century ago, pioneer American architects showed that the most unappetizing terrain could be turned to golfing account. This was done with increasing ease once earth-moving equipment replaced horse and scoop. Charles Macdonald's recreation of celebrated British golf holes on his National Links of America, on a windy site near Southampton on Long Island, was achieved and the course opened in 1909 by virtue of having moved enormous quantities of material and bringing in thousands of tons of topsoil. His masterpiece was complete with turf nursery and watering system.

Similarly, the building by George Crump of Pine Valley in New Jersey, cut through the middle of thick woodland and again requiring the

PING CREATOR *Karsten Solheim, with three early examples of his innovative putters*

re-siting of great amounts of material, produced a superb course wrested from a difficult site.

Elsewhere the demand for courses had been met rather more peremptorily. Tom Bendelow left his job as a New York newspaper compositor in 1895 and is reputed to have laid out 600 courses. This sounds unlikely until his methods are discussed.

He had a fine Scottish accent, which helped in any golf dealings in the early days of US golf, and could lay out two courses a day. First he would use a stake to mark the first tee, then march a hundred yards and stake a spot for a bunker, onward to mark where a mound should go, and on again to mark the green: all of his greens were either round or square, and were bereft of bunkers. Then lunch, one supposes, and on to the next town. At least he charged only $25 a time.

Nowadays the fees of big-name designers like Jack Nicklaus and Arnold Palmer, backed up by experienced course builders, can amount to as much as 25 per cent of the overall cost. But employing them pays off because the star's involvement helps sell the homes that go with so many courses. Meanwhile, course maintenance has become ever more expensive, because golfers, especially in America, demand fairways of a standard that at a quick glance can be mistaken for a green, and the greens must be perilously fast, which is what the professionals prefer also.

Costly search for pastures new

Pressure on course builders became intense as boom times in the eighties raised the tempo again. Europe and Asia in particular have kept and are keeping the architects busy. However, supplies of natural golfing land, such as Scottish links created by tide, wind, birds and animals, wild and domesticated, and the heathland of Surrey and Berkshire, are finite. Despite the availability of earth-moving equipment, designer seeds to suit the turf to the environment of soil and climate, and machinery that reduces the toil and labour costs of course maintenance, new courses cost more

VALDERRAMA REVAMP *Robert Trent Jones on the course he reshaped*

and more to complete.

Major course developments on reasonable ground add up to £2.25 million ($3.5 million). Draining a swamp in China, however, or building a course on a Japanese mountainside, and inserting the water hazards which are popular there, is a different matter altogether. But then merely refurbishing Penina reportedly cost £2.5 million.

Even a long-established club such as Ballybunion (1893) in County Kerry, on the west coast of Ireland, can run into construction problems on the choicest golfing linksland. The Old Ballybunion course has long been a favourite stop for British and American golfing tourists in general and for more distinguished Tourists like Tom Watson in particular, who will travel across from the US to play there before going on to a major event else-

where in the British Isles.

During the building in the 1980s of an additional 18 holes to a design by the doyen of architects, Robert Trent Jones, Ballybunion encountered a major problem: large amounts of sand, not in the characteristic clover-leaf shaped bunkers that are a hall-mark of Robert Trent Jones designs, but smothering one of the new holes.

The project had come about as a financial by-product of the enormous response of Irishmen and Ballybunion lovers world-wide to the club's appeal for funds to restore their celebrated short 7th, which the Atlantic had eaten away. An Italian system of stones in mesh baskets was used to underpin the restoration.

Surplus funds were deployed towards a new course, a highly desirable acquisition for the members, since their well-drained course was

sometimes in great demand when neighbouring clubs were weatherbound.

As this new course, recently renamed Cashen after the river reaching the sea at its far end, was taking shape, a sizeable sandhill overlooking the beach was removed by the river authority in the course of drainage works. Soon sand from the beach, no longer restrained by the mound, was sweeping inland, just as the final fairway grass was coming up, protected by the "shelter" grass which allows it to develop, then itself dies off. The sandhill had to be restored, and the fairways cleared – a penalty exacted, no doubt, for the crime of interfering with the natural topography.

This has not ended coastal erosion problems at Ballybunion. The restored sandhill is being kept in place by plantings of marram grass, and this is but a small part of the club's activities in defending their coastline from the Atlantic Ocean. They spend £100,000 every year on this work: 28,500 visitors a year, reports secretary/manager Jim McKenna, help to pay the bills at about £35 a round on the Old Course, £25 on the Cashen.

Financial difficulties with new lay-outs start when several hundred housing units are added to the equation, the property is slow to move and the cash rewards only start to flow after debts are being called in. How often in recent years has such a development been picked up for a relative song when it turns out to be break instead of break-even.

Environmental concerns pose further problems for course builders. Informed opinion is that an average of as much as 10 per cent of total outlay may be spent on finding how best to avoid damage to flora, fauna, water supplies and the landscape in general. The following pages enlarge on these concerns.

Welcome for golf no longer sure

Until the 1990s the global spread of golf seemed to be virtually unrestrained. now countries such as those on the Pacific Rim, which have gone through a period of massive economic growth, are begin-

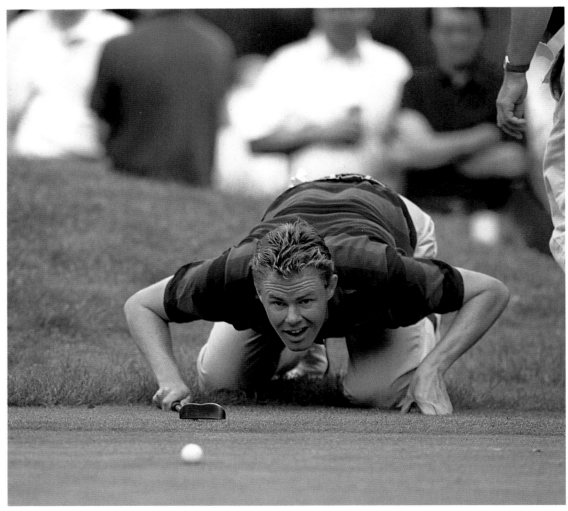

SWEDISH SURVEY *Joakim Haeggman checks his line at the 1993 Dunlop Masters at Woburn*

ning to consider the question of priorities. Some are pausing, to rethink the balance between increased economic activity and poorer quality of life, as flowers, trees, animals, birds, water to drink and irrigate, and even air to breathe are sacrificed to what might or might not be progress. The result is that not everyone is overjoyed to see the bulldozers move in, shaping the landscape into a golf course.

Planning authorities, and the public at large, in third world countries can and do take a very jaundiced view of course construction, especially peasants whose poverty makes the prospect of golf as a pastime laughably remote, and who may believe their crops are being robbed of water by an irrigation system on a nearby course or poisoned by run-off of over-used insecticides.

There is also a profound sense of injustice deriving from the game's perceived elitism. Golf is expensive, especially where course development is new, and there is much resentment of it where the surrounding population is poor, notably in places like the Philippines, Thailand, Malaysia and Indonesia.

The contrast between haves and have-nots was starkly presented during the European PGA Tour's first foray to Manila, where Fred Couples took first prize. Correspondents remarked on the close proximity of slums and poverty to the enormous clubhouse, offering all the comforts of the modern country club, that ran about one-third of the length of the final fairway. Leading players, whisked by helicopter back to their hotels, can have seen little of the "other" Manila.

Respecting the environment

In both Europe and the USA efforts are now being made to meet the concerns of maintaining the environment and strike a balance between recreational needs and possible despoliation of nature.

In America the USGA have striven to help preserve wildlife habitats and make clear the environmental benefits conferred by golf courses: among other projects they have co-operated with the Audubon Society and granted money for a Sanctuary Programme, encouraging clubs to show the way. Jim Snow and his USGA Green section have also been of great help as studies intensify in Europe to identify the criteria by which the wisdom of building upon a particular site can best be judged.

Touche Ross management consultants prepared a report for the

European Commission entitled "How Green is the Fairway?" that began with the daunting thought that if a similar supply of golf courses as exists in the United Kingdom (there were 3,678 at the beginning of the 1990s, or one 18-hole course per 25,000 inhabitants) were to be built in Europe, 10,000 courses would be needed – four times the present number. They would involve an additional five million players.

French construction reached a 10 per cent rate of annual increase between 1985 and 1991. In some areas, notably tourist regions, the figure was about 25 per cent. The UK figure for the 1983–93 period was 2 per cent. Rates of increase on the continent are now likely to slow because of rising public disquiet about such rapid change in land usage. Legislators, pressed by environmental groups, tend to ensure that protesters shall have ample time to examine and object to projects.

Planning permission is now difficult to obtain in Austria, Germany, Switzerland and Belgium, mainly on environmental grounds. Much earth-moving, big changes in the landscape, and loss of flora and fauna, added to accusations – here too – of golf's perceived elitism, produce an atmosphere hostile to construction. Two recently constructed courses serving Swiss urban areas, Golf de Bossey (near Geneva) and Golf de Basle, are sited mainly or wholly in France because planning permission could not be obtained inside Switzerland.

German clearances for building can take seven years, and there are strict controls: courses must be spacious enough to allow buffer zones for natural habitats; earth-moving and bunkers are closely monitored; greens and tees must be undersealed to permit water recycling.

Elsewhere course builders are less hobbled, though in southern Spain water shortage is a problem. It has been less acute during the tourist recession, but likely to return unless recycling and better water economy can be made to work.

In Sweden, whose leading professionals include names such as

Joakim Haeggman, Jesper Parnevik and Robert Karlsson have done much to make the game fashionable, the scale of growth in demand for golf can be gauged from recent annual rates of increase in the numbers of players ... up to 15 per cent. No nation is more aware of environmental issues, so that the golf union provides appreciation of the conflicting claims of use for the land in question. Land is limited in Sweden, and pressure upon existing golf facilities severe.

That is also very much the case in the Netherlands, where the authorities make a point of involving all interested parties in the environmental field when course construction is mooted.

It would seem logical to suppose that more golfing land has become available because of the Common Agriculture Policy payments of "set-aside" money to farmers who agree not to cultivate all their fields. (The UK rate is £200 per hectare, about £81/$126 per acre.) Many courses have indeed been the result, but not without criticisms about land being lost to food production forever. Golf courses designed for derelict sites are much more likely to get the planner's nod.

The EC report offers a chart of a succession of judgments to be made in deciding whether a project should or should not go ahead. Environmental damage or an unsound business plan would be immediate reasons for cancellation. If the environmental flaws can be righted in time, and if the social benefit exceeds the costs, the plan may win approval.

The accuracy of the initial judgements can only be assessed by regular monitoring, for instance, of the crucial link between the finished course and wide water usage, that is to say, grass. Rainfall apart, British courses need 100 cubic metres of water a day in July; Mediterranean littoral courses need all-over irrigation in summer, at 25 times the British volume. Thus the choice of grass is central to success. Native grasses in Britain need less water, but do not give the brilliant, lush colouring of US-style courses that have proved so attractive to leading European players, notably Nick Faldo.

As in southern USA, Mediterranean courses do well with Bermuda grass, and water can be saved with hybrid varieties. Water demand nevertheless remains high in summer, which may lower the water table and encourage saline intrusions into the supply, with possible deleterious effects on drinking water further down the drainage system.

The course architect must therefore be aware of what grasses will ease or exacerbate water problems. This is a subject upon which the Americans are having second thoughts, which may possibly lead to less use of the varieties of grass which produce the deeply attractive green tones on the fairways.

At a French course on the Mediterranean a neat solution was found to the problem of its turf being affected by a change in its water source. The villain was algae, so algae-eating fish were placed in the storage lake.

The way towards coexistence

Failure to confront the conflicting claims of leisure, the environment, and food production leads to golf schemes going off at half cock. Sometimes the construction stage is reached before any analysis has been attempted of the imperatives involved – even the elementary issue of what demand exists for a course in the first place. A 1995 poll of English clubs by the EGU showed that waiting lists totalled only 80,000 country-wide. Advertising for members is not uncommon.

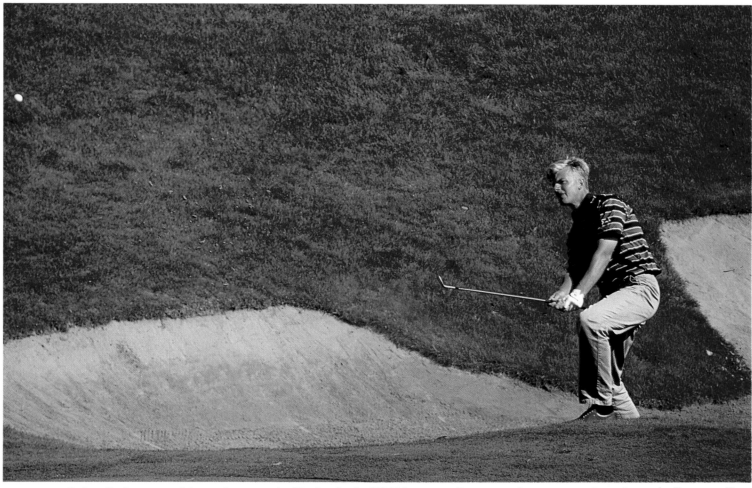

AGADIR INCIDENT *Robert Karlsson on a right royal course – the King's – for the 1994 Morroccan Open, an early season stopping point on the European Tour*

In Europe conservationists, and not just wildlife movements, are working hard to provide a set of guide-lines for course builders and maintenance staff. Michael Harvey, chairman of the trustees of the Golf Course Wildlife Trust, chaired a meeting in Brussels several years ago attended by representatives of 20 nations.

Many Continental golf organizations expressed the feeling that there was a negative image of golf. A rational strategy was needed to destroy that image, which was encouraging, as we have seen, a whole raft of obstructive legislation.

The meeting was attended by David Stubbs, Director of the European Golf Association Ecology Unit, based in Brussels and Dorking in Surrey. He subsequently led a study which early in 1995 resulted in the publication of *An Environmental Strategy for Golf in Europe*, a companion study to the massive USGA work on the subject.

Workers in many different disciplines have played a part in its production, among them Dr Anne-Marie Brennan, a wildlife consultant from Kent University, Bob Taylor, of the Sports Turf Research Institute, and archaeologists, anxious to ensure that construction does not destroy historical sites.

Michael Harvey would like to see an extension of the idea, already test-marketed, of a Golfers' Conservation Club, with its members spreading into clubs across the land, leading to the appointment of club conservation officers. There are many fairly cheap measures that can be taken to improve landscape values, especially if members are prepared to contribute a few hours of labour or gardening expertise.

A happy example at Wentworth

A fine example of how the manifold difficulties involved in course construction can be overcome is to be found just to the west of London, at Wentworth. Here the club's

pride in their third 18-hole course, the Edinburgh, is not founded merely on its popularity with professionals and members and the way in which it has eased pressure of use on the two famous existing courses. The West Course is the home of the Volvo PGA Championship and the World Matchplay Championship, while the East Course has also staged important professional and amateur events.

The third lay-out was at first to be called the South Course. The design of John Jacobs, teacher, Ryder Cup captain and European Tour pioneer, was accepted, while the club professional, Bernard Gallacher, and Gary Player were retained as consultants. The course was renamed in August 1990, when the Duke of Edinburgh opened it.

Since it was carved out of Surrey's Great Wood, just off the A30 road that links London with the south-west of England, it was bound to become a difficult planning proposition, because the site was not only in an area designated as greenbelt, but was also recognized as one of outstanding natural beauty.

The 150-acre site was bought in the late 1970s for a most reasonable £80,000, considering its position in one of the region's most desirable residential districts. The land was heavily wooded, and the original plan for its use by the club involved the construction of a course and golf centre surrounded by high-class housing.

Planning permission was initially refused, but the central idea of golf course use was not the main sticking-point, so all was not lost. Richard Doyle-Davidson, one-time managing director of the club, was a leading figure in the campaign to meet all

WENTWORTH PRIDE *The tree-lined majesty of the Edinburgh course, a model for meeting wildlife and botanical concerns: this is the par-4 fourth hole*

the concerns involved in building the course, and likes to think other clubs can learn from the way in which the club conducted that campaign.

It was based on the idea that the course could work with the environment, and not against it. A report commissioned from Liverpool University assessing how the new course would affect the local environment cost £10,000, but it favoured construction, and impressed environmental and wildlife groups who were in any case consulted. The Surrey Wildlife Trust were invited to manage particularly sensitive areas on the club's behalf. One such area is designated as of Special Scientific Interest.

Wet woodlands are a vanishing habitat in Britain, so that areas of that type, which supported flowers, toads and insects peculiar to Surrey, were given extra protection. Specimen trees were chosen, and the lines of fairways adjusted to protect them. A South Course Environmental Committee was formed. Doyle-Davidson represented the club's owners, and sat with the planning consultants and representatives of Wentworth Residents Association, Surrey Wildlife Trust and Run-

COURSE CONFERENCE *Gary Player (second left), John Jacobs (centre) and club professional Bernard Gallacher (right), map out Wentworth's third course*

nymede Borough Council. Doyle-Davidson says that the initial fears that restricted access to areas of interest to naturalists were dispelled, because footpaths were retained through the woodlands.

Long-term care of the club's estate was the end purpose of an overall Environmental Audit undertaken in 1990, by a group comprising landscape architects, experts in the field of ecology and landscape management from Liverpool and London Universities, and experts in forestry.

The stated aim is to improve conditions for golf while caring for the beauty of the landscape, protect and improve a wide range of habitats for wildlife, "establish long term semi-natural woodland cover which will be self-sustaining with limited maintenance and management, and develop woodland edge and off-fairway areas easy to maintain and manage."

The range of wildlife in the area revealed by the audit would surprise 99 per cent of the galleries and television audiences of Wentworth's chief events. Chobham Common nearby has two nationally rare items of vegetation, marsh gentian and marsh club moss, as well as marsh orchids.

The Wentworth area has spider species found only in Surrey and the New Forest in Hampshire: 40 per cent of all British spider varieties live there. Rare birds, including small falcons called hobbies, breed on the Ed-

inburgh course, and there are green and great spotted woodpeckers. Adders and great crested newts also breed there, and there are badger, deer, fox and (too many) rabbits.

The club also employed a PR man and a traffic consultant who looked at the increase in road use involved. All in all, it is estimated that £200,000 was spent on studies, PR and an explanatory video before planning permission was eventually obtained. The money proved to have been well spent.

It seems almost an afterthought to record that the third Wentworth course turned out well, and may host a European Tournament once it has matured. The first significant event played on it was the Peugeot Cup for assistant professionals, some of whom pronounced the course better than Wentworth's older ones. It is certainly a better viewing course than the West; its culminating feature, around the 18th, is an amphitheatre which could hide a battalion. With tall trees as a backdrop, this natural arena is sure to enhance the drama of a close finish.

A boon during construction was that a great deal of earth-moving was not required as the fairways were fashioned through the trees, avoiding the protected areas. Because of its sandy soil, the Edinburgh has proved playable when bad weather has closed down its more elderly neighbours.

THE RULES OF GOLF

Golf is a target ball game of stark simplicity, but it is governed by a wide-ranging and detailed set of rules and circumscribed by a code of conduct and an etiquette that are throw-backs to a more gentlemanly age.

In the beginning, and for several centuries after the game emerged as a cross-country sport, match play was the only form of golf. The object was to strike a ball with a club from point A (called a tee) into a hole at point B in fewer strokes than one's opponent. The contest was played over a stipulated number of holes in a set order. It could be single combat, or between pairs of players.

Games were organized person to person, on a private and individual basis, on the common land of such courses as Leith links and St Andrews. The idea of the club, as a sporting institution, is far younger than the game of golf: before the founding of the Gentlemen Golfers of Edinburgh (now the Honourable Company of Edinburgh Golfers) just over two and a half centuries ago, clubs were political in function.

There came a time when golfing man's competitive instincts reached a stage when a search for the best player became imperative. Hence the gift of the Silver Club by the City of Edinburgh to the Gentle-

SHORT AND SWEET *An 18th Century version of the Rules at St Andrews Museum*

men Golfers of that city. The winner of the Silver Club was to become Captain of the Golf: in modern parlance, champion. As such he was to settle all points of dispute concerning the rules.

John Rattray, winner of the first two Silver Club contests (1744-45), was undoubtedly concerned with the first code of rules, copied in 1754 by the St Andrews men away to the north in Fife.

To lift, or not to lift

These rules are simple and unequivocal. Though the player is never adjured in so many words to play the ball as it lies, the underlying thrust of the rules is unmistakably to that effect. Only if the ball landed in water or "watery filth", or shots came to rest so close together that strokes were impeded, could the ball be lifted. A player must, for the privilege of lifting his ball out of water, dropping it behind the hazard and playing on towards the hole, give up a stroke to his opponent. Obstructions, termed "break clubs", such as stones, were not to be removed, except upon "the fair green" – the putting surface. A lost ball cost a stroke too, the substitute to be played from the location of the errant shot.

St Andrews golfers played for their Silver Club from 1754 until 1759 not by a knockout process but on the basis that he who won more holes in his match than anyone else in theirs was the victor. This would

clearly not do: a weak opponent, rather than a brilliant winner, might settle the issue.

So it was decreed that the trophy would go to "whoever puts in the ball at the fewest strokes over the field, being 22 holes" … for not until 1764 did St Andrews amend their course to the now universally accepted 18 holes for a round. This invention of stroke play brought its problems.

The old play-it-as-it-lies rule of thumb could not survive in all circumstances. It was slow to die, however. Charles Macdonald, the first US amateur champion, a pupil of Old Tom Morris in the 1870s, wrote: "Touching a ball in play without penalty was anathema to me, a kind of sacrilegious profanity."

Provision had to made in stroke play for golfers to complete their rounds and submit a score no matter what difficulties they ran into. So

RULING NEEDED *An official is on hand as a ball search halts the Olazabal vs Stewart match in the 1989 Ryder Cup*

punishments for hitting into trouble, penalties for escaping from it, and definitions for every facet of play had to be minted and, over the years, reminted and refined. So varied is the nature of courses throughout the world that conundrums for the Rules of Golf Committees of the USGA and the R&A will never cease to present themselves. So their work is never done: for it is their joint responsibility to exercise authority worldwide, keeping the rules up to date amid changes in conditions and equipment and responding to the curious scrapes that golfers get into.

Modern terminology

There is plenty of variety in the forms golf can take. On top of the linchpins of single combat at match play and stroke play, there are threesomes, in which one plays against two, and each side plays one ball; foursomes (two against two, each side playing one ball); three-ball (three playing one another, with a ball apiece); best-ball (one plays against the better ball of two or the best ball of three); four-ball (two play their better ball against the better ball of two other players). In the foursome format, the partners play tee-shots at alternate holes, thereafter playing alternate shots; playing out of turn costs the hole in match play, two strokes in stroke play.

Disqualification follows in stroke play if the error is not corrected before teeing off at the next hole, or, where the last hole is concerned, leaving the putting green without declaring intention to correct the error.

American terminology is accepted world-wide where scoring is concerned: par means the score expected on each hole of a first class, i.e. scratch player. Birdie (one under par), eagle (two under), the rare double eagle or albatross (three under) developed from the day in 1899 at Atlantic City after George Crump's second shot at a par four fell close to the hole after hitting a bird in flight. There is an alternative version, that the origin is a comment about "a bird of a shot". Bogey is one over par (dou-

ble and triple bogey, etc. being self-explanatory).

Bogey used to mean the score achieved by the mythical Colonel Bogey, who made no mistakes, and therefore turned in the perfect score. The American system is clearly far more explicit, though the Colonel lingers on in older dictionaries.

The variations of the golf game are infinite, especially where the myriad betting formulas are concerned. Rules Committees have an opinion on betting too; it is frosty. Since private wagers are beyond the reach of the game's rulers, they make no attempt to police such gambling, and bookmakers take bets world-wide on professional tournaments. Where amateur play is concerned, the authorities frown on large-scale Calcutta sweepstakes and, on days of major club competitions, the purchase of shares in competitors with a view to receiving a dividend if investment has been made in the winning player.

"Vive la politesse"

Almost alone among sports, golf demands, but does not always elicit, total respect for opponents. Generally speaking, the better the golfer, the closer he or she comes to the USGA/R&A ideal. Etiquette comes first in the book of rules, the concept wedded to safety and consideration for others.

Players must be alert lest their practice swing injures a bystander, while absolute silence and immobility is demanded when a player prepares to hit the ball. Players must not dawdle, strike the ball before players in front are out of range, or fail to call following players through when a ball is being sought; three- or four-ball matches must let two-ball matches through, and golfers must not delay in leaving the green (by inference, this means also not standing about filling in score cards before moving off.) A group losing more than one clear hole on the players in

UNGENTLE SARCASM *René Vincent's drawing, "Gardening", in* L'Illustration, *1933*

front should invite the following group to go through.

It would be folly to suggest that all these counsels are followed with saintly forbearance, or even that the vast majority of players are aware of every one of the foregoing, not to mention further points of etiquette, such as that "Any match playing a whole round is entitled to pass a match playing a shorter round" and "A single player has no standing and should give way to a match of any kind."

There is also the matter of consideration for the course, in that players should smooth over marks they make in sand bunkers, repair pitch-marks (dents made in greens by approach shots), replace "divots" (portions of fairway turf dislodged in play ... though turf damaged on tees should *not* be replaced, lest a tee peg shift in a loose divot) and avoid damage to the holes themselves. Damage caused on greens by shoe spikes should be repaired only *after* putting is completed. However, repairs to old hole plugs and turf damaged by ball impact can be repaired before putting out.

In the writer's experience, one point of etiquette that is seldom ignored is that the great majority of players do take care not to walk on the line of other players' putts.

Professionals in general and top-class amateurs in particular will go further than the rule book on etiquette. On the tee, they will not drive off while a player is putting on a nearby green. This may lead to minor delay, but seldom causes ill feeling. The major cause of high blood pressure on golf courses is the failure to yield to other groups on the basis of the rules of precedence outlined above.

A basic cause of slow play, especially where groups of three or four are concerned, is the disinclination of players to get ready to play as soon as it is their turn. No. 2 of a quartet will delay his pacing out and surveying of his putt until No. 1 has performed the same sequence.

The rules are not the same for stroke play and match play. Suppose a player thinks his ball is damaged and unfit for play when he reaches his drive. Before lifting his ball to check, he must "announce his intention to his opponent in match play or his marker or a fellow competitor in stroke play." Then he must mark the position of the ball. He must not clean it (mud on the ball does *not* make it unfit for play) He must allow opponent, marker or fellow-competitor the chance to examine the ball.

The ball can be changed if it is found to be unfit for play. (When a ball breaks into pieces the stroke is cancelled, and another ball played from the same spot.) Any deviation from this procedure is punished in match play by the loss of the hole; in stroke play by a two-stroke penalty.

Since the usual penalty in stroke play for breaking a rule is two strokes, and in match play loss of hole, it is not permitted to indulge in both forms of the game at the same time: so a player keeping count of his opponent's strokes for submission for handicap purposes, of which more later, while also competing with him at match play has, according to the letter, and spirit, of the law, lost at match play and compiled an inadmissible card at stroke play.

It's no handicap

Golf has unique charms for spectator and player. It is possible to get a close-up view of players even in major championships. Furthermore, while an overweight, none-too-fit business man of 45 would never survive on a lawn tennis court even with the world's 100th-ranked player, or do more than just get in the way as a linebacker with the Dallas Cowboys, he could enjoy a game of golf against a top-class amateur, or a leading professional, and even hope to win if he played to his handicap. By which is meant the number of strokes that his ruling body consider to represent the difference between our plump businessman's golfing skill and that of the expert.

In principle, a player's handicap is, or should be, an accurate assessment of his ability to play to the standard scratch score (SSS) of a course. Great minds have been applied to

the intricate and thankless task of making these judgements which affect a golfer's prospects every time he enters a competition, or even plays a friendly match. Until 1983, a great many British players could not, consistently, play to their handicaps because they were awarded on the basis of their best scores.

Since 1983, performances are reckoned against the SSS of courses, after a model developed by the Australian Golf Union. The SSS computation starts with the length of a course. At 7,001 yards the provisional SSS is 74; at 4,100 it is 60.

The final SSS might be increased or lowered on consideration of general layout, sizes of greens and whether watered or unwatered, difficulties imposed by hazards, width of fairway, trees, rough, and prevailing weather conditions, together with the degree to which the ball runs on landing. Therefore the total *par* of a course will not necessarily equal the SSS, which must not be allocated hole by hole, but given only as a total for the course.

In the first place a player can obtain a handicap by submitting score cards. The national union or a delegated area authority is responsible for ratifying the handicaps of players with low or plus handicaps.

A player's handicap is effective wherever he plays, and can only be obtained by a member of a club affiliated to the national union. The USGA operates a patented system that depends on evaluation of 20 scores against two assessments of a course's playing difficulty, one for scratch players and one for players inferior to that standard.

The player in receipt of strokes from his betters on a golf course cannot choose where he will take them. The card of the course includes a stroke index, which will decree that if two strokes are to be given, they will be, for instance at Royal St David's, Harlech, taken at the 10th hole (stroke index 1) and third (SI 2). If 14 strokes were to be given, the receiver would get them at every Royal St David's hole except the 2nd, 9th, 11th and 18th. The SI figure is not an indication of a hole's degree of difficulty.

WINNER ON POINTS *Dr Frank Stableford, golfing "saint"*

Point scoring

One of golf's principal benefactors was Dr Frank Stableford, who has been called the patron saint of club golfers. His eponymous points system not only allows single matches to involve players of varying ability in a meaningful contest, but any number of players on a course – or courses. His system was first used at Wallasey on Merseyside in the early 1930s. A scratch player receives four points for an eagle, three for a birdie, two for par, one for bogey, none for double bogey. A player who has a stroke on any particular hole receives an extra point at each stage of this progression, so a par brings him three points, a birdie four.

Recent converts to golf cannot fully appreciate it, but those who were playing before 1952 may consider that the 1951 R&A/USGA rules conference included a majority of saintly figures. The conference was the first of its kind between the two ruling bodies, and issued uniform rules effective world-wide from 1952. One conference decision ended a hoary, old, and bitter controversy: the "stymie" was abolished.

A player was "stymied" on the green if he was unable to putt to the hole because his opponent's ball lay in the way. Unless the balls lay within six inches of each other, the only solution was either to loft the ball, or use the contours of the green to circumvent the obstacle: Old Tom Morris had remarked how skilful Allan Robertson had been at find-

ing the crumbling edge of a hole in such circumstances.

Traditionalists wanted to keep the stymie, to some degree because it had been part of the game for so long, but also because ending the stymie rule offered another opportunity to lift the ball, anathema to the old school of play-it-as-it-lies. Abolitionists considered that the essence of golf was that players should never be baulked in this way.

The USGA, among others, agonized about the matter, and polled the larger associations about it: 22 said keep the stymie, which had been in force since 1812, apart from one year. That was when the R&A abandoned the rule in 1833, but reimposed it the following year. Twenty-four associations said the stymie should be abolished.

Controversy was periodically renewed when famous matches were decided by stymies, as in Bobby Jones's 19th-hole win over Cyril Tolley on his way to the first leg of his Grand Slam in 1930, and the defeat, six years later, of the Scot, Jack McLean, in the US Amateur final by Johnny Fischer from Kentucky. English hackles were raised when the final of the English Close Amateur Championship in the crucial year of 1951 ended at the 39th hole where G. P. Roberts of Southport and Ainsdale beat H. Bennett of Buxton with the cruellest of stymies.

Seventeen years later the conference outlawed croquet putting: players may not putt with one foot on either side of the line of putt, as

FEATURES OF A GOLF COURSE *A standard golf course consists of 18 holes, each usually between 100 and 600 yards (91 and 549 metres) in length*

if with a croquet mallet. Like many other players, especially older ones who had developed a twitch using the traditional stance, Sam Snead had to resort to a posture known as the "side-winder", holding the top of the shaft with the left hand, then stroking the ball forward with the right hand lower down the shaft. Few believed croquet putting was golf.

One waive and you're out

Anyone who has served in the military will recognize the third section of Rule 1 (The Game) for what it is … golf's version of that service charge prohibiting conduct prejudicial to good order and discipline which, as every soldier, sailor or flying officer knows, means any conduct of which the Service disapproves in the slightest degree.

Golf's version is entitled "Agreement to Waive Rules", and says: "Players shall not agree to exclude the operation of any Rule or to waive any penalty incurred."

Rule 1 has already, in section two, brought the players to the realization that they are on their own. It makes clear that no player or caddie shall take any action to influence the position or the movement of a ball except in accordance with the rules. Nor are players to give advice

on play, or choice of club, to anyone except a partner, or their caddies … nor seek it, with the same exceptions. Penalty, loss of hole in match play, two strokes in stroke play. Penalties henceforward will be given in that order: first for match play, then stroke play.

Man is a litigious animal, and legislators are frequently outflanked by the expertise of the general public, aided by sharp-eyed lawyers, in finding loopholes in statutes. After more than 260 years of refinement, the rules of golf present a brick wall to the cheat. Admittedly, this is a strange claim to make of a game where cheating is easy, because the player is often out of sight of his fellows.

Here is the inner appeal of the game for in effect, as the totality of the rules make clear, the golfer's only opponent is himself. If he cheats, he has lost and the game has won: it usually does whether he cheats or not, but the difference is between honourable and dishonourable defeat. The stigma attached to the latter is a destroyer of character, and a quick way to lose club membership. Henry Beard has written, tongue in cheek one assumes, "The Official Exceptions to the Rules" with a sub-title of "at last a rule book that makes cheating legal" – but the *official* rule book accepts no exceptions to observing the rules.

TEEING GROUND *Tee-shots must be struck from within a rectangle two club-lengths in depth – but players can stand outside it to hit their shots*

OUT OF BOUNDS *The out of bounds line is that which joins inside points of fence posts at ground level. Therefore, ball on the left is out of bounds; the other two are in bounds*

UNPLAYABLE BALL *If a ball is declared unplayable in a bush, the player can (under penalty of one stroke):*
1 *Go back to play from where the previous stroke was played*
2 *Drop a ball within two club lengths of where the ball was declared unplayable, not nearer the hole, as shown in the shaded area in the diagram*
3 *Drop a ball behind the point where the ball lay, keeping that point directly between the hole and the spot on which the ball is played, with no limit to how far behind that point the ball may be dropped*

Playing by the rules

Let us now start at the beginning, on the tee. The player must arrive there with no more than 14 clubs. Six or seven was the usual complement for Harry Vardon and his rivals in the days of wooden, usually hickory, shafts. With the coming of steel clubs (legalized by the USGA in 1924, but not until 1929 by the R&A) and particularly with the refinement of matched sets, the temptation to carry a club for every length and variety of shot was powerful.

Lawson Little, winner of both British and US Amateur Championships in 1934–35, carried as many as 25. Opponents always of excess, and eager to encourage shot-making skills (veteran golfers were scornful of players who couldn't play a half shot with a six-iron to make up for lack of a seven-iron), the authorities called a halt at 14 clubs in 1938. Penalties are heavy for the unwary: one hole for each hole at which the infraction occurred to a maximum of two holes, or two strokes per hole, maximum four strokes per round. The clubs too must conform to strict regulations as to configuration.

The ball must conform to USGA/R&A specifications, and much money and effort are expended to make sure that it does. Briefly, its weight must be no more than 1.62 ounces (45.93 gm), and its diameter no less than 1.68 inches (42.67 mm). Crucially, the initial velocity of the ball must be no greater than 250 feet (76.2 m) per second, within a tolerance of 2 per cent.

Suitably equipped, which means without "artificial device or unusual equipment" and certainly without means of measuring distance or gauging the conditions, the golfer makes a start, mindful always that "the ball shall be fairly struck at with the head of the club and must not be pushed, scraped or spooned". Hitting the ball twice in the execution of a stroke costs a penalty stroke, i.e. the one blow counts as two. The golfer must be careful to take his rightful turn on the tee according to the rules of precedence. In a competition, that means following the draw order issued by the Committee, in the absence of which the order "should be decided by lot".

Low handicap golfers do not gain the honour, as the right to strike the first blow is called, because of respect for their greater expertise, though they often do by custom in friendly matches. Thereafter the honour falls to whoever last won a hole.

Our man should be equally careful not to place his ball nearer the hole than a line joining the twin tee-markers. Nor can he play from more than two clubs' lengths behind that line. At last, he steps up to make a start, only to find his ball has toppled off his tee-peg (not an essential item for teeing off) before he could make a swing at it. He is at liberty to replace the ball, and carry on: this happening involves no penalty, since no attempt to hit the ball was made.

If it falls off during the down-swing, and the golfer cannot check his swing, too bad – it counts as a stroke, even if the club makes no contact.

A tee shot struck from outside the proper teeing ground can be recalled by your opponent. You must play again: apart from this there is no penalty, but in stroke play the penalty is two strokes, and play again.

That would make three off the tee, which is also the answer when a ball is lost, or flies out of bounds. The score card tells what the boundaries of the course are, and what marks them: a line, itself out of bounds (OOB), a ditch, a fence, wall or stakes, in which last case the OOB line is the nearest inside points of the stakes or fence posts at ground level, excluding angled supports. The principle follows the soccer model: the ball is out of bounds when all of it lies out of bounds.

The player who fears his ball is lost can, to save time and an irritating walk back after a fruitless search, play a provisional ball. This constitutes the stroke and distance rule, in this case being provisionally followed in case the ball cannot be found in the statutory five minutes allowed. Opponent(s) or marker must be informed of the intention to play a provisional, which must be done before searching for the first ball starts: normally, that is before leaving the tee. The provisional can be played again, up to the point where the player believes his original ball might be.

If that stays lost, the provisional ball becomes the ball in play. A second ball can also be played when a disagreement occurs between players in a group about the right way to proceed, for example, what

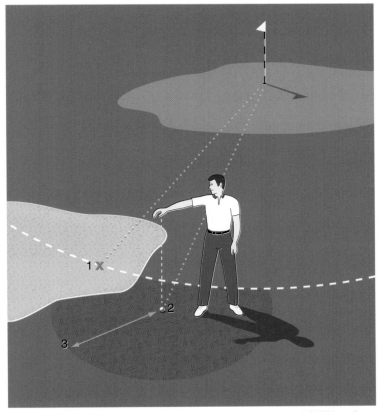

WHERE AND HOW TO DROP *A ball lying in ground under repair (GUR) at 1 must be lifted and dropped (without penalty) within one club-length of the nearest point of relief (2), and not nearer the hole (i.e. not between the dotted line and the hole). The ball is still in play as long as it rolls to no further than 3, two club-lengths from 2. If the stance to dropped ball is inside the GUR, the ball must be redropped. To drop the ball stand erect with arm outstretched to front or side and release the ball. The ball must not be dropped over the shoulder*

WATER HAZARD OPTIONS
1 *Play ball as it lies without penalty*
2 *Drop a ball outside the hazard within two club-lengths of the point where the original ball last crossed the margin of the hazard. Penalty one stroke*
3 *Drop, not nearer the hole, on an extension of line from hole through the line of entry: penalty, one stroke*
4 *Return to point where previous stroke was made: penalty, one stroke*

LATERAL WATER HAZARD OPTIONS
1 *Play it as it lies*
2 *Drop behind hazard on a line through hole and point of entry*
3 *Play from point of previous stroke*
4 *Play from shaded area, i.e. within two club-lengths of point of entry, no nearer hole or* **(5)** *shaded area on opposite side of hazard. Options 2, 3, 4 and 5 cost one stroke*

penalty should be imposed if any, or relief received. The player whose position is in doubt may play the first ball as it lies, the second with a drop, make a note of the score from both, and seek an official ruling at the end of the round, remembering not to sign the card until the issue has been settled.

The rules allow golfers to declare their balls unplayable at any time, except in a water hazard. The "unplayable" decision is entirely up to the golfer's sense of fair play. First, at the cost of a stroke, the golfer can follow the stroke and distance procedure, taking the ball back to where it was last struck. Second, the golfer can drop the ball, again with a stroke penalty, within two club-lengths, but not nearer the hole. Finally, the ball may be dropped any desired distance behind the unplayable spot, keeping that spot between the new position of the ball and the hole. This too costs a shot. "Drop" means releasing the ball while standing erect with ball at arm's length.

The most frustrating misfortune in golf is undoubtedly playing the wrong ball: which is why a distinguishing mark on a ball is a good and potentially match- or card-saving precaution. The penalty for playing the wrong ball, except in a hazard, is loss of hole, or two strokes. Disqualification follows in stroke play if the error is not put right before the miscreant tees off at the next hole. If the wrong ball played

PLAYING THE BALL AS IT LIES *Don't improve the lie of the ball (e.g. by pressing the foot into long grass behind the ball). Principle: play the ball as it lies. Penalty for violation: match play, loss of hole; stroke play, two strokes*

in stroke play belongs to an opponent, it must be replaced as nearly as possible to the position of the first stroke played in error.

The golfer is at liberty to lift a ball to identify it, if it is not in a hazard, and to replace it, but may not clean it. If was found in deep grass or mud, thence it must be returned.

Since lifting a ball to identify it in a hazard is not permitted, the golfer may play a ball in a hazard (defined below) when it cannot definitely be identified. This carries no penalty.

Next the golfer must be aware of penalties and rights attaching to hazards, defined as any bunker (usually termed a trap in America) or water hazard. Grassy ground near a bunker is not part of a bunker, which is basically a hollow filled with sand. Grassed areas within a bunker are not part of it. Little dells lined with grass are not bunkers and not hazards.

A water hazard is "any sea, lake, pond, river, ditch, surface drainage ditch or other open water course (whether or not containing water) and anything of a similar nature".

There are options in both types

of hazards. Play it as it lies is always an option, though the club must not touch the hazard except when the ball is being struck: so the club must not be grounded before the stroke is made. It is a good precaution never to ground a club in the rough either, for the grass, being disturbed, may move the ball, for which there is a one-stroke penalty.

A ball in a bunker which is also lying in casual water, ground under repair (usually delineated with a white line and labelled GUR by the greenkeeper) or in casts made by a burrowing animal can be dropped in the bunker without penalty, or outside it with a penalty stroke. It is sometimes impossible to find a spot clear of water in a bunker. Casual water is defined as an temporary accumulation of water visible before or after the player takes his stance.

Water hazards marked with yellow stakes or lines differ from lateral water hazards, which have red markings. Islands within a water hazard are part of it. First option with a ball in either is to play it as it lies … easier when the area is dry, but not impossible when wet. The club must not be grounded.

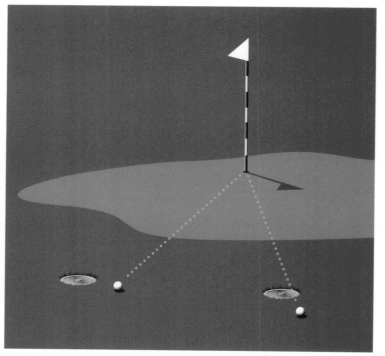

SPRINKLER BLOCKAGE *The ball shown on the right must be played as it lies, as the sprinkler head is not interfering with stance. The ball on the left can be lifted as sprinkler head is interfering with stance (though not in the case of a left-hander). No penalty*

INDICATING THE LINE OF A PUTT *A caddie or partner may indicate line of putt, but must not touch the green or mark it. Penalty: loss of hole, or two strokes*

Ins and outs

If a ball drops into the hole, and is forced out by a frog jumping from the hole, has the golfer holed out? Yes, as soon as the ball was "within the circumference of the hole and all of it … below the level of the lip of the hole".

Ace decision

Fearing a tee shot at a par three was lost, a golfer played a provisional, and could not find the original ball in a five-minute search. It was later found in the hole. Ruling: an ace, golfer's play on the hole complete once ball holed.

Water torture

Just out of bounds there is casual water in which a player must stand to hit a ball which is just in bounds. Can the golfer claim relief? No, such a condition must be "on the course".

Lucky bounce

A player's ball hit a rock and flew backwards into woods. He declared it unplayable, and dropped at original lie. His opponent's objection, on grounds that he was getting nearer the hole without playing a stroke, was rejected.

Taking the rap

When can a player not send for a replacement for a broken club? When it was not broken "in the normal course of play" – as when Ben Crenshaw in the 1987 Ryder Cup rapped his putter on the ground and snapped it.

In the cart

Players A and B were sharing a caddie car, in which B was sitting when A's shot hit it during stroke play. Ruling: his ball was stopped by their (mutual) equipment: two-stroke penalty on A.

Living things

Andy Bean won at Doral after escaping penalty when his practice swing near a tree detached leaves. It was ruled that this had not assisted him. Sam Torrance was penalized two strokes in Austria for bringing down a small branch with a practice swing.

If there is "reasonable evidence" that the ball is lost in the hazard, the player may, at cost of a stroke, play a ball as nearly as possible at the spot from which the original ball was last played; or "drop a ball behind the water hazard, keeping the point at which the original ball last crossed the margin of the water hazard directly between the hole and the spot on which the ball is dropped, with no limit to how far behind the water hazard the ball may be dropped". In the case of a lateral water hazard procedure is different; it lies along the general direction of play, so if it is not possible to drop behind it, a ball may be dropped within two club-lengths of either the point where the original ball last crossed the margin of the water hazard or a point on the opposite margin of the hazard equidistant from the hole.

Loose impediments (natural objects such as leaves and stones) and obstructions (artificial, man-made) present different options. The former may be moved, as long as they and the ball are not in a hazard: boundary fences and the like are not obstructions. Movable obstructions are what their name suggests … the rules are highly literal in their wording … but where immovable obstructions are concerned, relief without penalty is the general rule, unless the ball is in a water hazard.

The over-riding instruction is still to play the course as you find it, avoiding any temptation to improve lies or "moving or bending or breaking anything fixed or growing except in fairly taking your stance or making your swing".

Having finally reached the green, the golfer must never make a mark upon it to indicate a line for his putt, nor hit the flagstick with his putt, which costs the hole or a two-stroke penalty. Sand and loose soil are loose impediments *only on greens*, and can be brushed aside (but not pressed down), and balls may be cleaned before putting.

When a putt overhangs the hole, the golfer, having reached the hole "without unreasonable delay", is allowed 10 additional seconds to make sure the ball is at rest. If it falls in after that, the player is deemed to have holed out with his last stroke, but a penalty stroke is added.

Golfers must be men of their word to the last. If a putt is conceded, the offer may not be refused. The offer, once made, may not be withdrawn.

A golfer who seeks to absorb golf's 34 rules by competing at a board game called Masterstroke can be secure in the knowledge that this is by no means a Trivial Pursuit. Masterstroke has been put together by an acknowledged rules expert, Bruce Adams.

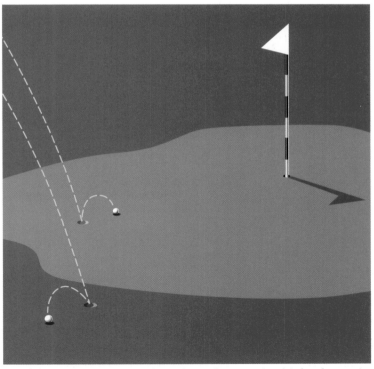

RUNNING REPAIRS *Repairing pitch marks on the green (top) is legal – repairing spike marks is illegal. Repairing ball marks off green is a violation, but permitted after putting out (below)*

THE HISTORY OF THE SWING

Some players, such as Bobby Jones and Sam Snead, are born great; some achieve greatness by sheer persistence, such as Ben Hogan and Henry Cotton; lesser mortals, short on both counts, labour in between.

The ball shapes the swing

Every bat and ball game is at the mercy of the men who make the ammunition, the ball, and the men who fashion the playing arena or, in the case of golf, amend what nature has provided.

Cricketers chat away endlessly about the ball's hardness, resilience, ability to retain shape, and the height of the seam; and that's quite apart from the question of how to keep the shine on the ball, legal and illegal aids thereto, and the state of the pitch. Tennis reformers want a bigger projectile, so that the power of the big servers is reduced and the public can watch rallies of more than two or three strokes again.

The golf ball has gone through even more radical changes, notably with its composition: boxwood, feathers stuffed into a leather sphere, gutta percha, wound rubber bands, liquid cores, solid cores, two-piece, three-piece, constant improvement of dimple patterns on the cover ... and at every stage different demands, complicated by wind and weather, have been made on the mechanics of making the ball fly. Books defining these flow ceaselessly from the printing presses, and it is a safe bet that the majority of golf books in any public library will be of the "Play Golf the Whatsisname Way" variety. Refusing to supply such a market would be unbusinesslike for publisher, teacher and (frequently) the teacher's ghostwriter, though wise golfers and reputable teachers know that personal instruction by a professional is the best way to success in the quest for a reliable swing.

One thought about the golf ball and how to propel it has remained a favourite through the years. As ex-

IN THE GROOVE *The unmistakable and reliable swing of Lee Trevino*

pressed by Harold Hutchinson in his classic and comprehensive 1891 study of the game in the Badminton *Golf*, and in various ways since by books, videos, magazines, and pros without number: it's a swing, not a hit ... very short and simple words containing a truth universally admired but, all too often, forgotten.

Hutchinson held that "hit" means a jerk with tensed muscles, whereas the golf swing involves gradual acceleration with flexible muscles. This does not preclude the application of great strength, but does preclude its misapplication.

Hutchinson played in the era which started with the solid gutty ball, which arrived in the middle of the nineteenth century, and finished with the lively Haskell, patented in 1898, with its wound rubber interior. Before these innovations the light and responsive feathery ball made its own swing rules. It fairly sprang off the club face, performing best in the dry. In the wet, especially when clumsily hit, the feathery would burst its stitches, and a careless iron shot would cut it.

Therefore it was necessary to sweep the ball away, so what is thought of as the old St Andrews swing was flat, and sent the ball flying away over the wide open spaces of what is now the Old Course. The favoured stance was closed, that is, with left foot in advance of the right, which had the additional advantage on windswept links courses (there were few of any other type) of keeping the ball low and running.

This method contrasts sharply with the model swing of the late twentieth century, which has become more and more upright, though Lee Trevino's swing, while scarcely a throw-back to Victorian times, has resisted the trend, and won him a fortune. Jack Nicklaus, himself an exemplar of the upright swing, defines Trevino's as "effective in that it is wonderfully well grooved". In other words, it is an action Trevino can repeat exactly and almost endlessly, an action that has stood the test of time deep into Senior status. He had the best stroke average five times on the PGA Tour. It is the repeatability of the swing that counts, rather than its beauty and technical orthodoxy or the strength of the player. This is what

MODERN MASTER *José-Maria Olzabal at Wentworth in the World Match Play*

Henry Cotton implied in his comment that anyone watching top class professionals setting off from the tee would rapidly realise there was more than one way to strike a golf ball with power and accuracy.

The coming of the solid gutty ball called for immediate adjustments, especially for such players as Allan Robertson, the champion of the 1850s, both in his play and his business, since he was a feathery maker. Though he and noted feathery makers like Gourlay felt threatened by the new ball, Robertson proved himself a true professional by mastering the art of clipping the gutty into flight, which called for accurate timing of the shot and firm wrists, and increased the value of iron club shots that came down hard on the ball, enabling the player to pitch the ball positively and stop it on the greens.

Every golfer has a friend who, once in a while, will excitedly make the claim that he has discovered the "secret" of golf. For Hutchinson, whose steadiness under pressure made him such a fine match player, the secret was accuracy in bringing the club back to the position it was in when addressing the ball. This, he wrote, "can best be accomplished by keeping under firm control all parts of the body whose free movement is not essential to speed of swing."

Thus there should be no swaying to the right (the movements of a right-handed player are specified throughout this section) involved in turning the body on its own axis. This simple idea of building up power by means of the body swivelling around the axis of the spine was scarcely challenged in essentials for half a century until refined by American researches into the full impact, and potential, of the Haskell and its derivatives as propelled by steel-shafted clubs. These researches are continuing, computer-aided, at USGA headquarters in New Jersey.

Hutchinson was not the first to publish an instruction manual. H. B. Farnie's *A Keen Hand*, which appeared in 1857, was described the clubs involved and their purpose, but fell far short of an attempt to analyse the mechanics of the swing.

GRIP VARIATIONS *Orthodox overlapping grip and (right) the now almost obsolete split-handed baseball grip*

Hutchinson's work, in contrast, was a bold and specific analysis. His starting-point was a closed stance, with the right foot two to three inches behind the left, as was the method of the feathery players, with their long-shafted, long-headed clubs that swept the ball away. This, he wrote, was the practice of most fine players, who lifted their left foot on to the toe at the top of the backswing, with the sole of the left shoe facing towards the green.

Though he did not speak of posture as often, or rate its importance as highly, as modern teachers, he was making a related point when he insisted that the upward swing was important because it must forecast the nature of the downswing to the ball. He held that the left hand provided power, the right guidance, so that the grip should be tight with the left hand, lighter with the right.

John Ball, the Hoylake champion, changed all this with a more upright, open stance that proved a winner, because it allowed a plane of swing that got the gutty up in the air. Ball was a ball-manoeuvrer supreme, and he would have been scornful of the modern professional practice of carrying wedges for all occasions,

sometimes as many as three or more.

He was able to open or close the club face to achieve his ends, which included keeping the ball low into the wind, or getting it up, with backspin, to pull it up quickly on the green. Bernard Darwin considered Ball's swing even more pleasing to watch than Bobby Jones's.

J. H. Taylor, first of the Great Triumvirate to win the Open, added significantly to the golfer's armoury with the spin he imparted to his iron shots, and his control over the ball in bad weather, in which he was a dangerous opponent. The story is told of him that while giving a playing lesson on course to Tommy Armour, he was asked how he contrived to get so much "stop" on the ball. Taylor replied that he would instruct Armour on that art as soon as he showed some signs of being able to hit his ball up to the hole.

Vardon officiates at a marriage

Harry Vardon was the next great innovator. He made a successful adaptation of the overlapping grip, with the little finger of the right hand crooked over the index finger of the left, first employed by Johnny Laidlay, the Scottish amateur. By this

means it was possible, in Vardon's phrase, "to wed the hands." The highest and lowest points at which the club is grasped are well separated, the thumb and first finger of the right hand at the lowest point of the hands, and the third, fourth and fifth fingers of the left at the highest.

Adding this to matchless timing, for he was said never to force a shot, Vardon created a classic model admired on both sides of the Atlantic. A contemporary account has it that the outstanding impression of watching Vardon play was of "utter ease and lack of physical effort."

The inescapable conclusion about Vardon's career is that he never thought about his swing until he had developed it. He had reputedly played only 20 full rounds of golf by the time he was 20. His writings confirm that it was not until he turned 21, and was established in his second professional post and five years short of his first Open win, that he began to think about why he had taken up an open stance, with upright posture.

Vardon put many a golfer on the right track, inveighing always against the straight left arm, which he considered to be the ruination of a golfer.

He certainly did not advise a tight grip with either hand, which "creates a tautening of the muscles ... the chances of executing a perfect stroke are remote." He began his swing in a fashion not taught today, dragging the club back and the hands inward: at the top of the backswing his arm was not merely bent but at a right angle. He held that the force of the swing would cause the arm to straighten at impact, which refutes accusations that he "hit from the top". Further proof is in pictures of Vardon taken at an advanced stage in his downswing. They show he was as late a hitter as the golfing world has seen, bringing his wrists into the equation at the last fraction of a second.

The only other player to attract as much veneration and fulsome praise as Vardon was Bobby Jones. Jones's instructional films and the flick books of his swing, which are now eminently collectable, display an upright swing with an effect of unbroken, rounded symmetry. This is as different as can be from pictures of golfers in the late gutty days.

Dick Aultmann points out in his work on outstanding swingers of the club that a picture of Jones, aged seven, at the top of the backswing shows no difference in essentials of posture from how he appeared as a mature player.

Like Sam Snead, Jones had natural rhythm and outstanding eye-hand co-ordination, so much so that a crack shot who was with Jones when he made his first attempt at trap shooting reported that Jones, unused to firearms, was soon regularly hitting the targets. But Jones was wise enough not to interfere with these natural gifts.

A search for means to control the lively Haskell-type ball quickly became a top priority as the new century dawned. Americans supplied the best answers, especially in approach shots, though Jock Hutchison's deeply grooved clubs that brought him the Open in 1921 also brought action from the authorities.

Henry Cotton's doctrine of the crucial importance of hand action, and training the fingers by practice to take up the correct tension on the club, helped him become the envy of all for his straightness off the tee. He believed teachers inflicted damage on their pupils by their (to Cotton's mind) injurious emphasis on body action. He did not need a full swing to send the ball enormous distances, and his swing attracted the epithet "grooved" before the American development of the notion.

Byron Nelson's great contribution to the swing, as he ran down one prize after another before and after the Second World War, was his ability to make best use of the firmer and more obedient steel shafts by virtue of using his legs, both of them, to drive through the ball. Hitting against the braced left side had long been the accepted gospel of the swing, ever since the days when Hutchinson was insisting that there should be no lateral swaying.

Vardon had implied that the use of the legs was part of the required swing sequence, in his practice of bringing the left heel back to the ground as he began his downswing. Now Nelson went further, and harnessed the power of his legs, yet achieved a straightness few could rival, and runs of tournament success no one has ever equalled.

Ben Hogan progressed from youthful hooker, by way of prodigies of practice, to perhaps the most complete master of ball control from tee to green that the game has seen. Tommy Bolt once remarked that Nicklaus watched Hogan practice; he never heard of Hogan watching Nicklaus practice. Hogan's slight fade and low flight were an insurance policy that paid off handsomely.

Nick Faldo remodelled and tightened technique in three years of hard labour, though not, as yet, with the same reward in major events. Comparing photographic studies of Hogan's action in the early years of his domination with its full flowering in the early 1950s, the impression is inescapable that everything became tighter, less flamboyant (if such a canard can ever be aimed in Hogan's direction) ... leg action and all other physical movements a paradigm of economy. The impression was that the whole production was so compact, there was so little left to chance, that very little *could* go wrong.

"Grooved" was indeed the name of his game, and of American teacher-technology since the Second World War. Jack Nicklaus and Tom Watson in particular have carried on in that grooved tradition, Watson with one of the most upright swings of all, sharp, speedy, yet compact.

John Jacobs, the English coach whose greatest contribution to golf is undoubtedly the major part he played in the creation of the European Tour, sums up the swing by reminding the player that "the grip largely determines clubface alignment at impact, that body alignment at address can directly affect the clubhead's path, and that posture before swinging largely determines its angle of approach."

Seve Ballesteros would get most people's vote as the player who has put this together most beguilingly as the possessor of the smoothest of all swings: harmony is the name of his game, allied to tremendous power. He also pleases the swing doctors, with his model posture at address. There has been no finer exemplar of Hutchinson's insistence

FILIAL REFLECTION *Jackie Snead, aged 12, surveys the grace of father Sam Snead's swing, 1956 vintage*

that it's a swing, not a hit. Ernie Els and Fred Couples are currently the next best.

Shedding light on putting

Frank Thomas and his USGA team of researchers are brave, or foolhardy, enough to be going into the mystic business of putting. At the 1994 US Open at Oakmont, and at certain 1995 PGA events, laser beams were used to take exhaustive measurements of putts as to length, slope, speed and borrow. Pro tour statistics over the last 20 years also come into the equation. Yips sufferers the world over will hope there is a cure in all this for those soul-destroying missed three-footers.

Early tees were, by rule, so close to holes that putting surfaces could scarcely be velvety in texture, and putting was sometimes better tackled as a chipping manoeuvre, a useful skill in any case in the days of the stymie. There is therefore a fine irony in the fact that it was largely through his putting supremacy that Willie Park Senior became the first winner of the Championship Belt back in 1860. He also won the Open on three other occasions, despite a tendency to foolhardy gambles through the green. Once on it, he usually proved the master. The historian Robert Browning tells how, as a boy, Park spent his evenings on a practice green of four holes, 25 to 30 yards apart. His best effort was five putts for the four holes.

Nowadays it is a useful putter who gets round, consistently, in less than 30 strokes on the greens. Pros on majors tours must aspire to around 28. The coming of better greens made it clear that putting is a game within a game. It still is, and one at which success has suddenly eluded even the greatest players, from Harry Vardon to Nick Faldo and Tom Watson. When it happened to Watson, he had already written one of the most useful of all instructional books, *Getting Up and Down*, subtitled *How to Save Strokes from Forty Yards and In*. It is a genuine stroke-saver. It is rather sad to read, in Jack Nicklaus's foreword to the book: "He [Watson] knows he isn't going to

ROLL ON *Putts went further and straighter when Bob Charles struck them*

miss many short putts, so he can be aggressive and take a run at a long putt or chip. Someday maybe he'll start missing some short putts and come back into the real world ..." This last conjecture is exactly what has happened to Watson, who would otherwise have added several majors to his tally.

This suggests that, however good the putting method, it will fail unless nerve and inspiration support it. Park believed in a pendulum stroke principle, using hands and arms. Watson's major points are keeping the eye over the ball, hands locked with forearms so that the putter is moved with the arms, which are locked to the shoulders, and (a crucial point) a consistent angle of bend in left elbow. Extending the arm, he believes, must break the bond with the shoulders.

Watson uses the term pendulum, but only as a tip to maintain a good rhythm: after hitting the putt, he advises, count one before looking up. As with all other strokes, deceleration of the clubhead as it reaches the ball is a cardinal sin, often caused by taking the putter back too far.

In between Park and what might be called the classic American "straight-line" putting technique espoused by Watson there were all sorts of contrivances, notably croquet putting, banned in 1968, and the Sam Snead side-winder style: a development of croquet putting but

with left hand high on the shaft, right hand much lower, this involved pushing the putter head through the ball while both feet remain the same side of the line of putt, i.e. in a legal position.

Desperate measures have been taken to combat putting failures. Henry Longhurst's cure, most radical of all, ensured he never missed another short putt: he retired from the game. Faldo has tried left hand below right, gone back to orthodoxy, then returned to left hand below right, and so on. Others have garages packed with putters, and many have gained comfort from the broomstick putter, long enough to cuddle under the chin, with one hand acting as a fulcrum, while the other pushes the putter head through.

Bernhard Langer's valour in the face of putting terrors is unrivalled. He has twice been in the depths, but rebuilt his game on the greens with his much copied ploy of gripping well down the shaft with his left hand, while holding his left forearm against the upper part of the shaft with his right hand. The shaft is thus made to act as a splint for his left wrist.

The far from encouraging fact for each and every struggler on the green is that the list of consistently great putters is much shorter than that of golf's "Legends". The six giants of the putting game are Walter Travis (once described as "a killer" on the green), Walter Hagen, Bobby Jones (who had no weaknesses, least of all perhaps when it came to a "must" putt), Billy Casper, Bobby Locke and Bob Charles, he of the inexorably rolling putt ... that is, four Americans (though Travis was born in Australia), the South African Locke and a left-hander, the New Zealander Charles.

Hagen's strength as a putter was two-fold. His hands, firstly, were those of a musician, with long slender fingers. Wrapping these around the grip, and with his weight on his left foot, he stroked through the ball in the approved US style of the straight-line putter, continuing the clubhead's path towards the hole for as long as possible.

Secondly, his mental toughness

was renowned. Who else would have asked for his closest rival at the climax of a US Open to come out and watch him putt for a win? Hagen rimmed the hole, went out on the town for most of the night, then beat his man in a play-off next day. Who else would provoke fate by saying there was no chance of his missing an eight-footer, because it was for several thousand dollars, and then sinking it?

Casper's method was almost frightening to watch: his stroke was the antithesis of Hutchinson's swing-not-hit gospel, for he gave his putts a thorough-going rap with an action that was almost all wrist. His putting average in winning the 1959 US Open was 28, and at Winged Foot too, notorious for its slopes.

Locke is held by many to be the greatest putter of them all. John Reece tells the story of how Norman Sutton gave an off-form and worried Locke a putting lesson just before the 1949 Open. Sutton had spotted that Locke was moving his body at impact. By the end of the lesson Locke had holed 50 putts in a row from four feet without moving any part of his body apart from his hands, with which, Sutton diagnosed, Locke had been gripping too tightly. Locke won that Open, after single-putting eight of the nine holes at which he had to escape from sand.

He won the following year, too, when at Troon he became the first Open champion to break 280. Locke is renowned, like Hogan, as a hooker who made good: but Locke, who stuck to his right to left flight, and was famed for his banana shots with wooden clubs that unerringly sought out the green, also reputedly hooked his putts, over which he took a long time, taking particular note of the nature and grain of the grass. But then his second putts, and he had fewer of these to play than most of his rivals, were usually tap-ins.

It is worth noting that the greatest putter took a lesson. Watson puts an question to the weekend golfer: "How many do you know who've ever taken a putting lesson?"

GOLDEN RAPPER *Bill Casper's putting put out the fire of Winged Foot's greens*

GOLF EQUIPMENT

From tee-peg to flagstick, golf can be one of the most expensive sporting journeys in the world. For all golfers, arming themselves with the right equipment is a vital prerequisite to the happy and successful pursuit of their game, and for many of them looking the part is a pretty serious business, too.

Never in the field of human recreation has so much been spent by so many to so little effect. The members of many a handicapping committee must think along these lines as they survey the sad and stratospheric figures returned in the monthly medal by fellow-members employing the most up-to-date and terrifyingly expensive confections of steel, carbon-fibre, exotic woods, rubber, leather and ceramics known as golf clubs, to belabour to no great effect a small dimpled spheroid that is itself a technological marvel, the result of approaching a thousand years of tireless search for the perfect projectile. But the viability of the whole subscription and green-fee lifeblood of a club, not to mention profitability of the bar and professional's shop, is a by-product of the restless search for improvement by average golfers, "the dogged victims of inexorable fate", as they have been called. Encouraged by the PR men, the golfer's watchword is that if spending a few hundred will do the trick, then let's go. Even playing well is not enough, for excepting always old whatshisname who has worn those velvet trousers and much-darned sweater since the days of the 1.62 inch ball, the golfer must look the part, and so must the bag that holds the clubs, the natty gloves that protect them and the trolley or cart that brings it along …

LEFT: **IT'S NOT JUST ROUND** *The three-piece ball of today is a technological marvel* RIGHT: **GOLF'S** *DERNIER CRI Expensively cast in search of more consistent striking*

Golf Equipment

GOLF BALLS

Defying the laws of aero-dynamics

The Haskell ball, called "a pill of quicksilver" by the great US Amateur Chick Evans, was not the work of a dedicated researcher. Coburn Haskell was something of a dilettante sportsman, who had married an heiress of the Hanna family. One day Haskell wound some rubber bands into a ball at the factory of his friend Bert Work, President of Goodrich Rubber. When his plaything slipped out of his hand, its liveliness gave Haskell the notion that changed the game. Just as the resilient, but costly, feathery ball had been ousted by the cheap, if stodgy, performer, the gutty, so now the gutty's days were numbered. The Haskell flew so far that it led to lengthening of courses, and re-siting of bunkers and other hazards taken out of play by the new projectile.

Progress with the Haskell ball was slow at first. The slender, dexterous fingers of Goodrich office girls were initially employed as the rubber-band winders, but clearly machinery was called for. Goodrich engineer John Gammeter provided it, and Patent 622834, granted on April 11, 1899, was made over to the firm. His complex machine wound two threads round a core, providing a balanced, homogeneous and highly resilient centre to the ball. David Stirk and his co-author Ian Henderson have gone so far as to say of Gammeter's machine: "If one single invention revolutionized golf, it was Gammeter's."

This was not an obedient ball, however, until James Foulis, the 1896

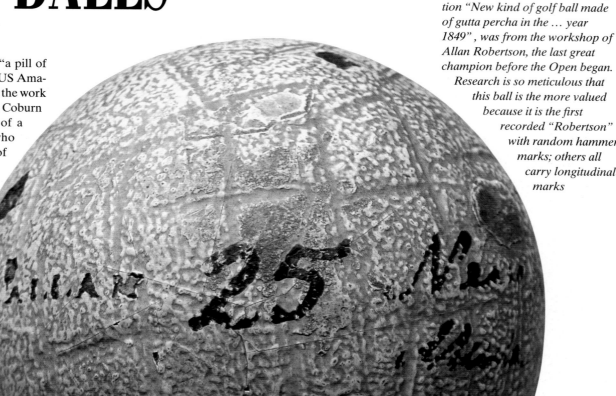

US Open champion, after putting new Agrippa "blackberry bump" patterned covers on a batch of (so he thought) gutties, found that one of them played wonderfully well. Curious, he cut it open. He found he had re-covered a Haskell and had found a cure for its flight problems.

Research has greatly improved the flight control exerted by the cover pattern, i.e. an arrangement of dimples, up to 500 of them covering 70 per cent of the ball's surface, usually based on the icosahedron pattern, with 20 repeating triangles. Spalding designers, acting on the thought that more dimples would give more lift and control, made space for them by making the ball bigger.

Oversize balls at 1.72 or 1.74 inches in diameter have contradicted one of the laws of aero-dynamics ... that a larger body moves more slowly through the air, just as the dimpled ball earlier disproved the law stating that smooth surfaces provide least wind resistance. The modern golf ball is *not* a simple spheroid.

It has encouraged in its train endless expansion of a mighty accessories industry: the simplest item, at first trademarked as the Reddy Tee, is the familiar wooden peg with a point at the bottom and a small concave cup at the top. It brought its inventor, William Lowell, a New Jersey dentist, much grief as he tried to protect his patent.

Haskell had varying fortunes as he tried to protect his invention. He was successful in America, but in Britain his 1905 suit failed because Capt. Duncan Stewart showed his design for a wound rubber ball with gutta percha cover which had been tried – unsuccessfully – 30 years earlier. Haskell must justifiably have thought the law an ass: his ball worked, made the game easier and pleasanter to play, opening its delights to millions.

FEATHERY SURVIVORS

Balls of leather and feather are often sold for thousands of pounds/dollars. The first (right) is still protected by its original paint. The second has lost most of its white paint, revealing the untanned hide that has been fashioned into an almost perfect sphere: it will have cost five shillings to buy 150 years ago. The third, though damaged, can still command large sums today.

SPOT THE ODD ONE OUT... *The ball in the middle of the third row is made of wood and was used during wartime rubber shortages. The rest are gutties. The wooden ball has aiming spots because they have to be struck on the end grain to avoid splitting. The first gutty in the first row is a fine example of a hand-cut gutty; it has red marks to its poles. The variety of gutty balls starkly contrasts to the gleaming uniformity of the modern Titleist balls below.*

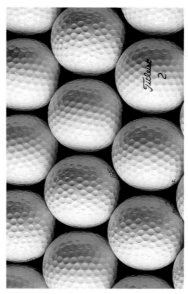

GOLF CLUBS

Club-making runs in the genes

Ironically, the best early clubs command higher prices than the most high-tech modern variety; clubs by Hugh Philp, who was made club-maker at St Andrews in 1819, are especially prized. His family and Robert Forgan's were linked by marriage, and Forgan, reputed to be the first to hand-hammer patterns on to gutty balls when it was found that smooth gutties performed poorly, carried on the club-making business after Philp died. Many famous makers began as Forgan apprentices. Forgan and Co. were based in Fife; other celebrated makers such as the Dickson and McEwan families, in the Lothians near Edinburgh.

David Stirk, in his study of the great club-makers, says they were born, not made. Family members who did not inherit the right genes usually left the business. The sheer volume of demand ended the era of the creators of the refined and beautiful club. George Cann was one such, and produced clubs for J. H. Taylor, whose playing success publicized Cann's products. But Cann soon became manager of a factory.

Wooden- and iron-headed clubs,

with hickory, ash or bamboo shafts, remained the norm until the late 1920s, when metallurgical progress ushered in the steel shaft, and the production of matched sets of clubs, which began to lose their tradition names and be known by numbers.

Brassie	No. 2 wood
Mashie	No. 5 iron
Spoon	No. 3 or 4 wood
Spade mashie	No. 6 iron
Driving iron (cleek)	No. 1 or 2 iron
Mashie-niblick	No. 7 iron
Midmashie	No. 3 iron
Pitching niblick	No. 8 iron
Mashie iron	No. 4 iron
Niblick	No. 9 iron

Note: "Cleek" was also a generic term for an iron club, while a "jigger" was an iron approach shot club.

The steel shaft, now replaced in turn by graphite, began to bring scores down because it behaved in a much more predictable manner than the wooden shaft, and gave better control over the new Haskell ball, which had revolutionized the game on its own account at the beginning of the century and within a decade or so drove out the gutty, certainly as far as the pros were concerned.

FUNCTIONAL DESIGN
The early rules of golf were a good deal less forgiving than they are today, with not many free-drops available, so a rutting iron (right), with long hosel and small head, was useful for extracting the ball from cart-tracks and other desperate lies. Equally handy, when a better opportunity for progress presented itself, was this square-toe iron (left) or a lofting iron (far right), also with a long hosel, current in the early part of the nineteenth century

CLUB MASTERS (TOP ROW)
Beechwood playclub by Dunn with leather face insert is shown with a driver, brassie and putter by the great Forgan, and a Morris playclub. Auchtlerlonie made the persimmon baffing spoon (bottom left); the remainder are by Ashford, two by Anderson, and the last is a rare Brand's Bulger driver. The top half of the Bulger grip was conventional, the lower part was equipped with a swivelling cyclinder to make the back-swing easier

WORLD WAR I ECHOES

Ely Callaway appropriated the name of the German cannon which fired shells many miles further than any other for his Big Bertha clubs. Ironically, his company has developed from a three-man concern bought in 1982 called the Hickory Stick Company, which made wedges and putters with steel shafts covered in veneer to make them look like hickory shafts. Renamed Callaway Golf, the company went public in 10 years, and has more than 1,000 employees

BIG IRONS

Like the metal "woods" the fashionable, and expensive, big irons are made on the principle of combining a thin striking face with as much of the weight of the club distributed around its perimeter as possible … all this to create a larger "sweet spot", so presenting the golfer with a greater margin of error when striking the ball. Large-headed clubs made out of graphite were already on the market when Callaway conceived the notion of a hollow perimeter-weighted metal "wood": the company spend $8 million (more than £5 million) a year defending designs against copyists

FAIRWAY FASHION PARADE

Men's fashions in golf began gaudily, continued plain, but are tending of late toward what the Victorian guardians of the game would have regarded as dandyish.

Red or blue tail-coats, cocked hats and buckled shoes were the thing when the first clubs held their competitions. Whether impelled by the need for economy or a Victorian distaste for show, players opted for knickerbockers and tweed jackets as the 19th century grew old: the average mid-century pro, to judge from pictures of the eight competitors for the Championship Belt in 1860, were a dowdy lot. Hats were still in favour, but cocked no longer, as prosaic flat caps and bonnets became the norm. Harry Vardon and the rest of the Triumvirate were most soberly clad. Plus twos and plus fours developed after knickerbockers fell out of favour, and are practical garments still much in evidence in fashionable clubs in Britain. Turn-ups in wet heather are a mistake.

Walter Hagen tended to flat caps, white slacks and shirts with bowtie at the time of his first US Open but, after the First World War, he set new trends. He soon became jacketless and hatless, with a short, carefully pomaded, centre-parted hair-style, set off by bright trousering and sweaters, and glittering two-tone brogues. Yet Hagen was seldom as brightly garbed as the Tour peacock, Jimmy Demaret, but then who was? The most famous single accessory of the 1940s and 1950s was the flat white cap Ben Hogan wore (and which he ordered by the dozen).

Looking good on TV

Television has empowered the manufacturers to sell modern styles in ever greater volume, since the advertising men have made leading pros, and not a few amateurs, into walking clothes-horses and billboards, kitting them out in the season's latest shade and style of trousers, shirts and sweaters, together with multicolour umbrellas and hats emblazoned with marketing messages. Payne Stewart, clad in outfits based on the colours of American football teams, has succeeded Demaret as latter-day peacock of the links. It all means big business, in which one of the world's great retailers of clothing, Marks and Spencer, have recently felt it worth their while to challenge the established suppliers. They burst on to the scene at the 1993 Royal St George's Open, after a six months' planning and production campaign ending in a scrum around their section of the main Exhibitors' tent, and lined foreheads elsewhere.

Upmarket, Nick Faldo's bright sweater styles decorated with colourful golfing images are to be seen on every course: so are high-crowned straw hats carrying the names of club-makers and so, to the chagrin of the traditionalist, is golf's version of the baseball cap. Fierce competition abounds in the wet weather gear market; even here, colour and fashionable cut are key weapons of the makers, who wage war with TV commercials.

From the fairway to the cat-walk

It would be interesting to compare the weight of clothes worn by Victorian women golfers with that of the short skirts of the 1920 flappers and the (apparently) featherweight shorts and tops that suffice, but only just, these days. They wore hats with huge brims, boaters, lace blouses, starched leg of mutton sleeves, long skirts, substantial undergarments that included whale-bone corsets, and were shod in button boots. The skirts were a bother in a breeze, especially when putting. The solution was the "Miss Higgins", a band of elastic material slipped over the knees and designed to restrain the skirt from billowing out at crucial moments.

The first woman, between the wars, to wear trousers caused more than a ripple. Grace Minoprio's play, in the 1933 English championship, made less of a stir. More modern players should pause before donning shorts or slacks, and take to heart the poet's lament about how his "sweeting" looked when retreating. Versace trousers, cashmere sweaters, designer blouses and shoes in pastel shades enliven the scene, though Alan Shepard has an irrefutable claim to have been the most expensively kitted-out golfer of all time. To hit shots on the moon as he did with a sawn-off 6-iron during the 1971 Apollo 14 mission, the first essential was a spacesuit.

PRETTY BUT...

Gracefully swaying ankle-length skirts and extravagant millinery fascinated magazine illustrators yet frequently frustrated the wearers. Joyce Wethered, the great British champion, pointed out that such encumbrances did not help in efforts to observe the game's golden rule: "Keep your eye on the ball." Many players resorted to the "Miss Higgins", a restraining band tied round the skirts which was useful when putting on a windy day.

TECHNICOLOR TRAVELLER

Payne Stewart (right) is famous for his colourful outfits, normally in colours of the NFL's American football (gridiron) teams. He will normally wear the local team's colours in the final round and here is playing on the US PGA winter circuit near San Diego.

BARE NECESSITIES

Barb Mucha, from Ohio, a three-time winner on LPGA circuit, putts at the 1995 Nabisco Dinah Shore tournament at Mission Hills, in what amounts to the modern lady professional's uniform.

225

COMPUTER-AIDED DESIGN

The thought that such instinctive grace as Seve Ballesteros displays when swinging a golf club could possibly be evaluated, let alone improved upon, by a box full of transistors sounds like a heresy punishable by a St Andrean thunderbolt. But in 1991 the USGA granted $2 million for their South African-born technical director, Frank Thomas, to expand their Research and Test Centre.

Part of the money is being used in a computer programme in which glass marbles attached to the club and to key points of a golfer's anatomy – shoulders, hips, elbows, wrists, knees, and ankles – are used as markers whose movements during the swing are picked up by infra-red cameras and fed into a computer. A model is produced on the monitor screen that shows precisely the path of each moving part, of players and equipment, that makes up the swing, from start to finish. The swing record is shown milli-second by milli-second.

Critics of photographic sequences of famous swings have pointed out that inadequate shutter speeds can falsify the position of various components of the swing at any given moment. Andy, the USGA Android, who on a monitor screen looks like a cross between the Michelin Man and a peacock displaying his tail feathers, overcomes these difficulties. What golfer *think* they are doing, and what Andy knows and records they are doing, can obviously be two entirely different things.

Thomas, as design engineer for a club-maker before joining the USGA in 1974, took the industry into the space age by his innovative use of graphite shafts. Not that he is about to tell people how to swing a club: this is not, he thinks, the business of the USGA. Teachers, however, are alert to the possibilities of using the Android to analyse and instruct.

What drives on Thomas's team

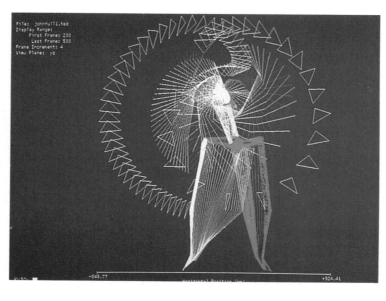

SWING TRUTHS ... *revealed by computer, milli-second by milli-second*

is the opportunity for original research. His assistant is Bernard Soriano, a Hawaiian with impeccable space-age credentials. After reading mechanical engineering at the University of California, Soriano worked on satellite guidance systems for Hughes Aircraft before joining the USGA, who co-operate with academics from Princeton, LeHigh and Brooklyn Polytechnic Universities in the study of the flight of golf balls and the efficiency of clubs in propelling them. Space-age materials, for example thermo-plastics, are already important ingredients in ball cores and covers.

A major strand in research as far as the day to day traffic on a golf course is concerned is the routine, long-established checking of balls submitted by makers, which must conform to R&A/USGA standards. The size (1.68 inches) test is carried out at 23˚C (±1˚), and to pass it a ball must fall through a 1.68-inch ring gauge under its own weight in fewer than 25 out of 100 randomly selected positions. It must be symmetrically spherical, a property measured by comparing the flight when speed (238 feet per seond) and differing

spin are imparted by a system of rubber rollers after the ball has been fired out of an airgun.

The balls are propelled down an indoor range, breaking through light screens as used to measure the velocity of a bullet. Computer evaluation follows. The use of a wind tunnel for this work was discontinued because creating the necessary laminar (smooth) flow of air was not possible, and the results were therefore flawed; hence the invention of this Indoor Testing Range (ITR) which turns the problem around and solves it by monitoring ball performance through the air.

A ball's initial velocity must not exceed 250 feet per second, and the average distance covered by the ball in carry and roll must not exceed 280 yards, plus a tolerance of 6 per cent, which will be reduced to 4 per cent as test techniques are improved. Testing for this is done on an outdoor range, with a centre-line within 2½ inches of level. The balls have been fired down it for many years by a driver-wielding mechanical device famously nicknamed Iron Byron, after that scarcely less reliable human swinger of that ilk, Nel-

son. As soon as the test ball comes to rest, the distance it has travelled is immediately transmitted to researchers by sensing devices known as geophones, buried the length of the test range. Iron Byron now has a clone beside it. Possibly, in this innovative age, the son of Iron Byron should be named Graphite Kite, after another model of consistency.

Soriano says that few balls are rejected, which means that the struggle to protect the skill factor is not without its successes. Despite the money and hype devoted to late twentieth-century golf gear, the balance between golfer, his or her gear, and the golf course has not changed very much. Thomas pointed out to the World Scientific Congress of Golf at St Andrews that the driving distances of the best professional players have increased only 12 yards since 1968 (he was no doubt excluding John Daly). Average *winning* scores improved by only one in 21 years.

CAD does the game a good turn

Computer analysis is also being used to determine how different clubhead designs perform, though the researchers are not yet ready to do more than make comparisons. The truth is that club design, despite all the manufacturers' claims made on behalf of their innovations, is not wholly based on scientific principle, because the type of pure research now being carried out has not previously been performed.

Once the best formulation has been established, Computer-Aided Design (CAD) will presumably do the rest. CAD is already being used, for example, in the highly successful perimeter-weighting of club heads: successful in the market place, at least. Duffers still need to practise, however, for they cannot be sure of buying success with money alone. That is a situation which golf's ruling bodies are watchful to prolong.

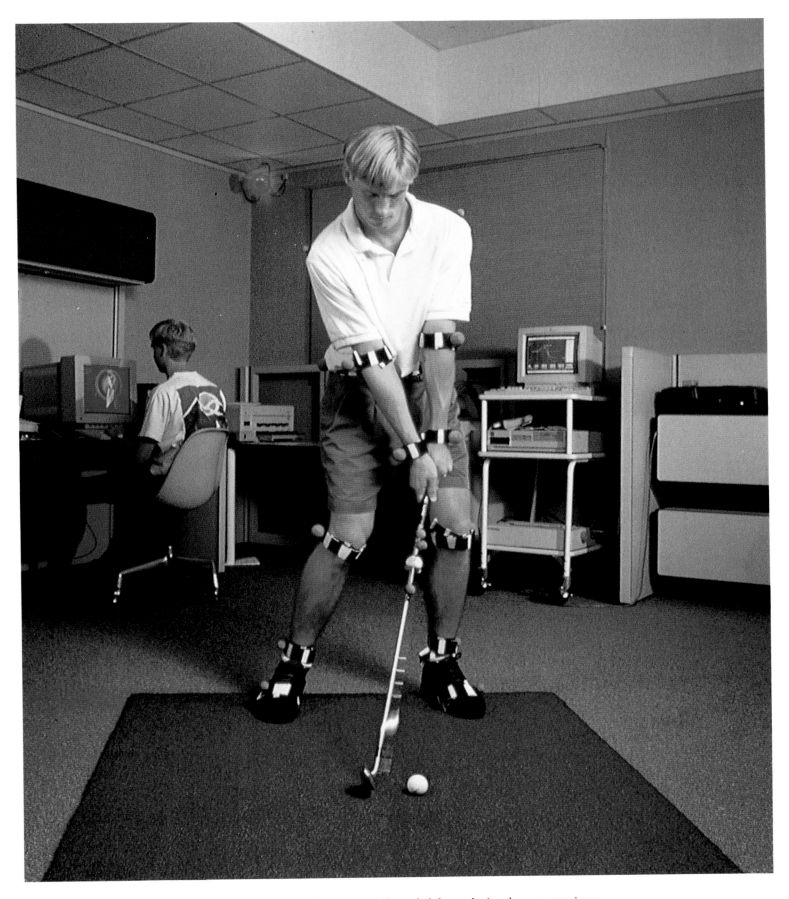

TELL-TALE KINEMATICS *Infrared cameras track the markers attached to the golfer and club, producing the computer image*

GOLF CULTURE AND GOLF POLITICS

Golf's inexorable conquest of Planet Earth has been hampered by wars, revolutions and charges of elitism, but never halted. Golf inspires the adulation of the crowd and fires the obsession of the collector, but it also harbours vestiges of racism and male chauvinism that continue to prove resistant even to the zealots of political correctness.

THIS GOLFING LIFE

John Hayes did his training on the roof of Bloomingdale's department store in Manhattan before winning the 1908 Olympic Marathon. Roof training is the *only* way many a Japanese golfer can practise the royal and ancient game, since the admission fees to clubs are in telephone numbers of yen, and space being limited in Japanese cities, some driving ranges (and there are about five thousand of them in Japan) are perched on the top of buildings. The Shiba driving range, reputedly the biggest, is on terra firma in Tokyo, if such a thing exists in Japan: it has three tiers.

For the Japanese, being a golf club member is a great source of "face". Here, obviously is a privileged, influential, not to mention well-heeled person. Japan's golfing population is uncertain, yet must be moving up towards 20 million, given that well over 20 million use either courses or driving ranges – and the sad fact is that more visits are made to driving ranges than to

courses. It's cheaper, by far, and it is still a sign of some affluence, and provides a fair amount of face, if you are seen to be in possession of a set of clubs.

Reliance on driving ranges for golf technique can have its drawbacks to judge by the actions of a group of competent-looking Japanese players observed recently on the Old Course at St Andrews. They were fine off the tee, but on turf they were in trouble. Could it be they had never hit a ball off a yielding surface of that nature?

Golf in the West can demand uncomfortable personal disciplines, such as getting up in the dark to reach a public course long before dawn, then to book a tee-time and wait until one's number comes up. It is just as onerous in the East: Jakarta in Indonesia has courses with a queue forming at 3.30 a.m. But it is not necessary to wait for daylight: there are floodlit courses for the super-keen and the insomniac from Los Angeles to Dubai.

Nothing new about a loud crowd

The present writer, after watching a Worplesdon Foursomes final late in September 1991, adjourned to the club's television set just as the Ryder Cup was reaching the climax of Bernhard Langer's final errant putt amid the sandy wastes of Pete Dye's Kiawah Island course in South Carolina, watched by a huge, brightly dressed, be-flagged crowd.

The difference in atmosphere was like a blow in the face. It was almost like watching a bar-room brawl after a scene from *The Importance of Being Earnest*. Only an occasional "Good shot" or restrained applause disturbed the autumnal peace of Worplesdon (off-line shots received the gentle therapy of silence); at Kiawah tribal howls of dismay or triumph bore witness to the effectiveness of the pre-Cup hype about the "War on the Shore".

It must be said that excesses of hero-worship have not diminished to any great extent over the years.

Young pros playing with Arnold Palmer, with his army in vociferous attendance, could find it daunting. If Palmer could arrange it, he would make his putt the last, for if it was not, an opponent would have to putt to the accompaniment of the army thundering off to the next fairway: they had not come to see tyros.

Macdonald Smith was less sympathetically treated at the 1925 British Open, when inadequate stewarding at Prestwick is held to have cost him the championship as he was buffeted by the crowd and lost the five-stroke lead he had taken into the final round.

Golfing relics for the aficionado

Golf is a wonderfully versatile advertising medium, which also makes it a collector's dream. Much of the ephemera connected with golf is collectable on aesthetic grounds, notably posters and art work on a wide range of objects – blotters, travel advertisements, pottery, any number of oil paintings, calendars, postcards and bookplates. There are few areas of human endeavour into which golf cannot be dragged to boost some product or other, and it has been a staple, until recently,

THE WONDERS OF MODERN TECHNOLOGY *Floodlit golf at the Emirates GC, host to the Dubai Desert Classic Tournament, an early-season stop on the European Tour*

SWINGING PARTY *American supporters raise voices and flags in triumph as the 1991 War on the Shore is won and the Ryder Cup regained at Kiawah Island*

229

for the tobacco trade. A mint set of golfers' cigarette cards issued by Cope Brothers of Liverpool in the 1900s will set you back £2,600 ($4,030). Postage stamps are a particular feature of golfing interest.

Phillips of Chester are among the acknowledged leaders in auction sales of historic golf equipment. Anything pre-dating 1800 is of immense value. Phillips issued a note of caution in one of their catalogues. they believe that no more than six or seven dozen clubs can safely be attributed to the eighteenth century. Two-thirds of these are irons, and the rest "play clubs", or drivers. Few putters of the period have survived: such clubs have, typically, square heads with no undercut at the toe, and the top and bottom lines of the clubs are parallel. Lucky finders of such a club can expect to raise far more than say the £1,800 made in 1994 by an early nineteenth-century lofting iron.

Members of a Highland club, Fortrose and Rosemarkie near Inverness, had a valuation done on a collection of old clubs which had lain for years in an unlocked cabinet beside the members' bar. The answer was a quarter of a million pounds; one club alone, a square-toed, dish-faced heavy iron, dating from the seventeenth century, was valued at £100,000 ($155,000). The collection was put in a bank, and replicas made. Even they were to be housed in a locked showcase.

Championship medals are in a class way above gold dust. Bobby Locke's four Open medals raised £82,000 ($127,000) – the 1949 Sandwich medal the costliest, at £24,150 – in a 1993 auction. The lovely Spode bowl in Imari, Japanese style, won by a Bow of Fife golfer in 1814, was bought for the magnificent collection being assembled in the Valderrama clubhouse on the Costa del Sol. Another treasure bought for the Spanish club was the £199,500 ($309,000) oil sketch *The Golfers, a Grand Match*, one of the best-known images in all of golf.

Other striking sales were of a book of rules from Musselburgh GC, which went for £30,000. Prices

MOST VALUABLE MEDAL *(middle bottom) from short-lived Caledonian Club, 1811–13*

are generally lower now than in the 1980s, partly owing to the absence of Japanese collectors, which is likely to be the more marked following the Kobe earthquake.

Satisfying the thirst for figures

Among modern golf's most praiseworthy developments, certainly at the top level of the game, are the excellent scoring systems that keep galleries in touch with tournament progress. Bob Harlow started the trend on the nascent US Tour in the 1930s, and they can be seen at their best at the Opens. Not only is there a giant board at the 18th, showing the leaders' scores and those of the players approaching the green, but at every green there is a board giving the position of the players approaching.

All has been brought to a fine simplicity, with red figures indicating that a player is beating par, black for over par. At Opens no detail is allowed to escape the media, whose working desks are faced with

huge boards detailing every score at every hole. Shortly after every notable round, there is a conference starring the player concerned, and documents detailing every stroke taken and with what club are circulated.

Every Monday since 1986, Sony have issued their world golf rankings. (Ping perform a similar service for women's golf.) This was

the first serious attempt to set the performances of golfers worldwide in order of excellence. Bernhard Langer was the first to head the "Sony", but has never been at the top since, for Greg Norman, Nick Faldo, Seve Ballesteros, Ian Woosnam and Nick Price had much the best of it over the rankings' first decade.

Points are awarded on the basis of official events from the various tours, and are related to the quality and strength of the players involved. There is a three-year roll-over, but most recent events are given extra weighting. Winning majors is the quickest way to climb the rankings.

Statistics in golf are beloved of the Americans; yet there are times when statistics seem particularly mendacious. A player may be high in the money list, yet according to his or her figures for driving distance, ability to reach greens in the regulation number of strokes, skill in getting down in two from a bunker, and average number of putts per round, not be top rank at any of these activities.

Winning tournaments is all a matter of getting it all together in the same week. For those who fail, there is always the consolation of the 19th hole, where the barman will (sometimes) be prepared to lend a sympathetic ear. One thirsty landlord, unwilling to wait that long for consolation, adapted his golf trolley to transport a fair selection of drinks. Traditionalists would call this cheating.

PITCAIRN'S POT *Golf's first-known prize, the Bow of Fife Bowl*

GOLF AND POLITICS

Racism in Golf

Race has been the greatest source of friction in golf. Racial problems started for the USGA right away. Their first president, Theodore Havemeyer, donor of the original US Open trophy, was faced with player rebellion at the second ever US Open, at Shinnecock Hills, on Long Island, in 1896.

The field was all white, except for two players. Both were entered from the host club. One was John Shippen, who worked at the club as a caddie. He had a black West Indian father and a Shinnecock Native American mother. The other was Oscar Bunn, a full-blooded Shinnecock.

Shippen's testimony, to the writer "Red" Hoffman, many years later, was to the effect that Havemeyer told the white pros that the Open would proceed with them or without them. Result: all present teed off for the 36 holes, over which the (one-day) Open was then played.

James Foulis, from the Chicago Club, became the first Scot to take the title. He won by three strokes from the defending champion, Horace Rawlins, thanks mainly to a second round of 74, a score not equalled until the coming of the Haskell ball, in the development of which Foulis was to play a significant part.

Shippen shared the first-round lead, finishing joint fifth in company with H. J. Whigham, Charlie Macdonald's son-in-law, who had won the Amateur title the previous day. No black man has come closer in the following hundred years. Shippen did play again twice, but did not make the top 20 either time.

Chances of black success were sharply curtailed by two factors. The first was economic, though there was, from 1928, a black equivalent of the PGA, the United Golf Association. When a black tour started up, even more intermittent and a good deal poorer than the PGA circuit, good crowds (of blacks) turned up, for not many had seen any of their race playing golf, certainly an elite sport where the black masses were concerned. White golfers played in these events, but there was no cross-fertilization, so to speak, in the other direction, for a compelling reason.

This was the second factor, namely a clause in the 1916 constitution of the US PGA stating that non-Caucasians could not be members. It was not deleted until 1961, and very few black pros managed to jump the gun and appear in PGA Tour events before that.

Charlie Sifford was the most notable of these. Born in 1923 in Charlotte, North Carolina, he began as a caddie, served in the US Army, later acted as private pro for the singer Billy Eckstine and won, almost routinely at one stage, the Black Open. He also won the Long Beach (54-hole) event, and the Puerto Rican Open.

Like many other blacks, he was barred from this hotel and that restaurant, and received death threats when he began to play on the tour. He was heckled when he was the first black to play in the South (in the Greensboro Open), and withdrew.

Money talks; golf listens

The end of the PGA's Caucasian clause came, in one sense, because of financial considerations. The Los Angeles Open always showed a laudable disregard for the clause, while George S. May took no notice of it, and carried on with his independent "World Championship" in Chicago, offering large purses and staging pro-ams with such black heroes as Joe Louis. Here and there states began to legislate against exclusion of blacks from courses.

But mostly the PGA clause stuck, Sifford usually having to omit the southern leg of the tour. The clause came under attack in the run-up to the 1962 US PGA Championship arranged for Brentwood, Los Angeles. In the previous year a letter from a black pro, Bill Spiller, to a lawyer about black exclusions from the pro tour led to a California state statute making it illegal to stage PGA tournaments on public courses from which blacks were excluded. Stanley Mosk, the State's attorney re-

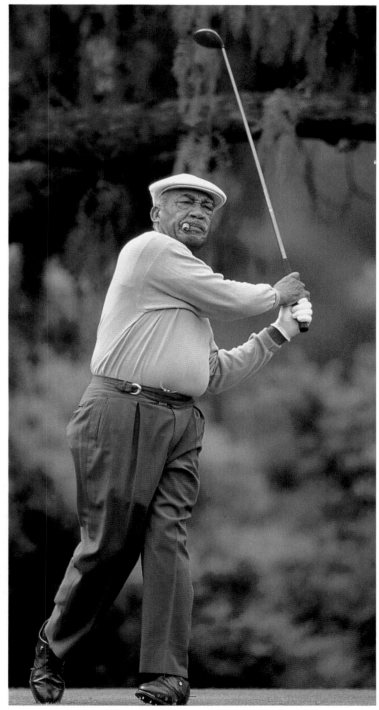

TRAIL BLAZER *Charlie Sifford, who challenged the Caucasian clause*

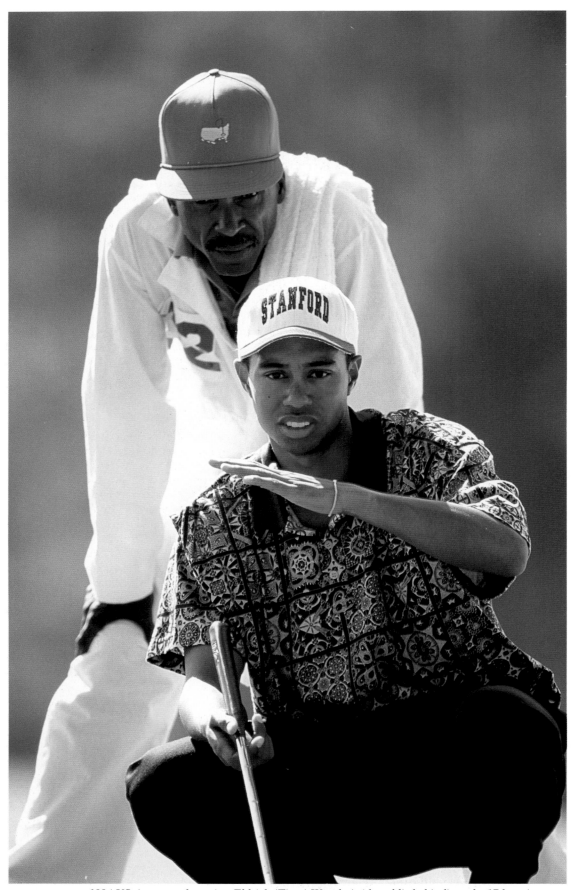

TIGER ON THE PROWL *1994 US Amateur champion Eldrick (Tiger) Woods (with caddie behind) on the 17th at Augusta*

sponsible for this, told other State's attorneys what he had done. Now the PGA were faced with purse losses on a grand scale. Totally without fanfare, they did the despised clause to death in November 1961. It made front-page news in the *New York Times*.

Sifford won the Hartford Open in 1967 and, appropriately, the LA Open in 1969. This was not enough to get him a place at the Masters, however, then the decision of past Masters. Lee Elder got in by winning a tournament after the Masters entry gate had been enlarged a little.

Sifford was turned down several times for club pro jobs at the end of his tour career, but was able to play on the Senior Tour.

Lucius Bateman, who died in 1972, was not so lucky. While his talent as a player can never be assessed, it is clear that he could teach. Tony Lema and Dick and John Lotz were among the boys he instructed who became tour players, a privilege denied to Bateman.

Shoal Creek gives an inch

Money, in the form of vested interest, had helped to expunge the Caucasian clause. It proved an irresistible force in support of the anti-discrimination front in 1990. Shoal Creek in Alabama, which had hosted the US PGA Championship once before, in 1984, had been chosen again, but the club was the centre of media attention long before the first player teed off.

Indeed, any teeing off at all seemed unlikely after the publication of a newspaper article by Shoal Creek's founder, Hall Thompson, which included the statement: "I think we've said that we don't discriminate in any other area except the blacks."

This bald statement of what, admittedly, encapsulated the opinions of a great many club members in the South, and not a few in the North, had the same potential to inflame emotions as South Africa's apartheid laws.

The wrath of black America and their supporters in the white community was at once directed at the

232

club, and the PGA must have had visions of Shoal Creek staging scenes comparable to those surrounding the desegregation of schools in the recent past.

It did not happen, because the threat of being involved, however remotely, in messy demonstrations, the danger of a boycott of their products and hence a costly loss of market share, prompted most sponsors of the ABC telecasts of the championship to pull out – which automatically meant no TV coverage.

Moreover, it was made clear by the USGA, PGA and tour administrations that none of their events would be staged by clubs who held to Hall Thompson's line. A positive PGA declaration, ostracizing "any club that has membership practices or policies that discriminate on the basis of race, religion, sex or national origin", had taken 29 years to arrive after the abolition of the Causasian clause.

On the regular tour the PGA moved the Centel Western Open from Butler National to Cog Hill, where it still is, sponsored now by Motorola. Poppy Hills replaced Cypress Point for the AT&T Pro-Am, and on the Senior Tour the Southwestern Bell Classic moved from Old Warson in St Louis to Loch Lloyd in Kansas City. Skokie, near Chicago, was replaced as site of the Ameritech Senior Open by Newby Stonebridge. There was also a move away from Amarillo Country Club on the Ben Hogan (now the Nike) Tour. Interlachen acquired the 1993 Walker Cup match when Chicago GC withdrew following the anti-discrimination rulings. Later, Tom Watson resigned from Kansas City CC when a Jewish applicant was blackballed.

Finally, Shoal Creek enrolled Louis Willie, a black Alabama businessman, as an honorary member just two weeks before the 1990 US PGA Championship, so battle commenced after all. No one was more grateful than Queenslander Wayne Grady, who won by three shots from Fred Couples for his one and, so far, only "major". In September 1990, Augusta National enrolled its first black member.

Four years later Eldrick "Tiger" Woods, America's first black Amateur Champion (and the youngest too), led Stanford University to victory in the Jerry Pate National Intercollegiate tournament at Shoal Creek. Woods, aged 18, was best individual, 10 under par. Hall Thompson was moved to tell Woods, who also has Thai and Indian blood, that he was a great player, and that he was proud of him.

Louis Willie is still the only black member at Shoal Creek.

Equal opportunities for women

When institutions as august (and often as adversarial) as Oxford and Cambridge Universities join in issuing a statement dissociating themselves from what they feel is "discriminatory and offensive", it makes front-page news. It certainly did early in 1995, when both seats of learning made clear their dislike of the membership policy of a club: no, not a golf club, but the London-based United Oxford and Cambridge University Club.

This (private) club excluded women from full membership. Women might join only as "lady associates" and so could not use the library. Lord Jenkins and other signatories of the joint statement began to resign *en masse* from the club.

If this news did not bring a slight blush to a great many cheeks at a good many golf clubs, it should have, for discontent about discrimination against women has soured golf for generations.

Although the cheap gutty ball was hastening the expansion of the game in late Victorian times, the chances of women becoming full members of a club were remote. Men of substance founded golf clubs: there were few women who could find the time or cash to play. In Victorian eyes, women were home-makers.

Scottish women were more fortunate, in that there were no restrictions against play on common land where the public links lay. As early as 1810 there was a competition at Musselburgh for the wives of the fishing community. At private clubs, springing up everywhere as

1900 approached, the outlook for women golfers was bleak. It did not mean there was no place for them in golf: Tom Dunn, the professional at Royal Wimbledon, had a daughter who made and mended clubs in his shop. Westward Ho! was among the few enlightened clubs who allowed women on their links. Musselburgh and Wimbledon founded ladies' clubs in 1872.

The women get together

Isette Pearson's energy and organizing ability gave the women's game a shape, a purpose and a championship, when the LGU was formed in 1893; she even managed to introduce a workable handicap scheme 40 years before mere males achieved agreement on the subject.

At almost exactly the same time, a number of women's clubs came into being, and of these Wirral Ladies, founded in 1894, and Formby Ladies (1896) are among the few survivors. The first women's club in America, the Morris County, New Jersey (1893), fell under the control of male members within two years of formation.

The general male attitude to women's golf was exemplified in the view of Lord Westwood in the Badminton *Golf*: "Ladies links should be laid out … on a smaller scale … [with] some longer holes admitting a drive or two of 70 or 80 yards … the posture and gestures requisite for a full swing are not particularly graceful when the player is clad in female dress." It was a wonder that any sort of stroke could be achieved in the female fashions of the time: large fanciful hats, long skirts on top of petticoats – not to mention whalebone corsets.

Wirral Ladies, 10 minutes by rail from Liverpool, was designed by Harold Hilton. The club was founded largely because ladies could not get into Royal Liverpool. Gentlemen were to be admitted as associates, a circumstance which must have sounded most satisfactory to the Wirral pioneers. The men paid a guinea (£1.05), the women three guineas entrance fee, and a guinea subscription. In 1907 Wirral were playing three other ladies' clubs,

Moreton, West Lancs and Formby. Wirral bought the course, too, though not until 1979 were the debentures for it paid off.

Wirral's most celebrated member was Doris Chambers (1883–1983). She always played at the gallop, and won the 1923 British Championship, which she celebrated with a lap of honour at her club on a gaily decorated draft horse. She captained the Curtis Cup teams of 1934, 1936 (Britain's first win) and 1948, and served with the First Aid Nursing Yeomanry in both world wars.

Gladys Ravenscroft, initially of Bromborough, was Wirral captain in her later years as Mrs Temple Dobell. *The Tatler* said she "was undoubtedly the 'flapper' of the 1909 Championship [and] shocked the gallery by playing with her sleeves rolled up." She lost in the fifth round that year, but took the British title in 1912, and in 1913 became the first Englishwoman to win the US Women's Amateur.

Northwood bigotry exposed

Lewine Mair's *One Hundred Years of Women's Golf* appeared in 1992, with a foreword by the Duke of York, which held that golf "is a game of equal opportunities and, with discrimination against women becoming a thing of the past …"

A fly-on-the-wall television documentary shown two years later by Britain's Channel 4 proved that to be an over-optimistic view of affairs. The film's producers were clearly on the look-out for a club with discriminatory possibilities, and in choosing Northwood, a London suburban club, they hit upon a propaganda jackpot for women golfers.

Not only did the club chairman have to resign after denying at the annual general meeting that he had threatened a (male) member with expulsion, which he clearly did in the TV film, but the second-class-citizen plight of Northwood's women members was brutally revealed. They paid subscriptions, but could not so much as speak at the AGM, let alone vote; nor could they play at weekends.

The upshot was that the board resigned and a new one elected.

Before the end of 1994, all members over 21 with two years' membership were granted full voting rights. The new board, said Press officer John Hawkins, deserved credit for "skilfully persuading die-hards" that the changes would benefit the club's reputation. The board did a thorough job. A 75 per cent majority was needed; they achieved 78.5 per cent. Similar changes were made at Tain in Scotland. Women's playing rights were not affected. Many Scottish clubs still do not grant equal rights to women.

The situation in the US is mixed. Minnesota state law specifically demands equal rights, but elsewhere many women go to law for such rights.

Marian Carr, secretary of the English Ladies' Golf Association, says the problem is slowly going away: new clubs in particular tend to start out on the right foot. It must be remembered that most women do play during the week, when many men cannot.

Women who insist on standing up for their rights, and who will step on any number of toes to get their way, are sometimes an embarrassment to the 80 per cent of members satisfied with the status quo. One advantage women do have is that it can be easier for them to get into a club than a man, since the competition in terms of numbers is less severe.

The World Tour

The long established, enormously prosperous and complex interests of the two most powerful professional tours, the America PGA and the European Volvo Tour, have, at the time of writing, made short work of a plan, put forward late in 1994 by Greg Norman and backed by Rupert Murdoch, for a World Tour of about eight events with fields composed of the world's top 40 players.

Many found it difficult to see what good Norman's circuit would contribute to the well-being of golf, in the US, Europe, or anywhere else for that matter, though it would clearly be of vast financial benefit to the fortunate 40 and to Mr Murdoch's satellite and Fox TV com-

DEFENDER *Ken Schofield made clear Europe's opposition to World Tour*

panies, who would show the events.

Furthermore, it was felt anything that would weaken the viability of golf's four major events must be resisted. The recent action of the controllers of the three majors played in America, in widening the entry to include more overseas players, was a wise move, aimed at protecting those events, because it heightens their world-class standing. Seldom recently have American players been in the majority in the Sony World Rankings top 10, but there is no doubt that overall the US deploy a far greater weight of talent than any other nation.

Norman's sales pitch for a World Tour went like this: "I want to finally see the Seve Ballesteroses, Nick Faldos, José-Maria Olazabals and Nick Prices playing against each other, week in, week out." The 40 would be made up of the 30 top golfers in the world, plus 10 invited players. A prize of $600,000 (£387,000) would go to the winner, out of a prize fund for each tournament of $3 million, and a $1 million bonus to the leading player at year's end.

Four tournaments would be staged in the US, starting at Atlanta the week before the Masters down the road at Augusta, one in Mexico, one in Canada, one in Scotland at Gleneagles, and one in Spain.

Jack Nicklaus seemed to be in favour, saying he had wanted it to

happen in America. Arnold Palmer counselled caution: think about the new tour, "but ... protect the US PGA Tour as it is today." Olazabal faxed his support; Bernard Gallacher did not. As Ryder Cup captain and member of the European Tour Board he had perhaps a more global view than most: "The World Tour is wrong," he said, "... it would send the wrong signals to long-term sponsors ... it wouldn't help young players to come into the game. It's a power struggle within management companies, backed by television."

Lanny Wadkins, the US Ryder Cup captain, concurred: "I think the public has seen enough greed from athletes." Wadkins spoke at a time when player power had blacked out the US baseball season, World Series included. The players' aim was to prevent a salary cap being applied by the club owners. At the time trouble was also brewing around the hockey rinks, which put that season on ice but not before the public, who were robbed of half the season.

For the Norman camp it must be said that the rise in standards outside the US has made clear the extent to which the free movement of players between one tour and another has been restricted. Ken Schofield, executive director of the European Tour, recognized this when he agreed that the top players

USPGA ULTIMATUM *US Tour boss Tim Finchem: "Players must choose"*

want to play more internationally, adding, "but that is the route the game is taking."

The immediate appeal of the Norman plan looked less than intoxicating when a poll revealed that none of the American players in the Sony top 30 would commit themselves to the World Tour.

Tim Finchem, who had recently been promoted to PGA Tour Commissioner to succeed Deane Beman, came down on the Norman plan within two weeks with a warning to his players that they would have to choose to play on one tour or the other.

Joe Dey, the first holder of Finchem's job, put forward a World Tour plan over twenty years earlier and retired in 1973 when it was not taken up. It involved 15 events from autumn to late summer. The sticking-point for Jack Nicklaus and others was that the stars *must* play in all of them. This smacked of nine-to-five salaried employment, inimical to the showbiz feel of golf.

Dey did introduce the first designated tournament roster, of three events that leading players had to enter, and Nicklaus and the other professionals complied. In fact, the main threat to the major tours may come from another direction.

Tour rules are basically the same either side of the Atlantic: members must play at in least 15 events in America; 11 in Europe. If they wish to play elsewhere when a tour event is available, they must ask permission. If this is given, it is often done with the proviso that the following year the players must enter the event they missed.

It will be left to the Federal Trade Commission to decide whether these restrictions violate the trust laws. Finchem's reaction to this danger – for if the verdict went against him the World Tour would have less trouble in attracting the stars – is to point out that the PGA Tour is not simply a set of golf tournaments, and that the PGA have done a great deal for charity and the development of golf in the US.

This is undoubtedly true, but

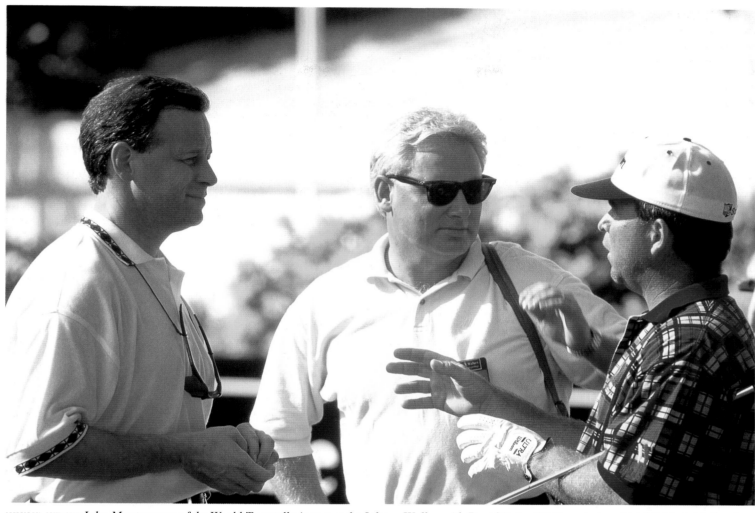

JAMAICAN JAW-JAW *John Montgomery of the World Tour talks it over at the Johnny Walker with David Yates (IMG, centre) and (right) Mark McCumber*

there is a history of courts being totally unimpressed by sporting bodies who imagine they can set up a body of rules which runs counter to common or statute law. Fine examples of this are the weakening of the British soccer transfer system after the players had recourse to legal action, and the total failure of cricket authorities to prevent Kerry Packer from starting his own matches featuring Test players.

So the established order prevailed, for the moment. A rethink of the World Tour plan, reduced to six events, attracted no takers, especially as the dates were a threat to established European events, and would interfere with long-term commitments made to sponsors.

The World Tour will not lie down

Despite its initial lack of progress, the concept of the World Tour is not dead by any means. The new tour appointed a executive director, John Montgomery, and at the Johnny Walker World (*sic*) Championship in Jamaica, a month after Norman's abortive scheme was unveiled, Montgomery was giving leading players further details about it. Nick Price and Seve Ballesteros were among the supporters of the concept, but Nick Faldo's conclusion was that it was not going to happen. "Nothing concrete" was his summing up, and he had one particularly awkward question to ask of its would-be organizers: "How do the tournaments rate when it comes to selection for the Ryder Cup team?"

Deciding how many Cup points should go to the winner of a 40-player "World" event, and how many to the victor in a US or European Tour event with the usual 150 field, might be a contentious business, especially where the players warring for the last Cup place were concerned.

Nick Price and Norman, first and second in the Sony rankings at the time, left the care of Mark McCormack's International Management Group in 1994. McCormack's opposition to the World Tour may or may not have been magnified by their defection, but his case against a scheme to fold such a tour into the existing major tours is strong.

The idea is to designate four events in each tour which all players good enough to qualify would be free to enter. McCormack thinks this would be unfair to the thirty-odd tournaments on each tour *not* chosen, whose sponsors and supporters had built up their events only to have them inescapably demoted in class. These events would inevitably become weaker.

The US, European, South African, Australasian and Japan tours held the second of their biennial meetings before the Players Championship in Florida, in March 1995. Their joint statement said much about improving "international scheduling" and international competition, which was to be done, by implication, by not upsetting the carefully and expensively constructed fleet of PGA apple carts.

How significant that not one word appeared on the burning subject of their discussions, the hoped-for World Tour. But then, like company directors threatened by asset-strippers – which is what the World Tour really is – the PGAs are undoubtedly wise to set out their own agenda.

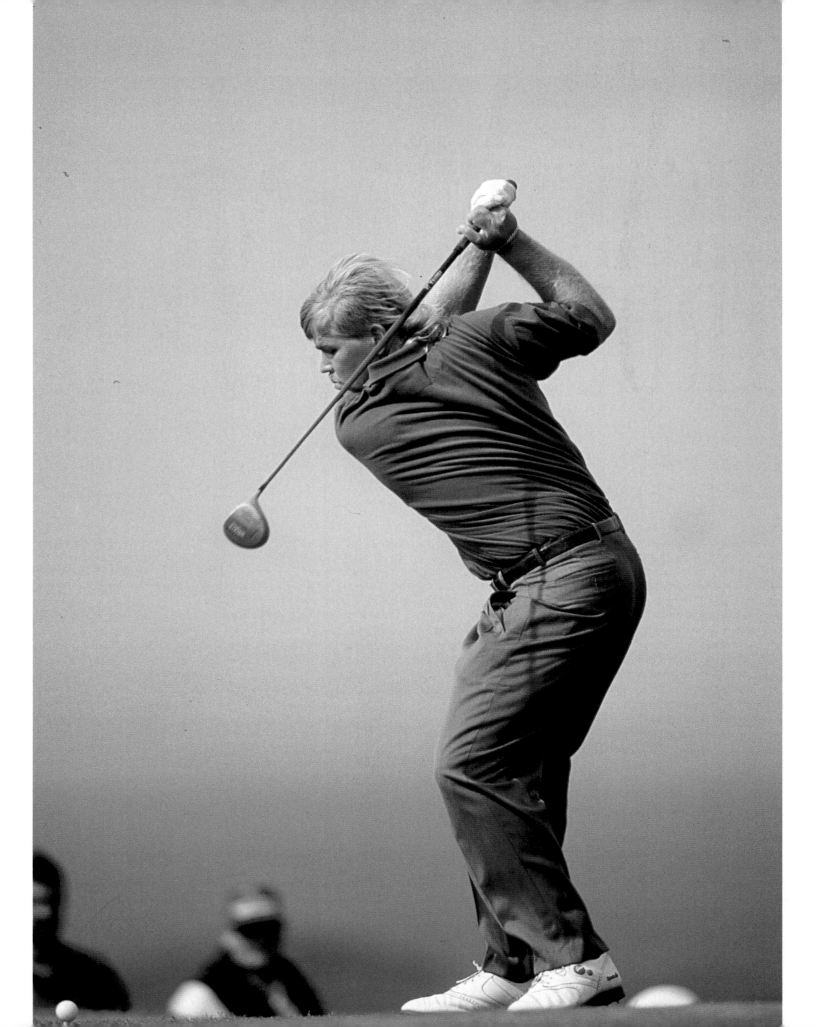

SCANDALS, DISASTERS AND TROUBLE-MAKERS

Golf is a game involving a projectile which may (legally) be dispatched at a velocity of up to 250 feet per second. Accidental death and destruction would seem unavoidable, while bad shots bring on suicidal tendencies.

In an age scarred by great suffering and slaughter in racial and religious conflict, words like tragedy and disaster, applied to strokes of ill fortune on a golf course, will seem to many to be inappropriate, incongruous, wild overstatements.

Yet the world must, for a giddy, disoriented and stomach-churning moment, seem to be coming to an end when a long-fought-for triumph is at the finger-tips, and then dashed away by a chance happening, or a Draconian punishment for a moment of carelessness, like Roberto de Vicenzo's card error that ruled him out of a Masters play-off.

Consider the thoughts of Richard Boxall, a European touring pro, as he was being carried off Royal Birkdale during round three of the 1991 Open Championship. Only three strokes behind the leader, perhaps 24 hours from immortality, his chances were suddenly ended when his left leg fractured as he drove off

GRIP IT AND RIP IT *John Daly applies his unvarying formula at the 1992 Open*

the 9th tee. He had won his first European Tour event the previous year; now his playing days might be over. They weren't, but he has not been so close to glory since.

Bobby Cruickshank from Granton-on-Spey never won a major, though this 5 foot 5 inch battler looked good at the Merion Open in 1934 when his ball hit a rock and bounced on to the green instead of sinking into a water hazard. Cruikshank joyfully threw his club in the air – and it came down on his head. Dazed, he finished joint third.

The slings and arrows

Fatal accidents are not all that uncommon, some of the most harrowing caused by clubs breaking, sometimes as the terrible result of a fit of ill-temper, as when Richard McCulough banged a club against a golf cart. The shaft broke, and flew up, cutting his carotid artery. Ian Cornwell may properly be recorded as the most unfortunate of golfers: he was struck twice, first on the leg and then on the head – which

knocked him out – by the same player, two groups behind, on the same round at Tehidy Park.

His fate was at least preferable to that of John Mosley, who in 1972 got into an argument about a green fee with a guard at Delaware Park, Buffalo. The dispute ended with a bullet from the guard's gun in

CRUTCH PUTT *Richard Boxall makes an early start on golfing rehabilitation*

Mosley's chest and he was "dead on arrival". His wife got more than a hundred thousand dollars in compensation from the City of Buffalo, and the guard got seven and a half years for second-degree manslaughter.

Tony Lema's death in 1966 is the only instance of a world-class professional being killed at the height of his powers. He and his wife Betty, and two other people, were killed when their light aircraft, flying them from the US PGA Championship at Akron to an exhibition near Chicago, crashed on to the 7th green of a course at Lansing, Illinois, and slid into a lake.

At least Lema had lived to enjoy an Open Championship triumph. By contrast, the mysterious death of John Douglas Edgar in 1921 is poignant in that, although he was considered by many to be an outstanding stylist, and was described by Tommy Armour as "the best golfer I ever saw", he was not granted time to fulfil his potential.

To start with, the First World War

237

cut years from his career, in which the outstanding feats were beating Harry Vardon by a distance in the 1914 French Open, and, having emigrated in 1918 to the US, winning the Canadian Open in both 1919 and 1920 against strong fields. Edgar, from Newcastle-upon-Tyne, wrote much admired instructional works, and his swing had elements that were not accepted as orthodox until the days of Byron Nelson 20 years on. Vardon predicted Edgar would become "the greatest of us all".

It was not to be. Edgar was found dead in a street in Atlanta, where he was a club professional. He had died from blood loss from a deep cut in his left thigh, which suggests that he is more likely to have been the victim of a robbery than, as the police theorized, a road accident.

There was no scintilla of doubt about the death of John White, the creative Scottish soccer international who was so central to Tottenham Hotspur's success: he was fatally struck by lightning while sheltering under a tree when his practice was halted by a storm over a north London club in 1964. Lee Trevino, Jerry Heard and Bobby Nichols were luckier when struck in 1975, but Heard was seldom a force again. Trevino needed surgery on his back.

UNLUCKY STROKE *Bobby Nichols, struck by lightning at the 1975 Western Open*

The mention of Vardon recalls what he must have felt was a tragic blow to his career, when ill health prevented his starting out in 1912 on a trip to America, for which he had arranged a passage … on the *Titanic*.

The game has seen mighty falls, none more spectacular than that of Marion Hollins, a powerful hitter who became US Champion in 1921, beating Alexa Stirling, who was trying for her fourth title in a row, by 5 and 4 in the final. Her father, formerly a partner of J. P. Morgan, lost a fortune setting up his own firm. His daughter made one.

She was a leader in the building of the Women's National Club on Long Island, which was not only an all-women club, but also entirely financed by women. An even bigger concept, the Pasatiempo club in the hills near San Francisco, rejoiced in a course designed by Alister Mackenzie. The club's opening day in 1929 offered an exhibition match comprising Marion and three legends of amateur golf, Glenna Collett, Cyril Tolley and Bobby Jones.

The following year the oil prospecting company she put together, with the help of Chrysler and Whitney money, hit the jackpot with its first well. Marion made $2.5 million, a vast amount in the depths of the Depression. Pasatiempo acquired a steeplechase course, race horses and polo grounds and a guest list that included leading financiers from the east, and Hollywood's finest, such as Mary Pickford, Jean Harlow and Will Rogers.

The Depression and the fact that she stepped a little too heavily on the champagne pedal at Pasatiempo led to money troubles, and Marion's health suffered when she refused medical attention after a severe concussion in a 1937 road accident. She had to sell her beloved Pasatiempo, and though she made an appearance in the 1940 Amateur, cancer killed her in 1944. Pasatiempo fell into disrepair, but better times returned, and it hosted the 1986 Women's Amateur, Kay Cockerill winning.

A candle-lit memorial service early in 1994 on the 18th green at

Moon Valley, Phoenix, mourned the passing of a more recent cancer victim, LPGA tour player Heather Farr, who was 28. A lone piper's lament was a reminder of how Heather had enjoyed the national music of the Scots at the closing ceremony of the Curtis Cup at Muirfield in 1984.

Yet, while they have breath in their bodies, golfers play on, as did the 43 competitors who entered, in 1933, for the first event for one-armed golfers; 37 of them had lost an arm in the First World War. The event has been held every year since. Even more amazing, a blind US golfer, helped by a coach who set him up for each shot, got round St Andrews in 88. British pro Ernie Jones lost a leg in the First World War, then made a career out of teaching in the US.

Daly, the demon and the drink

Like many other sports, golf is blessed, or beset, depending on their mood, by players whose talent is undeniable but whose temperament is not ideal. One such is John Daly.

One clue to his box-office appeal is his long sojourn at the top of the long driving statistics. Had he played one more round in 1994 he would have qualified to lead in that particular department of the game for the fourth year in a row. His driving distance figure in 1991 was 288.9 yards, the best for any of the 12 years in which the figure had been compiled.

He won $574,783 for 17th place on the money list in his first year on the tour, when he was named Rookie of the Year. Entering the 1995 season he has not achieved anything quite as spectacular .

Daly is big, and hits his weight – a fact he proved right away in commandeering the US PGA title at Crooked Stick in 1991. He went there as an unknown; four days later it was "Who's that playing with John Daly?" This Indiana course, one of Pete Dye's longest and most difficult, is well supplied with railway sleepers supporting pond banks, lots of rough toughened by heather, and greens with complicated, deceptive slopes.

The course is so long that David Feherty, who was seventh to Daly in the 1991 US PGA, said of it: "It's the first time that I've had to take the curvature of the earth into my shot-making calculations." Ray Floyd's conclusion about Daly's tee-shots there was: "I don't even drive that far when I go on vacation."

Add to this a confident short game, and you have a golfer to reck-on with: there is also a demon to reckon with inside the man, that prevents him from, so far, making the best use of the exemption to tour events that his US PGA title confers.

He began 1992 with the threat of a paternity suit from his girlfriend: they had split up before Christmas. They were reconciled by the summer, and daughter Shyna Hale Daly was born. Not long afterwards, Daly and his caddie Greg Rita, who had consumed "a few beers", were invited to leave a Newark-bound flight from Denver before take-off. Daly withdrew from the next tournament, the Buick Open, accusing a Buick official of starting rumours about him being drunk, and announcing that he would never buy a Buick. He managed to beat the 36-hole cut when he began his defence of his PGA title, but only by a stroke, and was 20 over par for the 72 holes at Bellerive, St Louis.

In September of 1992 Daly was back on top, taking the BC Open at Endicott, New York, by six shots. "The first tournament is not the hardest one to win. It's always the second one," said he.

His marriage to Bettye Fulford lasted only a year, and Daly was put on probation by the PGA Tour following an alleged assault on her at Christmas, 1992.

Daly really cut loose at Greg Norman's Open in 1993, by which time he had given up his excessive drinking and also got over a choco-late addiction. He drove the 421-yard 5th hole in practice, his ball stopping four feet from the pin. The 5th got its own back later, though Daly finished with a creditable tie for 14th place.

Complete with new girlfriend,

Paulette Dean, Daly was back in Britain for the Dunhill Cup at St Andrews in October. He, Fred Couples and Payne Stewart carried off the trophy and £100,000 each ($155,000), only Couples scoring better than Daly.

Next month Daly was suspend-ed indefinitely from the PGA Tour, after walking out midway through the second round of the Kapalua In-ternational in Hawaii. Commis-sioner Deane Beman said he had revoked Daly's probation.

So "Wild Thing" Daly – a not inappropriate nickname for a play-er whose watchword was "Grip it and Rip it" – did not start the 1994 Tour until March. He soon made two top-10 finishes, followed by a one-stroke victory in the BellSouth Classic. Again he drew the crowds, particularly at Augusta, where the netting at the end of the 260-yard practice ground had been raised to 65 feet in his honour, so to speak. It was raised further after Daly, at his third attempt, got a ball over the top of it ... but he finished tied for 48th place, with a last round of 78.

As in 1993, competition in 1994 ended early for Daly, who had in any case been hampered by lower back pain, after an unseemly car park scuffle with the father of a fel-low competitor at Akron's World Series in August. Daly had been ac-cused of driving into the group in front of him but Fuzzy Zoeller thought the accusation misplaced: "What we didn't read was that John was the second guy to hit ... Neal [Lancaster] hit first." Despite going through a drink rehabilitation pro-gramme early in 1993, Daly seemed to be finding it hard to adjust with-out his previous prop, the bottle.

Daly withdrew voluntarily from the Tour a month later, and suffered further blows to his pocket when Wilson Golf, Arnold Palmer's old employers and antagonists, and Reebok suspended Daly's contracts. Wilson's general manager Jan Thompson said his company would resume their relationship under a newly structured agreement "when Wilson is satisfied that John has met specific behavioural and perfor-mance objectives."

YEAR OF TURMOIL *John Daly had trouble in 1992 both on and off the course*

Fuzzy Zoeller's conclusion was that "When you're on top, they're shooting at you. And they're shoot-ing bullets. This one here was a direct hit."

Brown meets "Thunder" Bolt

Players of uncertain temper are not confined to the US Tour. Eric Brown, whose fiery spirit of compe-tition helped create a Ryder Cup record far above the British average, was quite ready to trade psycholog-ical punches with the leading Amer-ican club-thrower of his time (or any other, probably) Tommy Bolt.

Here is a small tragedy: Bolt was

considered by some to be among the top half-dozen at his profession, yet his skill has always been sub-merged in the public's conscious-ness by his tantrums. Salty, not to say toxic, legends attach to both these players. The truth of Brown's greeting to Bolt when they met in the 1957 Ryder Cup has been at-tested, however (though not Jimmy Demaret's assertion that the pair of them had been throwing clubs at each other from 50 paces). Once on the first tee, at Lindrick, Brown's invitation to Bolt to hit first was couched thus: "Your beat, sucker." Brown won 4 and 3.

"Thunder" Bolt, however, won the US Open the following year at 39, in his native Oklahoma, four ahead of Gary Player (aged 22). He led every round in heat and strong winds, and later passed the acid test of quality by keeping his game together in Senior competition.

If logos had been current in the 1950s, Bolt's would have resembled a javelin thrower, a reputation he nurtured by advising imitators to throw clubs *forward*, so as to avoid the trouble of having to retrace one's steps. Golf's favourite chestnut ends with Bolt's caddie explaining why the next shot is an easy two iron, not a nine iron as decided by Bolt: "There's only the two left in the bag."

A fulminating gallery of US golf's malcontents is presented in Al Barkow's books on the tour: notably Clayton Heafner, who would walk off the first tee if his name was wrongly pronounced by the starter, and Lefty Stackhouse, a Texan, who once beat a whole set of clubs into pieces against a tree stump, and another time refused help when he had thrown himself into a thorn hedge.

As the Irish-American satirist and golfer, F. P. Dunne, aptly put it: "…it's the kind iv game iv ball that ye play wit ye'er own worst inimy, which is ye'ersilf."

When is a scandal a scandal?

The scandal meter deep within us all is an untrustworthy instrument.

The prejudices that control it vary from generation to generation and by class, race, sex and a few other items.

When Maurice Flitcroft, a crane driver from Barrow-in-Furness, managed to finagle his way into the qualifying rounds for the British Open in 1976, scored 121 first time out and then withdrew, saying he had no chance of qualifying, all agreed: that *was* a scandal, and all the beleaguered R&A's fault too. So it had been in the same event in 1965, when Walter Danecki from Milwaukee (who said he was "after the money") scored 221 for 36 holes. Playing with Danecki can only have been unsettling.

Nowadays Open winners get six-figure prizes, but there was a sniffy response in 1900 when a sports good firm offered an *extra* $150 and a gold medal to the professional – other than Harry Vardon and J. H. Taylor – who made the lowest score in the Open at the Chicago club. The two Englishmen were considered sure things for first and second place, and that is where they finished, but to traditionalists the bonus sounded contrary to the spirit of the game. The USGA allowed it at the time, but never again would it sanction anything of that nature.

American spectators tend to accept the extreme partisanship of leading US Tour player Dottie Mochrie with rather greater equanimity than the British. Mochrie is reported to have made her plea-

TALENTED OKIE *Tommy Bolt's skills were obscured by his petulance*

sure plain when Laura Davies missed a putt in the 1994 Solheim Cup. "I don't really care," said Mochrie. "I know what it takes to play well and I know I am professional about it … I have to be happy with myself."

How far is Mochrie's behaviour calculated, and therefore scandalous, or spontaneous, and therefore merely regrettable? Either way, it was effective – and good box-office. Her attitudes were not copied by any other player on either side in a match of generally good humour and (although the phrase risks accusations of scandalous political correctness) sportswomanship.

A definite, abiding scandal in golf is slow play. Six-hour rounds in perfect weather on a course in top condition induced TV commentator Bruce Critchley to suggest after the 1994 Australian Open that the major tour bosses should follow the example of Brian Henning, the US

Seniors Tour commissioner; he tells each new recruit: "This is a four-hour tour … you must keep up."

Amateurs commit comparable crimes. Foursomes play can be brisk, but not, as in some matches in a recent Sunningdale Foursomes, if the player who is to play the second shot is still present on the tee when his partner drives.

The punishment fits the crime

The American novelist Henry James lived at Rye, England, close to a gem among links, but was so prejudiced against golf that his term for a course was "a series of beflagged jampots". Golfers are a forgiving lot, and tend merely to smile benevolently at such asinine jibes.

The depth of prejudice against what many folk think of as a suburban, middle-class, bourgeois pastime becomes clear when a plan for a £40,000 ($62,000) nine-hole course is scrapped, and approval is

Double-edged verdict

Cheating has ever been the worst scandal in golf, because it is an honour game, and no one is there to see you use the shoe wedge to ease your ball out of trouble. Some cheats seem to have a death wish as far as golf is concerned, like the young and skilful Scottish pro who, in full view of his fellow competitors trying to qualify for the Open, respotted his ball nearer the hole. His sentence of suspension was a heavy one.

Just as heavy, in its way, was the Nottingham Crown Court verdict reached in a libel case brought by John Buckingham against Graham Rusk and Reginald Dove, who reported him to the Sherwood Forest club's committee for cheating. Dove's evidence included expressions of disbelief at seeing Buckingham move his ball with his foot after his shot became stuck behind a tree.

The committee cleared Buckingham, who then sought to eradicate any lingering stain by suing for libel. The jury returned a verdict that was as palatable as Snow White's apple … poisonous in places. They found libel not proved because there was no evidence of malice on the part of the defendants in reporting Buckingham. The jury did not, however, want the verdict "to be perceived as proof that Mr Buckingham had definitely cheated".

He left Sherwood Forest, and could not afford to take further legal action against a newspaper that said an act of cheating would in future be known as a "Buckingham".

given for a £75,000 ($116,250) all-weather football pitch. The link is that both facilities were planned for inside the walls of Her Majesty's prisons.

The golf course was intended for Swaledale on the Isle of Sheppey in the Thames Estuary, and was "completely unacceptable" according to the Director General of the Prison Service, Derek Lewis; the Astroturf football pitch, full sized with landscaped flower gardens behind each goal, is for Parkhurst on the Isle of Wight, a maximum security prison for some of Britain's worst and most dangerous offenders.

Elmley prison in Kent, a category D, low-security gaol, not far from Swaledale, has a 13-hole pitch and putt lay-out, but it was not a burden on the tax-payers, having been built by the prisoners with waste materials. A prison spokesman added a no doubt unwitting touch of disdain by saying: "This golf course provides exercise for the elderly and less fit prisoners."

The influence of drugs

It is an error to suppose that because golf demands, almost alone among sports, a surgeon's touch and precisely applied power, there is no drug which will enhance performance. Dr Michael Turner of the British Medical Association says that drugs exist which would enable golfers to cheat pharmacologically.

It is indeed naïve to deny the existence of pain-killing drugs for abused elbows, muscle-building agents, and beta-blockers to steady the hands, as used by snooker players. All of these exist.

What does not exist is an overall testing programme. Amateurs can be tested, because it is a condition of receiving grants that they are subject to doping controls. Such a programme would incidentally be compulsory if golf were accepted as an Olympic Sport and professionals were involved in the Sydney 2000 Summer Games. The buck has been passed in the past from R&A to Tour authorities, and in the opposite direction.

The issue came to notice when Mac O'Grady, who as a player had a few high-profile disputes with former US Tour Commissioner Deane Beman, but who is making a comeback as coach to Seve Ballesteros and others, announced at the 1994 Masters that "seven of the top 30 golfers in the world are on beta-blockers." Sam Torrance said he had used beta-blockers in the distant past, but felt no benefit, Nick Price felt they had had a negative effect. There were no other admissions (though John Daly said a few months later that coke-snorting was going on, but no one took much notice). Nick Faldo neatly defused the issue: "I've even got grass on my spikes."

There would be great problems if testing were introduced on the Tours: what punishments should be imposed, and should the range of permissible drugs, especially ones for respiratory problems and painkillers, be wide or narrow?

The ruling bodies may, if ambushed by the discovery of a major drugs cheat, be left at the stable door watching the horse vanish into the distance. That *will* rank as a scandal.

GREENBRIER HIGH HINKS ... *and high-fives too as Brandie Burton and Dottie Mochrie (right) celebrate US progress in the Solheim Cup of 1994*

GOLF ECCENTRICS, COURSE CURIOSITIES AND BIZARRE HAPPENINGS

Oddballs abound in golf's literature, from P. G. Wodehouse's Oldest Member, by way of the hilarious Ring Lardner's diabolically truthful caddies and his hapless Mr Frisbie, to the country club satire of John. P. Marquand: these writers are outdone only by real-life characters, such as ...

A MOTLEY CREW

Harold Finch-Hatton

Eccentrics are frequently creative people. While practising his boom-erang throwing on the dunes at Harlech, no doubt to maintain his position in the Antipodean rankings as the Briton who could give the Aborigines a good run at their own game, Harold Finch-Hatton was spotted from the heights of Harlech Castle by the Crown Agent for Meri-oneth, William Henry More.

He went down to investigate, and the two of them got into con-versation. Finch-Hatton explained that he had recently returned from down under. The two men met again a few days later when More, who had little knowledge of golf, saw young Finch-Hatton at this even stranger, though royal and an-cient, pastime.

Finch-Hatton said: "Capital place for a golf links. Come on, let's lay one out ..." And so they did, says the club's historian, which is why Royal St David's, still under

ORDER & CONFLICT *Dame Ethel brought both*

the mighty shadow of Edward I's late thirteenth-century castle, was founded in 1894 on a made-to-mea-sure stretch of linksland, from which there is a view of Snowdonia which, once seen, is not easily forgotten. Finch-Hatton certainly had an eye for classic golfing terrain. More soon learned a great deal about golf, and for many years acted as secretary.

Finch-Hatton was the fourth son of the Earl of Winchilsea and Not-tingham, who had a gift for father-ing unusual offspring with highly developed sporting instincts. Harold's brother Denys was a big-hitting golfer, a celebrated hunter and pioneer aviator, a pursuit which cost him his life in a crash in Africa.

Not long before the First World War, Denys captained the Oxford University golfers in the Varsity Match. He achieved one of the greatest put-downs in the game's history when chided for conceding putts to a Cambridge player: "Do remember, Finch-Hatton, you are playing for your side and not for yourself." Finch-Hatton replied: "And do remember you are playing for neither."

Dame Ethel Smyth

Creative talent often comes with a powerful urge to swim against the tide. Dame Ethel Smyth was one such swimmer, making her mark as composer, writer, and equal rights campaigner (with the accent on votes for women) and, to a lesser degree, golf. Her musical works have long been neglected, though one of her operas *The Wreckers*, was revived at the 1994 Promenade Concerts at London's Albert Hall. Having stud-ied music at Leipzig, she turned from symphonies and operas to compose a battle-song, "The March of the Women", for the Women's Social and Political Union founded by Em-meline Pankhurst in 1903.

Just before the union began a window-smashing campaign in 1910, the two women practised stone-throwing, it is believed, on the 13th fairway at Woking GC. The practice was much needed, for the 13th almost lived up to its rep-utation for ill-luck as far as Ethel Smyth's dog was concerned: Mrs Pankhurst's first throw narrowly missed the animal. She and Ethel Smyth were soon scoring satisfac-tory hits on Government windows, and were briefly imprisoned in London's Holloway prison.

Ethel Smyth's rehabilitation with

CHARITY CAPERS *Mark Roe (in drag) and Robert Lee at a fund-raising event*

the establishment came with surprising speed. She was made Dame of the British Empire in the New Year's Honours of 1923. The new Dame was convinced that this turnabout was the result of her adroit handling of a skirmish in the war of the sexes at Woking, and the fact that Woking club member Lord Riddell was a friend of the prime minister, Lloyd George, who had evidently decided to let bygones be bygones, as far as militant women's movements were concerned: a house being built for him at Walton Heath had been blown up in 1913. Greens were dug up, and insurance cover had to be organized for the St Andrews clubhouse.

The Woking skirmish concerned male objections to women members (still temporary) taking a short cut leading past the men's changing-rooms. There was disquieting talk of no weekend tee times for women. A touch of humour from Ethel Smyth helped persuade the ladies to vote against using the short cut in future, a concession that was necessary, as she put it, "given the modesty of the British male".

Her attitude to the rules was not all it might have been, to judge from the report that when she lost her ball in a patch of heather, she sent to the greenkeeper's yard for a sickle to trim the offending vegetation. This is all of a piece with Victoria Sackville-West's valedictory judgment of Dame Ethel, who died in 1944 at 86: "Blinkered egotism could scarcely have driven at greater gallop along so determined a road. But although often a nuisance, Ethel was never a bore."

Count John de Bendern

The difference between an eccentric and a card is a matter of nice judgement: Count John de Bendern certainly qualified as a card, if one accepts the definition given by Arnold Bennett at the end of his eponymous novel as being "identified … with the great cause of cheering us all up". He played top-class amateur golf despite the intermittent, but still dreadful handicap, more usually suffered on the putting green, of being unable to take back the club.

Instead, in the same way that bowlers at cricket have felt unable to let the ball leave the hand, he would stand waggling club over ball on tee or fairway for what seemed an age before he could bring himself to strike. He still managed to capture (under the name John de Forest) the British title in 1932 at Muirfield. He was invited to play in the Masters at Augusta, and

SPIRITED PERFORMER *James Balfour of the Honourable Company of Golfers*

achieved immortality when deciding to step into the water to play a recovery shot at the 13th. Carefully taking off one shoe and sock, he took up his stance … placing his bare foot on dry land, the other, still shod, in the water.

Dame Margaret Ross

The most unlikely golf legend of them all concerns Dame Margaret Ross, said to be the original of Lady Ashton, the tragic, demented murderess in Donizetti's opera *Lucia di Lammermoor*, first performed in 1835. Dame Margaret was accused by enemies of her family of turning herself into a golf ball and spoiling their game by jumping into bunkers and wandering off line on the green.

"Singing Jamie Balfour"

The legends about James Balfour, better known as "Singing Jamie Balfour", secretary and treasurer of the Honourable Company of Edinburgh Golfers, elevate him to supercard and eccentric. Balfour was not only renowned as a singer of Scottish songs, but as a toper. It is said he had only to hear a cork being withdrawn to ask for "a glass o' that", whatever it might be.

Hence the tale about his fall into a pit on a building site. He asked a passer by to pull him out, but was refused, on the grounds that, once out, he would be unable to stand. Balfour then offered to run a race to the Tron Kirk for a bottle of claret. His rescuer must have thought this an easy way to obtain a bottle of claret, but Balfour set off at great pace and was waiting on the church steps, seemingly incapable of further progress, by the time the also-ran got there. "Another run to Fortune's for another bottle of claret," challenged the indomitable Balfour. He won that too; his two-bottle benefactor needed a sedan chair to get home.

THE RUB OF THE GREEN

Happy Valley

Golf began in Hong Kong in 1889, on a course which had no holes: tees, fairways and greens, yes; but holes, no. Foundation of the club, soon to be Royal Hong Kong, was mainly down to the enthusiasm of the Harbour Master, Robert Rumsey RN, and Gershom Stewart, who most fittingly became MP for Hoylake.

The inaugural course had no bunkers eicther, and for the explanation of this Chinese puzzle it is necessary to look to the military, who held the land. The course was laid out on the infield of the Happy Valley racecourse. Polo, football and hockey were played on it, and parades were held there too, though it was a marshy area, with a large pond in the middle, and the soldiers could foresee horses (and others perhaps) breaking their legs in holes.

Instead of bunkers, close mesh netting was laid down to catch errant shots. In place of holes, granite setts were placed on the greens which the players were required to hit in lieu of holing out. The research facilities of the USGA boffins would not be required to work out that hitting these setts was a far easier proposition than persuading putts to drop into a hole less than five inches across.

This happy (putting) state of affairs did not last long. The club acquired land at Deep Water Bay on the other side of Hong Kong Island. When the first course, complete with holes, was laid out there, it could be reached only by launch. It was improved, and re-opened in 1898. Later, golfers arrived by ponies, caddies making the steep trek over the hills from Happy Valley complete with tiffin. This, says the club historian Spencer Robinson, was always the same: cold saddle of mutton, cold gooseberry pie, and Watson's dry sherry … cost, one Hong Kong dollar.

Fanling

Now the club's main area of activity is on the mainland in the New Territories, which were annexed without seeking Chinese opinion, soon after the club was founded. Royal Hong Kong's three courses at Fanling are among the world's busiest.

The Hong Kong Open, thanks to the development of the Asian Tour, now facing competition from the Asian PGA Tour, has a most impressive list of winners. The first was Lu Liang Huan (Mr Lu), who later became pro at Fanling. Greg Norman, Peter Thomson, Kel Nagle and

Ian Woosnam also won the Open, always played at Fanling, whence Joe (the Pro) Hardwick has just retired. He succeeded Mr Lu, and among his pupils was Governor Chris Patton.

Between 11,000 and 12,000 Fanling golfers use the courses every week, including more than 100 Japanese a day, served by an army of 600 registered caddies. The register (popular since it involved having a photograph taken) was introduced to solve a rash of caddie troubles, including the time when a deputation of village elders came to request that an increase to 30 cents a day should be cancelled, because 30 cents was more than the average farm worker's pay.

Control was essential to ward off caddie strikes, during one of which 100 Sepoys were sent to act as caddies. Then there were difficulties at the nearest railway station, caused by crowds of would-be caddies fighting to get hold of members' bags.

Beware of tigers

Grave mounds were among the hazards in the early days at Fanling, as well as wolves and tigers. One tiger killed an Indian policeman, and there are still cobras about. There were countless jars of human bones too. The club paid 50,000 Hong Kong dollars in 1920 to compensate families for their removal.

A local rule bearing on tigers at an Indian course is at once helpful and disturbing: "A ball lying in a tiger's pugmark on the brown [which is the tropical equivalent of a green] may be lifted and placed without penalty." The Duke of Windsor was enabled, thanks to a local rule at Jinja, Uganda, to lift without penalty from a hippopotamus footprint. Another Uganda rule allows one to drop another ball if the ball in play comes to rest near a crocodile. An Arizona course has a similarly relaxed attitude (approved by golf's rulers) to dropping without penalty in case of an adjacent rattlesnake.

"Île Flottante de Golf"

Anyone who thought an île flottante was ice cream swimming in liqueur in a Parisian restaurant should visit Idaho, where the par three 14th hole at the Cœur d'Alène club is a movable feast – or beast if you miss it – because it is a floating green, surrounded by water. It is made of expanded polystyrene and is moved around daily, so that it can be a mere 100 yards from the tee, or as much as 175. *Flottante* also means vacillating and undecided, a state of mind easily induced by this novelty.

The only way players can reach it is by ferry. The designers actually had the nerve, as if all that water did not pose enough of a threat, to put a bunker each side of the putting surface. An enraged member may well have it torpedoed one day. The course was chosen as the most beautiful resort course in 1992 by *Golf Digest*. The ball-hunting concession for the lake must be worth a fortune.

ARBORIAL ANTICS *Nick Faldo trying a Spanish tree in 1993*

Seve Ballesteros considers such holes bad ones (like the island hole at Pete Dye's Sawgrass course in Florida, where the Players Championship is staged), for there are no shades of difference between complete success and utter failure from the tee: good holes punish by degrees, depending on the quality, or otherwise, of stroke.

Walt Disney Magnolia in Florida has armadillos, 1,500 magnolias, and a bunker on the 6th with a Mickey Mouse silhouette.

Tree irons and ladder of the law

Nick Faldo was upset to find that "his" tree by Pebble Beach's 14th hole was missing, victim of a storm, when he returned to the course in 1995 for the first time in three years. "I loved that tree," said Faldo, who had climbed it during the 1992 US Open in a vain attempt to find his ball, and raised a laugh by asking, when aloft: "Where's Jane?" Bernhard Langer did find his ball up a tree in a European Tour event, and played it out on to the nearby green, but didn't get his par.

Sir Simon Brown used a ladder when his partner Nigel Wilkinson, QC, put their ball on the Woking clubhouse roof: the intrepid Appeal Court judge, aged 57, used a putter and moved the ball to within a few feet of the pin. But he and Wilkinson lost the match for the Middle against the Inner Temple.

Till death us do part

Nearly every golfer who has played at all often at beautiful Ballybunion near Limerick on the west coast of Ireland, has sliced his opening tee shot one time or another into the village churchyard. Martin McDermott, of Los Angeles, who died aged 43, loved the course so much that in 1987 he had his body flown over to rest in that same churchyard.

McDERMOTT'S REST *Kilkenny Churchyard, near Ballybunion's first tee*

STRANGE BUT TRUE

Sounds a bit fishy

A golfer's hook has been known to catch a pike. Lennie Learmouth's hook at Wetherby, Yorkshire, landed his ball in a bunker, which was full of water. He used the rake to search for his ball and pulled out a 40-pound pike, which he believes had been marooned there when the River Wharfe returned to its normal course after the floods of the wet 1994–95 winter.

A few months earlier, America came up with an even fishier tale. Jerry Towns hit the green at the short seventh on the Woods Course, Cochran, Georgia. He was annoyed when it spun back into water at the front of the green, and amazed to see a 14-inch bass spit his ball back on to the green. This is entirely possible with a fish that size, said a professional bass fisherman. The ball ended nearer the hole than where it originally landed but Towns, shaken, missed the birdie putt.

Golfers are notoriously unsympathetic to the misfortunes of others, so the witticisms flowed when Worplesdon's captain Alec Justice gave a lift in a golf cart to the professional Alan Waters during the club's fashionable Mixed Foursomes, went off line a little and deposited him in the pond at the club's "signature" hole, the Pond Hole, all carry over a pond. The wags christened this "The Meeting of the Waters". It was said to be the only time the pro had gone into the pond.

Double eagles and aces

Holes in one are routinely described as shots in a million, though a statistical survey in the US established the odds for an average player at 42,942 to 1. There are thousands every year, and there have been some unusual combinations, like the man and wife who holed out on the same hole, but from the men's and women's tee respectively. Brothers once holed out, one after the other, at St George's Hill. Arnold Palmer

INDOOR CHAMPION *Enid Wilson tees off at the Grosvenor House Golf Ball, 1931*

managed a five-iron hole in one on consecutive days at the same hole. He had evidently got the range for ace number two, for it dropped straight into the hole from a great height, scarcely touching the sides.

Pride of ace must go to John Hudson. Bernard Gallacher won the Martini Tournament at Royal Norwich in 1971, but Hudson, then 25, commandeered the headlines (and a page in *Time* magazine). He holed out at the 195-yard par three 11th, and with his next shot holed out at the 12th, a par four of 311 yards. That is how Hudson went, uniquely for a major professional event, eagle, double eagle. He took 70 strokes for the other 16 holes, and in the end finished ninth.

Harry Vardon managed only one ace, so the hole in one is not essential to a successful career. In any case the double eagle, or albatross (three under par), really is something to shout about. There were 24 holes in one on the European Tour in 1994, compared to only four double eagles, though on the standard golf course of four par threes, four par fives and 10 par fours there are equal opportunities (statistically at least) to score aces and double eagles. The US Tour don't bother to list mundane holes in one, but managed three double eagles in 1994, the longest being the

527-yard 15th at Oak Hills, which Mike Donald negotiated with a driver and four wood. Several years in the 1980s were albatross-less.

Watch the birdie

Birdies, eagles and albatrosses are all very fine, but birds can be provoking: members of a Surrey club took to setting out on a different kind of round, armed with small-bore rifles, with which to cut down the number of feathered ball-thieves. The hunt gave rise to a neat headline, "Crows the Bogey". Three times British Champion Enid Wilson reports that visits to a small island off the St Enodoc course in Cornwall could be fruitful: birds nesting there sometimes had golf balls as well as eggs in their collections.

The increasing number of urban foxes can be a problem: one almost brought on apoplexy when a society member at a London suburban course who gave a sweet to a (begging) fox during the morning round saw the same animal make off with his ball in the afternoon.

When it comes to wildlife, the Wild Coast Country Club near Port Edward in South Africa is hard to beat, as Ernie Els will confirm. He was chasing Hendrik Buhrmann on the final day of the 1994 Wild Coast

Challenge when he almost stood on a yard-long, highly poisonous night adder. His previous shot was a 350-yard drive: his next took too much turf, and flopped into a pond. It cost a bogey six. Still shaken, Els hooked his drive on a next for a double bogey five, and finished joint second, five behind Buhrmann. "It's no excuse," said Els. "This is Africa and I've seen enough snakes before."

Four-legged friends

Among golf's most unusual caddies are surely the ones with four legs, a well-fitting white fur coat and a tendency, when piqued, to spit: llamas from South America. They carry two bags and cost $100 per round (llama handler included). The llamas are available for hire at Talamore at Pinehurst, North Carolina. Talamore is a Gaelic word meaning "land of great value".

Call the USGA stuffy if you like, but their contention that the use of llamas as caddies is not within the rules is indisputably correct. "Caddie" is defined as "one who carries or handles a player's clubs during play and otherwise assists him in accordance with the Rules". To start with, llamas have no hands. Their rating at club selection is not known to the present writer.

The world's oldest golfer

George Selbach lives in Florida, like many retired Americans but none among them can rival his claim to the title of the world's oldest golfer. He played nine holes in 44 strokes for a television programme at the age of 104. A few years further on, he now only watches the game – with a little putting on the side. Possessed of a fine short game, he held a course record at an Ohio club with 64. The name of the man who took that record from him brings home just what being over 100 means: it was Jim Barnes, US Open champion in 1921. Another way of putting it is to reflect that Selbach's father fought at Gettysburg. Beating his own age was routine for Selbach: he managed a 77 when 96, and two holes in one at 97.

CROCODILE HAZARD *Ball hunters may find the 13th at Sun City very unlucky*

CHRONOLOGY

"Tour guides," said John Betjeman, leave their clients "shipwrecked on a sea of facts." In case the dates listed below inflict similar sinking feelings upon readers, they should take comfort in the fact that there are only 10 truly significant dates in golf history. The first is not included hereunder, since painstaking research has failed to reveal when a Scottish shepherd invented the game. 1502: when James IV of Scotland stopped trying to stop people playing the game and took it up himself. *Circa* 1600: the invention of the feathery. 1848: gutta-percha ball. 1744: first club founded and rules codified. 1860: British Open begins. 1888: United States fuse lit in Yonkers. 1898: Haskell ball, and Gammeter's winding machine. 1926: steel shafts legalized. 1947: TV coverage of US Open.

1457, 1471 and under James IV of Scotland in **1491**: Parliament forbids golf and football for hindering military training

1502 Anglo-Scottish Perpetual Peace Treaty
James IV, first recorded golfer, buys clubs and balls

1513 James IV killed at Flodden

1553 Archbishop of St Andrews confirms right to play over links

1567 Mary Queen of Scots accused of playing golf a few days after the murder of her husband Lord Darnley

1592 Golf at Leith forbidden for interfering with worship on Sunday

1603 James I (and VI of Scotland) ascends English throne: he appoints a royal club-maker and encourages both his sons to play

1600 *(circa)* Feathery ball is introduced

1618 James I approves Sunday play … after worship

1637 Boy is hanged in Banff, Scotland, for stealing golf balls

1646 Charles I, prisoner of Scots, plays at Newcastle-upon-Tyne

1650 Charles II plays after being crowned King of Scotland

1689 Royal link with golf is broken as William III succeeds James II

1744 John Rattray, Edinburgh surgeon, wins first club competition for Hon. Co. of Edinburgh Golfers' Silver Club
First recorded code of rules

1754 St Andrews men set up similar Silver Club contest

1759 St Andrews men change Silver Club knock-out to stroke play

1766 Foundation of Blackheath club, first in England

1786 First mention of golf in US: Charleston club is founded

1834 Royal and Ancient title is conferred on St Andrews Club

1848 Gutta-percha is ball introduced

1856 Continent of Europe's first club is founded at Pau, France

1857 Inter-Club foursomes, first Championship Meeting, is suggested by Prestwick; won by Blackheath

1858 Robert Chambers wins individual Championship

1859 Death of leading professional Allan Robertson

1860 Willie Park wins Championship Belt offered by Prestwick for annual Championship, beating seven other professionals

1861 Tom Morris Senior wins first "Open" as Championship is widened to admit amateurs

1864 Westward Ho! (Royal) North Devon Club, founded

1869 (Royal) Liverpool Club formed at Hoylake, former race-track

1870 Young Tom Morris lands hat-trick of Opens at 19 and retains Championship belt

1872 Silver claret jug offered by Prestwick, St Andrews and Honourable Company of Edinburgh Golfers as perpetual trophy for Open. Young Tom wins again

1875 Young Tom dies, aged 24, soon after wife's death in childbirth

1878 Oxford beat Cambridge in first University match

1885 Royal Liverpool organize first British Amateur Championship, won by Hoylake member, A. F. Macfie, from Scotland

1888 Formation of St. Andrew's Club, Yonkers, New York, nicknamed the "Apple Tree Gang"

1890 John Ball is the first amateur and Englishman to win Open, at Prestwick

1891 R&A rule hole width at $4\frac{1}{2}$ inches, minimum 4 inches deep

1893 Ladies' Golf Union founded in Britain
Lady Margaret Scott wins first Championship

1894 J. H. Taylor first English pro to win Open, played in England for first time, at Royal St George's, Sandwich

1894 United States Golf Association formed

1895 USGA stages first Amateur Championship, won by Charles Macdonald from Chicago; Open won by Horace Rawlins, an English pro; and Women's Amateur, won by Mrs Charles Brown

1896 Harry Vardon, Channel Islander, wins British Open

1898 Coburn Haskell patents ball with gutta-percha cover over rubber bands wound under tension around core

1900 Vardon tours US and wins US Open by two shots from Taylor
Freddie Tait, former Amateur Champion, killed in Boer War

1902 Sandy Herd pioneers Haskell "Bounding Billy" all to win British Open from Harry Vardon and James Braid by a stroke
Rib-faced clubs introduced to gain control over lively "Haskell"

1904 Walter J. Travis lands first US victory in British Amateur at Royal St. George's using Schenectady centre-shafted putter

1905 British women's team beats US 6–1 at Cromer, Norfolk

1907 Frenchman Arnaud Massy is the first foreigner to win Open

1908 Old Tom Morris dies at St Andrews, aged 87

1909 Dorothy Campbell from North Berwick is the first to gain British and US titles in one season

1911 Johnny McDermott is the first American-born winner of US Open

1912 Jamie Anderson, Open winner 1877–8–9, dies in Perth Poorhouse

1913 Bostonian Francis Ouimet, aged 20, is the first Amateur to win US Open, beating Harry Vardon and Ted Ray in play-off at Brookline

1914 Walter Hagen wins his first US Open

1916 PGA of America founded: Jim Barnes wins first USPGA title

1919 R&A take over management of major British Championships

1921 Jock Hutchison is the first to take the British Open trophy to US
R&A and USGA rule ball must be not more than 1.62 ounces in weight and 1.62 inches in diameter
US beat Britain 9–3 in unofficial amateur international, Hoylake
British pros bt US 10½–4½ in unofficial international at Gleneagles

1922 Walter Hagen first American-born player to win British Open
US win inaugural Walker Cup match, National Golf Links

1924 Joyce Wethered wins fifth English Ladies' Amateur in a row

1926 Britain defeats US 13½–1½ in unofficial professional international at Wentworth
Bobby Jones wins British Open at Lytham
Jess Sweetser first American to win British Amateur title

1927 Hagen wins his fourth USPGA title in a row, his fifth in all
US beats Britain in the first Ryder Cup match at Worcester, MA

1929 Hagen wins his fourth British Open
R&A legalize steel shafted clubs, following USGA lead of 1926

1930 Bobby Jones Grand Slam: wins US and British Opens, British and US Amateurs, in same year

1932 Inaugural Curtis Cup match: US beats Britain 5½–3½

1934 Henry Cotton is first Briton to win the Open since 1923

1937 First US Ryder Cup away win, by 8–4, at Southport and Ainsdale
Harry Vardon, record six times winner of British Open, dies

1938 Britain and Ireland scores first Walker Cup win at St Andrews

1940 Johnny Laidlay, true inventor of the "Vardon" grip, dies aged 80

1943 Pam Barton, first Englishwoman to win the British and American Amateurs in same year (1936), dies in RAF air crash

1945 Byron Nelson wins 19 events in 31 starts, 11 of them in a row

1947 Lew Worsham beats Sam Snead in play-off for US Open at St Louis in first Championship to be televised (locally)
Babe Zaharias first American to win British Women's Amateur

1948 Ben Hogan wins first US Open, at Los Angeles

1949 Ben Hogan is almost killed, legs crushed, in road crash in Texas

1950 Ben Hogan recovers to win second US Open
James Braid, five times British Open winner, dies aged 80

1951 USGA/R&A Rules conference to rationalize golf throughout world: major decision abolishes stymie

1952 Britain and Ireland gains first Curtis Cup win over US

1953 Ben Hogan becomes the first (and only) golfer to win Masters, US and British Opens in one year

1954 Bob Harlow, guiding light of American pro Tour, dies

1955 Last day of Open at St Andrews is televised; Peter Thomson won

1956 Babe Zaharias, "Athlete of the Century", dies aged 42

1957 Dai Rees leads Britain and Ireland to first Ryder Cup win over US in 34 years at Lindrick, Nottinghamshire

1958 Arnold Palmer wins his first major, the Masters at Augusta: US Tour prize-money reaches record $1 million
Britain and Ireland retain Curtis Cup (won in 1956) with tied match, the best showing yet by the visiting team in the US

1959 Sam Snead's team regains Ryder Cup by five points in California

1960 Palmer wins Masters and US Open, the latter with a final round 65, then fails by a shot to catch Kel Nagle in Centenary British Open

1961 Bernard Darwin, greatest of golf writers, dies aged 85

1962 Jack Nicklaus, aged 22, beats Palmer in US Open play-off

1963 Bob Charles is the first left-hander to win a major – British Open
J. H. Taylor, last survivor of "Great Triumvirate", dies, aged 91

1965 Peter Thomson wins his fifth British Open at Royal Birkdale

1966 Tony Lema, 1964 British Open Champion, dies in air crash

1967 Francis Ouimet dies, aged 74

1968 Tour pros win fight for new USPGA division to run own affairs
Croquet putting banned

1969 Tony Jacklin becomes first Briton to win his national Open since 1951
Walter Hagen dies, aged 76

1970 Jacklin is US Open Champion by seven strokes

1971 Lee Trevino wins US, Canadian and British Opens in 3 weeks
Bobby Jones dies, aged 69
John Hudson holes successive tee shots at 11th (195 yards) and 12th (311) in Martini Tournament at Royal Norwich, Norfolk

1972 Britain and Ireland's second Walker Cup win in 50 years
European Tour gets under way

1974 Gary Player wins Open, with now obligatory 1.68 inch ball, at Lytham

1975 British Tour pros gain large measure of autonomy in separate PGA division

1979 Seve Ballesteros wins British Open, via BBC parking lot
US Ryder Cup foes now Europe, who lose, 17–11, in West Virginia

1980 Ballesteros becomes the first European to win the Masters

1985 Europe beat Trevino's US team in Ryder Cup at The Belfry

1986 Nicklaus is oldest Masters' winner, aged 46. Sixth win also a record

1986 Britain and Ireland women scores first European win by any team in US, winning Curtis Cup 13–5 in Kansas

1987 Nick Faldo wins his first British Open with final round of 18 pars
Ryder Cup further revitalized with European victory in Ohio
Sir Henry Cotton dies, aged 80
Bobby Locke, reputedly best of all putters, dies, aged 69

1989 Europe retains the Ryder Cup with the second-ever tie in the series
Britain and Ireland scores their first Walker Cup success in the US

1990 Faldo wins second successive Masters, then wins Open at St Andrews
US gains revenge in the Curtis Cup: 19–4 in New Jersey

1991 Europe lose Ryder Cup "War on the Shore" at Kiawah Island
US regains Walker Cup at Portmarnock

1992 Europe's women make it one-all in Solheim Cup at Dalmahoy

1993 Greg Norman's Sandwich Open is "the greatest" – Gene Sarazen
US take knife-edge Ryder Cup battle at The Belfry 15–13

1994 Nick Price (British Open, USPGA), Ernie Els (US Open), and José-Maria Olazabal (Masters) leave US without "major" winner
US women regain the Solheim Cup
US and European PGAs block Greg Norman's World Tour plan

INDEX

D

F

ACKNOWLEDGEMENTS

The publishers would like to thank the following sources for their kind permission to reproduce the photographs in this book: **Allsport**/Howard Boylan, Simon Bruty, David Cannon, Russell Cheyne, Phil Cole, Mike Cooper, J.D. Cuban, Stephen Dunn, Matthew Harris, Phil Inglis, Rusty Jarrett, David Leah, Bob Martin, Stephen Munday, Gary Newkirk, Mike Powell, Steve Powell, Gary M. Prior, David Rogers, Pascal Rondeau, Richard Saker; **Allsport Historical**/Hulton Deutsch Collection, Mirror Syndication International; **Bridgeman Art Library**; **Callaway**; **John B. Carnett/Popular Science Magazine**; **Colorsport**; **E.T.Archive**; **Mary Evans Picture Library**; **Hobbs Golf Collection**; **Phillips - Chester**; **Popperfoto**; **Range Bettmann UPI**; **Phil Sheldon Golf Picture Library**; **USGA**.